Elmer Epenetus Barton

A Business Tour of Chicago Depicting Fifty Years' Progress

sights and scenes in the great city - her growing industries and commercial

development, historical and descriptive

Elmer Epenetus Barton

A Business Tour of Chicago Depicting Fifty Years' Progress
sights and scenes in the great city - her growing industries and commercial development, historical and descriptive

ISBN/EAN: 9783337187828

Printed in Europe, USA, Canada, Australia, Japan

Cover: Foto ©Suzi / pixelio.de

More available books at **www.hansebooks.com**

⁕⁘ WHY IS THE DAVIS THE BEST? ⁕⁘

BECAUSE with the Vertical Feed the presser foot is always raised from the fabric when the feed takes place, and presents no resistance to seams or ridges, and the needle being in the fabric, moving with the Vertical Feed-Bar on the goods behind the needle, makes the stitches uniform in length, and renders it impossible to full one piece while the other is stretched. For the same reasons the machine is capable of sewing elastic goods, making a smooth and flexible seam with stitch alike on both sides; also of sewing any number of thicknesses without basting, operating with equal facility on the heaviest as well as the lightest fabrics.

BECAUSE it is Light Running, Simple in Construction and has a less number of working parts than any other machine. It has the greatest number of PRACTICAL attachments for doing every desirable style of work, all automatic in their action and made of the Best Materials, in the most Workmanlike Manner. It will do a greater variety of work than all other machines combined, and is the acknowledged Pioneer and Leader in Sewing Machine Decorative Art Work.

ADDRESS,

DAVIS SEWING MACHINE CO.,
46, 48, 50 Jackson Street,
CHICAGO, ILL.

Route of the Fast New York and Chicago Limited Express Trains.

LAKE·SHORE·AND
MICHIGAN·SOUTHERN·RAILWAY.

The only Route via **TOLEDO, CLEVELAND, BUFFALO** and **NIAGARA FALLS** to **NEW YORK, BOSTON, PHILADELPHIA, SARATOGA** and **INTERMEDIATE POINTS.**

The Great Double Track Route.   **Four Daily Through Trains.**

UNION DEPOTS.   **NO TRANSFERS.**   **STEEL RAILS.**
SAFETY BRAKES.   **NO FERRIES.**   **QUICK TIME.**

SPLENDID EQUIPMENT, MAGNIFICENT NEW DINING-CARS, PALACE SLEEPING AND DRAWING-ROOM COACHES, FIRST-CLASS EATING-HOUSES.

The only Double Track Railway between Chicago and Buffalo.

E. GALLUP, **F. I. WHITNEY,** **A. J. SMITH,** **A. G. AMSDEN,**
Ass't Gen'l Manager, Western Pass. Agt., Gen'l Pass. and Tk't Agt., Supt. Western Division,
CLEVELAND.   CHICAGO.   CLEVELAND.   CHICAGO.

A
BUSINESS TOUR OF CHICAGO

DEPICTING

FIFTY YEARS' PROGRESS.

SIGHTS AND SCENES IN THE GREAT CITY.

Her Growing Industries and Commercial Development,
Historical and Descriptive.

PROMINENT PLACES AND PEOPLE.

EPISODES IN USEFUL LIVES,

AND

LOCAL REMINISCENCES.

For the use of the Buyer, Shipper, Tourist, Investor, and all others interested in the growth and advancement of the Garden City.

FOR POPULAR DISTRIBUTION.

ILLUSTRATED.

CHICAGO:
E. E. BARTON, Publisher.
1887.

A Souvenir
OF
Chicago's Semi-Centennial.

It is with pleasure that we present you this copy of "A Business Tour of Chicago," as a review of our first fifty years' progress.

Being the result of an effort for its general distribution, both at home and abroad, it becomes at once the latest, most authentic and most complete representation of the great mercantile and manufacturing interests of the Chicago of today.

With the hope and belief that you will find it substantially beneficial and interesting for reference and other purposes, we remain,

Yours truly,

1887, BY E. E. BARTON.

A BUSINESS TOUR OF CHICAGO.

◁ SEMI-CENTENNIAL REVIEW. ▷

 IFTY years ago Chicago was first incorporated as one of the border towns of the public domain. Today it is the commercial metropolis of the great west, and is the third city in size in the United States. Though an infant in years, and situated in the center of a continent, its fame has gone forth to the ends of the earth. The activity, enterprise and prosperity of its business men, as well as their judgment, solidity and liberality, have become a proverb. The dash and brightness of its population, the beauty of its streets and edifices, the magnitude of its public improvements, its unequaled transportation facilities, its enormous trade, are things that fire the dullest imagination. Chicago is more distinctively than any other city the embodiment of all that is most characteristic of the American people—a people who have within the limits of a single century risen from poverty and obscurity to a foremost place among the nations. In a large sense it is typical of the age in which we live—the age of steam and electricity. The rapidity of Chicago's development has been without a parallel in ancient or modern times, and the brilliancy of its past is equaled by the promise of its future.

CHICAGO'S SITUATION DESCRIBED.

Chicago is situated in Cook county, Illinois, on the west shore of Lake Michigan, 960 miles by rail from New York. Dearborn observatory, three and one-half miles south and three-quarters of a mile east from the Chicago court-house, is in 41: 50: 1 N. latitude, and 87: 34: 8 W. longitude. The surrounding country is prairie land, with a loam soil, and a ridge runs north and south two miles or more west from the lake. The city is at an elevation of nearly six hundred feet above the level of the sea, but only fourteen feet above the lake. When it was originally settled, the elevation above the lake was not more than seven feet.

EARLY HISTORY.

As early as 1672, the French Jesuits had explored and mapped the whole of Lake Superior and the upper portion of Lake Michigan—then known as Lac des Illinois—as far south as Green bay. They had established themselves at various points, among which were the Mission de Ste. Marie de Sault; the Mission du St. Esprit, at La Pointe; the Mission de St. Fr. Xavier, at the head of Green bay; and the Mission de St. Ignace, at the outlet of Lake Michigan, nearly opposite Mackinac, on the north shore of the lake. At that time the English colonists skirted the Atlantic coast from Florida to Nova Scotia, without penetrating far into the interior. Elliot, in his missionary zeal, had explored only so far as Natick, six miles out of Boston; the Connecticut valley was still unoccupied.

THE GOOD PERE MARQUETTE.

The first white occupant of Chicago was Father Marquette, one of the Jesuit missionaries, whose name will always occupy a conspicuous and honorable place in the history of the northwest. He was attached to the mission of St. Ignace. On the 17th of May, 1673, accompanied by the Sieur Joliet, with two canoes and five voyageurs, he embarked on a voyage of exploration, his objective point being the great stream far to the west, which the Indians called by the impressive name of Mississippi, or Father of Waters. Coasting along Green bay to its head, then ascending the Fox river and descending the Wisconsin, one month after starting, he beheld the mighty current of the Mississippi, on which he floated as far south as Arkansas. In returning, he paused at the mouth of the Illinois, and, instead of proceeding on to the Wisconsin, ascended the latter stream, taking the Des Plaines branch, by which he passed by an easy portage to the Chicago river. Having reached Lake Michigan, he coasted along the west shore, and thus reached, after a canoe voyage of over 2,500 miles, the point of his embarkation.

So cordial had been the reception of the good father among the tribes inhabiting the valley of the Illinois that he resolved to return and erect among them the standard of the Cross; and the next autumn (1674) he arranged to carry out his design. It was late in October when, with a canoe and two voyageurs, he embarked. Reaching the mouth of the Chicago river, he ascended that stream for about two leagues, where he built a hut and passed the winter. It was on this voyage that the good father contracted the consumptive disease that caused his death early in the following spring. La Salle followed in the footsteps of Marquette. On one of his voyages, as early as 1670, he passed the mouth of the Chicago river, and in the fall of 1681, he passed by the Chicago portage, en route to the Mississippi. This portage was repeatedly used by his followers, but they made no permanent settlement at the mouth of the river.

THE FIRST SETTLEMENT.

By the treaty of Fontainebleau, in 1762, the vast territory east of the Mississippi passed into the possession of the British government; and the result of the Declaration of Independence, July 4, 1776, transferred this country to the United States. In 1800, the Territory of Indiana was organized, with Illinois as one of its counties. In 1809, Illinois county was made a Territory, and in 1818, it was erected into a State. In 1804, the government established a military post, with the title of Fort Dearborn, at the mouth of the Chicago. The fort was garrisoned by a single company of infantry. In 1812, on the declaration of war with Great Britain, the Indians gathered about the fort and made demonstrations of hostility. Captain Heald, who was in command, foreseeing that his supplies might be cut off, and availing himself of discretionary orders, undertook to retreat with his little command to Detroit, 300 miles distant; but he had proceeded less than two miles along the lake shore when he was ambuscaded, and only three of his party escaped massacre. In 1816, the fort was rebuilt and garrisoned by two companies of infantry. It was not until the close of the Black Hawk war, in 1832, that the region of southern Wisconsin and northern Illinois was thrown open to settlement. Emigration soon began to flow in with a surging tide, which has continued up to the present hour. A hamlet clustered around Fort Dearborn, which took the name of Chicago. As late as 1837, the year of its incorporation, flour was shipped from Ohio to supply the infant settlement.

BEGINNING TO GROW.

The first impulse communicated to the growth of Chicago was the passage, by the State legislature, of an act, January 18, 1825, for the construction of the Illinois and Michigan canal, and, in aid thereof, of the passage of an act of congress, March 2, 1827, granting to the State alternate sections of the public lands embracing a strip of six miles wide on either side of the projected canal; but it was not until 1836 that the work was entered upon, nor was it completed until 1848.

In 1831, Cook county, embracing Chicago, was organized. In the spring of 1833, congress made an appropriation of $30,000 for improving the harbor; and that same year a postoffice was established, John S. C. Hogan, who occupied a "variety store" on South Water street, being the first postmaster. The mail was brought weekly, on horseback, from Niles, Michigan. That same year witnessed the cession of all the lands in northern Illinois, amounting to about 20,000,000 acres, by the Pottawatamies, who removed farther westward. Chicago was incorporated as a town by a nearly unanimous vote; and to show the number of voters it may be said that twelve were in favor of and only one against the proposed measure. In explanation of the perverse action of the man who voted in the minority, it is to be stated that his residence was outside the proposed corporate limits.

In 1834 the poll list of citizens amounted to one hundred and eleven, and the amount of taxes reached $48.90; but this being inadequate for municipal purposes, the trustees resolved to borrow $60 for the opening and improvement of streets. The next year, however, grown bolder by the success of the former loan, the treasurer, "on the faith of the president and trustees," was authorized to

A BUSINESS TOUR OF CHICAGO—ITS SITE IN 1833.

A BUSINESS TOUR OF CHICAGO—EXPOSITION BUILDING.

A BUSINESS TOUR OF CHICAGO.

borrow $2,000, at a rate of interest not exceeding ten per cent., and payable in twelve months.

INCORPORATION OF THE CITY.

In 1837, Chicago became incorporated as a city, and William B. Ogden was chosen as its first mayor. The population in July of that year numbered 4,170 souls. The panic of 1837, which prostrated the business of other parts of the country, exerted for a time a discouraging influence on the infant city of Chicago. Speculation in lots, which had been wrought up to a fever heat, experienced a sudden check. Notes went to protest on every hand, and, to use an expressive phrase, the bottom fell out of business in general. Many men who had acquired large interests in the new city saw all their possessions slip away from them, and they were forced to begin life anew. But the depression was only temporary, and in 1840 everything was booming again.

IMPROVING TRANSPORTATION FACILITIES.

The early history of the trade and commerce of Chicago appears to have differed but little from that of most other western settlements, consisting at first of a small Indian traffic, but gradually growing as civilization began to advance into the then almost trackless prairie. Early settlement in Illinois, as in other western States, was confined almost exclusively to localities in proximity to rivers which could be made available for transportation. Hence, what trade there was went most wholly to such markets as it could be floated to. Chicago was not one of these, for while nature had provided a grand and free highway for commerce from Chicago to the eastward, there were no avenues for it penetrating to the interior until they were artificially created under the pressure of necessity.

For the first eighteen years of its settlement, the only trade of Chicago was such as it drew from the immediately surrounding country, with a limited traffic in such commodities of actual and pressing necessity as were demanded by the settlers within a distance of one hundred miles. All farm products were sold, when sold at all, at comparatively low prices; and the entire product of a wagon-load of the most available surplus of the farmer, when converted into such articles as he must buy, was scarcely sufficient to reward him for the time spent in effecting the exchange, to say nothing of the labor and capital employed upon his farm in its production. But notwithstanding the difficulties and embarrassments of both the producer and the merchant,

A BUSINESS TOUR OF CHICAGO—BOARD OF TRADE.

FIFTY YEARS' PROGRESS.

A BUSINESS TOUR OF CHICAGO—ART INSTITUTE.

the city had in 1848 increased in population to 20,000, and the taxable value of its real and personal estate, which in 1840 was less than $1,000,000, had risen to $6,300,000. Numerous wholesale establishments, for the sale of all kinds of merchandise, were in successful operation, and already the trade in cereals had grown to respectable proportions.

THE ILLINOIS AND MICHIGAN CANAL.

An important factor in Chicago's material development was the construction of the Illinois and Michigan canal, an artificial water-way connecting the city with La Salle, the head of steamboat navigation on the Illinois river. Work on this improvement was begun in 1836. Liberal appropriations of public lands were made by the general government in aid of the work. After protracted delays, incident to the embarrassed financial condition of the State, the canal was completed and opened for traffic in the spring of 1848.

A new era in the commercial prosperity of the young city now dawned upon it; and with the rapid settling and development of the territory contiguous to this new line of transit, and the facilities it gave for communication with the whole Mississippi valley, there sprang up a greatly enlarged trade, and an increased confidence in the stability and future greatness of the city. With the cheapened inland transportation was inaugurated on a largely increased scale the trade in lumber, which has from then until now exhibited a uniformity of growth scarcely less marked and noticeable than that in breadstuffs and provisions.

THE FIRST RAILROAD.

The introduction of railroads, at a later, but not distant day, was the next great step in the city's progress, and placed her on the solid foundation on which her subsequent wonderful development has been chiefly based. The first projected line—the original Galena and Chicago Union railroad, now a part of the consolidated Chicago and Northwestern railway—was in its inception and during all its separate corporate existence under the control, in all respects, of citizens of Chicago, and although financial aid in its construction and equipment was sought and obtained of eastern capitalists, it was always essentially a monument to the enterprise and faith of a few of Chicago's early citizens. This line was, after hard struggles, opened to the Fox river, some forty miles from the city, in 1850; and, although poorly equipped, it soon demonstrated the fact that although not furnishing as cheap a means of transit as water routes, it required but the construction of sufficient lines of railroad to make the great State of Illinois a very garden for production, and the home of a dense population. Other lines were speedily projected and built, until, within a marvelously short space of time, the city found itself the center of a system of railways diverging in every direction, all doing a prosperous and increasing business.

A BUSINESS TOUR OF CHICAGO—GRAIN ELEVATORS, NORTH CHICAGO RIVER.

It is worthy of remark, that although every principal railway line centering in Chicago has been built with special reference to Chicago's trade, and has brought with it increased commerce to the city, it has not been necessary to pledge the municipal credit or tax the body politic one dollar in aid of their construction, nor has the accumulated capital of the citizens been drawn on to any great extent for their establishment. Chicago lines of railway have, in view of the wonderful, vast and prospective growth of their traffic, been so eminently profitable that capital from abroad has been ever ready to embark in their construction, sometimes even when her own citizens could not comprehend the

A BUSINESS TOUR OF CHICAGO—THE GREAT AUDITORIUM BUILDING, CORNER MICHIGAN AVENUE AND CONGRESS STREET.

A BUSINESS TOUR OF CHICAGO—THE PULLMAN BUILDING.

those laid under contribution in the preparation of this sketch, remarked, "But few, even of our commercial community, are fully aware of the extent of our lake commerce, and many will be surprised at the statement that our custom-house returns show very much the largest marine business of any in the country. The comparative statement of the different customs districts is not now at hand, but such was an official statement promulgated within the last few months. The number of entries of arrivals at our custom-house during the season of navigation for 1870, was 12,739 vessels; and of clearances during the same time, 12,433 vessels. The navigation of the lakes, though running through but about seven months of the year, is the grand safety-valve by which all rates of transportation eastward are regulated, and by means of it nearly all our lumber and vastly the largest share of our farm products are moved, the former to and the latter from the city." Since the above was written the comparative magnitude of the city's railroad commerce has increased, but her lake commerce has undergone no diminution, and it will always be of immense importance.

necessity nor prospective profit of the investment. The fact that no drain has been entailed upon them by the building of railroads has left the citizens free to invest in mercantile or other enterprises of a local character, and has enabled them to meet municipal taxation for the extraordinary improvements necessary in a city requiring so much expenditure to make it convenient and enjoyable, without being oppressively burdened.

CHICAGO'S LAKE COMMERCE.

Whatever may be said of the advantages to the trade and commerce of Chicago resulting from her other means of communication with the world, the importance of the great highway provided by nature for the free passage of her shipping on the great chain of lakes must not be forgotten. Without the aid of this means of transportation, her warehouses would become over-burdened and choked, and her railroads could not be relieved of their enormous tonnage; in fact, but for this natural highway, no city would exist where now is so much of commercial life and varied industrial activity.

One of Chicago's historians, who wrote shortly after the great fire, and whose work has been among

A BUSINESS TOUR OF CHICAGO—THE TRIBUNE BUILDING.

A BUSINESS TOUR OF CHICAGO—FOUNTAIN AT GARFIELD PARK.

A BUSINESS TOUR OF CHICAGO.

THE GREAT FIRE.

In 1871 Chicago had grown to be a city of 350,000 inhabitants. Its material progress in nearly every direction had kept pace with this enormous numerical growth. In respect of the average individual prosperity of its citizens it was, perhaps, without a compeer upon the globe. In every city whose origin goes back to centuries, many quarters will be found to be rebuilt. What was good enough for the day when the struggle for existence perhaps was going on is not good enough when mercantile pre eminence has been secured, and a large number of members of the population have risen to opulence. It was the boast of an emperor of Rome that he found the imperial city brick, and he left it marble. This process had been entered upon in Chicago, and the structures in the business part of the city, for the most part, were of enduring materials and almost faultless in architectural arrangement. Field, Leiter & Co's store, for instance, was a more imposing structure than Stewart's, on Broadway, New York; the Tribune building was one of the best-appointed newspaper offices in the world; the First National Bank building, the Union building, the Chamber of Commerce, the Merchant's Insurance building, Drake's block, Honore's block, the Pacific Hotel, the Palmer House, the Bookseller's Row, the great station-houses of the Michigan Southern and the Illinois Central railroads, and other structures which might be cited, were models of architectural beauty. Many of the private residences on the North side, and on Michigan and Wabash avenues, attracted attention by reason of their good taste and appropriate surroundings. It

A BUSINESS TOUR OF CHICAGO—FOUNTAIN AT LINCOLN PARK.

is not meant to say, however, that Chicago, as a whole, was as solidly built as other cities of equal size which had been more plodding and commonplace in their development. This, indeed, would have been too much to expect. One of the inseparable conditions of such rapid growth as has been noted would naturally be the existence of many buildings of a makeshift character; many primitive buildings, good enough for the exigencies of their owners, would also naturally remain in use for a long time after they had ceased to be in conformity with the current styles as to either construction or durability. Side by side with such structures were to be seen others which would fail to ornament an insignificant country village. With the best flagging stone on the line of the canal, and readily accessible to the city, yet there were miles upon miles of pine yards, coal-yards, planing mills, sash factories, and other combustible structures.

The inflammable character of many of the buildings of the western metropolis furnished one of the important conditions of the terrible disaster which

'A BUSINESS TOUR OF CHICAGO—JEFFERSON PARK.

sidewalks. The tallest buildings, and of comparatively incombustible materials, were decorated with heavy wooden cornices, and roofed with shingles or a coal-tar covering. The river, winding through the heart of the city, was lined with immense lumber- overtook the city in 1871—the great fire, which was immeasurably the most destructive conflagration of modern times. The fire was started by the accidental overturning of a lamp, in a barn, near the corner of DeKoven and Jefferson streets, in a district built almost exclusively of wood. This accident occurred at about 9 o'clock on the evening of Sunday, October 8, 1871. The fire continued through that night and the greater part of the next day, lapping up great blocks of houses, and growing by what it fed on. It was finally checked by explosions of gunpowder in a line of houses on the south of the fire, and exhausted itself on the north by burning all there was to ignite.

The area burned over in each division of the city was as follows: West division (in which the fire originated), 194 acres; South division, 460 acres; North division, 1,470 acres. The total area burned was 2,124 acres, or nearly three and one-half square

flames sought refuge in the lake, and remained standing in the water for hours as the only means of preservation against the intense heat and the shower of sparks and cinders.

Among the buildings destroyed were the customhouse, postoffice, court-house, Chamber of Commerce, and nearly all the churches, railway stations, hotels, banks, theaters, newspaper offices, and buildings of a quasi-public character.

It is estimated that 73 miles frontage of streets was burned over, most of which had been improved with wood block pavements. These were partially destroyed.

The total loss has been estimated at $196,000,000,

A BUSINESS TOUR OF CHICAGO—JACKSON PARK.

miles, about four miles in length, and from one to one and one-half miles in width.

The season had been excessively dry; the rainfall in Chicago for the summer had been only 28½ per cent. of the average. There was a strong southwest wind, made a sirocco by the heat, and taking irregular, fantastic and uncontrollable offshoots and eddies, which spread the fire in all directions except west. The city fire department, though large and efficient, had been exhausted by an unusually extended fire the Saturday preceding, and the flames had their own way. Wooden buildings were scattered throughout the entire city, acting as brands to spread the conflagration. These were the main conditions of the fire.

The total number of buildings destroyed was 17,450, and 98,860 people were rendered homeless. Of the latter 250 perished in the flames or lost their lives from exposure. Thousands flying before the

of which $53,000,000 represented the value of the buildings destroyed, $58,710,000 the personal effects, and the remainder business stocks, produce and manufactures of every description. On the losses there was an insurance of $88,634,122, of which about one-half was recovered.

A vast system of relief was organized, which received the most generous aid from all parts of the world. The money contributions from the various States and from abroad were $4,996,782. Of this England contributed nearly $500,000. These funds, which were over and above the contributions of food, clothing and supplies, were made to last, under the careful and honest administration of a society of citizens, till the close of the year 1876. Out of them, temporary homes were provided for nearly 40,000 people; barracks and shelter-houses were erected, workmen were supplied with tools, and women with sewing-machines; the sick were cared for, and the dead buried; and the poorer classes of Chicago were probably never so comfortable as within the two or three years immediately succeeding the fire, while this colossal relief fund was being distributed.

The work of rebuilding the city was accomplished with marvelous rapidity. Immediately after the fire, the most sanguine persons predicted that it would require at least ten years to restore the build-

A BUSINESS TOUR OF CHICAGO—HUMBOLDT PARK.

ings that had been destroyed. But within three years the city was provided with buildings equal in capacity, and of two-fold value. The work was begun before the cinders were cold, and the population seemed to gain new ambition and new energy from the disaster.

The "fire limits" were extended so as to exclude the erection of other than stone, brick or iron buildings within a large area, and subsequently this prohibition was applied to the entire city. The result has been to make the new Chicago the most beautiful city in America, in its business centers.

The business and population continued to increase in spite of the disaster; indeed, the ratio of growth became larger. The solidity and permanence of this prosperity were confirmed during the panic of 1873, when the Chicago banks alone, among those of all the large cities of the country, were not compelled to issue certificates of deposit, but continued steadily to pay out current funds. There were few mercantile failures, and the business of the year following the panic still showed an increase.

THE CONFLAGRATION OF 1874.

July 14, 1874, another fire broke out in the heart of the city and swept over eighteen blocks, consum-

ing 600 houses, and leaving blackened ruins in its path. Fortunately, the area ravaged by the destructive element was occupied mainly by wooden structures, and the loss was light compared with that of the previous conflagration, aggregating only about $4,000,000.

THE GROWTH OF POPULATION.

The following is a table showing the growth of Chicago's population:

Date of Census.	Taken by	Population.
July, 1837	City	4,170
July, 1840	U. S.	4,479
July, 1843	City	7,580
July, 1845	State	12,088
September, 1846	City	14,169
October, 1847	City	16,859
September, 1848	City	20,023
August, 1849	City	23,047
August, 1850	U. S.	29,963
December, 1853	City	59,130
June, 1855	State	80,000
August, 1856	City	84,113
August, 1860	U. S.	109,206
October, 1862	City	138,186
October, 1864	City	169,353
October, 1865	State	178,492
October, 1866	City	200,118
October, 1868	City	252,054
August, 1870	U. S.	306,605
October, 1872	City	367,396
October, 1874	City	395,408
June, 1880	U. S.	503,185
June, 1886	City	750,000
June, 1887	Estimated	800,000

THE GROWTH OF WEALTH.

The material wealth of the city has kept pace with the population. Starting with a taxable valuation in 1837 of $236,842, which fell off in consequence of a panic to something over $94,000 in 1839–40, and made an astounding jump from $151,-342 in 1842 to $1,441,314 in 1843, again doubling itself the succeeding year, the increase has since been rapid and steady. The total valuation was $7,-220,249 in 1850; $37,053,512 in 1860, and $275,086,-550 in 1870. In October, 1871, the great fire consumed close upon $200,000,000 of property, yet, notwithstanding this enormous loss, the taxable valuation in May, 1872, only a few months after the fire, was $284,197,430, and it rose in the next two years to $303,705,140. Then the legislature passed a law transferring the duty of assessing and levying the taxes to the county authorities, their valuation being subject to revision by the State Board of Equalization. The result was a contest between the counties in the reduction of their tax lists, and the total valuation in Chicago, in 1875, was cut down to only $173,764,246, or something over one-half that of the preceding year. In 1880 the total taxable valuation was only $117,133,643, or less than one-half that of the year after the losses of 1871, although the actual values had been multiplied by improvements. In 1883 the figures were $133,230,-504. The revenues of the city were further restricted in 1879 by a law prohibiting the levy for municipal purposes from being raised above 2 per cent. on the valuation. The tax rate for all purposes is $3.41 on $100, but as that figure is considerably less than 2 per cent. on the actual value of property, one result of the present system is to give Chicago, which really enjoys a very light taxation compared with other cities, a most undesirable advertisement as a heavily tax-burdened city. The bonded indebtedness is $12,751,500, having undergone a gradual reduction from $14,103,000 in 1871, when it reached the highest point ever attained.

REAL ESTATE VALUES.

The comparative value of Chicago real estate affords an interesting illustration of the city's rapid growth. One example which may be cited is that of a piece of ground in an outlying district which sold in 1808 for $.50 an acre, and was resold in 1873 for $1,500 an acre. Land obtained forty-five years ago from the government at $1.25 an acre is now worth $10,000 an acre. Business property, which was sold in 1865 for $250 a foot front, with a depth of 125 feet, was resold in 1875 for $1,500 a foot front. Another piece of property, which was valued at $3,845 in 1860, was sold in 1872 for $100,000. These instances are not exceptional, but fairly represent the increase of values.

IMPROVEMENTS IN TOPOGRAPHY.

Nothing could have been more uninviting than the original site of the city. Ridges of shifting sands bordered the lake shore, while inland, and stretching beyond the range of vision, was a morass supporting a rank growth of blue-joint grass, with here and there a clump of jack oaks. Through this morass wound a sluggish river only flushed by the spring and fall freshets; and adjacent to its banks were pools of water, which were the resort of wild fowl. The river's mouth was barred by shifting sands, but the bar once passed, deep water was found within. For a mile its course was east and west, when it branched into two forks, running northerly and southerly. This stream, so uninviting, forms the present harbor of Chicago, and separates the city into three divisions—the North, South, and West. The watershed between Lake Michigan and the Des Plaines river—a tributary of the Illinois—was less than eight feet in height; and during flood time, communication could be made in a canoe without disembarking.

Such were the topographical features of Chicago fifty-six years ago. How wonderfully have they been transformed! The city commenced its growth upon the original surface; and so saturated was the soil with water that cellars and basements were from necessity dispensed with. The streets in many places presented an oozy mass of mud, and here poles were thrust down bearing placards "no bottom." The more frequented thoroughfares were planked; and when driven over, the planks were subjected to a churning motion, which caused the ooze to spurt up through the crevices. The gutters at the sides were filled with stagnant water, whose surface was covered with a green scum, the appropriate nidus of the cholera and other pestilential diseases.

LIFTING A CITY ON JACKSCREWS.

A series of public improvements was devised and executed, mainly under the direction of Mr. Chesbrough, as city engineer, which made Chicago one of the pleasantest and healthiest cities in the Union. A system of sewage was established for underground drainage, which required that the original surface in many places be raised eight feet. This change of grade involved the necessity of raising many of the largest structures in the streets adjacent to the river. Great brick blocks and hotels were thus raised, no portion of the business usually carried on within them being suspended on account of the raising, and no injury being done the structures. Under one great building there were placed no less than five hundred jackscrews, and for each jackscrew there was a man. Whenever the foreman fired a pistol, each of the five hundred men gave a twist on his screw, and in this way the whole mass, weighing many thousands of tons, was lifted as easily and uniformly as a steam crane hoists a building stone. Before many of the buildings were raised, the streets in front of them were filled up to the new grade, causing the first stories to be little better than basements; and it was the peculiar appearance of these buildings that led one of those wise Englishmen who used to spend a few days looking at this country for the purpose of writing a book about it to send word back to England that a man would be foolish to invest any of his money in Chicago real estate, for the city was likely to disappear any day, and that already many of the houses had sunk so low in the mud as to force the streets up in front of them. Meantime, however, the gigantic work of improvement went steadily on, and as it progressed the city become thoroughly drained, the houses admitted of cellars, and the streets became dry and solid.

CHICAGO AS IT IS.

The area of the city at the present day comprises 23,000 acres, and extends over seven miles north and south along the lake shore, and five miles east and west. There were 226,000 building lots of twenty-five by one hundred and twenty-five feet in 1875. The streets intersect each other at right angles. There is an inlet called the Chicago river, which runs from the lake nearly a mile west, then separates into two branches, one running northwest, the other southwest, thus separating the city into three divisions, which are connected by thirty-six bridges, and by two tunnels running under the bed of the river. This river gave the city its name. It was called by the Indians the Chacaqua, after the Indian god of thunder.

THE RIVER IMPROVEMENT.

The mouth of the river, in 1816, according to Colonel Long, of the topographical engineers, was at Madison street. It was a rippling stream, ten or fifteen yards wide, and only a few inches deep, flowing over a bed of sand. In the summer of 1833, the government entered upon the improvement of the harbor, or rather commenced the construction of one. The north pier was extended a short distance lakeward, a lighthouse was established, and an embankment was thrown across the old channel so as to divert the water to the new course. An unusual freshet during the next spring tore out the sand and left a practicable channel into the river. The pier has from time to time been extended, until now it reaches a distance of about three thousand feet.

Originally the river emptied into the lake, but a remarkable piece of engineering caused it to change its course, and, so to speak, "run up hill." The Illinois and Michigan canal, with which the main branch of the river is connected, was so deepened as to draw the water out from the lake. The canal empties into the Illinois river, and the Illinois river into the Mississippi river, so that since the improvement was made a portion of the water of Lake Michigan has flowed into the Gulf of Mexico. The Chicago river has been so deepened that the largest vessels may be towed into any of its branches, which are supplied with docks and water slips, affording a dockage capacity of nearly forty miles, more than twenty of which are already in use. The dock line is seven and one-half feet above low watermark.

The tideless river and an almost level plain afford almost unequaled facilities for receiving and distributing the immense freights that accumulate at Chicago.

THE WATER-WORKS SYSTEM.

To supply the city with pure water, Lake Michigan was resorted to as an unfailing reservoir. In the old works, established on the North side, the water was taken out near the shore. There were times when the current of the river, reeking with sewage, was borne against this portion of the shore. Besides, during the winter multitudes of small fishes collected about the strainers and gained admission to the pipes. A violent northeaster would so roil the water that it became necessary to filter it. To obviate all these inconveniences the plan was conceived of drawing the water through a tunnel from the lake, two miles distant from the shore. A shaft was sunk on the land side to the depth of twenty-six feet, and a "crib," pentagonal in form, forty feet in height,

A BUSINESS TOUR OF CHICAGO—THE TIMES BUILDING.

and ninety and one-half feet in diameter, was floated to the site in the lake and there anchored. It was then filled with stone and made to settle to its bed. An iron cylinder, nine feet in diameter, occupies the center of the structure, and penetrates from the water line to a depth of sixty-four feet, and thirty-one feet below the lake bed, where the tunnel commences. This is all the way excavated in a tough, blue clay, which offered no serious obstacles in the progress of the work. Its dimensions are five feet two inches in height, by five feet wide; and it is lined with two courses of brick laid in cement. Its capacity is 57,000,000 gallons daily. A tower, 130 feet in height, contains an iron cylinder, three feet in diameter, through which the water is forced by powerful machinery, and thence by its own pressure is distributed through the mains to the different parts of the city. These works, situated at the foot of Chicago avenue, and generally known as the North side water-works, are the main works of the system, and for a time furnished the entire supply. When the city's needs became greater, a second and similar tunnel was constructed, from the crib to the new pumping-works which were established on the West side, at the corner of Ashland and Blue Island avenues. This tunnel runs in a southwesterly direction under the city, passing twice under the bed of the river, and is two miles in length. The waterworks system as a whole is conceded to be a triumph of modern engineering, and is capable of furnishing the city with 104,000,000 gallons of water daily, through over 500 miles of mains and distributing pipes. It has been perfected at an expense of about $10,000,000.

CHICAGO'S STREETS.

The streets of Chicago were for the most part laid out on a liberal plan, which admitted of sidewalks ten feet wide then of a grass-plat in front of the residences, for the planting of trees and shrubbery, have been generally used in the business portion of the city. Macadam is used on the boulevards and on some of the streets. Outside of the business portion, however, the material used is largely cedar blocks, which, with the improved method of laying them, is giving very satisfactory results. Asphalt has been employed to some extent, but so far not with much success. The entire length of the streets of the city is upwards of six hundred and fifty miles, about two hundred and fifty miles of which are paved.

The city is laid out in rectangular lines, with the

A BUSINESS TOUR OF CHICAGO—CABLE CARS AND STREET SCENE, CORNER WABASH AVENUE AND WASHINGTON STREET.

with ample space for vehicles in the center. Twenty years ago, to a stranger from an eastern city, they seemed unnecessarily wide; but it was fortunate that this plan had been adopted, for on the introduction of street cars—the people's mode of conveyance—it was found that on either side of the track there was room for two teams to pass. In the improvement of the streets, the original surface was found to be ill-adapted to roadways; the soil was either sand or mud. Plank was first resorted to, and in 1854 twenty-seven miles had thus been laid; but it was found that with a mortar foundation and the churning process performed by each loaded vehicle in passing over, the planks soon formed a barrier to easy and safe locomotion. As far back as 1856 the introduction of Nicholson pavement began, and in the years between the war and the great fire it had a large run. Within the past five years granite blocks exception of several streets, which were constructed on the routes of the old plank-roads, and which consequently radiate to the northwest and southwest. The principal business streets of the city lie on the South side, where are congregated, within a space of about ten blocks square, nearly all the wholesale business of the city, and a large portion of the retail trade. This area contains the palatial business houses, hotels and public buildings whose magnitude and architectural beauty have added so largely to the fame of Chicago. In the residence quarters of the city are numerous palatial mansions. Red pressed brick is much used as a building material, but stone is the favorite. Of the latter there are many kinds, all varying in color, so that there is nowhere any sameness in the character of the coloring. There is equal diversity in the forms of the houses, there being but very little block building; each house, as a rule, is wholly independent in material, size, form and decoration. Joliet limestone, which is milky white at first, and after exposure becomes a rich, soft cream color, is in large demand. A deep, rich brown sandstone from Lake Superior is also much used. There is the dark gray, close-grained sandstone of the Buena Vista quarries, and a dozen other kinds of material, including the cream-colored pressed brick from Milwaukee, all of which affords an infinite variety of pleasing effects. The churches are generally constructed of rough-dressed limestone of a dark gray, which is a color eminently in harmony with their purpose. The winds, blowing al-

A BUSINESS TOUR OF CHICAGO—OLD WABASH AVENUE BAPTIST CHURCH, BURNED DURING THE GREAT FIRE OF 1871.

ternately from the lake and from the land, are sufficient to keep the city free from smoke, with the result that these richly-colored building materials are rarely obscured by stains.

THE STREET RAILWAYS.

The street railways of Chicago start from the business center, and radiate in all directions. The fare is universally five cents. The number of cars and the time-tables are arranged with due regard for public convenience. The first street railway in the city was laid along State street, and was commenced in the fall of 1858. The railways are operated by three companies, and comprise three systems, which correspond with the three divisions of the city.

The oldest of the three companies is the Chicago City Railway company, whose lines constitute the railway system of the South side. Within the past four years this company has largely substituted the cable plan of traction in place of horses. Its cable lines have an aggregate length of over twenty miles, and employ upwards of one hundred "grip-cars," which do the work of two thousand five hundred horses, and run an average of nine miles per hour, conveying one hundred thousand passengers daily. The total number of miles of track operated by the company is seventy-seven; number of cars, four hundred; average distance traversed daily, twenty-five thousand miles; average number of passengers carried daily, one hundred and twenty thousand. The powerful engines which operate the cable system of this company are located at the corner of State and Twenty-first streets. The North Chicago City Railway company operates the North side system of street railways. It was organized in 1859. The capital stock of the company is $500,000; number of miles of track, thirty-four; number of cars, two hundred and fifty-one; average distance traversed daily, nine thousand six hundred miles; average number of passengers carried daily, sixty thousand. The Chicago West Division Railway company was incorporated in 1863, succeeding to the franchises held by the Chicago City Railway company on the West side, and now oparates the lines in that division. The capital stock of the company is $1,250,000; number of miles of track, ninety-seven; number of cars owned, six hundred and thirty-four; average distance traversed daily, 21,620 miles.

BRIDGES AND TUNNELS.

The bridges over the Chicago river and its branches within the city limits number thirty-six. They are mostly built of iron and lighted by electricity. One of the most recent improvements in swinging bridges which has been adopted is machinery operated by steam.

The tunnels under the Chicago river are two in number. One at La Salle street connects the South side with the North side. The other, at Washington street, connects the West side with the South side. The Washington street tunnel was finished and formally opened to the public January 1, 1869, at a cost of $512,707. The La Salle street tunnel was completed and opened July 1, 1871, and cost $566,276. The Washington street tunnel is 1,608 feet in length. The length of the La Salle street tunnel is 1,854 feet. Each of the tunnels has a double driveway and a separate footway on one side, which is reached by stairs. The tunnels are wide, lofty, well lighted and ventilated, and each is fairly drained by means of a sub-tunnel five feet in diameter, which is connected with a steam-pump at one end.

FOUR HUNDRED MILES OF SEWERS.

The sewerage system of Chicago is extensive, well arranged and efficient, despite the engineering difficulties presented by the almost level character of the surface. Brick or pipe is used, according to the character of the drainage required and the soil through which the sewer runs. The total length of the sewers of Chicago is four hundred miles. Their

CHICAGO'S RAILWAY SYSTEM.

A glance at any good railway map will show the immense network of railway lines pointing directly to Chicago, or so connecting with other lines pointing here as to be fully available for traffic to or from

A BUSINESS TOUR OF CHICAGO—CHURCHES.

aggregate cost has been nearly six and a quarter million of dollars, or an average of $15,493 per mile. The cost of keeping them in repair averages $107.65 per year for each mile. There are about 13,000 catch basins and 15,000 man-holes.

this city. The manifold ramifications of these lines—all extending into territory more or less dependent upon Chicago as a market for its products or as a source of needed supplies—are so vast that it would be no exaggeration to say that every railway line in the country has an interest in catering to some extent to the commercial interests of Chicago. The city has long held undisputed title to rank as the greatest railway center on the globe, not less than forty-three thousand miles of track having their focus here.

The leading line entering Chicago is the Chicago, Milwaukee and St. Paul railroad. This magnificent corporation, the history of whose development would form an epitomized history of the northwest, has a capital of $150,000,000, and owns and operates 5,201 miles of road. Extensions aggregating several hundred miles are in course of con-

A BUSINESS TOUR OF CHICAGO—UNITY CHURCH, WASHINGTON PARK.

struction. The road knits Chicago to all sections of the north and northwest. It crosses the great states of Wisconsin, Minnesota and Iowa twice, and also taps Dakota by two lines. It controls important lines in northern Illinois, and numerous feeders in every direction. By an extension which it is now building to Kansas City, it will tap the business of the great southwest. As regards equipment it is one of the most complete railroads in the country, and in every respect it stands prominently forth as one of the great railroad systems of the world.

The Chicago and Northwestern is another great line which helps to bring the products of the north and northwest into the lap of Chicago.

The Illinois Central railroad has been one of the most important factors in the development of Chicago and the west. It was one of the first roads built, and has been the commercial backbone of Illinois, making its products marketable, and increasing its growth and wealth. It now covers fifteen degrees of latitude, and connects Chicago with the Missouri river and the Gulf of Mexico. The Illinois Central was the first railroad to introduce suburban trains, having commenced running them as early as 1856. To its management is largely due the development and growth of the beautiful suburbs south of the city, as its frequent trains made them even more accessible than some of the resident portions of Chicago that are reached only by the street cars. Upward of three million people are carried annually upon these suburban trains, and the number that go to South Park and Pullman sometimes reaches thousands per day.

The Pennsylvania railroad system has Chicago for its chief western terminus. Its eastern termini are at Philadelphia, New York and Washington; and it extends through New Jersey and Delaware, into Maryland, and as far south as Richmond, Va. It traverses Pennsylvania, Ohio and Indiana, en route to Chicago. Its tracks also go into Michigan, and through Illinois to St. Louis. The Pittsburg, Fort Wayne and Chicago is one of the principal trunk lines of this system.

The Chicago, Burlington and Quincy is another of the great railway systems centering in Chicago. Its main lines and branches stretch through Illinois, Missouri, Iowa, Kansas, Nebraska and Colorado.

The Michigan Central railroad is the great central highway of Michigan, which it ramifies in every direction, and brings tributary to Chicago the vast and fertile region bordered by Lakes Michigan, Erie and Huron. It operates upward of 1,500 miles of road.

The Lake Shore and Michigan Southern railway is another of the east and west trunk lines terminating in Chicago. Its main line, which is double-tracked, runs from Chicago to Buffalo, via Cleveland. Altogether it operates about 1,500 miles of railroad.

The Chicago, Burlington and Quincy railroad stretches from Chicago to Denver, and has 3,500 miles of road in Illinois, Iowa, Nebraska, Colorado Missouri and Kansas.

The Chicago, Rock Island and Pacific railway was the first railroad to reach the Mississippi from Chicago. It was opened to that river in 1854. It has absorbed a number of contiguous roads, and now operates 1,800 miles. Among its chief terminal points are Chicago, Peoria, Kansas City, Rock Island, Council Bluffs, Atchison, Davenport, Des Moines,

Leavenworth and Keokuk, Minneapolis and St. Paul. It reaches the two latter points on a leased line.

The Chicago and Alton railroad, with its leased lines, forms a grand trunk system, spanning the Michigan and Canada, to Portland, Maine, and the Atlantic coast, embracing, with branches and auxiliary lines, a total of 3,330 miles.

The Wabash, St. Louis and Pacific railway is a vast system of connecting lines, traversing the rich-

A BUSINESS TOUR OF CHICAGO—CHURCHES.

States of Illinois and Missouri. The total length of lines which it operates is about 1,100 miles.

The Chicago and Grand Trunk railway forms the western extension of the Grand Trunk railway, of Canada, by which it is operated, and with which it forms a continuous line from Chicago, through est sections of the States of Ohio, Indiana, Illinois, Iowa and Missouri, with a network of tracks aggregating 3,700 miles.

The Cincinnati, Indianapolis, St. Louis and Chicago railway, popularly known as the "Big Four," or the "Kankakee Route," constitutes a through line between Chicago, Indianapolis, Louisville and Cincinnati, and at the last two places forms through connections for all points in the south. It operates about 400 miles of road.

The New York, Chicago and St. Louis railway, better known as the "Nickel Plate," runs parallel with the Lake Shore and Michigan Southern, a few miles to the south. It extends from Chicago to Buffalo, via Fort Wayne, a distance of 513.28 miles.

The Baltimore and Ohio and Chicago railroad forms a part of the great Baltimore and Ohio system. It extends from Chicago Junction, Ohio, to Parkside Junction, Ill., from which point it enters the city on the tracks of the Illinois Central.

The Chicago and Atlantic railroad runs across the northern portion of Indiana, south of the "Fort Wayne Route," to a junction with the New York, Pennsylvania and Ohio railroad, at Marion, Ohio, in connection with which it is operated, forming an additional through line to the Atlantic coast.

The Wisconsin Central railroad is the latest great trunk line which has come into Chicago. It runs north and south through the entire length of Wisconsin, and has a line to St. Paul and Minneapolis, running east and west through the middle of the State after which it is named. It is the southern and eastern outlet for the Northern Pacific railroad. Its principal terminal points are Chicago, Milwaukee, Ashland, St. Paul and Minneapolis, and Portage.

The Chicago, St. Louis and Pittsburgh railroad has a total of 580 miles. The Pennsylvania company operates it.

The Louisville, New Albany and Chicago railway, better known as the "Monon Route," traverses the State of Indiana from north to south, and has for its termini Chicago, Louisville, Indianapolis and Michigan City.

The Chicago and West Michigan railway has a total of 410 miles. The Chicago and Western Indiana railroad owns a total of only about 52 miles, but is a valuable property.

The Chicago and Western railroad is a local line for switching purposes.

The Belt Railway company has a line beginning at South Chicago, and extending west about 11 miles, thence north about 11 miles, to a connection with the Chicago, Milwaukee and St. Paul railway, and connecting between those terminal points with all railroads entering the city. This road does a general transfer or switching business between the various railroads, and to and from the industries located on its own line.

CHICAGO'S WATER-WAYS—THE GREAT LAKES.

Chicago is the greatest fresh-water port in the world, and her list of entrances and clearances of vessels annually dwarfs that of many of the great seaboard towns. The chain of great lakes, on the shore of one of which she stands, are the avenues of a splendid commerce, extending to Manitoba in the far northwest, and to the St. Lawrence on the east, giving direct communication with Milwaukee, Erie, Buffalo, Cleveland, Detroit, and other important points, and access, via the Erie and Welland canals, to the Atlantic seaboard and European ports.

A BUSINESS TOUR OF CHICAGO—POST-OFFICE AND CUSTOM-HOUSE.

Over the lakes pass a large percentage of the direct imports of the city, which amounted in 1841 to $1,848,302, and in 1883 to $13,647,551, exclusive of duty. The lakes also provide a cheap route to the coal fields of Pennsylvania and the lumber regions of the north, and have made Chicago the distributing point for these commodities for the great northwest, and the greatest lumber market in the world.

The first vessel that arrived at Chicago was the schooner Tracy, which came in 1803, bringing soldiers and supplies for the fort. Until 1833 there was no harbor, and a sandbar prevented access to the mouth of the river. Vessels anchored off shore and were loaded and unloaded by lighters. In 1833 congress made the first appropriation for the improvement of the harbor—$25,000—and by the following spring vessels were enabled to enter the river. Lighthouses were built, but found ineffective, and the harbor was unprotected until 1870, when the present breakwater, stretching across the inlet, and enclosing the spacious inner harbor, with its lighthouse, was begun. In 1835 upwards of two hundred vessels arrived in port. In 1839 the first regular line of steamboats running out of Chicago was established. The boats plied between this city and Buffalo. The first clearance for Europe direct was made in 1856, by the steamer Dean Richmond. The first direct arrival from abroad occurred in 1857. The following table shows the arrivals of vessels in the Chicago district (including South Chicago and Michigan City) during the year 1886:

aded by a sandbar. The first vessel to enter the waters of the river was the Westward Ho, which was hauled over the bar by a team of oxen in 1833. This was the year in which the government began the improvement of the harbor. Before the close of 1834, the north and south piers had been pushed out five hundred feet, making a straight channel. In the spring of the latter year, and before the piers were completed to the length mentioned above, a freshet deepened the channel in the new mouth of the river so that vessels of heavy burden were enabled to enter. The government continued to

A BUSINESS TOUR OF CHICAGO—ILLINOIS CENTRAL DEPOT, AT SOUTH PARK.

	Coast trade.	Foreign trade.
Steamers, No.	4,484	58
Steamers, tonnage	2,246,072	23,915
Sail, No.	6,429	186
Sail, tonnage	1,545,877	60,454

The corresponding clearances were:

	Coast trade.	Foreign trade.
Steamers, No.	4,487	83
Steamers, tonnage	2,250,823	35,705
Sail, No.	6,211	424
Sail, tonnage	1,529,465	134,769

CHICAGO RIVER.

The Chicago river is an internal water-way of the city intimately connected with the lake, and forming an essential part of the harbor. Its shores are lined with docks bordered by mammoth warehouses, elevators, coal-yards, lumber-yards, etc., and it gives anchorage to the multitude of vessels plying in the lake. The original bed of the river was narrow and shallow. Near its mouth, it turned, abruptly southward, entering the lake by a crooked channel, which, as above noted, was block-

steadily improve the harbor entrance for many years, and expended large sums of money on the work. In 1857 there were six miles of dock along the banks of the river. Today there are twelve miles of slips and basins, and twenty-nine miles of river front, mostly docked.

THE ILLINOIS AND MICHIGAN CANAL.

The Illinois and Michigan canal taps the Chicago river at Bridgeport, four miles south of its mouth, and extends ninety-six miles, to La Salle, where it forms a junction with the Illinois river, and, by reason of the improvement of the latter stream, gives access to the Mississippi. Congress granted the right of way for this canal in 1822, and gave 284,000 acres of land in 1827. Work was begun in 1836, and the canal was completed for light-draught boats in 1848, the improvements having cost $1,848,-150. In 1869, the work of deepening the canal to nine and one-half feet, which was completed at a cost of $11,000,000, was begun. The pumping-works, which are an auxiliary of the canal, were enlarged in 1880 to a capacity of 60,000 cubic feet per minute. In 1882 the people of the State adopted a constitutional amendment, ceding the canal to the United States on condition that the government shall enlarge it to a ship canal, extend it to the Mississippi river, and maintain it free of tolls.

ORGANIZED TRADE BODIES.

Apart from the immense advantages derived from her natural position and unrivaled transportation facilities, Chicago owes her marvelous growth as a commercial center to the restless enterprise of her business men. No commercial community in the world has gained the credit for advanced and modern methods of doing business that attaches to the business men of this metropolis as a class. Any sketch of the history of Chicago which neglected to outline the development of its trade organizations would be obviously incomplete.

The most important of the various bodies coming under this head is the Board of Trade. Rufus Blanchard's work on Chicago and the Northwest contains a history of this organization, which is freely drawn upon in the following sketch:

THE CHICAGO BOARD OF TRADE.

At a comparatively early day in the history of Chicago as a commercial center, its then small number of merchants deemed it for their common interest to organize a board of trade. Whether or not the accomplishment of any special object was at that time had in view does not appear from any record now in existence. It is certain, however, that the eighty-two names, which, in April, 1848, were first enrolled as members of the board, were eminently representative of the general commercial interests of the city, then containing less than 20,000 inhabitants. Chicago, at that time had no public means of communication with the interior except by the stage coach and the "prairie schooner," but its favorable location at the head of lake navigation had already drawn to it a considerable volume of agricultural products, which were there exchanged for such needed supplies as could be procured only from the east. A brilliant future was, however, now believed to be dawning upon the infant city. The Illinois and Michigan canal, connecting the lakes, at this point, with the waters of the Illinois and Mississippi rivers, which had been in process of construction since 1836, was about to be completed, and doubtless the anticipation of important results to flow from this great achievement, as well as the prospective advantages of a railway system, which had then begun to assume tangible form, had more or less to do with the preparation of the merchants of the city for a united effort to meet the new and inspiring prospects of trade. Whatever may have been the object and expectations of the originators of the enterprise, it is certain that for several years it failed to accomplish very much of practical result, and its membership, in spite of the growth of the city, actually declined to but little more than one-half of its original number. In addition to occasional meetings for conversation on questions of a generally public character, there seems to have been an early attempt to establish a daily exchange. This, however, met with but poor success, and for several years various and sometimes novel expedients were resorted to for the purpose of securing the attendance of members at those daily meetings. The promoters of the organization, although discouraged by these fruitless efforts, clung to the idea that such a body ought to be sustained, and so kept it alive until its necessity became more apparent to others. By 1854 the influence of railroads as contributors to the development of the interior, and of the business of the city, became so marked in the increase of the grain and provision trade, which could be more advantageously conducted in a general meeting of buyers and sellers than in private offices, that the daily meetings on 'change begun to assume a new importance, since which there has been no ground of complaint as to the indifference of members engaged in those branches, in respect to their attendance.

In 1850, the board, originally a voluntary organization, became incorporated under a general law of the State, and in 1859 a special act of incorporation was obtained from the legislature, which has since remained the basis of the organization. Its general objects, as expressed in the preamble to its rules and by-laws, are "to maintain a commercial exchange; to promote uniformity in the customs and usages of merchants; to inculcate principles of justice and equity in trade; to facilitate the speedy adjustment of business disputes; to acquire and disseminate valuable commercial and economic information; and, generally, to secure to its members the benefits of co-operation in the furtherance of their legitimate pursuits." In order to promote these objects, an elaborate code of rules and by-laws has been adopted, these being amended or modified from time to time, as necessity or experience may seem to require. These rules and by-laws, while covering matters touching the government of the corporation, extend to detailed and specific regulations for the conduct of trade, especially that in flour, grain and provisions, in which a large percentage of the members are engaged, although among the members are representatives of almost every branch of trade in the city.

A BUSINESS TOUR OF CHICAGO.

The business transacted on 'change has grown to enormous proportions, and includes not only the sales of the vast amount of agricultural products seeking the Chicago market by the receiver from the interior to the shipper eastward, but also a volume of speculation in these products unequaled in any other city in the world. The facility with which this class of property is handled, and the fact are other than on commission orders; and these frequently aggregate many millions of dollars daily, the same property being re-sold again and again.

During its early years, the board was migratory, changing its quarters with the changing center of business in the city, but always, until 1865, clinging near to the river banks. In 1859 a building, at the time deemed ample in its accommodations for many

A BUSINESS TOUR OF CHICAGO—SHERMAN HOUSE, CORNER CLARK AND RANDOLPH STREETS.

that almost any conceivable quantity can find a purchaser for cash on any day in the year, renders the market an exceedingly inviting one for speculative operations; and they are engaged in, through the members of the board acting as commission merchants or brokers, by almost all classes of persons, not only residents of the city, but also those residing at remote points throughout the country, the latter far outnumbering the former. A very small per cent of the transactions made on 'change years, was erected for the use of the board; this was occupied early in 1860; at that time the membership had increased to about six hundred. With the impetus given to the business of the members of the board during the civil war, 1861-5 both in the volume of products seeking a market in Chicago, and in operations of a speculative character, which, although previously inaugurated, were greatly stimulated and increased during these years, the membership more than doubled, and its new quarters, although enlarged since first constructed, were found entirely inadequate to the necessities and comfort of those in daily attendance on 'change. As early as 1863, the question of enlarged accommodations again began to be seriously discussed, resulting finally, in February, 1864, in the consummation of an arrangement by which the members and others desiring to co-operate organized a building association, under an existing charter granted to the Chamber of Commerce some years previously, but which had never been actively organized. This charter was well adapted to the purposes of such an organization, and its stock of $500,000 was promptly subscribed, and the building contemplated was rapidly pushed to completion. At the outset of the enterprise, the Board of Trade contracted to lease so much of the building as its necessities required for the term of ninety-nine years, the rental being subsequently fixed at $20,000 per annum. The new building was occupied by the board in August, 1865, the membership numbering at that time over 1,400. The new building and exchange hall, at the time of its construction, was by far the largest and finest of any used for such a purpose in the country, and sufficed for all the needs of the board until it was destroyed by the great fire of October, 1871. Previous to the location of the board in its new quarters on the corner of Washington and La Salle streets, that portion of the city had been occupied as residence property, very little of any kind of business being carried on south of Randolph street. No sooner, however, had the location of the board been decided upon than the surrounding property began to appreciate in value, and business blocks rapidly supplanted dwellings, so that by the time the building was ready for occupation, it was surrounded by banks and business offices, entirely transforming the quiet streets of former days to the busy thoroughfares that have since remained.

The fire of 1871 found the affairs of the board in a most prosperous condition, the business transacted under its auspices being much larger than ever before. The shock produced by this great catastrophe was, for the moment, staggering; and as the members saw the results of their labor and effort thrown away in the wild scenes of those few brief hours, the feeling of despair was well-nigh overwhelming. The situation, however, was one that demanded action, prompt and effective. Temporary quarters were secured near the margin of the burnt district hours before the conflagration was stayed, and, rallying at this point, the members addressed themselves first to relieving the friendless, homeless multitudes, they for two days taking charge of the generous supplies sent from other cities and villages, distributing to the needy, and gathering together the scattered households. This duty being assumed by other organizations, the members turned their attention to business affairs, speedily adjusting outstanding engagements, and preparing for the proper care of the business that had scarcely ceased to flow in its accustomed volume. The receipts of grain in the city from October 9th to 31st aggregated over 3,750,000 bushels, notwithstanding the ability to care for such a business was greatly impaired. Among the first official acts of the board was its determination to re-occupy its old quarters as soon as they could be rebuilt, and the Chamber of Commerce having been formally advised to that effect, the latter corporation prepared at once for the reconstruction of the building, but on a much more substantial and elegant design than the one destroyed. The new structure was vigorously pushed to completion, and was formally occupied by the board October 9, 1872, just one year from the date of the destruction of its predecessor.

Within the building opened in 1872 were fought some of the greatest commercial battles in the history of trade. But even this arena became too small for the constantly expanding demands that were made upon it. The ninety-nine years' lease under which it was held was canceled, and a new, larger, and more elegant structure, located at the corner of Jackson and La Salle streets, was taken possession of in April, 1885. The new building has ground dimensions of $173\frac{1}{4} \times 225$ feet. The rear portion, which contains 100 offices, is 160 feet in height. The front part, containing the exchange hall, is 140 feet high, and is surmounted by a tower rising 304 feet above the ground. This is the tallest tower in the city. The structure is of Fox island granite. Its cost was $1,500,000. Four powerful elevators give easy access to all parts of the building. The exchange hall, which is approached by two flights of granite stairways leading from the Jackson street entrance, is 152×161 feet in floor dimensions, and 80 feet high. All its appointments are ornate and substantial, and it has been pronounced the most magnificent exchange hall in the world.

One of the brightest pages in the history of the board was the unwavering support it gave the country in the hour of its greatest need. With the echo of the first gun fired at the national life in 1861, the members of the board rallied to the support of the government, taking the most active measures to organize, inspire, and place in the field, those men who bared their breasts to the fury of battle, and finally achieved a victory, the fruits of which may be enjoyed by generations yet unborn. Many of the members gave emphasis to their patriotic emotions by personally joining with the "boys in blue," and sharing in the hardships and dangers of active military operations. Others contributed freely of their means to supply the needs of the soldier in camp, and of his family left behind. Three regiments of infantry and a battery of artillery were organized under the auspices of and bore the name of the Board of Trade, during three years of active service. Over these the board kept special watch, that they should not suffer for lack of anything that money or attention could supply, and on their account, together with contributions to others in the field, not less than $150,000 was raised and distributed by members of the board.

In other fields of benevolence the members of the board have heartily tendered their contributions of material aid. The devastations of fire, storm, pestilence and famine ever find them willing to lend a helping hand to the distressed, and assist as best they can to lighten the burden which these casualties from time to time place on some portion of their fellow-men.

That the men composing this body are, in general, possessed of unusual business ability, are remarkable for their quick perception of business possibilities, and are of untiring devotion to business affairs, will, perhaps, be freely conceded by all acquainted with their habits and modes of conducting those affairs. The best indication of their true manhood, however, is to be found in their generous treatment of the unfortunate, whether of their own numbers or of distressed humanity throughout the world.

OTHER TRADE BODIES.

The Produce exchange, which was incorporated June 11, 1874, has quarters at the corner of Lake and Clark streets, which are kept open from 8 A. M. to 5 P. M., daily. 'Change hours are from 2 to 3 P. M. The members, numbering about 500, are persons interested in the trade in butter, cheese, eggs, potatoes, flour, fruits, vegetables, and all kinds of country produce.

The Chicago Mining exchange was started in 1882. It has upward of 100 members, who meet daily between 11 A. M. and 2 P. M., at room 24, Portland block.

The Lumbermen's exchange is a strong trade organization, which has rooms at 252 South Water street.

The Drug, Paint and Oil exchange was organized in 1877. Its members are leading jobbers in and

A BUSINESS TOUR OF CHICAGO— DOUGLAS MONUMENT, AT THIRTY-FIFTH STREET AND LAKE FRONT.

manufacturers of the lines to which it is devoted. Its headquarters are at 51 Wabash avenue. 'Change hours, 11:30 A. M. to 12 M.

The Commercial exchange is an organization which facilitates transactions in groceries, and its membership is limited to residents of Chicago engaged in lines of trade identified with the grocery business. The exchange was incorporated in 1882. It is in a flourishing condition.

The Chicago Stock exchange was established in 1882. It has nearly eight hundred names on its roll of members. Its headquarters are 120 Washington street. It makes two calls daily, one for the sale of stocks, and the other for the sale of bonds. It grows in importance annually.

The Chicago Real-Estate board was incorporated in 1883, under another name, and took out fresh articles of incorporation, under its present name, in 1884. Its daily call-board sessions are held from 12 M. to 1 P. M.

The Builders' and Traders' exchange was organized in 1884. It has about five hundred members, composed of mechanics, manufacturers and traders whose vocations connect them with the building trades. The exchange rooms are at 150 La Salle street.

The principal trade associations, other than exchanges, are as follows: The Anthracite Coal association, Board of Marine Underwriters, Boss Horse-shoers' Protective association, Chicago Board of Underwriters, Chicago Boot, Shoe and Leather association, Chicago Brick-makers' association, Chicago Drapers' and Tailors' exchange, Chicago Jewelers' association, Chicago Liverymen's association, Chicago Master Masons' and Builders' association, Chicago Master Plumbers' association, Chicago Retail Coal Dealers' association, Chicago Vessel Owners' association, Chicago Cigar Manufacturers' and Dealers' association, Custom Cutters' association, Lumber Manufacturers' Association of the Northwest, National Association of Lumber Dealers, Pork Packers' association, Railway exchange, State Protective association (liquor dealers), Underwriters' exchange, Watchmakers' and Jewelers' association, and Western Railroad association.

The Lumber Manufacturers' Association of the Northwest, organized in 1873, aims to further the interests of its members by united action among them in everything pertaining to the lumber trade of Chicago and the northwest. It collects and publishes annually statistics of prices, sales, production and consumption of lumber, etc.

The Chicago Clearing House association was organized in 1865 and incorporated in 1882, its object being to substitute a safer and more convenient system of making collections than the old-time system of messengers. Many private banks make their clearings through members of the Clearing House association, and $7,500,000 changes hands at every day's proceedings.

THE UNION STOCK YARDS.

The great Union Stock Yards and the city of packing-houses connected therewith have long been prominent show-places of Chicago, and to the practical man constitute one of the wonders of the modern world. The yards are owned and managed by the Union Stock Yards and Transit company. The first stock yard founded in Chicago that attracted eastern capitalists to this market as a live-stock supply point was managed by John B. Sherman, who was the chief spirit in organizing the present Union Stock Yards, and has been actively identified with their management ever since. These yards were constructed in the year 1865, and were opened for business December 25 of the same year. The company now owns about a section of land, and over one hundred miles of railroad track, making a transit through the city, and running around and through different parts of the yards, all laid with steel rails, connecting with all the railroads centering in Chicago. Within an enclosure of three hundred and sixty acres is constructed the Transit House at a cost of $250,000, which is furnished first-class, and is kept second to none in the country, charges to stockmen being only $2 per day, or fifty cents per meal. In the center of the yards is a large two-story-and-a-half building, sixty by three hundred and eighty feet, with large wings extending south from either end, doubling the capacity of the main building. This is known as the Exchange building, and is divided up as follows: The large Board of Trade hall, main offices for Stock Yards' company, superintendent's, secretary's and treasurer's offices, telegraph and telephone offices, post office, restaurant 60x80, spacious saloon, packers' offices, offices for eastern shippers, barber shop, news stand, fruit stand, and about 150 offices for commission merchants, who take charge of and sell stock consigned to them; the Union Stock Yards National bank building, 40x60; twenty large hay barns, as many more large corn-cribs, twenty scale-houses, each containing one of Fairbanks' improved scales, with a capacity for weighing three or four car-loads of cattle or hogs at a draft; machine shops, depot building, printing office, and two dozen other buildings used to transact business pertaining to the receiving and shipping live stock, including the grand new horse sales stables and the experimental fat-stock barn. The water supply is furnished through the regular water-works by a half-dozen artesian wells, a standpipe, surrounded by a tower 150 feet high, into which the water is forced by a powerful engine and pumps on the spot.

Cable and telegraphic market reports from London, Liverpool, New York, Boston, Philadelphia, Baltimore, Cincinnati, Buffalo, East Liberty, Albany, and other markets, both east and west, are received here, and reports of this market are telegraphed each day to all eastern cities, Europe, and through commission firms to all parts of the western States and territories.

Over 230 acres of land are under plank and constructed as follows: About 150 acres are in cattle yards, and about 100 acres of covered hog and sheep pens; 2,000 cattle pens, sufficient to yard

25,000 cattle; 1,500 hog pens, sufficient to hold 200,000 hogs; 300 sheep pens that will accommodate 15,000 sheep; stabling for 2,500 horses; 2,000 car loads of stock can be unloaded and taken care of daily; over 20 miles of macadamized streets run through different parts of the yards, and over 50 miles of water and drainage pipes, forming a perfect network, run underneath the yards. There are about 10 miles of viaducts and elevated roadway. Nearly 1,000 men are constantly employed throughout the different departments.

The magnitude of the live-stock business conducted at the stock yards far exceeds what a casual glance at an aggregation of figures can possibly convey a correct idea of. A constant stream of cattle passing into these yards averaging ten per minute, of hogs averaging thirty per minute, and of sheep averaging four per minute for ten hours of every working day of the year, is a volume of animals that would, if it could all be seen, astonish even the best posted man in the trade, and yet such an array would fall short of the actual numbers brought to this great market for sale, slaughter, or distribution. The number of head of stock of all kinds received during the past year amounted to 8,314,934. The capital of the Stock Yards company is $1,000,000. The buildings are, of their kind, the finest in the country, and the arrangement of the yards is perfect in every detail.

CHICAGO AS A BUSINESS CENTER—THE CITY'S TRIBUTARY TERRITORY.

Any review of the trade and commerce of Chicago, however hasty and imperfect, would be essentially incomplete without some reference to the basis of that trade, and the reasons that may be adduced for its rapid growth and development. First of all may be noted the broad expanse of matchless agricultural territory, dotted with farm-houses, villages, and cities, stretching hundreds of miles northward, westward, and southward, all more or less (and the major part of it entirely) dependent upon the city, both as a market for its surplus productions and a source of supply for those necessaries and luxuries that tend to make life enjoyable, and that are produced or manufactured in other portions of this or of foreign countries. But scarcely less important than supply and demand, because by it only can either exist, is the means of speedy transportation demanded by an extended commerce; and this nature and art have supplied

A BUSINESS TOUR OF CHICAGO—ALLEN'S ACADEMY, TWENTY-SECOND STREET, NEAR CALUMET AVENUE.

for Chicago to a degree unequaled by any interior city in the land; so that, with lines by water or by rail, the city has come to be a center from which diverge in all directions ample avenues for conducting an almost limitless traffic, and through the influence of which the commerce of this city has been nourished and built up, and by means of which the great northwest has become populous, and the hitherto cheerless prairie has been converted into a paradise of happiness, prosperity and substantial wealth.

The States most intimately connected with Chicago, whose products, in a large degree, find a market here, and whose wants are here principally supplied,

A BUSINESS TOUR OF CHICAGO—CITY HALL, LA SALLE STREET FRONT.

are Illinois, Missouri, Iowa, Wisconsin, Kansas, Nebraska and Minnesota, with 470,170 square miles of territory, or 300,909,064 acres, which contained in 1880 a population of 10,415,634, being about the same as the population of the States of New York, Ohio, New Hampshire and Massachusetts together, upon a territory of 104,052 square miles. When we add to this list of States the territory of Dakota, with her 150,932 square miles, and the great State of Colorado, with her 104,500 square miles of magnificent arable lands, and reflect, even for a moment, upon the productive power of all this vast domain, and, moreover, that it has as yet scarcely begun to be peopled, we must stand amazed at the future which is spread out before this favored city, leaving out of the calculation the important trade of Chicago with the southwest, which is growing every year.

THE GRAIN TRADE.

Passing from theories of causes touching the wonderful growth of the trade and commerce of the city, and the means by which these have been developed, a brief reference to figures, setting forth what Chicago has done and is doing as a commercial center, will be interesting. Recognizing the agricultural interests of the west as the basis of all our commercial importance and prosperity, the trade in the products of the farm will be first alluded to. The first shipment of grain eastward from Chicago occurred in 1838, and consisted of seventy-eight bushels of wheat. This shipment was somewhat experimental in its character, and no more was forwarded until the next season. For several years subsequent, large quantities of flour were received in the city from New York State and Ohio, for local consumption, so that probably not until 1842 was there any balance of trade in favor of Chicago. In 1845 the shipments of wheat, and flour reduced to wheat (and in all the figures following, flour will be treated as reduced to wheat), exceeded 1,000,000 bushels. In 1848, the year of the opening of the Illinois and Michigan canal, the grain shipments exceeded 3,000,000 bushels. In 1852, when the influence of advancing lines of railroad began to be felt, the shipments reached nearly 6,000,000 bushels. From this time forward the traffic assumed most remarkable proportions, reaching in 1856 an aggregate shipment of over 21,000,000 bushels; and in 1860, the year preceding the outbreak of civil war, the grain shipments of Chicago exceeded 31,000,000 bushels. In 1880 they reached the enormous aggregate of 154,337,115 bushels, a point which has not been touched since, partly owing to the development of new channels of shipment. In 1885, the aggregate grain shipments were 135,587,021 bushels. In 1886, they were 129,636,678 bushels. The slight apparent tendency towards retrogradation which the shipments since 1880 have exhibited occasions no alarm, because its causes are understood, and it is known to be apparent rather than real. The mills of Minneapolis are all the time extending their influence with the old world, the port of Duluth is striving for the control of as much of the wheat trade of the northwest as escapes the flouring-mills, and the cut-off lines farther south are doing their utmost to obtain a diversion of the produce movement eastward in that direction. But this city has really been the market for it all, and never demonstrated her ability to care for and control the produce business of the great west better than during the recent years whose figures show the apparent falling off which has been noted. Chicago has carried the whole of the visible supply of wheat and other cereals, and our moneyed men have furnished the capital required to hold the greater part of it. The extent to which Chicago acts as a factor in produce is well illustrated by the wool movement of last year. The quantity passing through this city was actually smaller in 1886 than in 1885, and yet it is well known that the merchants of this city practically controlled the entire clip of the west, forcing the manufacturers and speculators of the seaboard to come here when they wanted to buy. It was handled here as much as are the goods of the grocer in his office, though a single barrel of sugar or molasses may never enter its door.

THE TRADE IN LIVE STOCK.

Next in rank of importance to cereals, in the products of the farm that find a market in Chicago, may be noted the trade in live stock. No reliable record of receipts and shipments in this branch of trade appears to have been kept until 1857, though for several years previous a considerable business had been conducted; and as a point for the packing of both cattle and hogs, Chicago had taken a respectable rank as early as 1850. The receipts of cattle in 1857 amounted to 48,524 head, increasing the following year to 140,534; and thenceforward the growth of the trade was steady and rapid. Last year's (1886) receipts of cattle amounted to 1,963,900 head, being the greatest in the history of the trade. The receipts of live hogs, which in 1857 amounted to a little over 200,000, have increased much more rapidly, though with not the same regularity as those of cattle. In 1880, the receipts amounted to 7,059,355. This was the greatest number of live hogs ever received in a single year. In 1885 the receipts were 6,937,535, and in 1886, 6,718,761. The number of dressed hogs shipped to this market in 1886 was 24,864. In the account of the stock yards, given in an earlier portion of this sketch, the magnitude of

FIFTY YEARS' PROGRESS. 33

Chicago's packing industry is hinted at. The following table exhibits the number of cattle and hogs packed in Chicago for the last twenty-three years, from March 1 to March 1. The figures of cattle packing for the last eleven years include city consumption.

Season.	No. of Cattle Packed.	No. of Hogs Packed.
1880-1	511,711	5,752,191
1881-2	575,924	5,100,484
1882-3	697,033	4,222,780
1883-4	1,182,905	3,911,792
1884-5	1,319,115	4,228,205
1885-6	1,402,618	4,928,730
1886-7	1,608,202	4,425,041

SOME OTHER LINES OF TRADE.

The city's trade in other produce amounts to an enormous aggregate. In 1886 the receipts of pork meats were 164,823,557 pounds; of lard, 88,454,118 pounds; of butter, 108,-122,119 pounds; of wool, 34,781,587 pounds; of hides, 85,980,053 pounds; of flaxseed, 7,002,573 pounds; of other seeds, 61,577,117 pounds.

The trade in coal, salt, and many other leading articles is in proportion to the demands of a country so dependent as is the northwest for the importation of these articles. The receipts of coal in 1886 were 4,056,-018 tons, and the shipments 906,205 tons. The receipts of salt for the same year were 1,274,203 barrels, and the shipments, 1,240,175 barrels.

THE LUMBER TRADE.

Chicago has for many years been the greatest lumber market in the world, and its trade in this line is still increasing. The business is conducted by upwards of 250 firms. The pine yards number 107, and there are 32 exclusive hardwood yards. The capital of the lumber trade of this city is estimated at $18,000,000, and the value of the total product handled at $40,000,000. The receipts during 1886 were 1,700,-000,000 feet of lumber, 800,000,000 shingles, 50,000,000 lath and 3,500,-000 cedar posts, added to which there were about 30,000 cords of wood, 1,000,000 railway ties (chiefly cedar), 31,000 cords of slabs, 20,000 cords of bark, 50,000 telegraph poles, and 2,000 piles. The shipments and sales for the year approximated 1,646,-022,806 feet of lumber, and 714,770,000 shingles.

THE IMPORTS INTO CHICAGO.

The articles imported at Chicago during 1886 included ale, beer, and porter, 5,856 packages; brandy, 1,001 packages; caustic soda, 14,309 drums; champagne, 941 cases; china and glass ware, 266 packages; coffee, 955 bags; dry goods, 17,559 packages; gin, 1,245 packages; fancy groceries, 7,145

A BUSINESS TOUR OF CHICAGO—LAKESIDE BUILDING, ADAMS AND CLARK STREETS.

STATISTICS OF PACKING.

Season.	No. of Cattle Packed.	No. of Hogs Packed.
1863-4	70,086	904,659
1864-5	92,459	760,514
1865-6	27,172	597,855
1866-7	25,996	639,332
1867-8	85,848	796,226
1868-9	26,950	597,954
1869-70	11,963	688,140
1870-1	21,254	919,197
1871-2	16,080	1,225,286
1872-3	15,755	1,456,650
1873-4	21,712	1,826,560
1874-5	41,192	2,136,716
1875-6	63,783	2,320,846
1876-7	824,898	2,933,486
1877-8	810,456	4,033,311
1878-9	391,500	4,960,956
1879-80	486,537	4,680,637

A BUSINESS TOUR OF CHICAGO.

packages; pig iron, 1,087 tons; Japanese goods, 1,894 packages; musical goods, 1,554 cases; cedar posts, 640,165; telegraph poles, 13,097; pickles, 2,749 packages; clay pipes, 1,302 cases; salt, 181,740 sacks; salt in bulk, 7,755 tons; stone, 5,526 tons; tea, 150,166 packages; railroad ties, 726,122; tin plate, 208,487 boxes; tobacco, 3,308 bales; whisky, 2,354 packages; wine, 10,191 packages. The value of imported merchandise entered for consumption, and the duties collected thereon at Chicago during 1886, were, respectively, $11,574,449 and $4,349,237.

WHOLESALE TRADE IN MERCHANDISE.

Following is a careful estimate of Chicago's wholesale trade in other leading articles of merchandise during 1886:

Groceries and confections	$58,800,000
Dried and California fruits	2,850,000
Dried fish	2,000,000
Fresh-water fish	565,000
Oysters	2,250,000
Canned salmon	725,000
Wooden and willow ware	2,500,000
Dry goods, etc.	65,750,000
Carpetings	5,300,000
Millinery, etc.	6,000,000
Clothing	23,000,000
Hats and caps	8,000,000
Furs	1,750,000
Boots and shoes	19,500,000
Leather and findings	2,250,000
Drugs and chemicals	6,250,000
Crockery and glassware	4,000,000
Coal-oils	5,500,000
Books	12,325,000
Paper	20,425,000
Paper stock	4,950,000
Wall-paper	1,252,000
Pianos	2,300,000
Reed organs	1,500,000
Other musical instruments	800,000
Musical stationery, etc.	400,000
Liquors, etc.	10,750,000
Carriages	1,485,000
Iron ore	2,700,000
Pig iron	14,000,000
Pig lead	3,870,000
Coal	22,675,000
Lumber	40,000,000
Tobacco	14,800,000
Jewelry	13,000,000
Iron, manufactured	18,000,000
Building materials	4,000,000
Miscellaneous	9,278,000
Total	$416,000,000

THE RETAIL BUSINESS.

The retail business of Chicago is on a par with her wholesale trade. No city in the world has finer stores, or merchants who better understand the wants of the trading public, or who display a more liberal spirit in catering to the comfort of their customers.

The aggregate clearings of Chicago for 1886 were $2,604,762,912.35, and for 1885, $2,318,579,003.

The clearings at the board of trade clearing house aggregated $100,665,007 in 1886, and $100,050,537 in 1885. The total receipts of the Chicago post-office during 1886 were $2,132,058.19, and the total expenses, $806,404.23. The average number of mails dispatched daily was 90, and the average number received, 95. The average number of letters, postal cards, etc., received and delivered was 315,754. This does not include newspapers, circulars, books, merchandise, etc.

The collections of internal revenue in the first district of Illinois for 1886 were as follows: On lists, $7,932; beer stamps, $1,045,558; spirit stamps, $5,765,614; cigars and cigarets, $394,881; snuff, $1,166; tobacco, $440,949; special tax, $247,264; oleomargarine, $78,641; total, $7,452,588; increase over 1885, $529,418.

The transactions in Chicago real estate during 1886 numbered 14,626, and the amount involved was $75,275,007. The corresponding figures for 1885 were 11,027 and $47,806,687. Following is a table showing the building operations in Chicago for five years past:

Year.	Buildings.	Frontage.	Cost.
1882	3,113	78,161	$15,842,800
1883	4,086	85,588	17,500,000
1884	4,169	98,782	20,689,600
1885	4,638	108,952	19,624,100
1886	4,674	112,302	21,324,400

CHICAGO MANUFACTURES — THE IRON INDUSTRY.

The growth of Chicago as a manufacturing center has been very great during recent years. One of the largest steel plants in the Union, comprising seven departments, covers an area of twenty-nine acres on the south branch of the Chicago river, with blast furnaces having a daily capacity of 330 tons, or an output of nearly 125,000 tons of pig iron annually. Following is a statement of the number of Chicago iron-works of various kinds in operation during 1886, the capital employed, the number of workmen engaged in each, and the value of the product:

Iron Manufactures.	No.	Capital.	Workers.	Product.
Rolling-mills	6	$11,450,000	7,940	$12,100,000
Foundries	40	2,825,000	3,200	8,500,000
Machinery, malleable iron, etc.	58	2,030,000	2,660	6,750,000
Boiler shops	20	500,000	1,430	1,430,000
Car-wheel works	4	1,050,000	1,465	4,650,000
Stove manufactures Steam fitting and heating	11	1,335,000	1,050	2,450,000
	6	200,000	400	600,000
Galvanized iron, tin, and slate roofing	80	350,000	700	1,500,000
Furnaces and ranges	10	150,000	140	275,000
Barbed wire	4	250,000	250	1,900,000
Wire-works	18	210,000	240	385,000
Miscellaneous	33	2,511,000	2,288	6,250,000
Totals	240	$22,881,000	21,633	$46,790,000
Totals, 1885	246	21,918,500	19,180	38,393,000

The total amount of wages paid to iron and steel workers in Chicago for 1886 footed up $12,543,000, as compared with $8,734,000 for 1885.

BRASS AND COPPER, ETC.

Following is a detailed statement of the brass and copper manufactures of Chicago for 1886:

Brass, Copper, etc.	No.	Capital	Workers	Product
Brass, copper and plumbers' supplies	21	$ 620,000	1,088	$ 2,200,000
Tin, stamped and sheet metal ware	30	1,500,000	2,000	4,000,000
Jewelry manufacturers	12	500,000	320	1,200,000
Watch cases and tools	8	250,000	380	1,880,000
Optical goods	2	50,000	40	160,000
Telegraph and electrical supplies	4	710,000	570	2,030,000
Smelting and refining and Iron and brass works	4	170,000	280	3,250,000
Miscellaneous	28	522,000	571	1,985,000
Totals	109	$4,122,000	5,249	$16,205,000
Totals, 1885	109	3,961,000	4,246	12,765,000

The estimated amount paid for wages is $3,202,750, against $2,380,000 in 1885.

IRON AND WOOD.

In manufactures using iron and wood combined, the business done in 1886 was as exhibited below:

Iron and Wood Combined	No.	Capital	Workers	Product
Wagons and carriages	60	$ 1,000,000	1,650	$ 2,750,000
Agricultural implements	3	5,000,000	3,700	11,850,000
Car and bridge builders	4	3,575,000	3,630	10,725,000
Elevators	9	895,000	795	2,252,000
Sewing machines and cases	5	415,000	423	920,000
Totals	81	$10,885,000	10,198	$28,497,000
Totals, 1885	85	10,000,000	9,250	26,000,000

The wages paid are estimated at $6,902,000, as against $6,000,000 in 1885.

MANUFACTURES OF WOOD.

The furniture trade and its allied manufactures are increasing in Chicago at a rate which point to this city soon being recognized as the head of this branch of industry in the United States. The largest manufacturing firm in this line in the country is located here, with a capital of $1,000,000 and several factories, giving employment to a force of 700 men. Following is an exhibit in detail of the work which was done in manufactures of wood in Chicago during 1886:

Manufactures of Wood.	No.	Capital	Workers	Product
Planing-mills, sash, doors, moldings, boxes, etc.	70	$3,350,000	4,500	$10,000,000
Cooperage	30	220,000	600	1,200,000
Furniture	200	4,000,000	10,000	15,000,000
Picture-frames and looking-glasses	52	400,000	1,000	1,000,000
Pianos and organs	9	450,000	850	1,675,000
Billiard tables	5	300,000	400	1,200,000
Miscellaneous	22	635,000	650	1,520,000
Totals	388	$9,355,000	18,000	$31,595,000
Totals, 1885	386	8,817,000	16,475	29,970,000

The wages in 1886 made an estimated total of $8,817,000, as against $8,035,000 for 1885.

BRICK, STONE, ETC.

The production of brick at the Chicago yards is given as 388,000,000 for 1886, against 335,000,000 in 1885, showing an increase of 53,000,000. The following table gives the statistics of the brick and stone industry of Chicago for 1886:

Brick and Stone.	No.	Capital	Workers	Product
Brickyards	67	$ 400,000	3,000	$2,716,000
Cut-stone contractors	24	1,000,000	1,200	2,500,000
Marble and granite works	30	750,000	500	2,250,000
Gravel-roofers	26	175,000	400	750,000
Limekilns	5	200,000	350	375,000
Terra cotta	1	100,000	350	500,000
Stained-glass	8	200,000	250	750,000
Totals	161	$2,825,000	6,050	$9,841,000
Totals, 1885	155	2,750,000	5,840	9,103,000

The total of wages is estimated at $2,545,000, as against $2,480,000 for 1885.

BUILDING.

The permits issued by the city building department for the year 1886 numbered 3,497, for the erection of 4,664 structures. The frontage covers 112,302 feet, and the cost of buildings is given at $21,324,400. This includes the erection of 1,703 sheds, the cost of which is not covered by the above sum.

BREWING, DISTILLING, TOBACCO.

The beer, liquor and tobacco interests of Chicago are of enormous proportions. The estimates for 1886 are as follows:

Brewing, etc.	No.	Capital	Workers	Product
Breweries	38	$3,750,000	1,000	$ 6,585,000
Malt-houses	23	2,000,000	400	3,500,000
Distillers and rectifiers	79	1,300,000	950	7,817,000
Tobacco and snuff	4	650,000	600	2,000,000
Cigars and cigarettes	430	1,250,000	1,750	5,350,000
Totals	574	$8,950,000	4,700	$25,252,000
Totals, 1885	570	8,850,000	4,840	25,345,000

The wages are estimated at $2,870,000, as against $2,850,000 in 1885.

CHEMICAL WORKS, ETC.

The establishments coming under this head are annually growing in importance. The soda and mineral waters and bottling business of Chicago is rapidly becoming an important branch of industry, and is fast driving out foreign products. The estimates are as follows:

Chemical works, etc.	No.	Capital	Workers	Product
Chemical works	6	$ 600,000	160	$ 1,000,000
White lead and paint manufacturers	14	1,100,000	350	3,350,000
White lead corroding works	2	750,000	200	1,000,000
Linseed oil and cake mills	7	1,250,000	135	1,700,000
Varnish	6	250,000	100	800,000
Glue and axle grease	5	450,000	500	1,000,000
Soap and candles	15	1,600,000	960	6,000,000
Soda, mineral waters and bottling	18	500,000	550	1,450,000
Totals	73	$6,500,000	2,955	$16,300,000
Totals, 1885	70	5,450,000	2,855	15,675,000

The total of wages was $1,535,000, as against $1,411,000 in 1885.

LEATHER MANUFACTURES.

The leather manufactories of Chicago and the

A BUSINESS TOUR OF CHICAGO.

business which they did in 1886 are shown in the following:

Leather.	No.	Capital.	Workers.	Product.
Tanners and curriers	19	$3,500,000	1,500	$ 5,500,000
Boot, shoe and slipper manufacturers	46	3,500,000	4,200	8,850,000
Saddle and harness manufacturers	5	200,000	260	1,000,000
Trunkmakers	9	225,000	320	800,000
Hose and leather belting	3	272,000	120	475,000
Totals	82	$7,700,000	6,400	$16,575,000
Totals, 1885	79	7,475,000	6,240	15,530,000

The wages paid foot up $4,225,000, as against $3,450,000 in 1885.

TEXTILE MANUFACTURES.

Another important branch of Chicago's industries is the manufacture of textile figures, as the following exhibit for 1886 will show:

Textiles.	No.	Capital.	Workers.	Product.
Men's and boys' clothing	42	$ 7,000,000	12,550	$17,500,000
Colored shirts, overalls, etc.	18	1,250,000	1,700	2,500,000
Men's neckwear	6	250,000	650	850,000
White shirts	86	300,000	800	1,250,000
Furs	3	300,000	250	600,000
Cloaks, suitings, etc.	16	1,300,000	3,800	3,850,000
Lace goods, fringes, dress trimmings, etc.	6	250,000	700	750,000
Millinery	8	275,000	1,000	900,000
Cotton mill	1	50,000	100	100,000
Totals	186	$10,975,000	21,500	$28,300,000
Totals, 1885	135	10,295,000	21,140	26,250,000

The estimated amount of wages paid was $7,100,000, as against $6,325,000 in 1885.

PRINTING, ETC.

In manufactures connected with the "art preservative," an immense business is done in Chicago. Following is the statement for 1886:

Printing.	No.	Capital.	Workers.	Product.
Printing, binding, lithography, newspapers, etc.	215	$ 2,600,000	1,950	$ 8,500,000
Bookbinding and pamphlets	20	500,000	800	1,250,000
Electrotype and stereotype	12	175,000	320	525,000
Type founders	4	500,000	500	925,000
Printing and writing inks	4	100,000	190	335,000
Totals	255	$3,875,000	3,760	$11,535,000
Totals, 1885	253	3,360,000	3,600	9,945,000

The wages make a total of $2,400,000, against $2,200,000 in 1885.

ALIMENTS.

The year 1886, for which the following statement was made, was not a favorable one for some branches of the industries enumerated, notably, the flour industry. Nevertheless the showing made is a striking one:

Aliments.	No.	Capital.	Workers.	Product.
Principal bakeries	30	$ 600,000	830	$ 4,890,000
Flour mills	3	400,000	120	2,124,000
Meal and feed mills	5	275,000	120	1,700,000
Coffee and spice mills	11	1,000,000	700	5,000,000
Baking powder, extracts, etc.	5	650,000	250	1,650,000
Confectionery	8	750,000	1,000	3,000,000
Preserves, canned goods, etc.	10	250,000	420	1,000,000
Vinegar and pickles	17	310,000	300	1,000,000
Sugar refinery	1	300,000	250	1,700,000
Totals	90	$ 4,535,000	4,050	$22,064,000
Totals, 1885	89	4,375,000	3,730	20,777,500

The aggregate amount of wages paid foot up $2,105,000, as against $1,865,000 in 1885.

MEAT-PACKING, ETC.

Following is a statement of the meat-packing and allied industries of Chicago for 1886:

Meat productions.	No.	Capital.	Workers.	Product.
Hog-packing	44	$ 7,000,000	10,000	$ 48,000,000
Beef-canning	3	3,500,000	5,850	23,750,000
Refined lard, lard-oil, stearine	4	3,000,000	3,000	14,000,000
Butterine	11	1,000,000	750	4,000,000
Sausage	18	350,000	250	1,300,000
Totals	80	$14,850,000	19,340	$91,050,000
Totals, 1885	79	12,800,000	18,500	85,240,000

The aggregate amount of wages for 1886 was $12,000,000, against $11,000,000, for 1885.

MISCELLANEOUS.

A number of industries which could go appropriately under any of the above headings are grouped in the following table, the showing, as in preceding tables, being for the year 1886:

Miscellaneous.	No.	Capital.	Workers.	Product.
Toy factories	5	$ 400,000	400	$ 750,000
Signmakers	12	80,000	100	400,000
Brushes and brooms	12	250,000	280	530,000
Feather dusters	6	80,000	250	200,000
Showcases	11	65,000	110	225,000
Glass	1	250,000	150	1,000,000
Corks	2	40,000	80	120,000
Paper boxes	9	150,000	700	600,000
Sails, awnings	12	300,000	325	1,000,000
Ship-yards	2	300,000	200	250,000
Totals	72	$1,915,000	2,595	$5,075,000
Totals, 1885	70	1,300,000	1,985	3,415,000

The wages approximated $1,412,500, against and $1,000,000 in 1885.

RECAPITULATION.

The manufacturing business of Chicago for 1886 and 1885 compares as follows:

	1886.	1885.
Number of firms	2,341	2,526
Capital used	$109,368,000	$101,651,500
Number of workers	126,430	119,025
Wages paid	$ 67,717,250	$ 57,780,000
Value of product	$349,079,000	$328,408,500

The last line shows a gain of $20,670,000 over the total for 1885, being about 6.3 per cent

SOME PERTINENT FACTS.

The business of the past year has fully met all reasonable expectations, and the city is true to her record in all that pertains to permanent gains and substantial wealth. While progressing in all departments of mercantile activity, she is constantly solidifying in those elements which in older communities constitute the substratum of commercial credit; not that the year has been free from periods of comparative dullness or exempt from disturbances.

The course of business of late years and its activity ushered in a period of prosperity, only to

A BUSINESS TOUR OF CHICAGO—INTER OCEAN BUILDING, 85 MADISON STREET.

meet with untoward events and forebodings calculated to arrest enterprise and create alarm. In spite of these disturbances, caused by a feverish state of European affairs, and by their sometimes hostile attitude, and notwithstanding serious outbreaks in our midst of impetuous and misguided laborers, frenzied by specious and criminally inflammatory appeals, the mercantile history of the past year is an exceedingly gratifying one. Had the labor troubles, which came like an epidemic and burst upon us with a murderous horror in the month of May, not occurred, labor would have been in increased demand, wages advanced, and that substantial prosperity, so long desired, would not have been delayed. All honor to the heroic police force, which, in that dark hour on the 4th of May, 1886, stood undismayed in Haymarket square like a wall of adamant for the public safety! But for that heroism, the terrors of that night would have been increased beyond the power of words to portray. Seven hearts were stilled. The red tide was stayed. Justice waits.

This tumultuous onslaught, so determinedly resisted and so emphatically condemned, will not be repeated. The people, tolerant of the largest liberty under the regulation of law, will not permit its excess to the detriment of good order or beyond constitutional limitations.

The stock yards strike, occurring in October last, was controlled with remarkable ability by the great packing firms of this city, composed of gentlemen of the highest integrity and utmost fairness. That all grievances of their employes, when properly presented, will receive their respectful and charitable consideration, cannot be doubted; that all attempts to obtain redress for alleged injustice, by violence or threats of persecution, will be summarily suppressed, is equally assured.

During the year 4,664 buildings have been constructed upon a frontage of 112,302 feet, at an estimated cost of $21,332,000; showing a very material increase in the number of buildings and in the valuation over the corresponding statement of 1885. In no other year have so many costly and elegant structures been erected.

Our coastwise and foreign trade, as a totality, makes an exhibit the extent of which may be realized by the following statement and comparisons obtained from the superintending special agent of the secretary of the treasury. The arrivals and clearances, foreign and coastwise, at this port, for the year ended June 30, last, are 22,006, which is 860 more than at the ports of Baltimore, Boston, New Orleans, Philadelphia, Portland and Falmouth and San Francisco combined; and 315 more than at New York, New Orleans, Portland, Falmouth and San Francisco; and 100 more than at New York, Baltimore, Portland and Falmouth.

When the agricultural and mining wealth contained in the vast regions lying north and west of this metropolis is thoughtfully considered; and when it is borne in mind that an immense population is destined to occupy those fields, and that unequaled facilities for transportation are provided by the great lakes, it is plainly seen that the foregoing facts, impressive as they are, will be dwarfed by the history of future years.

CHICAGO'S ÆSTHETIC FEATURES—BEAUTY OF THE CITY AND ITS ENVIRONS.

The attractions of Chicago are manifold. The boundless prairie on three sides and the waters of Lake Michigan on the fourth are its surroundings. The streets, blocks, drives, avenues and boulevards are as well defined and as regular in general as the squares of a checker-board. The streets are wide and roomy, and cross each other at right angles, and with mathematical exactness. Having sprung into existence almost instantaneously, nothing complex in the arrangements of the city mar its beauty or convenience. It is as level as a garden. Skillful engineers have succeeded in successfully draining the city by an excellent sewerage system. The climate is healthiancy of the Chicago atmosphere makes this vision of shining waters, white sails, distant spires, and green shaded drives highly fascinating. The huge elevators, looming up along the river front, the great wholesale stores, the imposing hotels and depots, suggest the enormous business interests of the city. The bridges that span the river are black with teams and carriages and people, and the intense vitality and movement of the scene can hardly be described in adequate words.

The suburbs are not less picturesquely attractive. Evanston, twelve miles distant, has the peculiar advantage of being situated on a natural knoll of rising ground, which forms the semblance of bluffs on the borders of the lake. The place con-

A BUSINESS TOUR OF CHICAGO—DEARBORN STREET, LOOKING NORTH FROM MONROE.
(CUT FURNISHED BY CHICAGO ENGRAVING CO.)

ful and invigorating, and the city is kept singularly free of all forms of malaria by the prevailing winds. The average death-rate for several years was 23.1 per thousand inhabitants, as compared with 25.3 in Philadelphia, 32.6 in New York, and 30.8 in Boston. The harbor is the best on the great lakes, and is quite picturesque as seen from the deck of an approaching vessel. The city and its surroundings, viewed from the water tower or the roof of a tall building, present a panorama of beauty. In one direction the eye takes in the miles of great business streets with their multitudes of people moving in seemingly inextricable confusion, and in another the green sweep of the parks and boulevards, built down to the very water's edge with stately mansions and trimly-kept villas. On a pleasant day the brilltains a population of about 10,000, and is worthy of a visit by those who desire to see the elegance of retired life. Highland Park, Glencoe, Lake Forest, Irving Park, Englewood, Hyde Park and Cheltenham are the names of only a few of many dozens of other charming suburbs, each having peculiar and varied attractions of its own, and all within reach by grand boulevards and by rail. No description of the suburbs of Chicago would be complete without some account of Pullman, a new city owned by the Pullman Land association. Contiguous to and really a part of Chicago, to which it owes its wonderful growth, it possesses features of interest to all visitors. Although only commenced in 1880, it has now a population of over twenty-five thousand, with gas and water works of its own, besides a park, hotel, market-house, schools, churches, library, etc. One of the special features of Pullman is that no liquor saloons are allowed within its environment, although the place is exclusively devoted to manufacturing. The green sward and leafy glades of Evanston remind the traveler of the green lanes of Kent. The gleaming waters of the lake and the gentle undulations dotted with mansions and villas present a landscape of natural beauty with which it would be impossible to compare the suburbs of any other city in the Union.

CHICAGO'S PARKS.

The parks, in many of which music is furnished during summer evenings, are among the most delightful of the attractions of Chicago. They are extensive, well planned, and beautiful, though many of them are yet in infancy. The principal parks are Washington and Jackson on the South side, consisting of two hundred and eighty-seven and eighty-four acres respectively, and including thirteen acres of artificial lakes. The drives and boulevards leading to these parks are superbly beautiful, the way for miles being lined with lawns, groves, flower-beds, etc. On the West side the Garfield park contains one hundred and eighty-five acres, the Humboldt park two hundred acres, Douglas park one hundred and eighty acres. On the North side Lincoln park has a frontage of about two and a half miles on the lake, and contains three hundred and ten acres. This park, like the others, is provided with an artificial lake, besides magnificent flower gardens, displays of birds, beasts and fishes, etc.

THE BOULEVARD SYSTEM.

The boulevard system of Chicago is a notable feature in the attractions of the city. Michigan avenue boulevard, 100 feet in width and three and a quarter miles in length, runs through a rich residence section on the South side, and is one of the finest drives in the United States. At its south end commences Thirty-fifth street boulevard, which connects with Grand boulevard. The latter leads to Washington park. Grand boulevard is 198 feet wide, and has a broad central driveway which runs between wide grass strips bearing double rows of trees. Outside of these are roadways, thirty-three feet wide,

A BUSINESS TOUR OF CHICAGO—STATE STREET, LOOKING SOUTH FROM MONROE.
(CUT FURNISHED BY CHICAGO ENGRAVING CO.)

one for traffic and the other for equestrians. Along the outer borders of the roadways are strips of grass bearing single rows of trees, and outside of these are the footways with a line of trees along the outer borders of each. Countless handsome residences line the magnificent thoroughfare on both sides. Oakwood boulevard, 100 feet wide, connects Grand boulevard with Drexel boulevard. The latter is considered the gem of the boulevard system. It is 200 feet in width, and a mile and a half in length. There is a broad central strip throughout its entire length planted with trees and shrubbery, and ornamented with winding walks, grass plats, and beds and borders of flowers and foliage plants. Drexel fountain, presented by the Messrs. Drexel, of Philadelphia, is one of the prominent ornaments of the boulevard, and gave it its name. Garfield boulevard, Western avenue boulevard, Douglas boulevard, Central boulevard, Humboldt boulevard and Washington boulevard, all have their special attactions. Lake Shore drive is a handsome part of the boulevard system, which, taken as a whole, is not surpassed, if equaled, by any system of drives in any other great city in the world.

BOAT SCENE IN LINCOLN PARK.

SOME OF THE NOTABLE BUILDINGS.

Chicago's public buildings include a large number of edifices which would do credit to any city in the world. The county court-house and city hall, which occupies the square bounded by Clark, La Salle, Washington and Randolph streets, is a notable structure, by reason of its cost and size, as well as of its tastefulness of design. Its east and west frontage is 340 feet, and its north and south frontage 280 feet. The style of architecture is modern French renaissance. The material is principally limestone, from the quarries on the Desplaines river. The columns, pilasters and pedestals are of Maine granite. The building is fire-proof. It was begun in 1877. Its total cost was about $6,000,000.

The federal building, which includes the post-office and custom-house, occupies the square bounded by Dearborn, Clark, Adams and Jackson streets, and also cost about $6,000,000. Its dimensions at the base are 342 x 210 feet. Its style of architecture is Romanesque, with Venetian treatment. The building is constructed almost entirely of stone and iron, and is fire-proof throughout. The finish of the interior is very rich.

The Exposition building, on the lake front, at the foot of Adams street, is noted for its size and the ingenuity of its construction. It was built by the Inter-State Exposition company. The building is 240 feet wide, nearly 800 feet long, and 110 feet high. It is surmounted by three towers, with ornamental domes, and has a broad gallery entirely around its interior. The arched roof, of glass, in a framework of iron, is the largest clear span roof in the world. The building was opened in the fall of 1877, with the first of a series of expositions of the products of art and industry, which have annually attracted thousands of visitors to the city.

MAGNIFICENT HOTELS.

Several of the Chicago hotels are magnificent examples of modern architecture. The Palmer house, at the corner of State and Monroe streets, is a fire-proof structure, which was erected at a cost of $2,000,000. Over half a million was expended in furnishing it. It is six stories in height above the basement, and has a frontage on State street of 281 feet and on Monroe street of 253 feet, and an L 131

ARMORY FIRST REGIMENT I. N. G.

feet in width, extending through to Wabash avenue. The fronts are of stone. The hotel was opened in 1873. An additional story was added in 1884. The structure contains 815 rooms. The wainscoting of the grand hall contains thirty-four kinds and colors of marble.

The Grand Pacific hotel covers half a square of ground, and fronts on Clark, Jackson, La Salle and Quincy streets. It is six stories high above the basement. The three main fronts are of stone. There are over 500 rooms in the house. It cost $1,300,000, the furniture costing $300,000 more. The Grand Pacific was opened in 1873. Like the Palmer house, it stands on the site of another hotel of the same name, which was destroyed in the great fire.

A BUSINESS TOUR OF CHICAGO—THE TREMONT HOUSE.

The Tremont house, on the corner of Dearborn and Lake streets; the Leland hotel, on Michigan boulevard and Jackson street; the Sherman house, corner of Clark and Randolph streets; and McCoy's New European hotel, corner of Clark and Van Buren streets, are all substantial and handsome edifices.

FINE DEPOTS.

The passenger depot at the corner of Fourth avenue and Polk street is a spacious and sightly structure, admirably adapted to the purpose for which it was built. The railroads which use it are Chicago and Grand Trunk, Chicago and Atlantic, Chicago and Eastern Illinois, Louisville, New Albany and Chicago, and Wabash, St. Louis and Pacific.

The Union depot, on Canal street, between Madison and Adams streets, has a less striking exterior, but its internal appointments are costly, tasteful and convenient, and favorably impress visitors with the wealth and taste of the city, of which it is one of the thresholds. The railroads which use the Union depot are the Chicago, Burlington and Quincy, Chicago, Milwaukee and St. Paul, Chicago and Alton, Pittsburgh, Fort Wayne and Chicago, and Chicago, St. Louis and Pittsburgh.

A MONSTER OFFICE BUILDING.

The Pullman building, Michigan avenue and Jackson street, is nine stories in height and fire-proof throughout, and is said to be the finest office building in the world. It is a dual structure, a court between the two parts assisting in the ventilation and lighting.

HANDSOME CHURCHES.

Many of the churches of Chicago are notable for their costliness and architectural taste. St. James' church (Episcopal), at the corner of Cass and Huron streets, is the oldest of its denomination in Chicago. The handsome stone edifice owned by the congregation in 1871 cost $200,000. It was destroyed in the great fire. The present church was erected in 1873. It is a sightly structure. The width of the transept is 100 feet, and the depth of the nave 173 feet. In the vestibule is a beautiful monument to the memory of members of the parish who died in the war. There are handsome windows and mural brasses, and in the tower is a fine chime of bells.

Union Park Congregational church, at the corner of Ashland avenue and Washington boulevard, is one of the largest church edifices in the city. It was completed in 1871 and cost upward of $200,000. It is Gothic in style, and built of rough-dressed stone.

The New England church (Congregational), at the corner of Dearborn avenue and Delaware place, stands on the site of the place of worship built by the congregation in 1865 and destroyed in the great fire. The present building was completed late in 1875, at a cost of $150,000.

The First Baptist church, at the corner of South Park avenue and Thirty-first street, is a fine stone edifice, which cost $80,000. It was erected in 1876. The church society was organized in 1833. By the destructive Chicago fire of 1874, the society lost a church edifice which cost $175,000.

The Second Baptist Church, corner of Monroe and Morgan streets, is one of the largest churches of this denomination in the country. It is a substantial brick edifice, with more pretensions to comfort than to appearance.

Immanuel Baptist Church, on Michigan avenue near Twenty-third street, is a handsome stone build-

A BUSINESS TOUR OF CHICAGO.

South Park Ave M E Church   L B Dixon Arch't

ing, in fifteenth century Gothic style. The spire is 216 feet high. The cost of the structure was $70,000.

Central church, in Central Music hall, is one of the notable religious institutions of Chicago. Its pastor is the learned, eloquent and progressive Rev. Dr. David Swing.

Chicago Avenue church is another of the independent churches of Chicago. Its place of worship, which is at the corner of Chicago and La Salle avenues, is a red brick edifice with stone trimmings. It seats two thousand people. The cost of the structure was $70,000.

The oldest church organization in Chicago is the First Methodist Episcopal church, which is the lineal descendant of a congregation formed in June, 1831. Since 1857 the church has followed the plan of devoting the lower story of its place of worship to commercial purposes, renting it out as stores and using the revenue in support of the church, and of other churches of the same denomination. Up to the time of the great fire over $70,000 had been contributed to other churches from this source. Since that time over $120,000 more has been distributed in the same way. The large four-story stone front building, at the corner of Clark and Washington streets, known as the Methodist Church block, is its place of worship. It cost $120,000. It has seven stores on the ground floor, and about fifteen rooms for offices above. The portion reserved for church purposes is on the third floor.

The Centenary M. E. church, on West Monroe street, near Morgan street, is one of the leading churches of Chicago. The church is an imposing stone structure, Gothic in style, ornamented with minarets, and cost $75,000.

Grace M. E. church, corner of La Salle avenue and White street, cost $100,000. It is a plain Gothic structure with gable front, and will comfortably seat twelve hundred people.

Trinity M. E. church, Indiana avenue near Twenty-fourth street, is one of the handsomest church edifices in the city. Its cost, including ground, was $142,540.

The First Presbyterian church, at the corner of Indiana avenue and Twenty-first street, is a handsome brick structure, with a spire 260 feet high, the tallest spire in the city. It is finished throughout in hard woods, principally black walnut, and has a seating capacity of 1,100. Its cost, including ground, was $165,000.

The Second Presbyterian church, corner of Michigan avenue and Twentieth street, is a massive stone building, in English Gothic style, with a stone tower and spire two hundred feet high. The tower is known as the Armour Memorial tower, and was built by Mrs. Barbara Armour, widow of the late George Armour, as a memorial of her deceased husband. In the spacious belfry is a cathedral-toned bell, weighing, with its mountings, three tons. The bell was given to the church by the children of Mr. Armour. The interior of the church is elegantly finished. The main audience room seats 1,500 people.

The Third Presbyterian church, at the corner of Ashland and Ogden avenues, is said to be the third largest Protestant church in the country. The two which surpass it are Plymouth church, Brooklyn, and Brooklyn tabernacle. It has nearly 2,200 members, and has established three churches out of the congregation, Re-Union, Westminster and Campbell park.

The Fourth Presbyterian church, corner of Rush and Superior streets, is a stone edifice, in Gothic style, finished and furnished in a very comfortable manner.

St. Mary's church, Wabash avenue and Eldridge court, is the oldest Catholic church in the city. It was organized in 1833. The present church building is a substantial stone structure, comfortably and durably finished and furnished.

The Cathedral of the Holy Name (Catholic), at the corner of North State and Superior streets, was completed in 1882, at a cost of $200,000. It is a stone structure, of the Gothic order, and seats 1,800 people. The interior furnishings are rich and in exquisite taste, and the organ is probably the most powerful in the city.

The Church of the Holy Name (Catholic), corner of West Twelfth and May streets, is a large and handsome brick structure, having seating capacity for 2,000 people. Its superb stained-glass windows, its numerous fine statues and its massive bell-tower and spire are worthy of note.

St James' church (Catholic), corner of Wabash avenue and Thirtieth street, is a Gothic structure, of stone, with a seating capacity of 1,600. It is accounted one of the finest church structures in the city.

St. John's church (Catholic), corner of Eighteenth and Clark streets, is a Gothic structure, of stone, strikingly handsome both in its exterior and interior. It seats 1,000 people.

Sinai temple, corner of Indiana avenue and Twenty-first street, is the leading church of the Jewish faith in the west. The building and ground cost $100,000. The membership includes about one hundred and fifty families, and is Reformed Jewish in faith.

St. Paul's church (Universalist), Wabash avenue, between Sixteenth and Eighteenth streets, is a fine stone structure of mingled Gothic and Romanesque architecture.

The Church of the Messiah (Unitarian), Michigan avenue and Twenty-third streets, is a sightly structure of stone. It seats 750 people. In the rear of the church is a fine two-story memorial structure, called "Mary Collier chapel." It contains the pastor's study and parlor, and a chapel for Sunday-school uses.

Unity church Dearborn avenue, opposite Washington square, is the largest of the Unitarian organizations in the city. The place of worship is of rough-dressed, stone, renaissance Gothic in its architecture. An industrial school for girls, in which sewing and housekeeping duties are taught, has been supported by the church for a number of years. A fine building for the school was erected at a cost of $20,000, from a fund bequeathed for the purpose by the late Eli Bates.

There are altogether nearly 300 churches in Chicago, of which 40 are Methodist Episcopal, 35 Catholic, 33 Evangelical Lutheran, 25 Congregational, 24 Baptist, 16 Episcopal, 16 Presbyterian and 14 Jewish.

THE BIBLE SOCIETY AND THE Y. M. C. A.

The Chicago Bible society, a branch of the American Bible society, has its depository at 150 Madison street. Its field is confined to Cook county, in which there are thirty-seven auxiliary societies. It employs about one hundred and fifty local agents in canvassing the city and county, and over half a million copies of the Bible have been circulated through its efforts.

The Chicago Young Men's Christian association has been in existence since 1858, and has upward of 3,000 members. It has a handsome and substantial building at 148 and 150 Madison street, which, with the ground on which it stands, is valued at $250,000. The library contains 3,600 volumes, and is free to all members. Handsome parlors, a reading-room, excellent baths and a well-equipped gymnasium are maintained. Sociables, lectures, and other popular entertainments are given. Railroad branches of the Y. M. C. A. are maintained at 4645 State street and 141 Stewart avenue. There is also an employment department, which is doing excellent work.

EDUCATIONAL INSTITUTIONS.

Chicago takes rank as one of the great educational centers of the country. Its public schools are numerous and admirable. It is the focus of a system of universities, theological schools and medical colleges unequaled elsewhere in the west. There are three public high schools, one in each division of the city, with altogether 1,500 pupils. The average cost of educating each pupil in the high school is about $48.25 per annum. The free primary schools and grammar schools, numbering about seventy odd buildings, are scattered throughout the city. They have an average aggregate daily attendance of upward of 60,000 pupils. The management of the schools is vested in a board of education appointed by the mayor and confirmed by the city council. There are fifteen members in the board. The total value of the school sites and buildings is nearly $4,000,000. The income of the public school system consists of the school tax from the State and city, and the income of the fund derived from rentals and sales of school lands, and from several special funds mostly bequests.

SKETCHES FROM WASHINGTON PARK.

The Northwestern university occupies a group of buildings at Evanston. The main structure, University hall, cost $110,000. The entire property of the university is valued at $1,500,000. The library contains 26,000 volumes and 8,000 pamphlets. It is especially rich in Greek and Latin classical literature. There is a valuable museum, a gymnasium, etc. The university embraces a college of liberal arts, providing classical, Latin and scientific courses, a course in modern literature and art, and special and elective courses; a college of medicine (Chicago Medical college), a college of laws (Union College of Law), a preparatory school, school of elocution, conservatory of music, department of art. The university is under the control of the Methodist denomination, but is unsectarian.

PRESBYTERIAN HOSPITAL, CORNER WOOD AND CONGRESS STREETS, S. V. SHIPMAN, ARCHITECT.

Cook County Normal and Training school, Normalville, Stewart avenue and Sixty-seventh street, was established by Cook county for the purpose of furnishing competent teachers for the public schools. Tuition is free to residents of the county. Non-residents are required to pay $30 per year.

The Union College of Law was organized in 1859 as the law department of the University of Chicago. About twelve years ago the Northwestern university was admitted to an equal interest and joint management in the school. The college occupies rooms at 80 and 82 Dearborn street.

St. Ignatius college, 413 West Twelfth street, is conducted by the fathers of the Society of Jesus. It embraces academic, collegiate, commercial and preparatory departments. In addition to the collegiate studies, the students are instructed in the doctrine and evidences of the Catholic religion. The college buildings are handsome and well arranged.

St. Xavier's academy, conducted by the Sisters of Mercy, is a boarding school for young ladies. It occupies a very handsome and commodious building on the corner of Wabash avenue and Twenty-ninth street.

St. Mary's Training school for boys is a Catholic educational institution at Feehanville, Cook county. The inmates are principally neglected youths. They are given practical instruction in the mechanical arts and the cultivation of the soil.

The Illinois Industrial School for Girls is located at South Evanston, in the old Soldiers' Home building, which was enlarged and remodeled for the purpose. It is managed by a board of directors, composed of gentlemen and ladies from different parts of the State. It is a training school for neglected and dependent girls under 18 years of age.

The Chicago Manual Training school, Michigan avenue and Twelfth street, originated with an association of gentlemen connected with the Commercial club, and was incorporated in 1883, and opened in the following year. It has a building which cost $50,000, and will accommodate about 300 pupils. The school furnishes instruction in mathematics, drawing, and the English branches of a high school course, and in the use of tools in shop-work of all kinds.

The Illinois Training School for Nurses occupies the wards in the county hospital. Pupils are required to undergo training for two years. The building and grounds known as the nurses' home, at 304 Honore street, are the property of the society under whose auspices the training school is conducted. The institution is supported by contributions, annual subscriptions, services to the hospital, private nursing and membership fees.

The Chicago Athenæum occupies the three upper stories of Nos. 48 to 54 Dearborn street. It provides facilities for intellectual and physical training, which are taken advantage of by upward of 1,000 persons every year. It is in charge of a board of directors, composed of sixteen prominent merchants and lawyers. There are day and evening classes in drawing, music, penmanship, elocution, mathematics, Latin, English and American literature, book-keeping, shorthand, type-writing, French and German. There is also a day grammar school, and a business school open to both sexes. The only condition of membership in the Athenæum is good moral character.

MEDICAL COLLEGES.

Rush Medical college has been in existence since 1836, and is the oldest medical college in Chicago. The college property is worth about $125,000. Its building is at the corner of Wood and Harrison streets, and is one of the most complete institutions of its kind on the continent. It has two lecture rooms, each with a seating capacity of 500, and thoroughly equipped. There are anatomical, physiological, clinical and chemical departments. The Central Free dispensary is connected with the clinical department, and 2,000 cases are treated annually in the county hospital.

Hahnemann Medical college was incorporated in 1855, and is the oldest homœopathic college in the northwest. The college building is at 2813 Cottage Grove avenue. It is a three-story and basement brick edifice. The hospital is a block away.

The Chicago Medical college is at the corner of Prairie avenue and Twenty-sixth street. The laboratories are well equipped, and the museum is an exceptionally large and fine one. The college was one of the first in the United States to adopt a full graded system of medical instruction, and one of the first to require a fair standard of general education in persons desiring to enter its portals.

The Bennett College of Eclectic Medicine and Surgery has a building at 511 and 513 State street, with accommodations for 250 students. Bennett hospital adjoins the college building in the rear.

The Woman's Medical College of Chicago is located at 337 and 339 Lincoln street, opposite the county hospital. It owns the brick building which it occupies. It is allopathic in its teachings, and is the only medical college in the west exclusively for women.

The Chicago College of Pharmacy has quarters at 415 and 417 State street, in a handsome brick structure that has a lecture room which will seat 400 persons. The college is admirably equipped for its work. In point of attendance it is the third in the United States.

The Chicago College of Physicians and Surgeons (allopathic) occupies a stone, four-story structure, with a tower 100 feet high, at the corner of Harrison and Honore streets. The architecture is Queen Anne style.

THEOLOGICAL COLLEGES.

The theological colleges of Chicago are numerous. They comprise the Chicago Theological seminary (Congregational), corner of Ashland and Warren avenues; the Presbyterian Theological Seminary of the Northwest, North Halsted street and Fullerton avenue; the Baptist Theological seminary, Morgan Park; the Garrett Biblical institute (Methodist Episcopal), on the grounds of the Northwestern university, and the Swedish Theological seminary (Methodist Episcopal).

CHICAGO'S LIBRARIES.

The Chicago public library, supported as a municipal institution, and free to all, has headquarters at the city hall, Washington, La Salle and Randolph streets, and branches in all parts of the city. The library has nearly 125,000 volumes, and circulates 500,000 per year. The nucleus of the library was presented to the city soon after the great fire, by Englishmen who were desirous of doing something to serve as a monument of English sympathy with Chicago in her great affliction.

The Chicago Historical society, which has been in existence since 1856, had, at the time of the great fire, a library of 100,000 volumes, and a large and valuable collection of pamphlets. Much of this material can never be replaced. All of it was destroyed in the conflagration. The library now comprises 10,000 volumes and 30,000 pamphlets. The society has a building at 140 and 142 Dearborn avenue.

The Chicago Law institute library comprises 17,000 volumes, and is one of the finest collections of legal works in the United States.

The Union Catholic library and the Young Men's Christian Association library, each comprises about 3,000 books, of a general character. Several of the public schools, and nearly all the private educational institutions, have good libraries, and the private libraries of many of the citizens of Chicago take rank among the finest book collections of their class in the country.

INSTITUTIONS OF ART AND SCIENCE.

The Art institute is an incorporated institution occupying a handsome brick building of its own, at the corner of Michigan avenue and Van Buren street. Nearly all the art societies in the city occupy rooms in the building or in some way make it their headquarters. The objects of the association are to maintain schools of art and design, form art collections and promote art culture generally. Annual loan exhibitions of painting, statuary, etc., are given. The initiation fees and annual dues of members of the association go a large way towards defraying the expenses of the institute. Connected with it is a school of instruction in drawing and painting, which is self-supporting. The Chicago Society of Decorative Art, the Chicago Art league and the Bohemian Art club, are among the organizations having rooms in the building.

The Illinois Art association holds annual exhibitions of works of art, and owns a number of fine paintings.

The musical societies of Chicago have done much toward the æsthetic development of the northwest. Among them are the Apollo Musical club, with a chorus of about two hundred voices and five hundred associate members; the Mozart club, the Germania mænnerchor, the Orpheus mænnerchor, the Chicago Musical club, and the Schweizer mænnerchor.

THE PERMANENT EXHIBIT OF BUILDING MATERIALS.

The permanent exhibit of building materials and improvements, open free to the public, at 15 East

Washington street, is an enterprise characteristic of the progressive and utilitarian spirit of Chicago. The management has no financial interest or consideration in the sale of any material shown, and the institution is supported solely by the rental of space to exhibitors. For those who build, this exhibit is a free repository of building intelligence. Being permanently established it is always at command and meets all requirements as they may occur. It gives an opportunity for comparisons of similar inventions and materials of a like kind. For those who are inexperienced and have but slight information of building improvements, this institution is an educator, and by the concentration of so much that

CRIMINAL COURT AND COUNTY JAIL.

relates to building it gives an opportunity for inspection of a great variety of subjects in a minimum quantity of time.

LITERARY AND SCIENTIFIC CLUBS.

Among the flourishing associations which exist for the study and encouragement of different branches of science are the Philosophical society, the Illinois Social Science association, the State Microscopical society, the Chicago Electrical society, the American Electrical association, the Western Society of Engineers, and the Chicago Numismatic and Archæological society. The Chicago Literary club is an organization which includes in its membership some of the brightest intellectual lights in the country. The Fortnightly is a literary organization composed exclusively of ladies.

The Chicago Woman's club has done a great deal of practical work looking toward the amelioration of woman's condition and the higher civilization of humanity.

SOCIAL ORGANIZATIONS.

The social clubs of Chicago are among the leading organizations of their kind in the United States. The Calumet club is the largest. Its building, at the corner of Michigan avenue and Twentieth street, is a palatial structure, covering an area of 81 x 183½ feet, and five stories in height. The Chicago club has a well-appointed building on Monroe street opposite the Palmer house. It is one of the oldest and most fashionable clubs in the city. The Union club is another aristocratic organization. It has a handsome and costly brownstone edifice, at the corner of Dearborn avenue and Washington place. The Union League club, the Illinois club, the West Side club, the Lakeside club, the Standard club, the Heather club, the Commercial club, the Bankers' club and the Press club are all flourishing social organizations. The Washington Park club maintains a fine race-course as well as a club-house, near Washington park. Its grounds are worth half a million of dollars.

The Chicago theaters and other public places of amusement are among the finest on the continent. Central Music hall, at the corner of State and Randolph streets, is particularly deserving of mention. The building covers 125 x 151 feet of ground, and is seven stories in height. It is of stone, and cost $215,000.

At Wabash avenue, Congress street and Michigan avenue, large gangs of men and teams are now making excavations for a building of truly mammoth proportions. This is the Chicago Auditorium. for which a number of wealthy men have raised $2,000,000. The structure will be 361 x 187 feet in ground dimensions, and ten stories in height, surmounted by a tower, rising 225 feet from the ground. The Auditorium is to have a vast opera hall containing 5,000 chairs, and with a total capacity, in such emergencies as a national convention, of 9,000 seats. This makes it the largest assembly room on the continent, and the largest one in the world available for miscellaneous public uses, as this is to be. Aside from the great hall the building will contain a hotel of 400 rooms.

CHICAGO AS A CITY OF CONVENTIONS.

On account of its lake breezes, its railway facilities, and its admirable hotels, Chicago has long been a favorite place for summer conventions. For this purpose it possesses a special advantage in having, in the main hall of the Exposition building, the largest place of assembly in the country, if not in the world. Chicago entertained the convention which nominated Lincoln in 1860, also the National Democratic convention of 1864, which nominated McClellan. Garfield was nominated here in 1880. Blaine was nominated in the National Republican convention, held in Exposition hall, in June, 1884, and two weeks later Cleveland was nominated by the National Democratic convention, held in the same place. Many of the denominational conventions make this city their place of meeting; and in the case of no national assemblage, political, religious, social or otherwise, has there ever been found any difficulty in caring for all who came, irrespective of numbers, and without inconvenience to other transient visitors.

CHICAGO'S NEWSPAPER PRESS.

The newspapers of Chicago have an individuality and enterprise that have made a reputation for them throughout the length and breadth of the land. At the head of the list are the Tribune and the Times. The Times was founded by the late Wilbur F. Storey. It occupies a handsome fire-proof building at the corner of Washington street and Fifth avenue, which cost $600,000, and is one of the best equipped printing-offices in the United States. The paper is independent in politics, with a strong democratic leaning. The Chicago Tribune is the leading republican paper of the northwest. It has a handsome fire-proof building at the corner of Dearborn and Madison streets, and is completely equipped with all the paraphernalia of a first-class modern newspaper. The Chicago Evening Journal is the lineal descendant of the first daily paper published in the city, and has flourished under its present title since 1844. It is a conservative family newspaper, in politics republican. The Times and Tribune are morning papers. The Journal is published in the afternoon. The Inter Ocean is a stalwart and influential Republican morning daily. The News is a flourishing journal which collects all the news of the world, and publishes a number of editions daily. The Chicago Herald is a handsome morning daily, bright in appearance, and newsy and entertaining in contents. The Illinois Staats-Zeitung is a newspaper published in the German language, and is the principal organ of the German-Americans in the northwest. There are nearly a dozen other daily papers, all of them enterprising and flourishing. Including the dailies, weeklies bi-weeklies, semi-weeklies and monthlies, the periodical press of Chicago has nearly 300 representatives.

THE CHARITIES OF CHICAGO.

The list of Chicago's charitable institutions is a long and creditable one. Mercy hospital, at the corner of Calumet avenue and Twenty-sixth street, was founded in 1848, by the Sisters of Mercy. It has a capacity for one hundred patients. Thirty-four sisters manage it. Its annual expenses are $20,000. The property of the hospital is valued at $260,000, but it is not free from debt.

Cook county hospital occupies an entire block, embracing twelve acres, bounded by Wood, Harrison, Lincoln and Polk streets. The buildings are all of red brick, trimmed with stone, built in pavilion style, with courts between, and well-lighted corridors connecting the four main structures. All the appointments of the institution are complete and modern. It has accommodations for upwards of five hundred patients.

The United States Marine hospital, on the lake shore, six miles north of the city, is a handsome four-story building, of granite, with ground dimensions of 300x75 feet, and accommodations for 150 patients. Its grounds are ten acres in extent. The hospital cost $450,000. Its maintenance is provided

RETAIL STORE OF MARSHALL FIELD & CO., CORNER WASHINGTON AND STATE STREETS.

for by a tax on the tonnage of all vessels. All American seamen are entitled to admission free of charge, and foreigners upon the payment of a small sum. There is a city office of the hospital, at room 20, post-office building, where applicants for admission can be examined.

The Presbyterian hospital adjoins Rush Medical college, on Wood street. It is a substantial structure of red brick. A board of twenty-eight managers directs the affairs of the institution. The doors of the hospital are open to patients of all creeds and nationalities, and the charges for board and treatment are nominal.

The Chicago Hospital for Women and Children, at the corner of Paulina and West Adams streets, affords a home for women and children among the respectable poor in need of medical and surgical aid; treats the same classes at home by an assistant physician; trains competent nurses, and maintains a free dispensary for the same class of patients. It is conducted wholly by women.

FIFTY YEARS' PROGRESS.

Hahnemann hospital, 2813 Groveland avenue, is the chemical annex to Hahnemann Medical college.

Bennett hospital is a four-story brick building, in the rear of Bennett Medical college. It has accommodations for fifty patients, and is owned and managed by the college.

St. Joseph's hospital, 309 Garfield avenue, is conducted by the Sisters of Charity. Patients who are able to pay for the treatment furnished are expected to do so. Others are received free.

St. Luke's Free hospital, at the corner of Indiana avenue and Fourteenth street, is under Episcopalian management, but admits patients without regard to their creed or nationality. Generous donations have

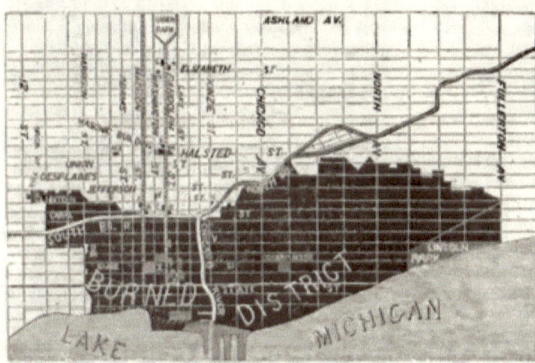

MAP OF BURNED DISTRICT—GREAT FIRE OF 1871.

placed it upon a solid financial foundation. The property is valued at $100,000, and the management have a handsome sum at interest.

The Woman's Hospital of Chicago is specially devoted to the treatment of the diseases and accidents peculiar to women. Patients are treated in the hospital and outside, and the expenses are met by the fees of paying patients and by donations.

The Maurice Porter Memorial hospital, at the corner of Fullerton avenue and Orchard street, was founded in 1882, by Mrs. Julia Porter, in memory of her dead son. Its object is the care of sick and injured children, for whom it has accommodations to the number of ten. The cost is all borne by Mrs. Porter.

The hospital of the Alexian Brothers is at 560 North Market street. Its building was erected at a cost of $45,000, and will accommodate one hundred. Only men are admitted, but there is a dispensary connected with it which is open to the sick and needy of both sexes. The expenses are met by subscriptions, solicited by one of the brothers.

The Michael Reese hospital, at the corner of Twenty-ninth street and Groveland avenue, is a handsome building, which was erected in accordance with the provisions of the will of the late Michael Reese, who left $90,000 for building and endowing the institution. The hospital is managed by the Hebrew Relief association, but patients are admitted without respect to the religious faith which they profess.

The Home for Incurables admits all classes of incurable patients who have resided in Cook county for twelve months or more. Those unable to pay are cared for without charge. The institution is located at the corner of Racine and Fullerton avenues. It is supported mainly by voluntary contributions.

Other charitable institutions in Chicago are the Old People's home, the Foundlings' home, the Servite Sisters' Industrial Home for Girls, St. Joseph's Home for the Friendless and Industrial School for Girls, the Chicago Home for the Friendless, the Burr mission, the House of the Good Shepherd, the Orphan Asylum of the Guardian Angel, the Chicago Orphan asylum, Ulich Evangelical Orphan asylum, St. Joseph's Orphan asylum, St. Vincent's asylum, the Chicago Nursery and Half-Orphan asylum, the Home for the Aged of the Little Sisters of the Poor.

The Chicago Relief and Aid society is an organization which has disbursed hundreds of thousands of dollars in charity.

The Newsboys' and Bootblacks' association maintains a home for indigent boys disposed to earn their own living. It conducts day and evening schools and a Sunday school.

The Washingtonian home, on Madison street, is a reformatory and asylum for inebriates. Most of the patients pay a small charge for board and attendance. The Martha Washington home is a similar institution for the care of women inebriates.

The Illinois Charitable Eye and Ear infirmary has a building at the corner of West Adams and Peoria streets. About three thousand patients annually are treated in this institution.

There are numerous other charitable and benevolent institutions and associations in Chicago, all doing noble work in their respective fields.

THE CITY GOVERNMENT.

The city government consists of a mayor and common council, elected once every two years by a popular vote. There are, as in other American

A BUSINESS TOUR OF CHICAGO.

cities, political districts called wards, each of which elects two members to the council. The council is vested with plenary powers as to taxes, appropriations, contracts, etc., but the bonded debt is limited by a provision in the constitution of the State to 5 per cent on the taxable valuation of all the property. The city government closed the year 1886 with every debt paid or provided for, and with a large surplus in bank. The following statements, compiled from the records of the various offices, give a comprehensive view of the work done by the city authorities during the year, and are interesting as showing the magnitude of the affairs of the great municipality:

For building, repairing and maintaining bridges and viaducts during the year, and maintaining the river tunnels, the canal pumping-works, etc., the Board of Public Works expended $384,100. In addition to this, during the twelve months, forty-three miles of streets were substantially paved, twenty-nine and one-half miles of which were new and improved streets, the remainder old streets. During the same period 3,331½ miles of streets were cleaned and kept in comparatively good condition. Nineteen and a half miles of new sewers were laid, at a cost of about $200,000, and fully that amount of water-pipe was laid during the same period.

The city treasurer's receipts during eleven months of the year, from general taxes and other sources, were $10,998,271.92.

The report of the fire marshal for 1886 shows the following interesting tabulations: Total number of fires during the year, 1,519; false alarms, 92; false still alarms, 153; second alarms, 50; second and third alarms, 3; third alarms, 10; special calls, 11; fires outside of the city, 41; buildings collapsed, 2. Total, 1,881. The losses and insurance on the same were as follows: Loss on buildings, $321,772; loss on contents, $1,131,130; total loss, $1,443,102; total insurance, $22,290,569.

The following is an approximation of the work done by the police department during the year: Number of cases prosecuted, 44,000; increase over 1885, 3,000. Amount of fines imposed, $200,000; less than 1885, $2,000. Largest monthly arrests, August, 4,949; least monthly arrests, January, 2,622. Arrests made by signal service, 20,000, being over 45 per cent of all arrests made.

The labor performed by the law department may be judged of from the fact that on January 1, 1886, there were two hundred cases pending against the city, seventy-three of which had been commenced during the preceding year.

The collections made by the city collector during the year aggregated $6,604,226, of which sum $2,051,330 represented the amount of licenses collected. Of the latter, $1,849,942 was derived from the single item of saloon licenses.

The health department reported the factory and tenement inspections made during the year as follows: Houses examined, 27,983, including 2:30,929 rooms, sheltering 56,113 families, comprising 258,477 persons, of whom 132,401 were males and 126,076 females. Of these persons, 51,677 were boys under 15 years of age, and 50,055 were girls under 15. Twelve thousand one hundred and nine notices were sent. There were 9,727 factories inspected, 20,872 stores, and 10,903 miscellaneous buildings. The number of persons employed in these stores and factories was 313,181, of whom 263,164 were males, 50,017 females, 4,313 boys under 15, and 1,528 girls under 15. The whole number of abatements made of nuisances and violations of law was 12,517.

The receipts of the water department for the year were $1,374,910.

CHICAGO'S CEMETERIES.

The resting places of Chicago's dead take rank among the most beautiful cemeteries in the world. Rose Hill cemetery, situated six and a half miles north of the city hall, is the largest. It comprises about five hundred acres of rolling upland. The main entrance to the cemetery is through an impressive, castellated stone structure, which contains a mortuary chapel. The grounds are beautifully laid out, and contain a number of artificial lakes, fed by an artesian well. The winding walks and carriage ways are macadamized. Innumerable costly and beautiful monuments of marble and granite rise above the turfy mounds, in pleasing contrast with the beautiful green of the ornamental trees and shrubbery. In summer time well-kept flower-beds add to the adornment of the place.

Graceland cemetery, which lies north of the city, about two miles from Lincoln park, comprises 125 acres of land. It is a park-like, beautiful place. Many of Chicago's distinguished citizens of the past sleep their last sleep within its peaceful borders, and many monuments, notable for their cost as well as their artistic features, mark the graves.

Calvary cemetery is the principal Catholic cemetery. It is on the lake shore, ten miles north of the city hall. Mount Olivet, south of the city, is another cemetery of the same denomination.

There are several Jewish cemeteries, owned by the Jewish congregations. Among the other cemeteries are Mount Greenwood cemetery, Waldheim cemetery, St. Boniface cemetery, Concordia cemetery, Forest Home cemetery and the Evangelical Lutheran cemetery.

A COMPENDIUM
—OF THE—
Prominent Wholesale, Retail & Manufacturing Interests
—OF—
CHICAGO IN HER FIFTIETH YEAR.

C. M. Henderson & Co.

Manufacturers and Jobbers of Boots and Shoes, Corner of Adams and Market Streets.

The inevitable conclusion of all human effort, whether in the domain of arts, science or commerce, is that some individual or coterie must and will hold the highest place, and possibly no class of men do more generously accord to an actual leader in trade his real position than gentlemen engaged in manufacturing and mercantile pursuits. The boot and shoe trade of this country need not be told that the house of C. M. Henderson & Co., of this city, have reached that representative position, since their status, is well recognized in the business world. The business, from which has been developed this really great house, was established originally in 1851, by Mr. C. N. Henderson, who, however, lived only long enough to place it in a substantial position, and upon his decease in 1859 the entire management devolved upon Mr. Charles M. Henderson, nephew of the founder, who was at that time a youth and had been connected with the house only a short time. The firm name of C. M. Henderson & Co. was at once adopted, and has continued unchanged to the present day. The firm have been burned out twice, once in 1868, and again in the memorable fire of 1871, when they were located on Wabash avenue, between Washington and Randolph, their stock, valued at some $400,000, being at that time utterly destroyed. Three weeks later, however, saw them again doing business in a temporary board shanty on Michigan avenue, corner of Congress street, where they were obliged to remain for three months, until the building at the corner of Wabash avenue and Van Buren street was completed, which they occupied for the ensuing year, and thence removed to the corner of Madison and Franklin streets. The marvelous increase of their business necessitated the occupation, in 1878, of the extensive building at the

corner of Monroe and Franklin, which in turn has again proved to be too small, and the increased facilities imperatively demanded have been lately sought in their present spacious premises, some 150 by 200 feet in dimensions, this entire six-story and basement building only affording accommodation for their salesrooms and offices. They have, in addition to this, three large manufacturing establishments, and these buildings altogether embrace more space devoted to the boot and shoe business than is occupied by any similar institution in the world.

Their sales are upwards of $3,500,000 yearly. They manufacture a great variety of goods, and make a leading specialty of the "Henderson Celebrated Red School-house" shoe, which has an unprecedented sale. They also make a specialty of gentlemen's sewed shoes, which are said to excel any similar goods in style and quality. Their ladies' and misses' fine sewed shoes are very superior, and the demand for their French and American kid and goat button shoes has become so great as to be specially notorious.

They received the first prize (a gold medal) for the highest grade of men's goods at the Centennial Exposition in 1876, but have vastly improved their styles and qualities and increased their facilities since then. They have rubber agencies, and are said to sell more rubber boots and shoes than any firm in the United States. In seeking for the causes that have led to these grand results, they may be briefly stated in a few plain words. The members of the firm, Messrs. Charles M. and Wilbur S. Henderson and Francis D. Everett, are among the leaders in the mercantile world, conducting their business upon a just and liberal policy, giving a customer the full value for his money without misrepresentation, and as they always buy for cash, they are enabled to offer to patrons such substantial inducements as careful buyers cannot afford to ignore.

L. B. Mantonya & Co.

Wholesale Commission Boots and Shoes, 227 to 231 Adams Street.

It would be difficult to find an instance that would be more readily accepted by well-informed business men as typical of Chicago's commercial enterprise than that established by Mr. Lucius B Mantonya in 1865. As a commission house where they can find a ready sale for stock, and in times of need secure ready cash, this house is always prepared to make liberal advances, Mr. Mantonya's motto being "semper paratus." His facilities for handling goods are such that in all cases quick sales and prompt returns are secured, while liberal cash advances are made on consignments. The business is divided into three distinct departments. In the private sales department, boots and shoes are received on consignment from manufacturers and jobbers, and where special bargains are offered. Another department is devoted to rubber goods, where the Boston Ideal Rubber Co's goods of every description are kept in stock, and for which Messrs. L. B. Mantonya & Co. are exclusive agents. Messrs. L. B. Mantonya & Co. handle no auction goods whatever. The house are also exclusive agents for the genuine Sucker boot, the Rochester Seminary shoe, the Society shoe and the Queen Anne shoe, also the men's Pilgrim and boys' Nabob shoes, synonyms of standard goods in the trade. To accommodate this large and valuable stock, very spacious premises are required, having occupied their present building, Nos. 227 to 231 Adams street, since 1885. Their eastern offices are at 49 High street, Boston; 142 Duane street, New York; and 333 Arch street, Philadelphia. Their references are of the highest possible character and include such well-known names as Carson, Pirie, Scott & Co., New York and Chicago; Atlas National bank, Chicago; and the Maverick National bank, Boston.

Mr. Mantonya is a native of Cleveland, Ohio, and a descendant of a famous Huguenot family.

James K. P. Pine.

Manufacturer of the "Lion Brand" Men's Linen Collars and Cuffs, 128 Fifth Avenue.

This firm has large houses at New York and Boston, which attend to the export trade as well as all the east, south and extreme west. A branch office in connection with these houses was opened in this city on October 1, '85, to supply the city and western trade generally, and already a good and steadily increasing business is the result. This branch office is located at 128 Fifth avenue, and occupies the whole of the first floor and basement. The manager, Mr. W. M. Wadsworth, is a thorough business man, and one who, thoroughly acquainted with the trade, is well qualified to watch over and develop this rising and important branch establishment. This office employs eight men as agents on the road, who take districts as far east as Cleveland and all north of Louisville. This house carries the largest stock of its kind, that is, purely men's collars and cuffs, of any in the trade, and the "Lion brand" has become so well known in the east that it is a household word. This branch supplies jobbers and retailers, and has not only a large country, but city trade also.

B. F. Chase Co.

Practical Sign Painters, 125 Fifth Avenue.

Those who imagine that art is not cultivated in this matter-of-fact, go-ahead city should pay a visit to the sign-writing manufactory of The B. F. Chase Co., located at 125 Fifth avenue. This is the oldest establishment of its kind in the city, dating back to 1845. Four years later the present head of the company became the proprietor, and continued so till last year, when the business was incorporated, having for its president, Mr. Chas. A. Chase; manager, B. F. Chase; and secretary, Fred. L. Chase. This firm are the originators of the beautiful carved wood signs which adorn some of the first-class mercantile houses, insurance offices, etc., of this city and elsewhere. They do a general sign-painting business, contracting for jobs of any magnitude and furnishing everything complete. Amongst others a large business is done in plain signs, in paint and gold, column signs, engraved, brass or white metal signs, wire signs, for hanging over streets, glass signs, etc. About twenty-five hands are employed constantly, of whom some are the most skilled artists that can be obtained. The work is carried on on the second and third floors of the building, also in premises forming part of the Times building. Orders are executed and shipped to all parts of the States and territories, some lately received being from Arizona, Dakota and New Mexico.

Myron L. Osgood.

Real Estate, Howland Block, Room 25, 182 Dearborn Street, Chicago.

The real-estate broker of Chicago has open before him an ample field for enterprise and usefulness, and many of our most prominent citizens are engaged in this important branch of industry, among whom none have more indubitably shown their capacity to rank with the very foremost than Mr. Myron L. Osgood. His business was founded four years ago, and by strict attention to business, faithful and conscientious zeal for the best interests of his customers, and fair dealing in all his operations, he has succeeded in securing a large and influential clientage. He is perfectly familiar with present and prospective values, both in and around this great city, and has upon his books many desirable bargains, including business, residence and manufacturing sites, improved and unimproved. He also secures money to loan on bond and mortgage, and in this branch is of the utmost service to both borrower and lender, procuring for the one funds with which to extend his business, and to the other a profitable and perfectly safe investment. The properties in which he deals are absolutely perfect as regards their title, and no estates are handled except those which are thoroughly safe investments. Mr. Osgood is a Massachusetts man by birth, and will be found a gentleman in every sense, well worthy of trust and confidence, careful, accurate and thoroughly honorable, whose great aim is the promotion of his clients' interests.

Servoss Furnace Co.

135 and 137 Lake Street.

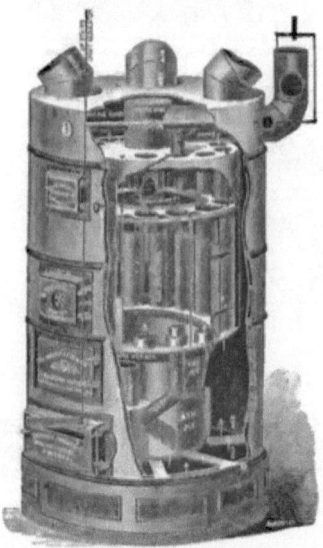

Prominent in the commercial world and representative in its special branch, stands the Servoss Furnace Co., who for the past twenty-five years have successfully covered the entire field of heating and ventilation. The company are the manufacturers of the improved Servoss "Electric Heater," "Automatic Fire Regulator" and "The Servoss-Ekstrom Kitchen Ventilator and Air-Renovator," the large demand for which, by the very best class of buyers, being a sufficient evidence of their excellence. The merits of the Electric heater are well known as regards economy in fuel and thorough efficiency in heating dwellings, stores, hotels, churches, halls and public buildings, while the Automatic Fire Regulator is capable of attachment to any kind of furnace, and will take care of the fire day and night with a large percentage of fuel saved. The company are also handling mantels and grates in great variety of styles and patterns, and in these, as in their own productions, have won a reputation on the merits of the goods and reasonable prices. The extent of their business, both in this city and abroad, makes this house a very prominent one even in Chicago, whose semi-centennial anniversary is now at hand, and as a memorial of which this review of her leading industries is issued. Like many others of our successful merchants, Mr. C. W. Servoss is a New Yorker by birth, while the characteristics which regulate the business policy of his house are such as to guarantee that business relations entered into with it will prove as pleasant as they must be advantageous to all concerned.

Portman Bros. & Co.

Manufacturers of Traveling Bags, 88 and 90 Lake Street.

Like many other branches of industry in the United States the manufacture of traveling bags has undergone a veritable revolution, while the competition has become so severe that only those fully alive to the requirements of the trade, and enterprising enough to utilize the very latest devices and appliances in the interest of speed and economy of production, can  hope for permanent success. Though established as recently as January, 1887, Messrs. Portman Bros. & Co. possess all the necessary qualifications to win success, and as regards skill, capital, care and intelligence, everything requisite is at hand. The appliances and machinery used are complete in every particular, and especially adapted for the most thorough and scientific prosecution of the work. The house confine themselves exclusively to traveling bags, and are the only ones in Chicago so to do, manufacturing them in over thirty-three varieties, while in quality and price they are prepared to compete with any in the country, and to offer every inducement compatible with legitimate business methods. Their trade includes many of the leading jobbers and dealers of our own city, and is rapidly covering the territory naturally tributary to Chicago, with prospects in the near future of the most favorable character. The individual members of the firm are Messrs. C. P. and Max P. Portman and A. C. Schmutz, the two former residents of some twenty-four years' standing, and the latter a native of this country, while the rapid development of their house fitly typifies that of Chicago.

Academy of Music.

Halsted and Madison Streets, Dan'l Shelby, Proprietor and Manager.

Though for many seasons the Academy of Music has been deservedly ranked among the most attractive theaters in the west, its former beauty was mere admirable. The opera chairs have been given a bronze gilding, the floors are covered with rich new Brussels carpets, and the whole interior decorated to conform to the wall treatment. The curtain, the work of Messrs. Sosman & Landis, is beyond doubt the handsomest hung in any Chicago theater. It is a portraiture of numerous excellently executed figures representing a scene entitled "Rewarding the

A BUSINESS TOUR OF CHICAGO—ACADEMY OF MUSIC, HALSTED AND MADISON STREETS.

display compared with its present rich and tasteful charm. The auditorium is a veritable dream of loveliness. The vestibule has been done over in delicate blue, and is very inviting. The walls of the auditorium, both up stairs and down, have been uniquely and very artistically treated, and the color tones of the house are composed of a harmonious blending of golden browns, olives, malachite greens, relieved by crimson, gold and silver. The effect is Bull Fighter," and is an enlarged reproduction of a painting by a Spanish artist. Manager Shelby can with perfect propriety claim to have one of the model theaters of the country. The past success of this theater is a sufficient guarantee that the public appreciates the manager's exertions to make this the most popular and most comfortable theater in the city. It is always in the lead with first-class attractions only, which are changed every week.

Rand, McNally & Co.

Printers and Publishers, 148 to 154 Monroe Street.

Wherever, on the American continent, railways are known or books are read, the name of Rand, McNally & Co. is familiar. Their time-tables, folders, guides, and tickets are found in railway offices everywhere; their atlases, maps, and directories are seen in the business offices of every city and town; and their book publications have hosts of readers throughout the length and breadth of the land.

The history of this house exemplifies in a striking manner the rapid development for which American institutions are celebrated. Starting little more than a quarter of a century ago as a job and book printing-office, it soon became the largest establishment of the kind in Chicago. Soon after railroad ticket printing, wood engraving, map engraving, miscellaneous book publishing, etc., were introduced; and, steadily developing, the establishment has become unrivaled in the world at the present day. The miscellaneous book department is the latest addition to the company's business, and during the few years it has been in existence, its "Globe Library" and other special publications have earned a wide popularity. Other familiar publications of the house are the "Bankers' Directory" and the "Bankers' Monthly," the "Lumber Directory," the "Business Directory of Chicago," the numerous tourists' and travelers' guides bearing the company's name, the "Indexed Atlas of the World," the "Standard" map of the United States, etc. In short, there are few establishments in the world whose names are so widely or so favorably known as that of Rand, McNally & Co. They occupy the large six-story building at 148 to 154 Monroe street, Chicago, where a map may be followed from the hands of the compiler to the bins of the stock room, or a book may be traced from the pen of the author to the cases in the shipping room.

Heath & Milligan M'f'g Co.

Manufacturers of Mixed Paints and Dry Colors, Etc., 170, 172 and 174 Randolph Street.

The Heath & Milligan Manufacturing company commenced their business in a small way in 1851, and by industry and sound business qualities their trade grew with the growth of the city, and though burnt out twice, once in 1870, and again in the great fire of the succeeding year, they recommenced each time with renewed life and vigor. In 1881 the firm became a corporation with a paid-up capital stock of $250,000, and of which Messrs. Monroe Heath is president, Elliott Durand, vice president, E. W. Heath, secretary, and James S. Smale, treasurer. This house is now one of the largest and most complete of its kind in the United States. The premises occupied here are of large extent, centrally located, and admirably adapted for the trade carried on. They consist of the whole buildings comprising Nos. 170, 172 and 174 East Randolph street, each containing five stories and basement. The top floor and basement are used for storage, the second, third and fourth floors for grinding and preparing the paints and dry colors, while the first floors are used as packing rooms, sales rooms and office. A force of 175 hands is employed constantly, 175 grinding mills are in constant operation, worked by an engine of 150 horse-power. Twenty-five hundred gallons a day are made of the mixed paints, four tons daily of dry colors, two tons daily of oil and Japan colors, while six large grinding mills turn out daily fifteen tons of white lead and paste paint. Orders are not only shipped to all parts of the United States, but to Canada and Mexico. A very heavy stock is carried, the largest of any house this side of New York city. The business is still rapidly increasing, the approximate sales for last year amounting to over $800,000. None but the best materials are employed, and the firm are so well known that their name alone is a sufficient guarantee of the quality of their goods.

Moorhead-McCleane Company.

Galvanized Sheet Iron, Corrugated and Crimped Roofing Iron, Office and Warehouse, Lake and West Water Streets.

In crossing to the West side, over the new Lake street bridge, visitors will first notice the handsome new Jones & Laughlins block on the right-hand side. One of the most important firms carrying on business in this building is that of Moorhead-McCleane Co., manufacturers of galvanized sheet iron, corrugated and crimped roofing iron, special widths sap pan and sheet iron. The works of this company are situated at Pittsburgh, Pa., and are the largest of the kind in the country. Their Chicago business is cared for by their agent, Mr. W. E. Stockton, who has held that position since 1881. He is a thoroughly practical business man, and one who has the interests of the company at heart. Through him they do a most extensive trade among the western and southern States. At their warehouse on Lake and West Water streets they carry the largest stock of galvanized iron goods in the city. Persons interested in this line of manufacture would be consulting their own interests to call and inspect the stock of Moorhead-McCleane Co.

Lawrence Ambs & Co.

Manufacturers of Fine Scales and Weights, 81 and 83 North Clinton Street.

A branch of industry in which the greatest amount of skill and accuracy is required, and in which the ingenuity of the artisan is taxed to its utmost, is the manufacture of the delicate scales and minute

weights in use by the chemist and druggist, in which he makes a specialty. This business is in the hands of a few firms, and one of the best known is that of Messrs. Lawrence Ambs & Co., of 81 and 83 North Clinton street, manufacturers of fine scales and weights. This firm occupies a light and spacious factory facing on Clinton street, which is fitted up with the most intricate and delicate machinery, and they give employment to six skilled workmen. Mr. Ambs, who is at the head of the business, is a native of Germany, where he learned his trade. He came here in 1877 and established himself in business on his own account in 1880. Being a most expert workman he is enabled to personally supervise his staff of assistants, and the excellence of the work turned out by him has established their reputation throughout the United States.

Grier & Jack.

Wholesale Lamps, Glassware and Fruit Jars, 18 Lake Street.

In the wholesale lamp and glassware trade this firm has attained an enviable reputation among the representative establishments of its kind in the city, and, although established as recently as 1884, under the present name, yet each member of the firm has been in the business since 1861, succeeding the old firm of Wheeler, Chapman & Co. and Chapman, Grier & Co. Every facility is at hand for the prosecution of the business under the most favorable auspices, while the experience of Messrs. Henry B. Grier and Albert Jack, the proprietors, guarantees the permanency of their success. The stock is extensive and well selected, embracing everything desirable comprehended under the general head of glassware, lamps, globes, chimneys, chandeliers and fruit jars, the variety of the latter being specially complete, while the goods are offered at such prices as enables them to compete with any house in the trade. The building occupied is a spacious five-story and basement structure, well lighted and conveniently appointed and arranged for the proper storage and display of the stock, while externally the handsome front presents an attractive and showy appearance, adding much to the metropolitan aspect of that portion of the street. Taken in any respect, whether in the extent of its stock, the magnitude of its salesrooms, or the scope and volume of its transactions, this house ranks as a representative one and a fair exponent of the present stage of progress of the lamp and glassware trade of the western metropolis at the close of the fiftieth year.

The Exhaust Ventilator Co.

Mechanical Air-Movers and Contractors for Heating and Ventilating, Corner of Polk Street and Third Avenue.

The subject of ventilating is one which occupies much attention, but in many cases it is as necessary in cold weather as in warm. Wherever it is required that the air shall be frequently changed, exhaust fans rotating by steam or natural ventilation are more or less affected by the varying winds and the condition of the atmosphere outside, hence are not to be depended upon. The Exhaust Ventilator Co. was organized about six years ago, and has offices in Boston, New York, Philadelphia, London (England) and in this city at corner of Polk street and Third avenue. Mr. L. G. Fisher is president, and Mr. L. Litchfield manager of this branch. This company's system acts independently of the weather, and is secured by patents granted to Messrs. Altebrand and Blackman, the first of which dates from 1877, and the last 1883, and by them assigned to this company.

The Blackman inventions have resulted in a form of blades which delivers the maximum amount of air and has a feed area two-thirds greater than that of the old forms; so that these fans give the largest volume of air at the lowest horse-power. Besides carrying a large stock of fans of their own manufacture, this company is prepared to supply any form of machine for mechanical air movement, including pressure or blast fans. The use of these ventilators is universal and applied to all large buildings, offices, manufactors, etc., in all parts of the world. Upon application a list of buildings ventilated by this company and parties using this wheel will be furnished, and plans will be submitted, or advice given where the facts are stated, gratuitously. References in this city are to Chicago Tribune, First National bank, Commercial National bank and Chicago National bank.

In no instance has the introduction of an exhaust or other form of ventilation by this company for any use been followed by complaint. Full information, catalogues and price lists will be sent free on application to the offices before mentioned.

Globe Foundry.

R. M. Eddy's Sons, Proprietors, 41 to 55 East Indiana Street.

This is one of the largest and most important establishments of the kind in the west. They turn out all kinds of heavy and light castings for boiler fronts, buildings, machinery, etc. In the heavy casting line they have no superior, and their trade is very large and extensive. The business was established in 1865 under the firm name of Gardner & Eddy, which was changed in 1869 to R. M. Eddy, and in 1884 to the present firm of R. M. Eddy's Sons. The premises occupied are large and commodious, having dimensions of one hundred by two hundred feet and four stories in height, with a large basement. Every facility is found in this establishment, and they are prepared at all times to turn out large and special jobs on short notice. From sixty-five to one hundred men are employed, according to the amount of work on hand. The business has increased year by year, until now it amounts to over $100,000 annually. Both members of the firm are experienced foundrymen and well acquainted with every feature of this trade. Correspondence is solicited, and estimates are furnished for castings of all kinds.

W. Seng & Co.

Manufacturers of Furniture Fixtures, 224 E. Washington Street.

Mr. Seng has patented some eight or nine devices which are used in the construction of various articles of furniture, such as reclining and barber chair fixtures, bed-lounge legs, locks and extensions, crib and rocker fixtures, universal joint for arm-chairs, etc.

The latest invention is that of a drill-press of four spindles represented by the cut.

This tool is automatic in every respect, oils its own work, feeds its own drill, stops feed and returns table instantly to starting point. The operator has to put the work in and take it out. A boy of ordinary intelligence can operate it with ease and do the work of four ordinary presses, besides a great saving in oil and drill. You can work one, two, three or four spindles at once. This firm employs from four to eight hands and makes goods either for stock or order, and goods are sent out to all parts of the country, and a large city business is also transacted. The sales are chiefly to manufacturers of furniture, and a business is done of over $10,000 yearly. Mr. W. Seng was born in Germany and came direct to Chicago in 1856, when the number of inhabitants was only about one-tenth of its present population.

Commercial Laundry.

Annie Lindner, Proprietress, 83 North Clark Street.

At this location is the well-arranged Commercial laundry, which is under the charge of Miss Annie Lindner, who began business about eight years ago, and has given such satisfaction that a large and influential trade has been established. The special feature of this laundry is handwork, so that persons who patronize this place may rest assured of not having their clothes spoiled by excessive use of starch on over-heated machinery. Goods are called for and delivered to any part of the city free of charge, and all orders by mail will meet with as prompt attention as though delivered personally. Perfect order prevails at this establishment, and none but efficient help is employed. Her specialty is family washing, for which she charges thirty-five cents per dozen for rough-dry work and one dollar for finished work.

The Great Four-Track Route, over the New York Central
AND HUDSON RIVER AND BOSTON AND ALBANY RAILROADS.
Western Department, 97 Clark Street, Room 10, Chicago.

W. B. JEROME, General Western Passenger Agent.

One of the first inquiries generally made by persons intending to become interested in any manner at large commercial centers is, "Are the transportation facilities adequate, and will they be commensurate with the growth of future business?" In this respect Chicago is exceptionally fortunate, and we have only to point to Lake Michigan on the east and glance for a moment at the great steel highways that either make this city their terminal or initial objective points to be able to answer such a question decidedly in the affirmative. By connections made with the trunk lines in other cities, Chicago is enabled to maintain direct travel from ocean to ocean.

that it is the only line having a depot in New York, thus being able to land its passengers in the heart of the city and save them the annoyance of "ferry transfers." Those who have traveled over this route between Chicago and the metropolis, along the eastern bank of the historic Hudson, through the lovely Mohawk valley (famed in poetry and prose), are unanimous in praising the unrivaled scenery presented to their enraptured view.

Limited express trains are run over this route between Chicago and New York in both directions, making the trip in the remarkably fast time of twenty-five hours.

GRAND CENTRAL DEPOT, NEW YORK.

Among the oldest of these connections are the New York Central & Hudson River and the Boston & Albany railroads. They were among the first to enter Chicago for business and have kept steadily in advance of other eastern lines by affording first-class facilities to the traveling public. The New York Central, being the most direct line between Buffalo and New York, is enabled, with its connections, to run solid trains between New York, Boston and Chicago. The special advantages it offers as to speed and safety are unsurpassed by any road in America; two of its four tracks, laid with steel rails, being used exclusively for passenger traffic, and two for freight. This, with the entire absence of grades or short curves, makes traveling safe and comfortable.

Another very commendable feature is the fact

The connection of "The Central" with the Boston & Albany road (at Albany) makes it the short line to Boston and all New England points. The growth of business on these roads, especially in the western department, is synonymous with that of Chicago itself. This department, under the management of W. B. Jerome, embraces all the territory west and south of the State of Ohio and the Dominion of Canada. Mr. Jerome, having had some sixteen years' active experience in an official capacity with other leading railway lines before taking charge of this territory some three years ago, is consequently well acquainted with the intricate details of railroad management, and takes great pleasure in giving the public any necessary information regarding the lines he represents.

John V. Farwell & Co.

Wholesale Dry Goods, Notions, Woolens, Carpets and Upholstery, Monroe and Market Streets.

The fact that Chicago has permanently retained the supremacy as the great national emporium of the western and middle States, is almost entirely due to the enterprise and energy of her leading merchants and importers, who have by their untiring industry and thorough knowledge of the requirements of the public, enlarged their business and increased their stocks in a ratio proportionate to the calls of the vast trade concentrated in this city.

In the wholesale dry goods trade the representative house is that of Messrs. J. V. Farwell & Co., devoted exclusively to dry goods of any house in the world. The building is imposing in appearance and an architectural ornament to the city, being eight stories in height and handsomely finished. Internally the store, or rather series of stores, is a hive of busy, well-ordered industry, each one of the eight floors containing 52,200 square feet of space, every inch being utilized for the accommodation of the firm's enormous stock, accumulated from all the leading manufacturing centers of the world. The stores are most handsomely fitted up with every modern convenience and improvement, including steam freight and passenger elevators, electric bells, electric lights, telephones and telegraph, while a thorough system of organization pervades every department of the immense establishment, each one of

A BUSINESS TOUR OF CHICAGO—JOHN V. FARWELL & CO'S. WHOLESALE DRY GOODS HOUSE, CORNER MONROE AND MARKET STREETS.

whose immense establishment, corner of Market and Monroe streets, is one of the sights of Chicago, and takes rank with anything of the kind either in Europe or America. The gigantic business transacted here really began its marvelous growth in 1854, when John V. Farwell became the junior member of the firm of Cooley, Wadsworth & Co., which soon afterward became John V. Farwell & Co. The rapid growth of trade compelled an early removal from the original location to Wabash avenue. Here the house made rapid progress and was enlarging its connections and developing upon the most substantial and conservative basis when the calamitous fire of 1871 swept away their entire establishment, which had been seriously damaged by fire only a short time previously. Messrs. Farwell & Co. were not to be deterred by the magnitude of these reverses, and with characteristic enterprise and perseverance selected a favorable site on Monroe street, erecting thereon a large building, where they remained until removing into the Farwell building, which is considered to cover the largest superficial space the firm's six hundred employes being systematically trained to his duty.

The firm reaches out by its direct personal representatives to all the markets in Europe and America and is a complete wholesale emporium for dry goods, woolens, notions, carpets, upholstery, etc., representing the choicest fabrics of these classes of manufacture throughout the world, adapted to the wants of buyers from all parts of the country and selected with especial reference to the assortments required in each of the various departments of their business. The stock embraces foreign and domestic silks, satins, velvets, dress fabrics in all textures, white goods, linens, domestic cottons, laces, ribbons, embroideries, shawls, wraps, etc., furnishing and upholstering goods, blankets, flannels, hosiery, gloves, underwear, carpetings, both imported and domestic, mattings, yankee notions, fancy goods and kindred articles.

The firm is the most active and extensive importing house in the city, and ever foremost to exhibit the choicest season's novelties, keeping experienced resident buyers in the European and eastern markets. Buying so largely as Messrs. John V. Farwell & Co. do, and possessing such perfected facilities, the firm is universally noted for its splendid display of goods and the lowness of its prices. Associated with Mr. John V. Farwell in the co-partnership are Messrs. Charles B. Farwell, John K. Harmon, John T. Chumasero and John V. Farwell, Jr. They combine that strength of talents and resource for which this house is celebrated, while the wise and prudent management characteristic of their commercial career reflects the greatest credit upon all concerned. Mr. John V. Farwell, during his lengthy, active identification with engrossing commercial pursuits, has, as is well known, found time to engage in many philanthropic and beneficiary enterprises, and is one of Chicago's most public-spirited citizens, whose efforts for the advancement of the western metropolis are duly appreciated and will forever link his name with the noble cause of humanitarian progress. In commercial life he and his able co-partners have ever adhered to the most stringent code of business ethics and have advocated the policy of equity and honor on all occasions, supporters of national as well as individual rectitude. Mr. Charles B. Farwell has been time and again honored with the suffrages of his fellow-citizens, whom he has ably represented in numberless responsible and honorary public offices, and has lately been deemed worthy to wear the mantle of the late lamented hero, soldier and statesman, John A. Logan, whose unexpired term in the senate of the nation he has been called to fill. Upon all questions of the hour the firm stands a unit, on the side of progress and is a thorough exponent of the best methods in mercantile life, upon which substantial basis their immense trade has been developed, which includes all the leading dry goods houses of the western, middle and southwestern States, their annual sales aggregating many million dollars, no house contributing more largely to Chicago's permanent commercial prosperity and financial importance.

Isa A. Eberhart

Dealer in Chicago Lawn Property, 182 Dearborn Street.

The great demand for choice suburban property, together with the steady rise in values, affords the best evidence of Chicago's growing wealth and prosperity. Experience shows that to the thrifty artisan, the salaried clerk and the moderate business man, these suburban offerings have proven of inestimable value in permitting them to acquire a pleasant home at a reasonable price, apart from the turmoil of city life, and in a healthful location. Without wishing or intending to institute comparisons, while referring to suburban properties, justice only is served when Chicago Lawn is named as one of the finest building sites surrounding Chicago, and which offers superior inducements to those desiring cheap homes or an investment for speculation. Since being put upon the market only a year ago, over 200 of these lots have been sold. Mostly to American families for immediate improvement. It is located southwest of Chicago, on the Grand Trunk railroad, at Sixty-third street, the highest ground anywhere in that vicinity, and considerably higher than either Chicago or Englewood, the commutation fare being only that of the street-cars in most cities, while the town has all the conveniences of schools, churches, stores, post-office and express office. Mr. Isa A. Eberhart, 182 Dearborn street, is offering at present these lots upon unusually favorable terms, accepting monthly payments and even assisting his customers in building their homes. Mr. Eberhart, whose son is editor of the "Insect World" at the Lawn, is a native of western Pennsylvania, and was for many years engaged in the ministry, while in business life he has achieved a success and reputation accorded only to those whose transactions are based on the strictest probity.

Kroeschell Bros.

Boiler and Steam Fitting Works, 4 to 12 Michigan Street.

This house was established six years ago and has continued with a large trade ever since, until now they employ from fifty to seventy-five experienced workmen in the manufacture of tubular, locomotive and upright boilers, oil and water tanks, sheet iron work, heating of buildings, connecting of boilers, engines, pumps, pipe-fitting and brass goods. The plant they occupy consists of 125 feet on Michigan street, with a depth of 100 feet. The buildings are well arranged for the work, and fitted with the best machinery and appliances for the rapid prosecution of this business, a twenty horse-power engine being used. One of the specialties of this firm is the manufacture of Kroeschell & Bourgeois' patent feed water heater, represented in the accompanying cut.

Although only manufactured since 1883, it has met with great favor by the trade. It is superior to all other heaters in the following respects: That by introducing the exhaust from above, the temperature of water is raised faster and higher than by any other heater; it keeps boilers free from scale; it does not cause back pressure to engine; by its simplicity of construction it will require less attention; saves boiler repairs; saves from 15 to 30 per cent. in fuel. The great trouble with other heaters, caused by the early and frequent corroding of flues, is obviated in this heater, the material of the tubes being the best brass. The price is lower than any other on account of simplicity. Being manufactured at their factory and under their direct supervision, they are enabled to guarantee every heater in all respects.

The members of the firm, Chas., H. A., Albert and Otto Kroeschell, are natives of Nashville, Tenn., from whence they came and located in Chicago in 1862.

The Tourists' Paradise.

Famous Resorts of the Northwest Reached by the Wisconsin Central Line.

Each succeeding year, when the first bright freshness of the spring foliage has disappeared to give place to the dust and dryness of the fierce June sunshine, when the gentle showers of early summer have been superseded by the sprinkling-cart and garden-hose, and the spring overcoat discarded for the linen duster, when the business man begins to hug the shady side of the street on his daily trips to and from his office, a very large proportion of the people of our great cities turn their thoughts toward the country and commence laying plans for the annual summer vacation, which, in these days of rapid money-getting and high-pressure living, has become an indispensable element in the calendar of every man of wealth and woman of fashion whose line of life has been cast in the seething, bubbling, tumultuous swim of modern metropolitan existence.

Until within a very recent period, the tide of summer travel has set almost exclusively in the direction of the fashionable, though long ago exhausted, resorts of the east. Saratoga, Long Branch, Newport and the White mountains are like an old edition of some standard line of authors, whose pages have been thumbed and turned so repeatedly that there is neither pleasure nor instruction to be derived from their further perusal. California and the Pacific slope appear to have been so completely overdone by guide-books and circulars as to have reached a hackneyed stage of "innocuous desuetude" long before its attractions are exhibited to view, and, besides, the time occupied in visiting those distant scenes would consume a considerable share of the average American's midsummer holiday season.

During the past decade, however, a new Eden of enchantment has gradually but irresistibly developed to draw within its delightful circle an ever-increasing throng of pleasure-seekers from all parts of the Union. Wisconsin, the summer paradise of the fashionable world, the angler's Mecca of inexhaustible resources, the huntsman's bonanza, the invalid's acme of sanitary perfection, in short, the complete Utopia of the tourist and pleasure-seeker, presents an innumerable array of charms which each recurring season attract thousands of the nation's wealthiest citizens to our lovely State.

BAD RIVER.

Waukesha, "the Saratoga of the West," endowed by nature with climatic and scenic advantages which her eastern namesake never possessed, and whose fame as a water-cure, where lost health and vigor may be renewed or subtle disease baffled and defied by the simple efficacy of her Bethesda and Silurian springs, has been heralded to the remotest quarters of the globe. As a fashionable social resort alone, Waukesha has achieved a national reputation. Within an hour's drive of the city, upon the loveliest of roads winding through shady groves and over rustic bridges spanning rippling rills fresh from their fountain source, are to be found from twenty to thirty of the most beautiful little lakes in the world, transparent as crystal, their edges overhung with drooping grasses and clinging vines and their verdure-clad shores lined with picturesque cottages and rural homes, while steam yachts and miniature sailing craft with snowy canvas and swanlike outlines speed along over the rippling blue surface of the foreground in delightful profusion. All of these lakes are plentifully stocked with every variety of American game fish and the most improved tackle and seductive bait is provided at a moment's notice for all who care to indulge their piscatorial fancies. Nothing has been left undone by nature to fit this region for a perfect suburban home, and with all due deference to the vaunted lakes and crags and castles and glens of European legend and guide-book, it is scarcely an · exaggeration to claim that, for summer resort purposes, the lake region in the vicinity of Waukesha is unsurpassed on either continent.

Gus. Lindholm's Express.

72 to 76 North State Street.

Besides the large express business done by Mr. Lindholm he is also an extensive dealer in coal, wood and coke. The business was begun some years ago with only a one-horse wagon, and Mr. Lindholm is now the proprietor of one of the largest express businesses in the city. He is persistent and painstaking in all his work, and satisfaction is guaranteed on every order received, and at moderate prices. His business is divided into three departments, teaming, general expressage and parcel delivery. In the first he has some of the largest trucks in use in Chicago, and he has permanent contracts with the large merchants to do their hauling. Besides doing a general express business all over the city, he has his regular customers who have his call cards, and four trips are made daily all over the city. The parcel delivery is complete in every respect, and for ten cents persons can have articles delivered at their homes in any part of the city. Mr. Lindholm is a native of Stockholm, Sweden, and came to this city in 1869.

N. G. Levinson & Co.

Wholesale Jewelers, No. 114 Dearborn Street.

Mr. Levinson has been in the business for the last five years, having been located in his present position the whole of the time. He carries a full line of jewelry and watches, and the latest designs and novelties are to be found in his stock. All the articles he handles are of the very best quality and can be depended upon to give satisfaction.

The business is exclusively wholesale, and goods are supplied by agents to all parts of the central and western States, from Ohio to Kansas and Nebraska.

Mr. Levinson has been connected with the business for the last fifteen years and his long experience enables him to purchase the best class of goods, and those most likely to please the taste as well as the pocket of the public.

A full stock is kept in all branches, so that retailers will find here just what they need, the best in quality and lowest in price.

Aug. Hirschfeld.

Merchant Tailor, 106 Fifth Avenue.

One of the oldest established firms in the trade is that of Mr. Aug. Hirschfeld, who occupies the ground floor of No. 106 Fifth avenue. He commenced this business at 127 North Clark street eighteen years ago, and after his loss in the great fire he re-established his business in the same locality, where he remained for ten years. He has only occupied his present site for two years. The business is large, and numbers amongst its customers some of the leading men of the city, his garments being always superior in style and perfect in fit. The manufacture is confined solely to men's clothing, which is supplied to city customers, the cloth being obtained from eastern and also from city houses. The stock kept is medium, and of the best quality. Mr. Hirschfeld, a Saxon by birth, is always ready to execute orders on short notice, and made up in a manner that cannot fail to be satisfactory. He trusts the cutting out to no one, preferring that branch of the business himself, and does his best to give complete satisfaction.

L. Nitschkowsky.

Merchant Tailor, 130 South Clark Street.

It will never be possible to make to order as cheaply as to buy ready-made clothing, but there is a great difference in the prices charged at different houses. No firm in the city make more cheaply goods of first quality and best workmanship than Mr. L. Nitschkowsky, who has his establishment at No. 130 South Clark street, room 5. He commenced business in 1864 on the North side, where he was burnt out in 1871. For the last ten years he has been located at the place he now occupies, enjoying a steady and increasing amount of patronage.

He uses the best domestic material and imported goods only, and employs workmen thoroughly skilled and experienced in the making-up department. As an instance of the hold he retains on his patrons it may be noted that he has orders from Florida, Nebraska, etc., from those who dealt with him while residing in this city.

Mr. Nitschkowsky prides himself on his good name; he has always acted fairly and honorably by all who have favored him with their patronage. He came to this country thirty-two years ago, when the city had only one-tenth of its present population, and during the whole of the time since then has been engaged in his present line of trade.

Chas. T. Wilt.

Manufacturer and Dealer in Trunks, Traveling Bags, Etc., 40 East Madison Street.

In that of Charles T. Wilt, Chicago possesses a house of more than ordinary importance in the manufacture of trunks, traveling bags and ladies' satchels.

Mr. Wilt is a gentleman of great versatility of talent, having become proficient as a printer, and also a thoroughly learned lawyer before leaving his native city, New York, whence some thirty-two years ago he came to Chicago. In 1862 he founded his trunk business at No. 24 N. Clark street, and soon developed his trade, opening his factory at No. 222 on the same thoroughfare. The business growing he found it profitable in 1869 to open another establishment at No. 100 Lake street. In 1883 Mr. Wilt occupied his present eligible premises, No. 40 Madison street, where is displayed the finest and most complete stock of solid sole-leather Saratoga and sample trunks, traveling bags and ladies'-satchels of every description to be found in the west. The large factory comprises the spacious four-story and basement building Nos. 198 to 204 Kinzie street, wherein a large force of skilled and experienced trunk-makers are engaged. Throughout the establishment the greatest order and system prevail, which is at once an evidence of Mr. Wilt's judicious management, while the good judgment and taste displayed in the production of stock indicate thorough experience in the business and an intimate practical acquaintance with the wants of a critical trade.

James Pittaway.

Teas, Coffees and Spices, 26 and 28 River Street.

Among the many houses who handle these commodities in Chicago may be mentioned that of James Pittaway. This gentleman occupies extensive premises at 26 and 28 River street, and is engaged in business as a wholesale dealer in teas, coffees and spices. He handles the choicest kinds of these goods that can be bought in the eastern markets, and his trade extends throughout the western and northwestern States. In the matter of spices he does a very fine local trade among the grocers and retail houses. Mr. Pittaway has been in the trade for thirty years, and during that time his perseverance and experience combined have given him a recognized place in the market, and he is looked up to as one of our most reliable traders in this class of goods.

Richard Irwin.

Draper and Tailor, No. 41 North State Street, Chicago.

At this establishment garments are made of good material, and in the most elegant and latest styles. The proprietor Mr. Richard Irwin, is one of the most popular drapers and tailors of the city of Chicago. He has been in the business for over ten years, and during that time has had the patronage of the most influential citizens of the Garden City. His facilities are unsurpassed, and he keeps a force of twelve skilled workmen, whose labors are conducted under his own direct supervision. His transactions average $15,000 per annum, and the business is rapidly increasing. He is a native of Canada, and came to Chicago in 1868.

Gannott's Laundry.

2135 Wabash Avenue.

Gannott's laundry is well arranged and equipped for the rapid prosecution of the business. Six to eight assistants are employed to help with the work, while machinery of the latest and best patterns is used. Mr. Gannott established the business twelve years ago, at his present quarters, and by perseverance, good work and a personal supervision of all the branches has built up a large and steadily increasing trade. The best of order prevails, and all goods are received, checked, done up and returned in splendid condition. There are no chemicals used in the work, and the best of satisfaction is given. Special rates to hotels and restaurants. Mr. Gannott was born in Germany, and came to Chicago in the spring of 1872.

David J. Braun.

Manufacturer of Stamped and Spun Metal Goods, Etc., Office and Factory, 70 West Monroe Street.

The well-known and prosperous house of David J. Braun, of 70 West Monroe street, is extensively engaged as a manufacturer of stamped and spun metal goods, wire workers, chandelier trimmings, etc. He makes a specialty of the manufacture of the well-known electric kerosene lamps, a most useful invention, and one in great demand among his numerous customers. Mr. Braun is a German by birth, but has been a long while in this country. He has been engaged in his present business for the last twelve years, and has established a large and ever increasing business among the principal lamp and gas-fixture dealers in the country. His goods have a first-class reputation on the market, and as Mr. Braun is a thoroughly practical man, he makes it a point to turn out nothing but first-class work.

N. Barnett.

Dealer in All Kinds of Coal, Coke and Wood, Office and Yards, 3121 to 3125 Cottage Grove Avenue.

Energy and enterprise, when well directed, invariably lead toward success in all the walks of life, a notable instance of which being found in the prosperous career of Mr. Napoleon Barnett, the enterprising coal dealer of Cottage Grove avenue. Though born and reared in Montreal, Canada, Mr. Barnett has resided in the United States for some twenty-one years past, during fourteen of which he was engaged as a contracting mason and plasterer. In 1879, however, seeing a favorable opening, he established his coal business at Nos. 3121-25 Cottage Grove avenue, his present site, where he enjoys every facility for conducting his business under the most favorable auspices, his storage accommodations being ample, the yards themselves desirably located, while purchasing, as he does, in large lots direct from the mine, he is enabled to quote the lowest ruling prices. All kinds of hard and soft coal are dealt in, as well as coke, wood and kindling wood, in quantities to suit. Under his management this business has developed into one of the largest in this section of the city, having reached the snug sum of $25,000 per annum. Mr. Barnett is a gentleman well known in business and financial circles, and has attained success upon an honorable basis of equity.

T. E. Copelin.

Stoves, Furnaces, Ranges, Hardware, Etc., 37 North State Street.

The stock of this standard house is entirely new and consists of stoves, furnaces, ranges and shelf hardware of almost every description. A full line of kitchen utensils of the latest designs is carried, as well as all kinds of hardware specialties and housefurnishing goods. Mr. Copelin is agent for the celebrated M. & D. wrought-iron ranges and also the "Monitor" stoves and ranges of Wm. Resor & Co., Cincinnati, Ohio, and makes a specialty of kitchen outfits for hotels, large residences, etc., in which correspondence is solicited. All kinds of stove work and jobbing in tin and galvanized iron is done here. The facilities are such that all orders meet with prompt attention. Fine grinding is also done, as well as nickel-plating and polishing. The prices for goods and work are very reasonable. Mr. Copelin is a native of this city and has long been connected with the business interests of Chicago.

Bakenhus & Mueseler.

Manufacturers of Carriages, Trucks and Wagons, 95 and 97 East Indiana Street.

Prominent among the establishments engaged in this important branch of industry is that of the firm of Bakenhus & Mueseler, located at Nos. 95 and 97 East Indiana street. This firm has acquired a merited popularity throughout the city and environs for the superior quality of vehicles turned out, and their uniform reliability. The business was begun seven years ago, on the corner of La Salle avenue and Illinois street, but was removed to the present eligible and commodious quarters two years ago. The blacksmithing, wood-work, paint and finishing departments are all well arranged for the rapid prosecution of work. Only the best material is used, and the best class of workmen are employed. Both members of the firm are veterans in this business, it being their life trade. Many improvements have been made by them, which have not only helped to establish their reputation for good work, but have added to the general character of this line of industry in Chicago. Every description of work is made to order, while repairing is promptly and satisfactorily executed. All persons having work of this kind will do well to consult this firm before going elsewhere, as their prices are reasonable, and work first class.

Home Laundry.

10 Rush Street, Mrs. A. Moller, Proprietor.

The name of this laundry is appropriate, for it is a home laundry in the full acceptance of the term. Every piece is done by hand, and with great care, under the direct supervision of Mrs. A. Moller, who has a practical knowledge of how everything in this line should be done. She has been established in business for the past six years, and has never wanted for patronage, as the work has won a trade very desirable and remunerative. She carries a small stock of gents' wares for the accommodation of her laundry patrons. The office hours of this laundry are 7 to 12 P. M.; Sundays, 6 to 9 A. M. It will pay you to patronize the Home laundry.

G. A. Mariner & Co.

Analytical and Consulting Chemists and Assayers, 81 South Clark Street.

Science has made rapid strides in the last twenty years, and to its researches we are indebted for much of our knowledge, comfort and commercial success. To no branch does this apply more particularly than to the chemical analyses of the various materials and products that surround us. The leading firm of analytical and consulting chemists in the city is that of G. A. Mariner & Co. They have been engaged in this profession for thirty years, and have achieved just renown, having been called upon to decide in many difficult cases. They accept all kinds of substances for analysis, but make a specialty of waters and ores. They have lately been engaged upon the analysis of soaps for the government and water for various of the railroad companies. The articles sent here are too numerous to be mentioned, but whatever they are, the firm do not fail to give all the substances and quantities used in their composition. Both Mr. Mariner and Mr. Hoskins, the two leading members of the firm, are well known in the highest circles of scientific and business men, and are highly esteemed, both for their skill and their upright and honorable character. No firm stands higher in public estimation, nor possesses ability of a higher order in this profession. As assayers they have had long experience, and are adepts in the profession, their decisions having always been proved to be correct.

C. H. Fargo & Co.

Manufacturers and Jobbers of Boots and Shoes, 116, 118 and 120 Market Street.

The boot and shoe trade of Chicago possesses no better exponent than the house of C. H. Fargo & Co., wholesale manufacturers of these goods. The large business conducted by the well-known gentlemen constituting this firm was originally established in January, 1856, under the style of Bill, Fargo & Kellogg, the former retiring in the following year. In 1858, upon the retirement of Mr. Kellogg, Mr. Bill again became a member of the firm, the house of Fargo, Bill & Co. continuing the business for the subsequent five years, when, Mr. Bill retiring, the firm of Fargo, Fales & Co. was formed, Messrs. C. H. Fargo, H. D. Fales and S. M. Fargo being the members. This style continued until Jan. 1, 1871, when Mr. Fales withdrew, and Mr. John Benham was admitted, under the firm name, as it now stands, of C. H. Fargo & Co. Like many of our other leading mercantile houses, so the birthplace of this firm was on South Water street, No. 43, occupying successively, as their growth required increased facilities, No. 57 Lake street, Nos. 48 and 50 Wabash avenue and Nos. 40 and 42 Randolph street, where the greatest holocaust of fire in modern times in almost the twinkling of an eye reduced their business to ashes, entailing a net loss, over and above insurance recovered and stock saved, of over $80,000. Nothing daunted, within a week after the fire, before the ashes were cooled, in fact, the business was resumed at Mr. Fargo's private residence on Wabash avenue, from whence, upon the restoration of order, a few months later, the firm removed to State street near Twelfth, where they remained until the spacious five-story and basement building on the corner of Madison and Market streets was completed, when they moved into it, occupying it for eleven years, when they moved into their present large, spacious quarters. Messrs. C. H., C. E., S. M. and F. M. Fargo compose the present firm, Mr. C. H. Fargo, a native of Berkshire county, Mass., having been at the head of the house since its first organization, and, with only two exceptions, longer in continuous business than any man in Chicago, this city being in no small degree indebted to him for the advancement of her material interests, while in the development of the manufacturing industry belonging to his own field of labor, he undoubtedly occupies a foremost position. The firm manufacture a full line of men's, women's and children's boots and shoes of all kinds, and in addition carry a full stock of eastern made goods, and a complete line of the best makes of rubber goods, and are also the original patentees and manufacturers of the celebrated sole-leather box-tip shoes, which fully met the want that existed, doing away entirely with the unsightly appearance of the metal tips, while retaining the desired durability. For several years past the firm have devoted special attention at their factory in this city to the manufacture of a fine class of shoes for ladies' wear, employing some 125 skilled workmen, while 200 more find steady employment in the production of a general line of boots and shoes at their factory in Jackson, Mich. Thus briefly has been sketched the salient points in connection with the rise and progress of this great jobbing and manufacturing house, a business that has been conducted with consummate skill and untiring energy, until now their great volume of trade, still on the increase, reaches yearly into millions, and extends over every State and territory in the Union, while the liberality characterizing the policy of the house has always made business relations between them and their customers both mutually pleasant and profitable.

Charles Himrod & Co.

Dealers in Pig Iron, Rooms 60, 61 and 62, 115 Dearborn St.

One of the oldest men in this part of the country connected with the pig iron trade is Mr. Charles Himrod. For upwards of twenty years he has been a manufacturer and dealer. In 1881 he established the firm of C. Himrod & Co. This firm are large dealers in all the leading brands of pig iron, and are the sole agents for the celebrated Deerlake, Vulcan and Detroit (Michigan) brands. Brierhill, Calumet and other well-known kinds of pig iron are also largely handled by the firm. They supply manufacturers and foundries in all parts of the western States, having customers as far out as Omaha. They have also a large city trade, and are known as thoroughly reliable business men. Their rates are always as low as those of any firm in the trade, while the quality of their supplies is unequaled. The city offices are located on Dearborn street, No. 115, rooms 60, 61 and 62. Mr. Himrod, senior member of the firm, served during the war in the 83d Pennsylvania infantry, receiving his honorable discharge at the close of the war.

Elmer & Anderson.

Manufacturers' Agents and Commission Merchants, 267 and 269 Franklin Street.

Among the great hosiery and notion houses for which the Garden City is justly noted, none have succeeded in establishing and maintaining a higher reputation, alike for the standard of excellence of the goods handled and upright dealing, than Messrs. Elmer & Anderson, manufacturers' agents and commission merchants. The firm was organized some eight years ago, though both Messrs. T. H. Elmer and Geo. F. Anderson were for ten years prior each independently engaged in the same line. They have occupied their present spacious premises for five years past, where they are prepared to show an assortment of hosiery, notions, knit goods and gossamer clothing unsurpassed in extent and variety in this city, and in which, being the direct representatives of the producers, they are able to name the manufacturers' bottom figures. A large and influential patronage has been built up, both at home and abroad, and few possess better facilities for promptly placing large consignments.

A BUSINESS TOUR OF CHICAGO.

The Union Steamboat Co.

Thos. T. Morford, Agent, Market Street, Between Washington and Randolph.

Chicago has now its large connections by rail with every town and village of importance in the States, but in the early days of its existence, the waterway was the only easy means of transporting goods across the continent. Foremost among the freight-carrying lines of steamboats which have connections

in this city is the Union Steamboat Co., which has connections at Buffalo with the New York, Lake Erie and Western R. R., and at Chicago with all western railroads. This company was incorporated in 1868, with head offices at Buffalo; the general manager being Mr. W. Bullard, Buffalo, while Mr. T. T. Morford is the manager of the Chicago agency. This company runs a daily line of large freight propellers between Chicago, Milwaukee and Buffalo, carrying grain, flour, sugar and general merchandise. The celebrated fast steamers Tioga and H. J. Jewett, which make the run between Buffalo and Chicago in less than three days, are comprised in this line, and also two larger steel steamers, to be called the Owego and Chemung, now being constructed at Buffalo. Besides these they have a fleet which plies between Lake Superior points and Buffalo. This company executes bills of lading to any port in Europe. They employ about two hundred men at each port, Buffalo and Chicago, and an average of twenty-five hands on each boat. The docks here have a frontage to the river of four hundred feet, and are one hundred and fifty feet in depth. The warehouses and offices occupy the whole block on Market street, between Washington and Randolph. These boats carry only freight, the average amount received, both ways, being two thousand tons daily, during the season.

Isaac Shillington.

Livery and Boarding Stable, 210 and 212 Indiana Street.

The fine livery and boarding stables of Isaac Shillington are located at this point. The premises occupied are 50x100 feet in dimensions, and well arranged in every particular for the livery business. The stables contain a number of fine horses, and in the carriage-house may be found every description of wheeled vehicles. Turnouts are furnished for shopping and pleasure riding on reasonable terms, liveried drivers being provided when desired, and stylish rigs of every description are to be had, all of which are entirely new. Telephone orders, by number 3077, receive prompt attention. The business was begun in 1873 by the present proprietor, who has been a resident of this city since 1858. He has had long experience in the livery business, and as a judge of fine horses has no superior in Chicago.

Garden City Cigar Mfg. Co.

26 Rush Street.

At No. 26 Rush street is located the establishment of the Garden City Cigar Manufacturing Company, Richard Bradel, superintendent. They are wholesalers and retailers of the best grade of Havana cigars, besides prominent manufacturers of the fine brands of domestic cigars. They call special attention to their new brand, "The Grip," which is copyrighted and just being introduced to the public. Their other noted brand, "Private Stock," is so well known to the Chicago smokers that comment of its fine qualities is unnecessary. Mr. Bradel has half a dozen skilled workmen to aid him in his business, and all his stock is choice hand-made cigars. His trade is entirely local and amounts to 250,000 cigars annually. Mr. Bradel is a native of Saxony, and opened up business in Racine, Wis., in 1861, and came to Chicago in 1881

Hotel Woodruff.

Corner Wabash Avenue and Twenty-first Street.

The new and elegantly appointed Hotel Woodruff is in every way a representative establishment among the fine hotels of the west; in truth, it has never been called upon to compete with other hotels, for since it was first erected, in 1872, it has always had a select and influential patronage from the best families of our city, and when they are away to the seaside or mountains during the summer months, their places are filled by southern tourists who for years have made this model hotel their home while in the city. The hotel was built by Mr. H. N. Woodruff especially for J. W. Boardman in 1872, and was then known as the Woodruff hotel. At Mr. Boardman's death in 1874 his wife assumed charge, and to her enterprising management and liberal business policy is due its present success. A few months ago the house was entirely remodeled, refitted and painted inside and out, and the name was also transposed to read Hotel Woodruff. It is located on the southeast corner of Wabash avenue and Twenty-first street, just far enough away from the business center to be free from the noise and dust, and near enough to the lake to receive its cool, refreshing breeze. By means of the cable cars, which run by the door every three minutes, one is in direct and rapid communication with all the railroad depots, steamboat wharfs, parks, places of amusement, etc. The interior appointments are most pleasing, fully in keeping with the exterior appearance. On the first floor are located the offices, ladies' reception room, gentlemen's reading room, private office and telephone room and also the large, beautiful dining hall, which is one of the finest in the city. The large, handsome parlors and suites of rooms are found on the second floor, while the other floors contain the airy and roomy sleeping apartments. The house contains every modern convenience which science and skill can produce, the building being lit throughout by Edison's incandescent light, the plumbing and ventilation also being perfect. Upwards of one hundred employes are connected with the house, and every department is run with that regularity and precision which marks good management. The cuisine of Hotel Woodruff stands unrivaled, the catering for it being conducted on the basis of the greatest liberality, which insures only the best and rarest of everything that the market affords, while the culinary department is under the management of a distinguished chef, giving the utmost satisfaction in this line to all guests. The proprietor spares neither time, pains nor expense, making everything comfortable for her guests, who ever remember their delightful stay at the Hotel Woodruff.

Jos. Downey.

Mason Contractor and Builder, 159 La Salle St., Room 94.

Mr. Joseph Downey, whose office is at room 94, 150 La Salle street, holds a prominent place among his fellow-craftsmen, not alone from his long residence in Chicago, but also from his well-known capabilities as a mason contractor and builder. The time in which he has been established in business is, of itself, enough to rank him among the foremost of his class. For more than fifteen years he has been actively engaged in his calling, and many buildings in this and neighboring as also more remote cities bear evidence of his handiwork. While making Chicago his home, Mr. Downey has not been confined to this city alone, as his work in adjoining States will show. Among the number of buildings erected by him here and in the vicinity are the Chicago and Western Indiana railroad depot, known as the Polk street depot, and the Cook county poor house, at Jefferson, a few miles out from the center of the city. Mr. Downey also built and is part owner of the Columbia theater. Very many private buildings in the city have been built by him, and all bear marks of a master hand. Among those abroad, the Missouri State Lunatic asylum at St. Joseph, Mo., is probably one to revert to with most pride.

The Rascher Map Publishing Co.

162 La Salle Street.

The Rascher Map Publishing company, at 162 La Salle street, was begun ten years ago, when three volumes were published; now there are twelve volumes of Chicago and suburbs. The fine maps of this company are the most complete and perfect published, being prepared from accurate surveys by efficient draughtsmen, so that a person can tell at a glance the class of building in any spot in the city. Mr. Chas. Rascher, the manager, is founder of the company, and by his efficient and earnest work has succeeded in establishing a system very valuable to all business men. These maps are not confined alone to this city, but are published by this company of all the western cities. They are sent out all over the world, being used by the various insurance companies, so that after a big fire they can tell at a glance what losses have been sustained by their company. Corrections are made on these maps from time to time, so that they are strictly reliable.

Judd's College

116 Monroe Street.

This institution occupies a high position among the many institutions which give to Chicago its unusual educational facilities. In this college the aim is not to gather a crowd of pupils, and then claim that the large number in attendance is evidence conclusive of the merit of the school, but the rather that a limited number may have the full advantage of a thorough course of painstaking instruction either individually or in classes.

Regular day, special afternoon and evening sessions the year round, give the young and middle-aged men and women excellent opportunities to acquire a practical knowledge of book-keeping, Munson's shorthand, penmanship, grammar, German, commercial law, business arithmetic, correspondence, geography, spelling, reading, etc., at very reasonable rates. Teachers and others at a distance frequently take advantage of the course by mail. While it is not so desirable as attending the college, still good results have been obtained by this method. Prof. F. F. Judd, the principal, has spent the past eight years in this particular line of work, devoting his spare time to the examination of tangled accounts, opening and closing books, etc., until he now occupies a prominent position as expert accountant and teacher of commercial branches.

E. L. Brainerd.

Real Estate, 125 Dearborn Street, Room 10.

Mr. E. L. Brainerd has been engaged more or less for fifteen years in real-estate transactions, and has now just placed his valuable subdivision of forty-five acres, in South Englewood, on the market. This property lies between Eighty-seventh and Ninetieth streets, and between Loomis street and Center avenue, ten miles from the court-house, on the Rock Island and Pan-Handle railroads. The streets are being laid out, and sidewalks and trees put in. Good well-water abounds, and the land is dry and well drained. The lots are 126 feet deep, with an alley fourteen wide in rear. The low price of from eight to fifteen dollars per foot frontage is all that is asked. The owner, Mr. Brainerd, has erected a residence for himself, and other houses are rapidly being put up here. Besides this property, Mr. Brainerd owns seventy acres more in this neighborhood about to be subdivided. He has had a long acquaintance with the city, and no man is better posted in real-estate matters, or better qualified to handle property or make investments.

M. H. Lowell.

Artist and Dealer in Oil Paintings and Frames, 183 Madison Street.

Much good work may yet be done in all parts of this country in elevating the tastes and cultivating art instincts in the people. Besides, what tends more to the adornment of a home than the presence on the wall of a few good pictures? M. H. Lowell, an artist, is doing his best to supply this want, and employs on an average sixteen artists in producing a class of oil paintings that, while not beyond the reach of the middle and even poorer classes, yet are so pleasing in subject and well executed as to be desirable. Their manufacture of genuine oil paintings occupies the third and fourth floors (each 35x80 feet) of No. 183 Madison street. All kinds, qualities and subjects are treated here, being painted from nature, sketches, copies or imagination, the latter being chiefly those of the cheaper class. Prices range from $1 to $250, the higher priced being genuine works of art and fit to compare with many on exhibition in picture galleries; indeed, some have been sent to exhibitions in New Orleans and elsewhere. The bulk of the sales are to jobbers from New York to California, Montreal and Winnipeg to Florida and Texas. Many are also shipped through jobbers to China and Australia. Mr. Lowell is also a dealer, and has on hand productions from some of the most noted artists of modern times.

Victor Lassagne.

Restaurant Francais (Elite) for Ladies and Gentlemen, 77 and 79 South Clark Street.

The French are proverbially the most skilled caterers in the world, this industry having been developed to the rank of a science in that country, and consequently those of experience who have embarked in similar pursuits here have been uniformly prosperous and successful. Few in Chicago, however, have obtained that hold upon the public favor equal with the Restaurant Francais, so ably conducted by Mons. Victor Lassagne, which since its very inception, twenty-two years ago, near the old Board of Trade building, being at that time known as the Board of Trade restaurant, has continuously commanded the patronage of the best class of the city. Mons. Lassagne was born in France in 1827, at Bagnols-sur-Ceze, Department du Gard, and at the age of twenty came to the United States and located at New Orleans, from whence, just prior to the war, on account of his well-known union sentiments, he was obliged to come north. After the close of the war, in 1864, throughout which he gallantly served his adopted country, filling the responsible office of chief musician, he decided to locate himself in Chicago. In the great fire of October, 1871, he suffered a very severe loss, his place of business being then located where now the Pacific house stands. Nothing daunted, however, he at once re-established himself, and as soon as practicable secured his present central and eligible premises. The Restaurant Francais is handsomely furnished, and the service is first class, while the cuisine, in charge of a distinguished French chef, a friend and acquaintance of the proprietor in old France, leaves nothing to be desired. Spacious rooms for private parties are on the second floor, and service is had until midnight. In the management everything has been reduced to a complete system. The best that the market can afford is to be found in the menu, while the stock of wines and liquors is procured direct from the most famous foreign houses. Mons. Lassagne is an active, enterprising and clear-headed business man, and is peculiarly fitted for his vocation, in which he has achieved a well-earned popularity and success.

A. Schrader.

Bakery and Confectionery, 1019 West Madison Street.

Mr. Schrader has one of the finest and most attractive establishments in this part of the city. He does a large business, and has a fine stock of all kinds of confectionery, cakes, pies, ices and soda-water. This bakery is noted for the fine quality of

FIFTY YEARS' PROGRESS.

its bread, which alone draws a large custom. The premises occupied consist of first floor and basement, and are well arranged for the rapid prosecution of business. Steam power is used, and every modern appliance necessary for this trade can be found here. His creams are most excellent in flavor, and are much sought after by families in the vicinity. Mr. Schrader has been in the business for over six years. This is his life trade, and he superintends the filling of all orders received. He is a native of Germany, and came to Chicago in 1868.

John J. Inkersell.

Groceries, 1006 West Madison Street.

Those who wish to secure fine and choice groceries will always find them at the popular and well-known family grocery store of John J. Inkersell, located at No. 1006 West Madison street. His store is well stocked with a complete line of staple and fancy groceries of every description, and no one can fail to be suited who pays him a visit. Great care is taken in his selection so as to always keep on hand a fresh stock of goods. He has been a resident of Chicago for a number of years, and thoroughly understand every feature of the retail grocery trade. Although only established in business since Nov. 21, 1885, he has succeeded in building up a large and lucrative trade among the best families of this section of the city.

I. Blumenthal.

97 1-2 North Wells Street.

Mr. I. Blumenthal is a manufacturer and dealer in all kinds of vermin exterminators. His premises are located at No. 97½ North Wells street. His is probably the most successful article of its kind in the market, and will effectually exterminate roaches, ants, moths, fleas, water-bugs, mosquitoes, lice in animals, etc., and all kinds of insects on flowers and plants, and will exterminate rats and mice. It is sold in all parts of the United States. Contracts are also taken by Mr. Blumenthal to exterminate any of the above-named vermin. The best of references are given, and all orders meet with prompt attention. His patrons comprise Marshall Field & Co., Brunswick, Balke & Co., H. Schultz, and other large firms in the city, including hotels, restaurants, business and private houses. None of his insect powder contains the least bit of poison, and never loses its strength.

The Corey Car and Mfg. Co.

Successors to Francis W. Corey & Co., 87 North Ashland Avenue.

This company are successors to Francis W. Corey & Co., who begun the business in 1873 at La Porte, Indiana, but in 1885 was changed to the present company. They are manufacturers of all kinds and styles of side, end, rotary and bottom dumping cars

of any desired capacity. These cars are made from the best seasoned oak, or from iron throughout, and are for use in railroad grading, parkways and landscape grading, brickyards, stone quarries, lime works, gravel pits, mines of every description, sugar and cotton plantations, levee building, coal and ore docks, tunnel work, peat works, and for logging and narrow gauge railroads. All the wheels are thoroughly chilled and annealed, while the best skilled labor is employed in every department. They also manufacture all kinds of portable track, frogs, switches and curves, as well as iron platforms and all styles of hand cars, for section work and patrol or telegraph service. Their works contain the latest and best improved machinery used for this kind of business. Thirty-five skilled and experienced hands are employed, while their trade extends not only all over the Union, but to South America, Cuba and Mexico.

James H. Rice Co

Importers of Polished, Rough and Crystal Plate Glass, 13, 15 and 17 Quincy Street.

The growth of Chicago as a business center has not only been very rapid, but its history is one of advanced strides toward the position it now so creditably occupies. Every department of commerce has kept pace with this marvelous growth, and today are to be seen the colossal results of the ability and energy of her citizens, in which the glass trade forms a most important branch, one of the leading representatives being the James H. Rice Co. The business was established just after the fire in 1871, by James H. Rice, and conducted with eminent success, the result of which is the present stock company, which was organized January 1, 1884, with a paid-up cash capital of $100,000, and whose officers are Messrs. James H. Rice, president; J. M. Vernon, treasurer; and E. Flanigan, secretary. The company do an extensive wholesale and retail business, importing direct every grade of polished, rough and crystal plate glass, and handling large quantities of English, French and American window-glass, also French plate and German mirrors, colored, embossed and enameled glass. To accommodate the immense stock carried, a removal was effected, at the opening of the year, from their former location, Nos. 80 and 82 Adams street, which had been occupied by them so many years, to their present spacious premises, Nos. 13, 15 and 17 Quincy street, a modern constructed six-story building, one hundred feet square in dimensions. The stock carried embraces the choicest goods in the market, and the resources of the company are such that the largest orders can be executed promptly and on reasonable terms.

Wilber Mercantile Agency.

Special Direct Mercantile Reports, Offices 182 and 184 Dearborn Street.

The Wilber Mercantile agency was established in 1872, and during the intervening period it has effectually demonstrated its usefulness in the commercial world. In every town in the Union and Canadian provinces they have as a representative a responsible attorney, some 8,000 in number, through whom, by an ingenious system of blanks, special direct mercantile reports may be obtained, and debts collected. Its attorney lists are published annually and revised by supplemental issues monthly, thus rendering them more reliable than any others in existence. Each attorney is supplied with the attorney list and supplemental issues, thus enabling them to use it as a medium through which they may transact their own law and collection business, and, as a result, attorneys by the thousands testify that more business comes to them through the Wilber agency than from all others. The advantages are manifest and have not failed to commend themselves to the leading business houses in the country, from whom indorsements are daily received; a few from Chicago being quite sufficient, among whom are Armour & Co., John V Farwell & Co., Sprague, Warner & Co., Reid, Murdoch & Fischer, John A. Tolman Co., Hart Bros., Leopold Bros. & Co., Kohn Bros., Phelps, Dodge & Palmer, Greensfelder, Florsheim & Co., Selz, Schwab & Co., S. A. Maxwell & Co., James H. Walker & Co., Giles Bros. & Co., Daily Inter Ocean, Chicago Tribune and Chicago Times. Subscribers are entitled, first, to make inquiries regarding delinquents; second, to obtain special direct mercantile reports and the prevention of making bad debts; third, the best possible assistance in collection of accounts. Another marked feature is that when a firm is interrogated by the agency's representative as to their financial standing, the replies are taken down by them in writing and filed away as statements to obtain credit, so that if untruthful, and a loss occurs to the seller, the firm becomes liable to criminal prosecution. The agency deals only with wholesale and manufacturing houses, and it is needless to say are doing a large business. The officers of the agency are Messrs. M. D. Wilber, president, now United States district attorney for the eastern district of New York, located at Brooklyn, New York, and E. J. Wilber, secretary and business manager in charge. The general offices are at Chicago with branches in all the leading cities.

L. Eaton.

Dentist, 235 State Street.

The profession of dentistry unites both mechanical skill and theoretical knowledge in a degree peculiar to no other profession, while among dental practitioners in Chicago, few have attained a finer reputation than Mr. Eaton. He has had many years' experience, and began the practice of his profession at Elmira, N. Y., removing to Chicago in 1870, and established his office at No. 94 Washington street, where in the great fire of 1871 his entire outfit was destroyed. He has been in his present central location continuously for the past eleven years. Dr. Eaton has built up a large and influential practice, including among his patrons many of our leading citizens and families. As a dentist of rare professional skill and ability he is unequaled, while the satisfactory manner in which he covers every branch of his profession has won the confidence and esteem of the entire community.

I. Jonas.

Merchant Tailor, 22 Rush Street.

Mr. Jonas has a fine trade, and a standard reputation in Chicago for good work, fine material, and for perfectly fitting and stylish garments, and his patronage is among our best people. A stock of select patterns of the latest styles is kept constantly on hand in his store from which to make selections. Clothing is also cleaned, dyed and repaired at very reasonable rates. Mr. Jonas is a native of Germany, and came to Chicago in 1882, but did not begin business until March 1, 1885. His trade at present is very good and rapidly increasing.

H. G. Medcalfe & Co.

Prescription Druggists, 72 North Clark Street, Between Michigan and Illinois Streets, Telephone No. 3158.

This house keeps constantly on hand a superior quality of goods, and satisfaction is rendered in the compounding of prescriptions. The business capacity and judgment displayed in the management of this establishment has attracted a large and first-class patronage, which is rapidly increasing, and today they enjoy as large a measure of success and maintain as high a reputation as any similar concern in the city, not only with the general public, but with the medical fraternity as well. The business dates its origin back to 1859. This house has many standard preparations, but chief among them is Syrup of Red Spruce Gum for coughs and colds, Elixir Aperient and Corn-cure. These three have many warm friends, not only in the west, but throughout the east and south, where many can be found who will testify to their unqualified merit. They are also western wholesale agents for Dr. M. M. Townsend's Hay Fever, Asthma, and Catarrh Remedy, so popular with the public. Dr. Medcalfe was a native of Baltimore, Md., and a graduate of one of the leading medical colleges there. He was a surgeon in the regular army during the late war. Early in 1859 he came to Chicago to begin the business described above. At his death some seven years ago, his eldest son, Mr. H. G. Medcalfe, succeeded to the business.

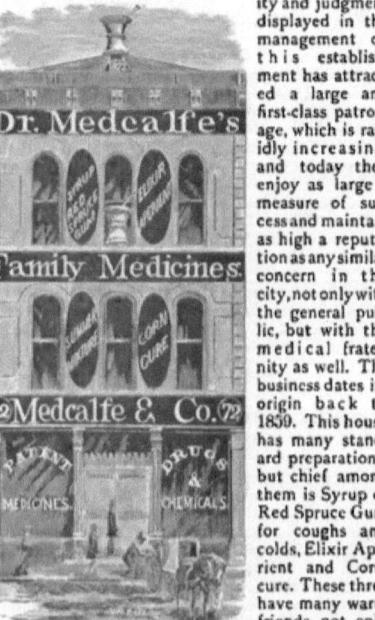

C. W. Fullerton.

Attorney at Law, 94 Dearborn Street, Chicago.

Mr. C. W. Fullerton is well known in this city in connection with law and the bar and honorable conduct in the transaction of legal business. He has at the present time a subdivision of about one hundred acres in Lake View, just outside the city limits, bordering on Fullerton avenue, and only 3½ miles from the court-house. This land is for sale for manufacturing purposes. This district is admirably suited for such purposes, being very convenient to the river, lake, city and railroads. The well-known reaper factory of Deering & Co. is in close proximity, as are also several others of almost equal note. This land has been in the possession of the Fullerton family for the last fifty years, and there has been but one conveyance since the original grant was made; the title is therefore clear and unquestionable. This land is for sale in lots of ten acres and upwards. Mr. Fullerton's office is located at 94 Dearborn street, to which all communications should be addressed.

A. H. Andrews & Co.

Manufacturers of Fine Office Furniture, Bank Fittings, Etc., 195 and 197 Wabash Avenue.

The business of this house is that of special lines of furniture, as they do not manufacture common household goods. The list of the manufactures

includes office furniture, bank counters and railing, opera chairs, parlor folding beds and school furniture or desks and all kinds of school merchandise or apparatus. The well-known reputation of this firm appears to have been largely due to a determination, from the very outset, to select the best material for their stock, and never to trust the reports of the country lumber seller who claims that his wood had been so many months or years in seasoning, but do their own kiln-drying by a new process in what is known as the Noyes lumber dryer, which they find very valuable in preparing lumber for their purposes. Their one hundred varieties of office desks, samples of which have been seen in the various expositions, are their own best advertisement and have needed no special notice. Many lines of railway have also adopted their desks, specially designed for offices and stations of railway companies. The bank fittings of the firm are well known, especially throughout the northwest and the south. To this department they have added the new and stylish brass work for gates or wickets, which is very superior and of original designs. The improved opera chairs, designed by this house, have attracted much attention, with their various appliances, both for comfort and reduction of space. The Andrews folding beds are made in various designs, several of which are highly artistic, and represent dressing cases, bureaus, book cases, etc., while some have the addition of a writing table. In addition to these specialties thus briefly mentioned, the firm have always manufactured that staple article called the public school desk; also the various articles under the head of school merchandise, such as globes in a very large variety, maps, blackboards, etc., and as is well known, A. H. Andrews & Co. have for years led off in this line of manufactures. All in all, this house is a standard one, on this fiftieth year of our history as a municipality.

Fred. G. Frank & Brother.

**Brokers and Dealers in Bonds, Stocks, Notes, Etc.,
99 Washington Street.**

The firm of Fred. G. Frank & Brother have been for the last eight years dealers in bonds, stocks, notes, etc., and are members of the Chicago Stock Exchange. These brothers, having had over twenty-one years' experience in some of the largest houses in this city and New York, commenced on their own account, and have succeeded in establishing a large and widely connected business. A specialty is made of investment and foreign exchange, both in specie and notes. Loans are negotiated, exchange and drafts issued on European banks and houses. An office of this kind is one of the most useful in transmitting or receiving sums of money from abroad. The firm itself is well known in the business communities of the city as one of the most reliable and rising business houses of the class existing. The offices are central and easily accessible from all parts of the city, and any wishing to transact any business of the nature quoted above will not do better than by paying F. G. Frank & Bro. a visit.

Ivison, Blakeman & Co

Publishers, 149 Wabash Avenue, John C. Ellis, Manager.

The American educational system is unquestionably the finest and best organized of any in the world, and naturally requires text books of the very highest order, with the publication of which the time-honored name of Ivison, Blakeman & Company will always be inseparably connected. The founder of this great business, Mr. Henry Ivison, was born in Glasgow, Scotland, in 1808, and at twelve years of age came to this country, and found congenial employment in a Utica, N. Y., store. In 1830, seeing a favorable opening in Auburn, N. Y., he entered into business there on his own account, and in 1840 removed to the city of New York, to form a co-partnership with Mr. Mark H. Newman in the publication of school and college text books. In 1856, Mr. Phinney was admitted to the firm, and shortly after, as the business grew in volume and importance, Mr. Birdseye Blakeman became a partner. In January, 1882, three years prior to his decease, Mr. Ivison, after having been the honored head of this house for upwards of thirty years, retired and transferred his interests to his son, Mr. David B. Ivison, who, however, has been an active partner since 1864. During 1868, the demand of the firm's western trade had become so large that a branch was opened in Chicago, with S. C. Griggs & Co., which arrangement continued until 1870, when the firm opened an office and store-room at No. 133 State street, where the premises and stock were destroyed in the great fire of October, 1871. They promptly reopened at No. 273 West Randolph street, and in 1872, when rebuilt, removed to Nos. 133 and 135 State street, and eventually, in 1882, occupied their present eligible and central location, at No. 149 Wabash avenue, which contains an extensive and complete assortment of the firm's publications, embracing well-known text books in nearly all branches of study, by such eminent educators and litterateurs as Horatio Robinson, C. W. Sanders, Wm. Swinton, Asa Gray, James D. Dana, David A. Wells, Arnold Guyot, LeRoy Cooley, and others, and which are pronounced the best by the most experienced and successful teachers in our schools and colleges east and west. For some years past the management of the Chicago house has been in the charge of Mr. John C. Ellis. Ivison, Blakeman & Co's publications are perfect specimens of the typographical and binder's arts. They are collectively known as "The American Educational Series of School and College Text Books," and are introduced at prices which afford a substantial inducement apart from their intrinsic merits.

M. D. Rider

**Wholesale and Retail Dealer in Blank Books and Stationery of Every Description, 129 La Salle Street,
Four Doors North of Madison Street.**

The expenses of this house are low, and as the business is all conducted on a cash principle, the proprietor is enabled to quote as low rates as any retailer in the trade. Besides a large retail local business, this house does a considerable wholesale trade, both in the city and outside, in all parts of the States, north, south and west, even supplying goods as far as California. Mr. M. D. Rider commenced in this business six years ago, at 170 East Madison street, where he continued till his removal to 129 La Salle street in May of last year. He manufactures, on the premises, blank books of all kinds, to order, while his general stock is obtained direct from eastern manufacturers. A standard line of goods of all grades is kept on hand, and one well worth a visit from anyone interested in or requiring goods in this line.

M. Thome.

**Importer of Hair Goods, Hair Bazar, 157 State Street;
Wholesale Depot, 138 and 140 Wabash Avenue.**

The house of M. Thome, importer of hair goods, is one of the oldest engaged in this branch of business in the west, having been established in 1871 at No. 157 State street, and which is still the location of the retail hair bazar. In 1880 Mr. Thome entered the wholesale trade, and was fortunate in securing the present eligible and spacious premises, where more than seventy-five skilled hands are employed in manufacturing all kinds of hair goods, which for superiority of workmanship and finish are unexcelled, while being himself a direct importer of human hair from Europe in large quantities, he is enabled to secure the best qualities of hair, and to quote such prices for his goods as to defy competition. Mr. Thome is a German by birth, and has been a resident of this city for many years, where he is highly esteemed as an energetic, clear-headed business man, honorable and fair in all transactions. Of the stock but an inadequate idea can be conveyed. Suffice it to say that it includes everything desirable in the nature of human hair goods, and that the goods themselves are what they should be, and their prices correct, is best attested in the liberal patronage that Mr. Thome has always been able to command.

A. S. Barnes & Co.

Publishers, 263 Wabash Avenue, Chicago.

As publishers of the newest, best and handsomest school books in the world, the house of A. S. Barnes & Co. may fitly be considered the representative firm not only of Chicago, but of the country. Strictly speaking, the house in this city, which is under the management of Mr. Chas. J. Barnes, is a branch of the New York house, Nos. 111 and 113 William street, and since coming here early in 1869 their business has developed with the growth of the west. Among their more noted publications may be mentioned Steele's Scientific series, Barnes' Drawing series, Barnes' Short Studies in English, Barnes' National Copy Books, Barnes' New National Readers, Barnes' General History of the World, Barnes' New Arithmetics, Barnes' Elementary Geography, Barnes' Complete Geography and a large number of other school and college publications. Many of these works have reached an enormous sale, as, for example, Barnes' New National Readers with an annual demand for half a million copies, and Barnes' Brief History of the United States with a sale of over 150,000 copies. The success of the house, brought about by the exercise of ability, energy and a strict adherence to mercantile honor, is in every respect typical of Chicago's remarkable progress.

Columbia Rubber Stamp Works.

Sellschopp & Klockmann, Proprietors, Manufacturers of Rubber Stamps of Every Description, Banking and Business Stamps, Etc., 183 and 185 S. Clark St.

The trade in rubber and metal stamps for mercantile use is one that has of late years grown in a remarkable degree, one of its leading representatives being the Columbia Rubber Stamp works, which, though established as recently as 1885, has attained a patronage and position in the trade seldom accorded houses of much older origin. Messrs. P. F. and H. A. Sellschopp and A. Klockmann, the proprietors, are gentlemen of large experience in this business, in which they were engaged in Germany, their native land, prior to coming to this country, four years ago. The factory employs a large force of skilled workmen, and possesses every facility for the manufacture of its various specialties, among which are the latest improved rubber stamps of every description, banking and business stamps, notarial and corporate seals, steel stamps, stencils, badges, hotel, baggage and pool checks. A large stock is carried, and all orders are executed promptly at reasonable prices. The superiority of all work turned out, and the liberal methods on which Messrs. Sellschopp & Klockmann conduct their business has won for the Columbia Rubber Stamp works a large and prosperous trade.

R. Ralston Jones.

Resident Engineer for Pittsburgh Testing Laboratory, 20 Portland Block.

Mr. Jones has been a citizen of Chicago for several years, and as the resident engineer for the Pittsburgh Testing laboratory is known to the scientific fraternities of Chicago generally as a peculiarly active man in this line, and as one who has done his share in advancing his profession to a higher plane of usefulness. Mr. Jones is also the agent here of the Thayer Manufacturing company, who are manufacturers of car bearings, babbitt metals, etc., and also for the Solid Steel company, of Alliance, Ohio, manufacturers of steel castings of all kinds. He is a member of the American Society of Mechanical Engineers, and also of the Western Society of Engineers, and was at one time for some years in the employ of the government as engineer. The Pittsburgh Testing laboratory, for which Mr. Jones is resident engineer, are inspecting and metallurgical engineers and chemists, and test iron and steel, both chemically and physically, in a most thorough manner, and guarantee accuracy in all cases as to any statements sent out from this laboratory, and mine owners, mine inspectors and prospective buyers cannot find a more reliable institution with which to place their patronage.

The Geo. F. Child Adjustable Parlor Chair Co.

281 Wabash Avenue.

This house was organized Oct. 2, 1885, for the purpose of manufacturing the G. F. Child adjustable parlor chair, which they are prepared in the most scientific way to manufacture in all of its varieties and styles. They use nothing but the best material and employ none but skilled workmen. Manufacturing nothing else, it receives their full and undivided attention. They guarantee their chairs to be all claimed for them, in principle, construction and durability. A careful examination of the chair will reveal the fact that the inventor has surpassed his highest imagination, and has produced, upon scientific principles, and in an artistic way, one of the most used and useful articles in the interest of humanity. Nothing approaching it, is to be found in the United States or elsewhere. The Geo. F.

Child adjustable parlor chair to be appreciated must be seen and used. During the illness of Gen. Grant, when the chair was first shown to the people of Dayton, Ohio, it was proposed among the prominent citizens of that city that one of these chairs be ordered and made in elegant upholstery, and sent as a token of esteem from the people to the illustrious soldier; accordingly such was done, with result as follows: New York, June 6th, 1885.—(Special telegram to the Cincinnati Commercial Gazette.)—General Grant and his family are greatly pleased with the new and elegant easy chair which the old hero has received from the citizens of Dayton, Ohio. It is a piece of marvelous workmanship, and many a politician would be happy could he but get in as many positions as the new chair. The upholstering is extremely rich and elegant, and, as Mrs. Grant says, "makes the parlor look quite plain." Today the General drew the chair up to the window and reclined on it for an hour with a smile of satisfaction on his face. The old chair in which he spent so many weary hours has been consigned to the attic, and when the General wishes to lie off and be comfortable he chooses the chair which the kind-hearted people of an Ohio city sent him.

Peter Smith & Co.

Manufacturers of Carriages, Buggies, Etc., 78 and 80 Michigan Street.

Mr. Smith is one of the oldest and most prominent manufacturers of carts, buggies, carriages, milk, express, delivery and truck wagons in Chicago. The business was established in 1803, May 1. His large shop is equipped with every facility in the way of machinery, tools and appliances for turning out the most durable and easy-going vehicles. About twenty-five competent workmen are employed, and Mr. Smith sees to it that none but the best material is used, and none but the best and most satisfactory work is turned out. He not only sells largely to the city trade, but also ships his goods to all parts of the west and northwest. Mr. Smith is a native of Germany, and came to Chicago in 1842. This is his life trade, and he is thoroughly conversant with every feature of it, and readily merits the success attained by his energy and perseverance. He is ably assisted in the business by his son, George A. Smith, who has been connected with the trade since 1881.

Charles Creamery Co.

F. R. Jackson, Manager, 68 and 70 North State Street.

Through the Charles Creamery company, located at 68 and 70 North State street, it is possible for the people of Chicago to secure as fine, pure creamery butter as is sold in any market in the world.

This has been accomplished by the above company, whose business is confined strictly to the retail trade. The butter is put up in four and eight pound packages at their creamery at Ossian, Iowa, shipped here and distributed to all parts of the city weekly. They also receive daily strictly fresh eggs, every one of which is stamped, "Guaranteed strictly fresh by Charles Creamery company." The business was begun by C. W. Williams in 1880, at Ossian, Iowa. Two years later a branch was established in this city, which is under the management of Mr. F. R. Jackson, who sees to it that every patron receives the best of satisfaction. The cut above is a view taken from life, and represents the source that has rendered Charles Creamery company so popular.

Riverdale Distilling Co.

264 to 270 Kinzie Street, A. Junker, General Agent.

The premises of the Riverdale Distilling company in this city consist of their offices and warehouse, and are three stories in height, with a large basement, and are 50x160 feet in dimensions. The location is central, and all that could be desired for the business. Their distillery is located at Riverdale, Cook county, Ill., and the whole plant covers sixteen acres. The distillery is equipped with all the most improved modern appliances. They are distillers and rectifiers of alcohol, cologne, French spirits, gin and whiskies, and their products have a standard reputation, their trade extending all over the United States, and aggregating many thousand dollars annually. Upwards of a million bushels of grain are used during the year, and one hundred hands are employed by the company. This company also handles the reliable and noted "Fermentum" compressed yeast, in which line they do a large business. The officers are as follows: A. Junker, president; J. J. Kissinger, treasurer; and H. Wischemeyer, secretary. They have every facility for filling all orders promptly.

Fred. Kaempfer.

Taxidermist and Dealer in Singing and Fancy Birds, Parrots, Goldfish, Etc., 169 East Madison Street.

This is the largest business of its kind in the west, and was established in 1857, on Wells street (now Fifth avenue), but as this did not prove a good locality, Mr. Kaempfer rented a store on Clark street, and afterwards on Madison, where it was burned out at the big fire of 1871. After keeping a temporary store on the West side for a year, in 1872 he removed to 127 Clark street, where he was doing a good trade for nearly fifteen years. The steady increase of his business forced him to look for larger quarters, which he found at his present store No. 109 East Madison street, a much larger and more commodious place. This large and varied assortment includes in its category singing birds of all kinds and particularly the fine singing Hartz mountain canaries, which Mr. Kaempfer receives from the most experienced and successful bird raisers in Germany; a fine variety of all other fancy birds and talking parrots of the best species of this bird; cages in large numbers and designs; also, birdseeds of all kinds, and Kaempfer's prepared mocking bird food, which is favorably known all over the country. Besides, he keeps a complete stock of taxidermist materials, tools, instruments and a full assortment of bird and animal eyes, oologists' instruments and entomological apparatus; foreign bird skins, mounted birds and animal heads, in fact, all that a collector and naturalist may need. Fred. Kaempfer Jr., his able assistant and oldest son, has charge of the business at the store on Madison street, while Mr. Kaempfer himself attends to the preparing and mounting of birds and other specimens of natural history, at his large shop and studio at 250 Elm street. In connection with this he has a fine show or private museum of stuffed birds and animals, all of his own mounting, comprising a large and complete collection of North American and European game birds, a beautiful case of humming birds of sixty different species, containing all the scarce varieties. A large number of finely mounted heads of buffalo, elk, moose, deer, antelope, bears and so forth are shown. Mr. Kaempfer learned taxidermy from his father, a noted taxidermist in Germany, and has spent his whole life in the study and practice of that art, and is now assisted in his workshop by his youngest son William, and other skillful taxidermists.

John W. Masury & Son.

New York and Chicago; Manufacturers of Paints and Varnishes; Chicago Office, Masury Building, 190, 191, 192 Michigan Avenue.

The extensive house of Messrs. John W. Masury & Son is not only the oldest established, but also the most prominent American house engaged in the manufacture of fine house, car and carriage paints and varnishes. The headquarters of the firm are located in the city of New York, Bennett building, corner Fulton and Nassau streets, with three large factories in Brooklyn, the best equipped of the kind in the world, and which give employment to upwards of four hundred hands, two of the establishments being devoted to the manufacture of paints, and the third to varnishes. The business was founded in New York in 1835, and, during its half-century of existence has met with a remarkable measure of success. The firm decided to open a branch house here in 1877, and located at Nos.

138 and 140 Wabash avenue, but the firm, in order to better accommodate its business, purchased a central site and erected their present splendid warehouse, Nos. 190, 191 and 192 Michigan avenue, into which they moved in 1881. The premises are six stories and basement in height, sixty by one hundred and seventy-two feet in dimensions, and

especially constructed and arranged for the storage of the enormous stock of paints and varnishes always carried here. Mr. M. J. House, a gentleman who brings to bear vast practical experience and an exceptionally perfect knowledge of paints and varnishes, is in charge as manager of the Chicago branch. Messrs. J. W. Masury & Son keep in stock a complete line of house paints, including railroad colors (tinted leads), liquid colors, pure colors in oil and distemper, carriage and car paints, all carefully and scientifically prepared, and are the most economical, durable and brilliant of any in the market; also large quantities of the celebrated varnishes manufactured by this house.

A full line of artists' tube paints are also manufactured, which the most eminent artists in the United States pronounce in every way superior to any others manufactured in this country or in Europe.

The branch house in Chicago is directly represented to the trade by a force of ten men on the road, while a staff of over thirty find steady employment in the various departments of the Michigan avenue establishment. A significant fact in connection with the reputation of this house is that almost if not all others guarantee their goods "equal to Masury's," thus according them "the standard of quality."

Simpson, Hall, Miller & Co.

Manufacturers of Fine Silver-Plated Ware, M. N. Burchard, Manager, 137 and 139 State Street.

The development which has attended the manufacture of electroplated ware is now admitted to be largely the result of the distinguished enterprise of Messrs. Simpson, Hall, Miller & Co., who, in their persistent efforts to better their products, have actually forced other manufacturers to follow suit or be debarred from participation in the benefits of the trade. The house was originally founded in 1834, by Mr. Samuel Simpson, the pioneer of the electroplate trade, and as the business grew, the firm of Simpson, Hall, Miller & Co. was formed, whose interests were eventually capitalized in 1865, the company being duly incorporated under the old familiar firm name and style, the present officers being Messrs. Samuel Simpson, president; Clarence H. Brown, treasurer; Andrew Andrews, secretary; and G. W. Hull, superintendent. At Wallingford, Conn., they possess the largest and best equipped factories in the country, in their line, for the manufacture of electroplated table silverware of all kinds, and also of the celebrated Wm. Rogers knives, forks and spoons, of which they have the sole control; in fact, Mr. Rogers personally is in charge of this department of the factory. In 1884, they opened their Chicago branch, at No. 160 State street, in charge of Mr. M. N. Burchard, who had been connected with the company since September, 1883, and than whom none are better acquainted with the wants of the western trade, with which, as a member of the St. Louis house of Cheever, Burchard & Co., he had been identified for upwards of thirty years. In April, 1885, the present spacious salesrooms were occupied, wherein a display of silver-plated and Rogers ware is made, the like of which cannot be duplicated in the west, while their perfect manufacturing facilities enable such prices to be quoted as absolutely defy competition, the trade developed making their house the most prominent alike both west and east, and the representative exponent of the silver-plate industry of the United States.

The Bee-Hive.

State Street, Opposite the Palmer House.

No review of the industries of Chicago commemorative of her semi-centennial celebration would be complete without mention of the Bee-Hive, the distinctive bargain house of the city as regards everything in the line of dry goods, fancy goods, millinery, etc., yet although cheap in price, the quality is of the best, and it is only through the command of large capital and constant attention to the market that Messrs. Morgenthau, Bauland & Co. are enabled to quote bargain prices. The store is large, and the goods and fittings most tastefully arranged, while there is not an article, imported or domestic, which the Bee-Hive cannot furnish to accommodate the purse of the rich and the poor alike, from the most expensive silks of Lyons to the cheapest calicos, the handsomest India shawls to the modest sack, there is nothing wanting to suit all conditions and tastes. To give an idea of the tremendous volume of business continually done, it may be mentioned that three hundred employes are always kept at work, while the double store has recently been enlarged by taking in the adjoining building. Its location, directly opposite the Palmer house, is considered the best in the city for the retail trade. The great specialty of the house is their millinery department, in which branch they excel every establishment west of New York city, keeping, as they do, the most complete assortment of hats for ladies, misses and children, and all kinds and styles of materials used for trimming purposes. The Bee-Hive receives during the seasons weekly shipments direct from Paris, and are thus enabled to show the latest novelties simultaneously with the most fashionable milliners in New York city.

Fred. P. Buell & Co.

General Fire Insurance, 175 La Salle Street.

Among the prominent fire insurance firms in this city is that of Messrs. Fred. P. Buell & Co., than whom none have been more fortunate in establishing and maintaining a high reputation, and certainly none enjoy a larger share of well-earned success. Established in 1880, and conducted on sound business principles, it was not long before the firm of

Fred. P. Buell & Co. reached a front rank in their line. Mr. Buell has enjoyed a long and valuable experience as an underwriter, through his prior active connection with well-known companies, and possesses special facilities for placing large lines without delay. Some of the oldest and most reliable insurance agents in the city have placed all the brokerage business they formerly did into Mr. Buell's hands. He also places risks for some of the largest firms in the west and northwest. Risks are placed in any State in the Union, and none but the best and most reliable companies are represented. He is a native of Hamilton, Ill., and an old resident of Chicago, in whose mercantile circles he is esteemed a gentleman of unmistakable ability, keen intelligence and unswerving integrity, with whom those who place their commissions will find their interests carefully guarded in every particular.

There is no establishment in Chicago that shows more conspicuously the rapid development and improvement in the art of photography than that of J. K. Stevens' gallery, in the McVicker theater building. This is the result of the close personal application to every department of his chosen profession. Mr. Stevens began the business on the West side twenty-seven years ago, near the corner of Madison and Halsted streets, and built up one of the largest galleries on that side. In fact, ever since the inception of his business here, he has been one of the recognized leading artists in Chicago. In 1874 Mr. Stevens moved to the South side, and after various changes, finally, two years ago, located in his present central and commodious quarters. His gallery occupies two floors, his reception rooms being handsomely furnished and equal to any drawing room in elegance and comfort, and his operating department is equipped with all the most improved modern apparatus and appliances. Mr. Stevens employs from twenty-eight to thirty skilled and experienced assistants, at the head of whom is L. W. Stevens, son of the proprietor. Mr. Stevens possesses every facility for turning out first-class work in the most prompt and satisfactory manner, while his prices are very moderate. Photography in all its branches is attended to, special attention being given to children's pictures, and in this line he has won a reputation second to none in Chicago. His work is not alone confined to this city, as is proven from the fact that in one day his order book had fifteen States and Canada represented upon it. Mr. Stevens has been a resident of Chicago for over thirty years, coming here from his native State, New York. By a life study of his chosen profession he has contributed much to the advancement of modern photography in this city.

McCormack Bros.

Homœopathic Pharmaceutists, Rooms 34, 35 and 36 Quincy Building, 113 Adams Street, Opposite Post-Office.

This house is engaged in the preparation of all the various drugs, chemicals, simples and therapeutical appliances of the homœopathic pharmacopœia and enjoys an extensive and increasing patronage from the Atlantic to the Pacific. A leading feature of the business is the manufacture of staple homœopathic products for the general drug trade, consisting of tinctures, triturates, pellets, liquids and other remedial agents peculiar to homœopathy. These remedies are furnished in any and every degree of attenuation to suit the notions of the prescriber or the demands of the consumer, and are sent out from the pharmacy in shape most convenient for handling, dispensing or administering them. They are furnished to the trade and for general use in the well-known regulation homœopathic vials of hyaline glass of uniform size and shape, which are carefully sealed with their combination capping to guard as far as possible against evaporation or contamination through external influences. It is understood that retail druggists do not generally have sufficient time nor the necessary conveniences for the preparation of homœopathic medicines, and are unable to prepare them for themselves on a small scale so accurately and economically as can be done by manufacturing pharmacists like McCormack Bros., who devote their skill and attention to the business on a large scale; hence it is that the products of this pharmacy are in such active demand by the retail drug trade throughout the country, to whom they are sold in any quantities required. Another feature of the McCormack Bros'. business is the furnishing of family cases of selected homœopathic remedies, for family or individual use, with books describing the disorders to which they are applicable, and giving directions for their proper administration in all ordinary cases. Thousands of families have procured them and can testify to their great convenience and value in the treatment of common ailments. McCormack Bros. also furnish veterinary cases of homœopathic remedies adapted to the diseases of all domestic animals, including horses, cattle, sheep, hogs, poultry, etc. Horse-owners, stock-raisers, farmers and all others having the care of animals find these remedies of the greatest service in curing the diseases to which animals are subject. None but skilled and trusty assistants are employed in manipulating and preparing the McCormack Bros'. remedies, and the utmost care is taken to produce them in absolute purity and perfection. From modest and moderate beginnings this house has built up during the past ten years an extensive patronage among jobbers and retailers of drugs, and their remedies have become known and valued in thousands of households from one end of the country to the other. For further information concerning the remedies or the business of the firm, address McCormack Bros., homœopathic pharmacists, rooms 34, 35 and 36, 113 Adams street, Chicago.

ing on basis of estimate. The machines are manufactured in Chicago, a spacious foundry and machine shop, at the corner of Jefferson and Fulton streets, being utilized for this purpose. These machines may be ordered either direct from Mr. Whitcomb, rooms 31 and 33, Commercial National Bank building, patentee and sole proprietor, or through his traveling salesmen, by whom he is represented in all the mining districts. The Consolidated Coal Co., of St. Louis, have over one hundred of them in use in their mines. They are also in use by W. P. Rend, of Chicago, the Bloomington and Springfield Coal Co., of Springfield, Ill., the St. Louis Ore and Steel Co., Brazil Block Coal Co., the Tennessee Coal, Iron and Railroad Co., in the Pratt mines of Alabama, and many others.

Geo. D. Whitcomb.

Proprietor Harrison Mining Machine, Rooms 32 and 33, Commercial Bank Building.

Every day mining becomes more and more dependent for its success upon labor-saving machinery, the production of which, of different kinds, is a business engaging the attention of the most talented business men of the country. The introduction of the now justly celebrated Harrison Mining Machine

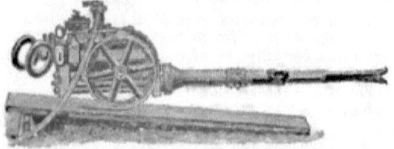

has wrought a veritable revolution in this industry, constructed, as it is, substantially, and from the best materials, and yet with such simplicity as to preclude the possibility of any derangement of its parts. The machines require only one operator and one laborer to run them, and will do more work for each cubic foot of air consumed than any machine in use. They are manufactured in two sizes, respectively, the "light" and "heavy" standard, the former, when mounted, weighing only five hundred pounds, and will shear five feet in height and four and a half in depth; the latter weighing seven hundred pounds, and of corresponding power. These machines are in successful operation wherever mining is carried on, and are so reasonable in price as to be within the reach of all. A feature of the business is in examining mining properties and furnishing machines and estimates, with machines subject to sale after work-

The growth of musical literature is a pleasing indication of the rapid increase of refinement and culture throughout the country, and no city in the United States has become a more important center for the trade in this line than Chicago. In music typography and printing, no one is better fitted by natural ability and experience than Mr. H. S. Bigelow. He was formerly located in Boston, but removed to Chicago in 1883, where he occupies suitable premises, admirably arranged and equipped with every facility and convenience for the business, and is now prepared to furnish on reasonable terms electrotype plates for sheet music and music books of all sizes and styles, while his arrangements with artists are such that every variety of cover illustration can be had at short notice. In mechanical execution his work is unexcelled, his composing rooms being stocked with a most extensive supply of new type, comprising all the latest styles, and to which additions are constantly being made as new designs are issued. While being practical in every department of his art, Mr. Bigelow, in achieving success, has built up a standard reputation for the artistic merit of his work.

Bogue & Hoyt.

Real Estate Agency, 182 Dearborn Street.

The late course of events in the financial world has fully demonstrated that there is no form of investment so safe and with such sure returns as real estate, and especially is this the case with regard to realty in the western metropolis, wherein prudent and judicious investments are more popular than ever. Prosecuting an enterprise in this direction is the house of Bogue & Hoyt, one of the oldest and leading in the real-estate trade, and one which has contributed largely to the development of property interests in Chicago. This house was originally established in 1867 by Mr. Geo. M. Bogue, the firm composed of himself, Henry W. Hoyt and Hamilton B. Bogue, having been organized in 1883, these gentlemen being among the best known members of the real-estate fraternity, and who have developed a large and permanent trade. Their connections are of a most superior character, including among their permanent customers many of our capitalists and investors. As real-estate brokers, they have carried through many of the heaviest transactions on record, devoting themselves to securing the best possible bargains for investors who can always implicitly rely on their sound judgment as to present and prospective values of the residence and business section of Chicago and its vicinity. The firm transact all branches of a general real-estate business—buying, selling, exchanging, renting—including the negotiation of loans on bond and mortgage, the collection of rents, and the placing of insurance risks at lowest rates with the most reliable companies. A prominent specialty with them is the management of estates, in which line they enjoy an especially high reputation and have permanently retained the confidence of property owners. They have recently directed their attention to fine residence property, such as that on Drexel and Grand boulevards, Kenwood, Hyde Park and the like, in which their books contain some of the choicest selections. Their business methods have met the permanent approbation of our leading citizens, while their appreciation of values together with their extensive acquaintance renders their services peculiarly valuable to owners of realty and intending investors.

C. M. Linington.

Importer and Jobber of Fancy Goods, Notions, and Five and Ten Cent Counter Supplies, 200, 202, 204 and 206 Randolph Street.

This business occupies the second floor of the above mentioned numbers, covering an area of eighty by one hundred and eighty feet. It was first established twenty years ago, and has been located at various places, chiefly in this immediate neighborhood, till last year the present premises were occupied. The stock consists of fireworks, tinware, iron and steel hardware articles, cutlery, perfumery, tools, toys, dolls, toilet and shaving requisites, musical instruments, valises, canes, satchels, pens, stationery, pencils, brackets, optical instruments, glassware, pipes, combs, ladies' work baskets, etc., etc. The chief specialties are five, ten, twenty-five, forty-nine and ninety-nine cent counter goods, and these are supplied at a cost not to be met with in any other house in the United States. The supplies are obtained direct from the manufactories, and in such large quantities that special rates are quoted. The house also imports largely, direct from Europe,

many of the leading novelties. The bulk of the trade is with country houses in all parts of the States and Canada. A large stock is always on hand, and a well-illustrated catalogue is sent gratis on application to the proprietor.

Kesler Bros.

Real-Estate Dealers, 146 La Salle Street, First Floor.

In reviewing the real-estate interests of Chicago the business naturally divides itself into two great subdivisions, brokerage and dealing, the latter including those whose transactions are confined to their own property exclusively, and among these the firms engaged in the erection of buildings for sale naturally take precedence.

One of the most widely known firms thus engaged is that of Messrs. Kesler Bros., who have for years made a specialty of building and selling residences in Chicago and vicinity, and are all the time planning new and beautiful designs in cottages and two-story houses, or, in short, any kind of house a purchaser may want, with all modern improvements and built of elegant material, which they are prepared to sell at prices which must insure speedy enhancement in value, and upon terms which even include monthly payments. The firm are offering an opportunity to procure a home, to neglect which is nothing short of improvidence. Messrs. S. W. and A. E. Kesler are natives of Ohio, and have been established in business here since 1868, and are universally respected, as they are widely known throughout our leading financial and business circles.

R. H. Sanborn & Co.

Western Agents for Celluloid Collars and Cuffs, 143 Fifth Avenue.

Though introduced to the public but a few years ago, the utility of celluloid collars and cuffs has been amply demonstrated, and their merits are now universally recognized. Large amounts of these goods are annually sold in Chicago to supply points near and far throughout the west and south, the great bulk of which business is done by Messrs. Sanborn & Co., who became established in this city in 1879 as western agents of the leading manufacturer of these goods. Their offices and salesrooms, located at No. 143 Fifth avenue, are well adapted to their business, the firm carrying a large stock in all the latest styles and supplying all western jobbers and retailers in their line in this city, in addition to the large outside trade built up by their traveling salesmen, while the prices named for these superior goods enables retailers to place them within the reach of all. The members of the firm are thoroughly experienced and practical gentlemen who spare no pains to render satisfaction in every instance, while the growth and prosperity of their house is the best possible proof of the high estimation in which Messrs. R. H. Sanborn & Co. are held by the trade.

Alsip Brick Co.

Brick Manufacturers, Office, Room 73, 159 La Salle Street, Yard on 43d Street, West of Ashland Avenue, and Chicago and Hamlin Avenues.

Like many other branches of industry in the United States, the manufacture of bricks has undergone a veritable revolution, quite in keeping with the rapid march of progress, while the competition has become so severe that only those fully alive to the requirements of the trade and enterprising enough to utilize the most approved machinery in the interest of speed and economy can hope for permanent prosperity in the future. The house of Messrs. F. and W. H. Alsip, lately merged into the Alsip Brick Co., is one of our best known and most highly esteemed as well as largest manufacturers of brick, having turned out over forty million last year, and has had an extended and honorable business career, dating its foundation to the year 1871. The firm possesses all the necessary qualifications to win success, both as regards skill, capital and intelligence. Everything requisite is at hand, while the appliances and machinery used are complete in every particular, and specially adapted for the most thorough and scientific prosecution of the work. The yards at 43d street west of Ashland avenue, and Chicago and Hamlin avenues, are very spacious, and employ 500 to 700 men in the season. Constant improvements are being made, many of them of great magnitude and at heavy expense, but the results of which place them in a position to promptly supply the demand and at the same time maintain the high standard of quality which first gave them their prestige. Messrs. Frank, Wm. H. and Frank B. Alsip, the first a Pennsylvanian and the latter two Iowans by birth, are members of our Builders' Exchange, and in the very prime of life have developed a business of more than usual magnitude, and reflecting the highest credit upon the fair fame of our city.

A Great Railway.

The Chicago, Milwaukee & St. Paul System.

The Chicago, Milwaukee & St. Paul Railway company now owns and operates nearly fifty-six hundred miles of thoroughly equipped road in Illinois, Wisconsin, Minnesota, Iowa, Missouri and Dakota.

Each recurring year its lines are extended in all directions to meet the necessities of the rapidly populating sections of country west, northwest and southwest of Chicago, and to furnish a market for the products of the greatest agricultural and stock raising districts of the world. In Illinois it operates 320 miles of track; in Wisconsin, 1,220 miles; in Iowa, 1,575 miles; in Minnesota, 1,125 miles; in Dakota, 1,190 miles; in Missouri (now building), 150 miles, and the end is not yet. It has terminals in such large cities as Chicago, Milwaukee, La Crosse, St. Paul, Minneapolis, Fargo, Sioux City, Council Bluffs, Omaha and Kansas City, and along its lines are hundreds of large and small thriving cities, towns and villages. Manufacturing interests are cultivated, and all branches of trade find encouragement. The railway company has a just appreciation of the value of its patrons, and its magnificent earnings are the result of the good business tact which characterizes the management of its affairs. The popularity of the line is attested by the fact that, notwithstanding the strongest kind of competition of old and new lines, the Chicago, Milwaukee & St. Paul railway continues to carry fully sixty per cent. of all the business between Chicago, Milwaukee, St. Paul and Minneapolis. It is the best patronized route to and from all points in Wisconsin, Minnesota, Dakota and Iowa, and on the completion of its Kansas City line, in 1887, it will undoubtedly take equal rank with the older lines leading to and from the southwest.

On all its through lines of travel the Chicago, Milwaukee & St. Paul railway runs the most perfectly equipped trains of sleeping, parlor and dining cars and coaches. No effort is spared to furnish the best accommodations for the least money, and, in addition, patrons of the road are sure of courteous treatment from its employes.

Take it all in all, the Chicago, Milwaukee & St. Paul is the peer of any railway in this or any other country.

Henry Jansen.

Direct Importer and Dealer in Rhine Wines, 163 and 165 Washington Street.

The largest importer in this city of Rhine wine exclusively is Henry Jansen. Some of the finest casks in the world may be seen here made of solid oak, of finest grain, and carved so elaborately as to be quite works of art. The premises occupy a space of 50x100 feet, and contained at time of visit an average stock, that is, 150 casks of 80 gallons each and 600 cases of bottled wines. The trade is both wholesale and retail, of which the bulk is with retailers, wine and spirit dealers. A large and growing outside business is also prosecuted. Mr. Wecker commenced this trade here in 1873, but was bought out by the present enterprising proprietor in 1880, since when the sales have increased 300 per cent. Mr. Jansen imports direct through the Chicago custom-house, and sells at low rates. His wines, being of the finest quality, command a ready sale and give satisfaction.

Eastland & Duddleston.

Butchers, 83 and 85 Fifth Avenue.

Perhaps the largest retail establishment in the city for all kinds of butchers' meats is that of Eastland & Duddleston. The store is large, occupying two buildings thrown into one, Nos. 83 and 85 Fifth avenue. The store is a model of neatness and cleanliness and is so centrally located that it is within easy reach of all parts of the city. The basement and part of the store are used for the reception and keeping of meat. Vast ice rooms, holding the products of six hundred cattle, form a sight worth seeing here.

No butcher's establishment in the city possesses such accommodations for the reception and keeping of meats in the warm weather as we have here.

The store has a frontage of thirty-five feet on Fifth avenue and a depth of one hundred feet in the rear. This firm has been established ten years, the last seven of which have been spent in their present location.

A specialty is made of supplying hotels, clubhouses and restaurants, while a large trade is with families and private residents.

The firm has a widely extending business, and one that includes many of the most influential and well-known citizens amongst its customers. Their efforts are to secure patronage by fair dealing, supplying only the best class of meat and at the regular market prices, and in this they have been most successful.

Wm. Henning.

Manufacturer of Vinegar, Nos. 115 and 117 North Avenue.

Just west of Clybourn avenue is located the extensive vinegar works of Wm. Henning. His large factory, fifty by one hundred and twenty-five feet in dimensions and four stories in height, is well arranged for the business. The vinegar and compressed yeast produced by Mr. Henning are manufactured by the most scientific and approved methods and apparatus, and in quality and general excellence have a standard reputation. His vinegars are noted for their purity and freshness and find a ready sale throughout all parts of the east, west and northwest, and are much sought after by the city merchants in this line. The business was begun in 1872 in a small way and is now one of the largest in the city. Mr. H. is a native of Germany and came to Chicago in 1862.

John J. Davis & Co.

Successors to R. W. Sweet & Co., Jobbers of Cigars, 274 East Madison Street.

Among the various interests which diversify the industries of Chicago none deserves more prominent mention than that of the cigar trade, giving employment as it does to large numbers of skilled operatives and forming in many ways an important item in estimating the manufacturing and commercial importance of this enterprising and thriving city. One of the most popular and energetic houses in the jobbing department of the trade is that of John J. Davis & Co., succeeding on January 1, 1887, to the business of R. W. Sweet & Co., established in 1883. The aim of the house is to place before the trade an honest cigar at a reasonable price, one worthy of the good opinions of smokers, and by scrupulously maintaining the high character of their well-known brands, "B. O. E.," "Old-Timer" and "La Inocenta," to retain the patronage so lavishly bestowed upon their predecessors. Commodious and well-appointed premises, are occupied, in the very center of the business district, and a full and complete stock of both imported and domestic cigars carried, the reliability of which is demonstrated by the steady demand arising for these goods wherever introduced, while the facilities and resources of the house enable them to quote prices difficult to duplicate elsewhere. Mr. Davis has long been identified with the trade, to whom he is well known as a gentleman of strict integrity and reliability, and under whose guidance this prominent house possesses every assurance of even still further increased prosperity in the future.

Frederic Gaylord.

Real Estate, Room 31, 175 Dearborn Street.

The rapid growth of the city of Chicago abundantly demonstrates that those who effected judicious investments in realty years ago made the wisest possible use of their capital. Mr. Gaylord has fine properties on Calumet avenue, Forty-seventh street, Garfield boulevard and Woodlawn avenue, where he has at all times choice building sites at bargain prices. He has resided in this city for over twenty years, and was formerly engaged in the wholesale grocery business, having, however, for twelve years past devoted his attention to real estate.

Michener Bros. & Co.

Packers and Curers of the Celebrated "Banana Brand" of Hams, and Dealers in Provisions Generally. Office, Room 211, Insurance Exchange Building, 218 La Salle Street.

The packing trade is admittedly one of the greatest factors in the remarkable development of the commerce of Chicago, and one of the leading houses in this line is that of Michener Bros. & Co., packers and curers of the celebrated "Banana Brand" of hams, whose packing house at the Union Stock Yards is equipped with all the most improved modern machinery and appliances, and wherein thousands of workmen are employed constantly. The hams are cured by a process which adds to the flavor of the meat, renders it free from all injurious substances, and the unpleasant taste of excessive salt so often noticed in those of other packers. Though their specialty is the "Banana Brand" of hams, of which a large sale is had all over the United States, Messrs. Michener Bros. & Co. are also extensive handlers of provisions generally, and possess complete facilities for promptly filling all orders at the ruling markets, both Messrs. J. Hart and W. W. Michener being members of the Board of Trade. The house is an old Philadelphia one, having been established there in 1843, while the Chicago branch was opened eight years ago, and has proved to be eminently successful, doing a business which extends all over the world. The extent of its operations has made this house a prominent one even in Chicago, the center of the packing trade, while the inducements offered to patrons are of the most advantageous character.

Enterprise Wire Cloth Mfg. Co.

Frederick Voss, Proprietor. 67 and 69 West Monroe Street.

Wire work and railings now enter largely into the interior fitting and decoration of our large business houses, and we find some of the largest manufacturing firms engaged in this class of work. One of the oldest and most prosperous houses engaged in this business is that of Frederick Voss, of 67 and 69 West Monroe street, whose establishment is known as the Enterprise Wire Cloth Manufacturing Co. He does a large business throughout the States as a manufacturer of architectural and decorative wire and iron work, bank and office railings, elevator guards, window guards, stair rails, iron fences and wire cloth and wire goods of every description. His large factory here gives employment to forty-five men. The business was started fourteen years ago under the style of Keily & Voss, but two years ago Mr. Voss succeeded to the entire control of the concern.

Spalding Lumber Company.

Lumber Manufacturers, 248 South Water Street.

Foremost among the great lumber receivers of Chicago today is the Spalding Lumber company. In 1861 Mr. Jesse Spalding commenced, in a small way, on the Wisconsin side of the Menominee river, in Green Bay, locating yards in Chicago at Lumber and Mitchell streets, south of Twelfth street. The timber was cut and run down the Menominee river. At that time the manufacture and sale of four million to six million feet for an entire season seemed very large. Twenty-three years ago Mr. Spalding purchased the Cedar river property, thirty miles north of Menominee, on Cedar river. The product of the mills on the Menominee the past season was forty million feet of lumber and of those on Cedar river thirty million feet. Sales for the season were about $1,000,000. Besides doing an immense business on the cargo market, Mr. Spalding also had yards in Chicago up to four years ago. It was then determined to abandon the retail trade. It is all wholesale now, and so completely is the trade in hand that no firm or company can sell cheaper, when it comes to sharp competition. In bringing the product of their mill to Chicago they employ a line of barges of their own.

The Hon. Jesse Spalding has long been a representative citizen of Chicago and the State, and has held various positions of honor and trust, all the way from city alderman up. He was also a member of the National Republican convention of 1880. As collector of customs of the port of Chicago he inaugurated and enforced many changes and reforms and put the affairs of the custom house on a practical, business-like basis. As popular as he is wealthy, everyone in Chicago business circles knows "Uncle Jesse Spalding."

The Thomson & Taylor Spice Co.

34 to 40 South Water Street.

The spacious buildings containing many acres of floor room from 30 to 40 South Water street are occupied by the Thomson & Taylor Spice Co. This is the largest house in the trade in this country, and about the oldest, being established in 1865. They

are direct importers of spices, coffees, indigos, etc., and are also manufacturers of the various grades of ground spices and coffees, mustards, baking powders, flavoring extracts, dry and liquid bluing, hops and herbs, seeds, etc. They are also the proprietors of the famous Red Cross lye and other grades of lye and potash. This firm employ over 150 workmen in their factories, and their business outside of Chicago is with the jobbing trade exclusively, selling no goods to the retail trade. The company was incorporated four years ago, and its officers are Alex. M. Thomson, president; James E. Taylor, vice president; Geo. Thompson, secretary and treasurer.

Murphy & Company.

Varnish Makers, 262 Wabash Avenue.

Varnish is one of the most important of all the aids to external decoration, and few articles of manufacture have a more varied field of usefulness. Much of interest might be written of its history and mysteries, its manufacture and application, the transformation of the fossil gums, hidden for ages in tropical sands, into the mirror-like luster upon coach or piano, and of the progress made in the methods of its manufacture in the past few decades. It is not more than a single generation ago that the itinerant varnish-maker traveled from place to place and melted in the kitchen pot a mixture of gum, oil, and turpentine sufficient to supply the carriage-maker with enough "varnish" to last until his next yearly visit. Today the manufacture of this article employs enormous capital and extensive plant. Murphy & Co. are undoubtedly, whether considered by the quality of their products or the extent of their operations, the leading house in their line in this country, and have a history which is in full sympathy with the spirit of the age. Their business was started in 1864 in a very modest way at Newark, N. J., which place is still the general headquarters, No. 238 McWhorter street, and where their plant, in its completeness and capacity for the production of fine goods, is without an equal in this country or in Europe. The company have also extensive works at Cleveland, Ohio, No. 566 Canal street, and are erecting on Twenty-second, Dearborn and Butterfield streets, in Chicago, works that will rival their Newark plant in capacity. They have offices at No. 231 Broadway, New York, and carry in storage full lines of stock at No. 300 S. Fourth street, St. Louis, and at No. 262 Wabash avenue, Chicago; the latter a building fitted up with huge indestructible, fireproof tanks especially for their purpose, the average stock therein carried being 35,000 gallons. The company's total storage capacity closely approximates 500,000 gallons, and this one fact alone carries with it the assurance of uniformity of quality, an all-important element, which no other statement could give. The foundation of the remarkable success of this company lies undoubtedly in the complete knowledge of the business possessed by its managers, who are not only practical varnishmakers, but practical business men. They undertook to make only goods of a standard quality, and never wavered from this policy. Manufacturing a full line of coach, railway, cabinet and other varnish, their product goes wherever varnish is used, but the larger portion of their business is in railway and fine coach goods and the higher grades of cabinet varnish. The Chicago depot, which is under the charge of Mr. F. H. Taylor, supplies not only the vast city trade, but also that of the northwest, the Cleveland house supplying the middle west, and the St. Louis house the far west and southwest, while their New York department caters to the wants of the balance of the union and their export trade, which is large.

George Beaumont.

Architect, 115 Dearborn Street, Chicago.

Much of the prosperity and beauty of a city depends upon its architects, and those of Chicago have much to look back upon with pride. One of the leading men in the profession is Mr. George Beaumont, with office located at 115 Dearborn street. This gentleman has been in the profession seventeen years, and has spent much of the earlier part of his time on the continent of Europe, studying in nearly every city of importance there.

In 1879 he received the medal of the Leeds and Yorkshire Architectural Society for the best class of drawings.

He has been connected for six years with this city, much of which time was spent in the capacity of superintendent to the well-known late firm of Wheelock & Clay. He is prepared to execute plans and designs for any class of work required, and is with his assistants kept busy executing orders in this line.

He has superintended the building of some of the largest and handsomest residences in the city, the cost of which has in some instances reached over $200,000. Though Mr. Beaumont is still a young man, he has achieved much success and has been recognized for his talent both here and abroad, being a member of the Royal Institute of British Architects, London, and first vice president of the Chicago Architectural Sketch club.

Wm. M. Dale.

Manufacturing and Dispensing Chemist, Corner Clark and Madison Streets.

There is perhaps no branch of business which requires a higher degree of proficiency and business capacity than that of the chemist and pharmacist, and in this connection we speak of our visit to the "City Prescription Drug Store" under the proprietor-

ship and management of Mr. Wm. M. Dale. The premises occupied are most central, being located in the northeast corner of Clark and Madison streets. The store is fitted up in the most thorough and attractive manner, and contains the largest and most complete soda and mineral water fountains in the west. The store is amply stocked with pure drugs and chemicals, all popular and desirable patent medicines, perfumeries and toilet articles in great variety, and in fact everything to be desired in a first-class metropolitan establishment of this description. Careful attention is given to the preparation of physicians' prescriptions, which is under the supervision of Mr. Dale and his corps of experienced clerks. Mr. Dale enjoys a high reputation in this line, and possesses the highest qualifications as a practical pharmacist, and has the confidence and esteem of the medical profession generally. Mr. Dale is a native of Scotland, where he was born, in 1842, and came to Chicago in 1865, two years after which he commenced business in a small way at No. 155 Clark street. He moved to his present premises in 1879, and so marked and rapid has been his progress that at the present time his

Elgin National Watch Co.

General Office, 76 Monroe Street.

In no department has American genius been more satisfactorily rewarded than in the manufacture of fine watches, among which the celebrated "Elgin" is universally accorded the leadership in all the markets of the world. This business was organized and duly incorporated as "The National Watch Company of Chicago, Ill.," Aug. 27, 1864, with a capital of $100,000, the incorporators being Benjamin W. Raymond, Howard Z. Culver, Thos. S. Dickerson, Geo. M.

Wheeler, Philo Carpenter, W. Robbins and Edward H. Williams. In 1865 the company was re-organized by special charter, with a capital of $500,000, and the title changed to the National Watch Co. On Jan. 28, 1869, the authorized capital was increased to $2,000,000, and the name again altered to that of the Elgin National Watch company. The factory is situated at Elgin, Ill., on the banks of the Fox river, and the area included in the works contains 27 acres, 22 of which were presented to the company by the citizens of Elgin, who likewise donated 13 additional acres to accommodate the cottages of the employes. The manufacturing premises consist of a splendid series of buildings, admirably arranged and fitted up with every appliance and convenience that art and science have devised for the prosecution of the business and the comfort and safety of the operatives. The machinery is magnificent and unsurpassed in this country or Europe, the tools and appliances being miracles of accuracy and exactness. The drills for probing the orifices in the jewels to admit the shaft on which the wheels revolve are almost as fine as the filaments of a spider's web, while the gauges used to measure the correctness of the aperture thus made are so delicate as to indicate the thirtieth part of a hair or the ten-thousandth part of an inch. The cutters which are employed to form the teeth of the 'scape wheel out of the solid metal are sapphires ground down to the proper shape in diamond dust and oil, and then inserted in small wheels or discs, and so fine do they cut that the chips which they can remove are only the thirtieth part of the thickness of a hair, and this infinitesimal portion can be cut from any part of the tooth, so easily are their motions controlled. A coil of wire weighing a pound, and worth $5, is divided and worked into 300,000 screws worth about $4,000. These screws, which to the naked eye resemble rifle powder, are finished in all respects as perfectly as those larger ones with which everyone is familiar, having counter-sunk heads, threads and grooves for the reception of the screw-driver. The threads are cut with perfect accuracy by means of discs, and of a fineness not visible to the eye except by the aid of a microscope. Many of the tools and machines in use in the Elgin National Watch company's factory are the inventions of employes of the corporation, about 2,300 skilled and experienced operatives being constantly engaged. One great distinguishing feature of the Elgin watches is the simplicity of their construction. In some foreign watches there are as many as 600 different parts, rendering them a perfect labyrinth of cogs and wheels, which complexity of construction necessarily increases their liability to derangement, and which in the Elgin is lessened two-thirds, and the friction at least one-half. Again in the Elgin there is a perfect uniformity of parts, by which every watch of the same class is a duplicate of every other. In addition to these advantages the Elgin watches have, in common with others of American make, some peculiarities in invention which are secured by patent. Mr. T. M. Avery, the president, is widely known as one of the representative manufacturers of the United States, and worthily presides over the rapidly increasing business of the Elgin National Watch company. Messrs. J. W. Scoville, vice-president, and Wm. G. Prall, secretary, are able and widely known business men, of inflexible integrity and devotion to the company's interests. The enterprise of the Elgin National Watch company is not only a source of pride to the citizens of Chicago, but to the whole of the United States, while the officers, from their training and education, are well qualified to carry on this vast business and with the greatest satisfaction to their numerous patrons in all parts of the world.

B. F. Fitch.

Dealer in Paper Hangings, Window Shades, Paints, Oils, Glass, Zinc, White Lead, Varnishes, Brushes, Etc.

194 Twenty-second Street.

On entering the establishment of B. F. Fitch at No. 194 Twenty-second street, it is found to be stocked with a fine grade of wall paper, window shades, paints, oils, glass, zinc, white lead, varnishes, brushes, etc., in fact everything to be found in a first-class establishment of this kind. He employs from eight to ten competent workmen to assist him, and every class of work in this line is done with neatness and dispatch. Mr. Fitch is an old and experienced workman and

FIFTY YEARS' PROGRESS.

understands fully every branch of his large business, superintending personally all orders given to his charge. He has been established at his present quarters for the past twelve years, and the large patronage received, which is throughout the city, is evidence of the success he has achieved. He is a native of the State of Pennsylvania, and has been a resident of this city since he began business twelve years ago. He was in the late war as a volunteer from this State, and served acceptably as a lieutenant of company E, 129th regiment, Illinois volunteer infantry.

E. W. Blatchford & Co.

70 North Clinton Street.

The well-known shot-tower on the West side is a landmark in Chicago, and serves to point out the place of business of one of the most enterprising and prosperous firms in Chicago. We allude to Messrs. E. W. Blatchford & Co., of 70 North Clinton street, manufacturers of lead and tin pipe, sheet and bar lead, pig lead and block tin, solder and antimony, antimonial, leads, linseed oil and oil cake, babbitt metals, stereotype, electrotype, type metals, copper and spelter. They also make a specialty of the manufacture of shot, of which they turn out hundreds of tons annually. Their enormous factory and shot-tower at North Clinton street is one of the best equipped in Chicago, and gives employment to over 100 workmen. They have a very large trade among the wholesale city houses, but by far the larger part of their goods are shipped throughout the country. They are a very solid and reliable firm, and spare no pains to retain the patronage they have once acquired. To deal with them once is to deal with them always. Mr. E. W. Blatchford is a thorough specimen of an American business man, and is highly respected among the trading community.

Geo. F. Kimball.

Importer and Dealer in Polished Plate and Window Glass, 45 and 47 Jackson Street.

The natural and acquired advantages which have contributed to make the city of Chicago a commercial center of such an important character within one short half-century have also induced here the establishment of enterprises which have become justly celebrated far and wide, throughout the length and breadth of the United States. Such an one is that conducted by Mr. George F. Kimball, which, since its inauguration in 1879, has obtained a liberal and influential patronage throughout the entire west. Mr. Kimball is an extensive importer of plate and window glass, and carries a large and valuable stock of American window glass, and French and German mirrors, to accommodate which a spacious six-story building is occupied—seventy-five by one hundred and twenty-five feet in dimensions. The goods carried by this house are of the very best obtainable, while its resources are such that the largest orders can be promptly executed at bottom prices.

J. H. Wallace.

Dealer in Pine and Hardwood Lumber, 242 South Water Street.

The rapid growth of Chicago abundantly demonstrates the wisdom of those who early entered the lumber trade, the rise of which, with but a few brief intervals, has been rapid and permanent. In 1870, seeing the advantage of the opening afforded in the lumber trade to energy and perseverance, Mr Wallace, who for the five years prior had been identified with the dry goods trade at Decatur, Mich., established this house, which has since obtained a constantly increasing patronage, and whose annual sales now exceed ten million feet. The yards are located at North Branch and Eastman street, and are provided with every facility and appliance for the economical shipping and handling of lumber. Though pine is largely dealt in, hardwood lumber is the specialty of Mr. Wallace, in which the trade can at all times depend on being supplied with promptness and dispatch at the lowest market rates.

W. H. Reid.

Draper and Tailor, and Men's Furnisher, 163 Twenty-second Street.

One of the leading drapers, tailors and gents furnishers that have been foremost in promoting the standard of elegance in dress is W. H. Reid; and in making a tour of the business interests of Chicago, we did not omit to visit this popular resort of all who appreciate elegant, neat fitting garments. Mr. Reid is located at No. 163 Twenty-second street, telephone 8200. This now representative house dates its inception from 1862, and when first started was located under the old Matteson House, which was then situated on the corner of Randolph and Dearborn streets. Being a first-class tailor, and turning out work of the most excellent character, his trade grew rapidly, and he has always been recognized as among the foremost tailors and drapers of this city. His fine stock of goods consists of imported and American cloths, cassimeres and suitings of the latest styles and patterns. None but experienced cutters and workmen are employed, and perfect fits are guaranteed in all cases. The large trade of this house necessitates the employment of forty or more hands. In 1871 the big fire took all that Mr. Reid had, and after the fire he began again at his present premises, and is one of but a few who paid one hundred cents to the dollar after the fire. Mr. Reid has two sons, who also have large establishments of the same kind, and during each year Mr. Reid takes a trip to New York and makes selections for his trade. Mr. Reid also carries a large and fine stock of gents furnishing goods. He has been a resident of Chicago since 1855, coming here from New York, and to his effort as much as any other one man's is due the advancement this branch of industry has made in this city.

Chicago Desk Manufacturing Co.

Manufacturers of Office Desks. Office and Factory, Corner of Peoria and Kinzie Streets.

The largest concern in this line in the city is the Chicago Desk Manufacturing company, of Peoria and Kinzie streets. The factory is a handsome six-story brick building, sixty by sixty-five, and there are eighty workmen employed. The company is exclusively engaged in the manufacture of office desks, and they turn out a large number annually. Their business is nearly all transacted outside the city, and there is a great demand for their goods in all the principal cities in the States. This is an incorporated company, and the business has been established for eight years. The following gentlemen are the officers of the company: Lars L. Skielvig, president, and John H. Minges, secretary and manager. They formerly did business at North Desplaines street, but they moved into their present handsome premises last year. This is a thoroughly representative concern, and it is well established on a sound commercial basis. It is under good management, and contains within itself all the elements of success.

McHugh & Enright.

Iron Foundry, Machinery and Light Castings a Specialty, 199-205 North Halsted Street.

The large iron foundry of McHugh & Enright, at Nos. 199 to 205 North Halsted street, was formerly known as the Standard Foundry, and has been in operation for a number of years, although the present proprietors have only had charge of it since September, '86. Through their energy, enterprise, and the practical experience they have brought to bear upon the business, they have been able to win a large and influential trade. Their specialty is machinery and light castings, and any fine work that is to be done can be turned out by them in the best manner. Their telephone number is 4398, and all orders received in this manner meet with prompt attention. The foundry is fitted up with all the latest machinery and facilities for the rapid and perfect prosecution of their work, and they employ a large corps of practical and experienced workmen, who are under their personal attention, and every job that leaves their establishment may be relied upon as being perfect in every respect. Both members of the firm are skilled foundrymen, this being

their life trade, and as they are hard and earnest workers, they have succeeded in establishing a connection with the prominent iron merchants of the city and surrounding country.

Gates Iron Works.

50 to 58 Clinton Street.

The Gates Iron Works, of South Clinton street, are engaged in the manufacture of a class of machines that are invaluable to our great railroad and mining interests. They are principally concerned in the production of their celebrated rock-breaker, known as the greatest rock-breaker and ore-crusher on earth, guaranteed to do three to six times more work than any crusher in use. They are in great demand by the principal railroads for breaking ballast, etc. In addition they manufacture mining machinery. The works are owned and operated

by an incorporated company, of which Mr. P. W. Gates is president; Ralph Gates, vice-president and superintendent; and J. L. Fargo, secretary and treasurer. Their plant is supplied with all the necessary machinery adapted to their heavy work. Mr. P. W. Gates, who is the head of the concern, started in the iron trade, on the banks of the Chicago river, in 1840. The business increased, and for many years was one of the largest manufacturing establishments in Chicago. In 1871, he says, he thought he would retire from active business and improve his real estate. He says he soon found that he was not competent to carry out the program of the gentleman loafer, and started out again with his sons in the machinery business. The result has been the getting up, perfecting and introduction of the greatest rock-breaker on earth.

Mathias Peters.

Manufacturer of Upholstery, Drapery and Millinery Trimmings, Fringes, Tassels, Gimps, Cords, Etc., 229 Fulton Street.

A business that has its importance among the furniture men of Chicago is that carried on by Mr. Mathias Peters, at 229 Fulton street. He is a manufacturer of upholstery, drapery, and millinery trimmings, fringes, tassels, gimps, cords, etc. Mr. Peters started this business in 1872. His factory is a handsome brick structure, cornering on Fulton and Sangamon streets. He gives employment to fifty workpeople, and is generally as busy as he well can be. He manufactures none but the very best articles, and his trade is entirely among the first-class houses. His principal customers are among the furniture supply houses and large dry goods establishments. Mr. Peters is a native of Germany, but he has resided in this city since 1870.

We would also call attention to the Peters power spinning wheel, invented by Mr. Peters. It is something entirely new for the manufacture of cords and gimps. The lightest and heaviest, as well as the finest work, can be done with this wheel, combining accuracy, speed and economy. It occupies but one-third the space of the old wheel, and requires but little power to drive it, and, owing to the simplicity of mechanism, will effect a saving of from ten to fifteen per cent. It has the following advantages: It does not require a boy to run it; it runs both right and left, without crossing the band; it has a brake to stop it instantly; it can be operated by a single shifting cord attached overhead; it requires oiling but once a day. It can be seen in operation at his factory in Chicago, and at the factory of Walliser, 617 and 619 Arch street, Philadelphia. The inspection of manufacturers is invited.

Mullen Bros. & Co.

Woolens and Tailors' Trimmings, 264 and 266 Madison Street.

Like many others of the leading mercantile houses of Chicago, that of Messrs. Mullen Bros. & Co. was formerly located at Milwaukee, where it

was established in 1856. In 1880 they opened a branch in Chicago, which proved a complete success, and was followed three years later by the removal of the entire business to this city. The firm occupy very spacious and eligibly located premises, and carry one of the most complete and extensive stocks of woolens and tailors' trimmings to be found in the country, the great European manufacturing centers, as well as the leading American mills, being represented in large variety. The firm have nine traveling salesmen on the road constantly, representing them to the trade in all parts of the west and northwest, while the house is fully prepared with all necessary facilities and resources to execute all orders not only promptly, but with that intelligent understanding that has made their efforts so highly appreciated among their patrons. The house is in every respect a first-class one. Messrs. Andrew and James Mullen and Charles Catlin, the proprietors, experienced merchants, are recognized exponents of the various branches of metropolitan trade, and they well merit the high degree of prominence to which their own energy and enterprise have attained.

Hill's National Builder.

**Hill Standard Book Co., Publishers, 103 State Street.
Established March, 1885.**

Hill's National Builder is the acknowledged representative of one of the foremost industries in the world. It is a mammoth monthly illustrated journal of practical building, containing all the way from thirty-two to forty-eight pages, bound and trimmed like a magazine, printed upon the best quality of book paper, and is one of the handsomest publications issued, typographically speaking, besides containing valuable editorial matter, and market quotations as to lumber, sash, doors, blinds, brick, stone, iron, glass, building hardware and everything pertaining to the erection of a building from foundation to roof, to the dealers in which its advertising columns, with its large circulation all over the Union, must necessarily be of great value. An especial feature is the complete set of practical working drawings in colors, with full details, specifications and estimates, accompanying each number. This work is in charge of Thomas E. Hill, author of "Hill's Manual," "Hill's Album," and other popular works, assisted by Mr. Geo. O. Garnsey, one of the leading architects of Chicago, where he has been actively engaged in his profession for the past twenty-five years. Of the many publications started in these interests in the United States, *Hill's National Builder* very early in its history has attained a recognized position, while the ability, energy and liberality displayed in its management must lead to greatly enhanced success in the near future.

The Hiram Sibley Fireproof Warehouses.

Nos. 2-18 North Clark Street.

In taking a perspective review of the commercial interests of Chicago for the past fifty years, we must not fail, in our "Business Tour," to give an account of the visit made to "The Hiram Sibley Fireproof Warehouses," at Nos. 2-18 North Clark street. They are grand specimens of solid and beautiful architecture, and are the first strictly *fireproof* warehouses erected in this city. They will long stand as a monument of the energy and enterprise of the owner, whose favorite maxim is *"that the preservation from destruction by any cause of value in* any form is economy in business." This, together with the fact of there being a lack of sufficient first-class storage accommodation in Chicago, was the origin of these warehouses. They have a frontage on North Clark street of 200 feet, and a depth of 240 feet on the river. This includes the warehouses A, B and C. The structures A and B are completed and in active operation. It is contemplated to erect building C in the near future.

Building A contains the boilers for hoisting and heating purposes, has the main machinery of the warehouses in its basement, and is eight stories in height. The main floor, on Clark street, is planned for stores, with large plate-glass windows, four of which are occupied by the firm of Hiram Sibley & Co. for their general offices and the retail department of the Chicago branch of their seed business. Above the main floor are elegant offices, with every modern convenience, for the use of brokers in merchandise, agents of out-of-town business concerns and transportation companies. The four remaining floors are used mainly by Hiram Sibley & Co. for the cleaning and storage of field and grass seeds, of which they are doing a large and constantly increasing business.

Building B, immediately back of and adjoining A, and covering the same area of 80x200 feet, is ten stories in height, and is adapted throughout to the safe storage of large stocks of goods and merchandise. Here are placed the four large steam elevators, built by Hale & Co., after special patterns for these buildings, running from basement to top story, one of them having the capacity of carrying a loaded truck of 15,000 lbs. weight to any floor. Loaded teams enter by an arched driveway from Clark street to the center of building B on the main floor, and rapidly dispose of their loads, entirely under cover of the building.

Building C, is intended to be an exact duplicate of building B, with the addition of appliances and space set apart for cold storage.

The exterior of the warehouses is a departure from the nondescript style usually employed in buildings of this character, and presents a very fine appearance. The Clark street front, of Anderson pressed brick and iron, with terra cotta details, and its liberal display of glass, is very effective; and the river and railroad fronts, while somewhat plainer in detail, are strong and imposing. The broad pilasters, running up from the foundation to long projecting arches at the ninth story, seem to add to the already great height of the building, the whole forming a harmonious structure of massive and pleasing proportions, which does credit to the taste of the builder and skill of the architect and designer.

The extraordinary size and facilities of his warehouses enable him to offer the advantages of first-class fireproof storage to other business houses, where the same views of the close economies in business prevail.

One noticeable feature is the large iron letters on the top of the building. They are eight feet in height and can be seen a long way off. Mr. Sibley is also the noted seedsman of this country. He bought out, several years ago, the large business of Briggs Bros. The main house is located at Rochester, N. Y., and the western branch in this city. This department of the business, together with the warehouses, is under the charge and personal direction of Mr. F. A. Warner, who has had many years of experience in the seed business, and been an active member of the Chicago Board of Trade since 1879. There is kept constantly on hand a choice and select stock of timothy, blue grass, orchard grass, red top and Hungarian, clover in all standard varieties, the finest mixtures for lawns, and a variety of popular imported grasses, sorghum, broom corn, millets, seeding flax and buckwheat, also Sibley's Pride of the North, Yellow Dent and other tested varieties of seed corn. Garden and flower seed, together with all kinds of implements for their cultivation, are kept on hand by this firm. They are prepared to receive consignments of seeds from growers or dealers who desire to hold for higher prices, and have no facilities of their own for cleaning and storing. If desired, all seeds will be re-cleaned and put in proper shape for the market, or held in store at reasonable rates. These warehouses are absolutely fireproof, and, besides all facilities for general storage, have a department for the receipt of bonded goods also. For further information address Hiram Sibley & Co., Chicago, Ill.

Dunlap & Co.

Palmer House Block, 171 and 173 State Street.

The name of Dunlap & Co. has long been inseparably connected with the finest trade in gentlemen's hats in this country, and whose retail stores in the leading cities are to be found located in the very center of trade, viz: In New York City at Nos. 178 and 180 Fifth avenue, and No. 179 Broadway, near Cortlandt street; in Philadelphia, at No. 914 Chestnut street; and in Chicago, in the Palmer house, at Nos. 171 and 173 State street. The firm employ hundreds of hands and operate three distinct and separate factories, two in New York, one for silk and opera hats at Nos. 191 to 195 Seventh avenue, and the other for straw goods at Nos. 132 and 134 South Fifth avenue, while the felt hat factory is in Brooklyn, at Nos. 72 to 88 Nostrand avenue, the latter having been destroyed by fire in 1880, entailing a heavy loss, but was immediately rebuilt, and is now in operation on a larger scale than ever. Seeing the desirability of representation in this city, Messrs. Dunlap & Co. as early as 1868 established their branch here. They have agencies established in all the large cities of the union. The Chicago branch is under the efficient management of Mr. James P. Brewster, who is prepared to show the largest and most stylish assortment of gentlemen's hats in the city. Only the best grade of hats is to be found in this establishment, and every one is sent from their large factories in the east, and contains the die or trademark of Dunlap & Co. The prices in all cases are the same, as this firm considers they have no competition for these goods, and do not deviate from an established price the country over.

The firm have ever aimed to lead, in the attainment of which as to quality and styles large sums are expended annually, with the result that the productions of their factories are unrivaled even by the finest London or Parisian importations, and the demand for which is rapidly increasing all over the country.

Sautter & Apking.

Manufacturers of Men's, Boys' and Youth's Boots and Shoes, Nos. 66, 68, and 70 West Lake Street.

Among the many notable business houses in Chicago that have taken a prominent position in the commercial world, we mention that of Messrs. Sautter & Apking, manufacturers of men's, boys' and youth's pegged, nailed and machine-sewed boots and shoes, of Nos. 66-70 West Lake street. This firm occupies two floors in the building, and employs sixty workpeople, and they have facilities for turning out 125 cases of boots and shoes a week. Mr. J. Sautter is a native of the kingdom of Wurtemberg, Germany, while Mr. Apking was born in New York State, and they have been associated together in business since 1880. They formerly occupied premises at the corner of Lake and Franklin streets, but their increased business required increased accommodation, and in May, 1886, they moved to their present location. They have a very large city trade, selling directly to the retail dealers, and they are gradually pushing their goods into the country. They turn out the very best of goods, both as regards workmanship and material, and as they sell direct to the trade without the intervention of jobbers, they are enabled to compete favorably as regards terms.

Selz, Schwab & Co.

Boots and Shoes, Nos. 192, 194, 196, 198 and 200 Franklin Street.

In the wholesale manufacturing boot and shoe trade of the west, the house of Selz, Schwab & Co., of this city, may be fitly considered a representative firm, the development of their business aptly typifying the growth of commerce throughout the west. They have neglected no opening that presented itself nor failed to retain the trade which the unsurpassed quality of their goods and their liberal terms have secured. They carry a complete stock in all the various grades, and in their factory give employment to over nine hundred skilled artisans, besides an army of clerks, while their traveling salesmen are constantly on the road all over the States west of the Alleghanies and as far south as the Rio Grande. They occupy very extensive premises at Nos. 192 to 200 Franklin street, six entire floors, each two hundred by one hundred and fifty feet in dimensions, being occupied. The house makes a specialty of fine boots and shoes, which have never yet failed to win their way when introduced, such is their superior quality and correct price. The success of this house has been typical of Chicago's remarkable progress.

Simeon Farwell & Co.

Manufacturers and Jobbers of Men's Furnishing Goods, 244 and 246 Monroe Street.

As an essentially representative house, the firm of Simeon Farwell & Co. are standard in this line. As manufacturers and jobbers of men's furnishing goods they are second to none and possess unsurpassed facilities in their factory for the production of these goods at a minimum cost, over three hundred hands being constantly employed. The house is an old one, Hamill & Laskey Co., the founders, having been for years in the business. The present firm was organized August, 1885, and is composed of Simeon Farwell, H. S. Farwell and Stephen Laskey, practical, experienced manufacturers, and thoroughly conversant with the wants of their critical trade. A full line of men's furnishing goods is made, and a large stock carried at their spacious storerooms, in this city, fifty by one hundred and seventy feet in dimensions, while a specialty is made of their celebrated diamond brand S. F. & Co. farmers', miners' and mechanics' garments, which are unsurpassed for quality, durability and workmanship. The house enjoys an enviable reputation among jobbers and first-class retailers, wherever introduced. Indeed, to the care and attention personally bestowed by these gentlemen upon all the processes of manufacture, is largely due the success of this reliable firm.

National Boiler Works.

J. Bee, Proprietor, 56, 58 and 60 Fulton Street.

A visit of interest is to the National Boiler Works, Mr. Joseph Bee, proprietor, at Nos. 56 to 60 Fulton street. Here we find a scene of activity and thrift at once indicative of the importance and standing of this firm. A large force of workmen is busily engaged in the manufacture of all kinds of marine,

locomotive and stationary boilers, and sheet iron work of all kinds. In another part of the works boiler heads and flue holes are being flanged by machinery in the most thorough manner. This is the specialty of these works, and the jobs turned out of this department give the best of satisfaction as regards durability and finish. The latest and best improved machinery is in use here, and every facility is had for the rapid and perfect prosecution of work. The premises occupied are 60x130 feet, besides ample space for storage and handling of all material used. The business was begun by Mr. Joseph Bee in 1867 in a small way, but by energy and industry he is now at the head of one of the largest and finest establishments of this kind in Chicago. The trade is large and increasing each year. Products from these works can be found not only in all parts of this city, but throughout the west and northwest.

Ries & Co.

Ladies' and Gents' Furnishing Goods, Nos. 251 to 255 Monroe Street.

Few branches of mercantile pursuits demand closer knowledge of the wants of the trade to insure successful results than the ladies' and gents' furnishing goods trade, and therefore it is that only those thoroughly conversant with the business in its every detail ever attain even comparative success. Among those engaged in this line in this city who have attained well-merited recognition, none have achieved greater prominence than Messrs. Ries & Co. The members of the firm, Messrs. B. Ries and M. Guettel, are both Germans by birth, and on coming to the United States, while still quite young, settled in Chicago and organized their house in 1878, on Franklin street, as importers and jobbers in ladies' and gents' furnishing goods. In 1882, in order to procure enlarged facilities, they removed to Nos. 207 and 209 Monroe street, and which in turn, in January, 1886, was found to be inadequate to accommodate their largely increasing trade, necessitating a further removal at that time to their present spacious premises, one hundred feet square in dimensions. Their trade is general and comprises a well-selected and complete assortment of ladies' and gents' furnishing goods, including gloves, hosiery, neckwear, underwear, shirts, and every article, in short, to be found in a well-ordered and strictly first-class establishment. Four traveling salesmen are constantly on the road, and a large staff of clerks are engaged in the house, in promptly filling orders from customers in all parts of the west, who have been attracted and permanently retained by the reliable quality of their goods, their reasonableness in prices and by the liberal policy which has always characterized the transactions of Ries & Co.

A. C. Mather & Co.

Manufacturers and Importers of Kid Gloves. Wholesale Depot, 122 and 124 Market Street.

Of those houses that have attained distinction in this industry few have the complete equipment and the valuable experience of A. C. Mather & Co., the fine goods bearing his name having an estab-

lished reputation, and are standard in all the principal markets of the west, northwest and south. The factory in this city employs a large force of skilled operatives in turning out these unsurpassed goods, and a large stock in all sizes and colors is necessarily carried to promptly fill the orders daily pouring in from all over the country. In fact "The Mather," on account of its reasonableness in price and admitted superiority in quality, has all but driven from the market the many comparatively worthless grades of imported kids, and is a formidable rival of even the most expensive Paris makes. This house has been established for the past eight years, and occupies an essentially representative position, its proprietors esteeming time and money well spent in maintaining the high reputation these goods have attained.

Garden City Stool Co.

Office and Factory, 427 and 429 Blue Island Avenue.

The Garden City Stool company next claimed our attention. The officers of the company are as follows: G. W. Schultz, president; Andrew Fuertsch, secretary; and Geo. Fuertsch, manager. We found,

on entering the first floor, a large and varied stock of piano, organ and store stools, of fine pattern and superior finish and workmanship. One can gain some idea of the magnitude of this establishment when we say that they turn out over forty thousand of these stools annually, and that their trade extends to all parts of the United States. Their office and factory is located at Nos. 427 and 429 Blue Island avenue being two stories in height, and covers an area of fifty by sixty-five feet. The business was begun in 1882 on South Canal street, under the name of Fuertsch & Pitts, and was incorporated under the present name last October.

A force of thirty men are employed, and the best of satisfaction is guaranteed in all cases. Their designer is now employed in completing various modern and beautiful specimens for their new illustrated catalogue, which will be issued in the near future, and will be a surprise for the trade.

Merchants Safe Deposit Co.

78, 80 and 82 La Salle Street.

An unusually interesting place to visit is the vaults and safes of the Merchants Safe Deposit Co., at 78, 80 and 82 La Salle street. The two vaults, which are very long and occupy 40 x 150, contain no less than 6,000 safes—all fire and burglar proof. These vaults are owned by the Merchants National Bank Co., and occupy the space underneath that bank's office. The president of this Safe Deposit Co. is C. B. Blair, Esq.; treasurer, C. J. Blair; and manager, G. E. Purington.

This company allow larger safes and more room than any other company for the same money. Their system of safes is unequaled for massiveness, strength and beauty. They are protected by double combination improved time locks and guarded by armed men night and day. These safes are for rent at from $5 per year and upwards, for the safe keeping of money, bonds, jewelry, deeds, abstracts and valuables of every description. The company also receive for storage trunks and packages, paintings silverware, etc. Office hours are from 9 a. m. to 5 p. m.

Bookwalter, Kelley & Co.

General Commission Merchants, 78 South Water Street.

Our next visit was to one of the most active and enterprising houses engaged in the produce commission business in Chicago. The co-partners—S. Bookwalter, S. G. Kelley and C. H. Bartlett—are business men possessed of a wide range of practical experience, and have developed a large and growing trade, including among their correspondents leading producers and dairymen throughout the western States. They are located at No. 78 South Water street, near State, and possess every facility for the prompt disposal of large consignments of butter, eggs, poultry and country produce generally, numbering among their customers our principal marketmen and dealers; also selling to eastern points. They have an extensive trade throughout the west, from Montana to New Mexico. Dealers in search of choice creamery and fresh dairy butter are referred to this house, as they make a prominent specialty of this article. They are all driving merchants and good judges of all kinds of produce. The firm has retained the entire confidence of our leading financial circles, being known for its legitimate methods, and has attained a record at once a credit to the co-partners and an abundant guarantee to all who have mercantile transactions with them.

Wold & Wulff.

Undertakers and Livery, 177 West Indiana Street.

Messrs. Wold & Wulff's, of No. 187 West Indiana street, is one of the best known undertaking establishments on the West side. They have been in business here during the last fifteen years, and have succeeded in establishing a most respectable connection. Their rooms are fitted up in a most elegant manner, and they carry a large stock of caskets, coffins, and all the usual articles found in a house of this description. In connection with their undertaking business they run a livery stable at No. 4 Peccary street. Mr. Wold was born in Norway and came to Chicago a quarter of a century ago, while Mr. Wulff is also a native of the same country and has been a resident of this city for the past twenty-two years. Their telephone number is 4636.

Stotz, Woltz & Co.

Manufacturers of Furniture, Factory and Office, 57, 59, 61, and 63, Illinois Street; Warerooms, 193 Wabash Avenue.

Prominent among the many houses of Chicago is the old and noted firm of Stotz, Woltz & Co., whose large factory and office is located at Nos. 57, 59, 61 and 63 Illinois street. Their mammoth factory

covers an area of one hundred by one hundred and eight feet, and is three stories high with a large basement. They also own and use a large building on Indiana street. They are manufacturers of all kinds of furniture, but run as a specialty store, bank, drug-store and saloon fixtures, and hardwood finish for residences and public buildings. All their goods are turned out in the most workmanlike and artistic manner, the designs being unique and original with the firm, as they have their own pattern-maker. They employ a large force of hands, including over one hundred skilled and experienced workmen. Their goods are all reliable and give the best of satisfaction, while their finishing work in buildings cannot be surpassed and meets the approval of the most exact and critical. This firm has performed many important jobs, not only in this city, but all over the country, notably of which is the finishing work of the government's new custom-house at St. Louis, as well as the one in this city. The business of this firm was begun in 1863 in a small way, and their success and prosperity has been the result of good material, good work, and close personal application to all branches of their large business. Both members of the firm are natives of Germany, and have long been residents of the Garden City, which they have successfully helped to build up and improve.

William Neff.

Dealer in Flour, Meal, Hay, Feed, Etc., 1064 West Madison Street.

This house carries a full supply of flour of all brands, meal, hay, feed of all kinds, and country produce. Mr. Neff was, at the time of his death, one of the oldest residents and merchants of Chicago, coming here way back among the 40's. The business has been established since 1873, and the premises are well arranged for the business. The best the market affords can be found here and is sold at reasonable prices. Mr. Neff was a native of Vermont and was connected more or less all his life with the farm produce business. He was at different times town clerk, school director and justice of the peace of the township of Cicero, which this suburb of Chicago was formerly called. All in all, this is one of the standard houses in the section of the city where located.

Bernard H. May.

Manufacturer of All Kinds of Rattan, Reed and Willow Ware, Etc., 95 and 97 East Indiana Street.

On our visit to the establishment of Bernard H. May, at Nos. 95 and 97 East Indiana street, we found nearly a score of people busily engaged in the manufacture of all kinds of rattan, reed and willow ware. In this line Mr. May makes a specialty of reed and rattan chairs. Although only established since September, 1885, he has built up a large and rapidly increasing trade. His patterns are of the latest and most approved styles and meet with ready sale among the city merchants. All work is first class and under the direct supervision of the proprietor, who is skilled and experienced in this line of manufacture. Mr. May is a native of Chicago and has shown much talent and enterprise in the successful business he has established, and we heartily recommend him to our many readers desiring work of this class, feeling assured that they will be fairly and courteously treated.

Fitchburg Machine Works.

Manufacturers of Machinists' Tools, No. 59 South Canal Street.

The Fitchburg Machine Works, of Fitchburg, Mass., have a large repository at No. 59 South Canal street, where they keep in stock a large variety of machinists' lathes, planers and drill presses. This is a partnership company, of which Messrs. J. L. Chapman, Harrington Sibley, and Jos. S. Wilson are the proprietors, and their Chicago business is under the efficient management of Mr. C. F. Wardell, a gentleman well and favorably known throughout the country. Mr. Wardell is also agent for the sale of the Taylor Manufacturing company's, of Chambersburg, Pa., engines. These latter include Taylor's high-speed automatic engine, the Tiger agricultural and Tiger portable engines, and the Clipper vertical engine and boiler. Also the Prospect Machine and Engine company, of Cleveland, Ohio. Mr. Wardell has been in business in Chicago for twenty-five years, and is always willing to consult the wishes of his patrons in every particular.

Chicago Foundry Co.

Manufacturers of Rolling Mill, Blast Furnace, and Every Description of Heavy Castings. Office and Works, Corner Redfield and Stein Streets.

We would invite the reader to step in with us to examine one of the important industries of the Garden City. We refer to the large establishment of the Chicago Foundry company on the corner of Redfield and Stein streets. They are manufacturers of rolling mill, blast furnace and every other description of heavy castings. The business was begun in 1870 under the firm name of Dyer, Lamb & Co., and was incorporated seven years later as the Chicago Foundry company, the present officers being E. Dyer, president; T. S. Kirkwood, vice-president; W. W. Flinn, treasurer; and H. A. Keith, general manager. The plant of the company consists of over three acres, while the foundry proper is sixty by one hundred and fifty feet in dimensions.

A greater part of the work of this foundry is for the North Chicago rolling mills, although their trade in other parts of the city is also very large. About one hundred and fifty hands are employed, and about 10,000 to 15,000 tons of iron is used annually. The men connected with this business are well known, not only among the iron merchants, but to the business men of Chicago, as alive to every interest which tends to promote the general welfare of the city in the iron trade.

Putnam Clothing House.

131 to 133 Clark Street, 113 and 117 Madison Street, C. M. Babbitt, Resident Partner.

Here may be found at all times a stock of ready-made clothing of the finest grades and most elegant styles, manufactured expressly to meet the requirements of the better class of trade. The best material only is used, artistic cutters are employed, and the most reliable workmanship characterizes every garment. Numerous new features in the

clothing trade have been introduced by the enterprising proprietors of this model establishment. The members of the firm are wide-awake, energetic business men, who have had long experience in this line, and are thoroughly conversant with the wants and requirements of the trade. The order department, for the special convenience of customers at a distance, is a feature which commends itself to all desiring perfect fitting garments at reasonable rates. The premises occupied by the "Putnam Clothing House" are eligibly located, in the very heart of the city, and the vast improvements which have just been made place it in the front rank of the handsomely fitted clothing houses of Chicago. The place is well lighted by thirty Brush electric lights of two thousand candle-power each, eight of which illuminate the exterior. In the main store, on Clark street, their large stock of men's clothing is tastefully arranged, and experienced and obliging clerks look after the wants of the many patrons. The Annex, or boy's and children's department, is entirely separate, the main entrance of which is at No. 117 Madison street, although connection is also had with the main store. It has lately been finished in the most complete and handsome manner—large plate-glass windows, beautiful mahogany mantel, open fire-place and every convenience and luxury to be found in a first-class hotel parlor, which at once makes it the finest and most handsome boys' and children's department in the city. This house has a large establishment in Boston, where they manufacture all their own goods, doing the largest trade of the kind in New England. As they retail all their goods at wholesale prices, it can be readily seen at what low rates goods can be had at this establishment. The business was begun by Mr. Abraham Putnam, in 1852, on Randolph street, and has met with a successful career from its inception. In February, 1886, the present company was formed, consisting of Miner, Beal & Babbitt, the latter being the resident partner. The policy of the Putnam clothing house is to have but one price, and that the lowest; to make no false representations, and furnish only reliable articles at reasonable rates; and the high character and large experience of the manager of this house are a sufficient guarantee that this policy will be persistently adhered to.

Rudolph Born.

Wholesale and Retail Hardware, Cutlery and Mechanics' Tools, 99 West Randolph Street.

A striking example of what enterprise and well-directed energy can do, is shown in the subject of this sketch. Few houses in this business have acquired a better reputation or have built up a better trade than Mr. Rudolph Born, wholesale and retail dealer in all kinds of mechanics' tools, hardware and cutlery. He occupies commodious quarters at No. 99 West Randolph street, which is suitably arranged and stocked with as fine a supply of goods as can be found in the city. As a dealer in mechanics' tools he has no superior, and keeps the best and finest lot of specialties to be found in this line. We will only mention Morandi's improved kerosene glue-pot, for which he is sole agent. It is the handiest, cheapest and best glue heater in use. Gives out no odor or smoke. It costs but three cents a day for oil, and requires but little attention. They are made entirely of tin and copper, and are very light and strong. Mr. Born has been established in business for a long term of years, and he is now ably assisted by his sons. All orders meet with prompt and satisfactory attention.

Vessel Owners' Towing Co.

240 South Water Street.

The fleet of fine tugs seen constantly plying in the harbor bearing such names as "Protection," "Van Schaick," "Satisfaction," etc., belong to the V. O. T. line—the Vessel Owners' Towing company. It was the practice among tug owners in Chicago, as at other ports along the lakes, to blackball the vessels of certain owners on the slightest cause, and refuse to tow them. Often a vessel, for several days at a time, could not secure a tug to bring her in or take her out of the harbor. It was to crush out this sort of foul play that the vessel owners held meetings and finally organized this tug line of their own. The successful organization of the company was due mainly to the energy and determination of Captain

James L. Higgie; this was in April, 1871, and he has been the president of the line ever since. At one time there were fourteen boats, but some of the smaller ones were disposed of, and larger, more powerful ones built, and there are now eleven of the finest craft of their class on the entire chain of lakes. The list of stockholders include Captain Higgie and such extensive lumbermen and vessel owners as A. A. Carpenter, A. G. Van Schaick, J. H. Witbeck, John R. Lindgren, Thomas Hood, William Johnson, the N. Ludington Lumber company and the Spalding Lumber company. The capital stock is $75,000. J. L. Higgie is president, A. G. Van Schaick, treasurer, and George D. Kirkham, secretary and superintendent.

Albert Galloway.

Steam Heating and Ventilating, 198 Jackson Street.

This is undoubtedly an age of progress, and in no branch has greater perfection been attained than in the production of steam and hot water heating apparatus for warming and ventilating public buildings, private residences and green-houses, the desideratum being to secure a pure as well as a warm atmosphere, at a reasonable outlay of expense. To this important branch Mr. Galloway devotes his entire attention, having established his business in Chicago more than twenty years ago, and by reason of his practical experience is able to determine upon inspection what system will prove to be most serviceable and economical in any given case, many elements being necessary to be taken into consideration in addition to the architectural features of the building, its exposure and the size and number of rooms to be heated. A large assortment of heating and ventilating apparatus is carried in stock, and experienced workmen employed, thus enabling him to promptly execute all contracts, however large, many of the most pretentious buildings in the city having been equipped through this house, than which none occupies a higher position in the commercial world, and those contemplating building operations will do well to consult Mr. Galloway, and thereby secure, at a reasonable cost, that perfect warmth and ventilation so essential to health in this rigorous and variable climate. He is agent for the large house of T. C. Joy, of Titusville, Pa.

Geo. P. Harris & Bro.

Copper, Brass, Tin and Sheet Iron Works, 62 and 64 West Lake Street.

The enormous capital invested and the number of workmen employed in the metal trade of Chicago have combined to render it a branch of industry of the first magnitude. A representative house in this line of business is that of Messrs. Geo. P. Harris & Bro., of Nos. 62 and 64 West Lake street, manufacturers of copper, brass, tin and sheet iron goods. They make a specialty of distillery, brewery and steamboat work and engineers' supplies, and special attention is called to their kettle and column. The combination is apparent to all distillers at a glance. Heavy bronze and brass castings and brass finishing of all descriptions are done. Their large and well-equipped factory occupies two floors, and is fitted up with all the latest improved machinery. Their principal customers are among the distillers and the brewers, and they ship their goods to every part of the States and Canada. They have been at their present factory for two years. Messrs. George and Arthur Harris are Englishmen and came to this country thirty-three years ago. They use the best of material, and all the work passes under the master's supervising eye, and in this way they have succeeded in acquiring the confidence of the public.

entire floors are occupied, each 150x250 feet in area, and though large as the floorage is, it is still inadequate to accommodate the immense stock of furniture, carpets, stoves, desks, show cases, etc. There are some thirty-seven departments exclusive of the manufacture of store, office and drug fixtures, a branch recently added, and one in which great prominence has been already attained. Mr. Revell has found the desideratum, elegance and cheapness, and without wishing to institute any comparisons, the simple fact remains that this house can fit up a store or office complete on short notice, with fixtures fully as elegant and at a price less than half that of any other house in town. The concern throughout bears the marks of enterprise and judicious management, Mr. Revell being satisfied with a small profit on every article and relying upon the extensive patronage to make the returns,

a policy which doubtless has been the keystone to his success. Their building has lately undergone great change by the addition of a new story, two new passenger elevators, and nine new departments, including silverware, crockery, woodenware, mantels and curtains.

Alex. H. Revell & Co.

Furniture, Carpets, Stoves, Desks, Show Cases etc., Corner Fifth Avenue and Randolph Street.

As a great metropolis Chicago, in this, the semi-centennial anniversary of her birth, can justly pride herself upon the possession of mercantile establishments in every line which are fully the equal of anything found in the city of New York. In the line of furniture, carpets, and house furnishing goods generally the house of Alex. H. Revell & Co. fully maintains the reputation of Chicago in this respect. The business was established in 1876 upon such an insignificant amount of cash capital that, were it stated, the fact would be entirely disbelieved, to such immense proportions has the business been developed in so short a time. Six

L. Heller & Co.

Wholesale Jewelers, 240 Adams Street.

In more ways than one has Chicago eclipsed the metropolitan greatness of her eastern rival, New York, and in no sphere of activity more satisfactorily than in the wholesale jewelry trade, a leading exponent of which is the well-known and popular house conducted by Messrs. L. Heller & Co., whose name for the past eleven years has been synonymous of that energy and enterprise through which this substantial development has been effected. This house confines itself exclusively to the jobbing trade, in which they possess special facilities for filling the largest orders promptly and on reasonable terms. They carry a large and attractive stock in all the finer and medium grades of gold, plated and jet jewelry and novelties. They have a large and growing demand throughout the entire west in addition to their extensive city trade. A leading feature of this house is their ability to secure all the *new* leading novelties in the jewelry line, and particularly so in the way of the latest patents in cuff and collar buttons, before any other firm in the city, so that all their patrons will be the first in their town to secure the latest styles and quick selling articles. Any new patent offered by this firm the trade may buy without any hesitation as nothing in that line is added to the stock before it has been given a thorough and practical test and the results show a positive merit.

The house was established in 1870, and under Mr. Heller's attentive management has obtained a most influential connection among the most famous jewelry manufacturers in the United States. The gentlemen at the head of this house are well and favorably known in the business world, and have placed it upon a substantial basis.

Newman Bros.

Manufacturers of Organs, Nos. 38 and 40 South Canal Street, Corner of Washington:

This popular firm are not only wide awake to every interest of their many patrons, but, by their ability, experience and skillful workmanship, are enabled to place before the public an organ of the most modern pattern, fine finish and rich tone, unsurpassed by any other instrument of the kind in the country. The business was established in 1856 in a small way, but the merit of their fine instruments soon became known and appreciated, calling upon them for greater facilities, which are found in the large factory they now occupy.  Today their trade extends to all parts of the globe, and for church, chapel, lodge-room and parlor use, the Newman Bros. organs take the lead. They have taken out several patents from time to time for the improvement of their organ, prominent of which may be mentioned their pipe-coupler swell, which is only used in their organs. This is the only invention ever introduced into a reed organ whereby the tones are so modified and softened as to resemble the rich, mellow tones of a pipe organ.

The personnel of the firm is Charles, Gustavus and John Newman, all practical men, having had years of experience in this line before beginning business for themselves. They employ upwards of one hundred skillful workmen, and are able to turn out two hundred and fifty instruments a month. Their prices are reasonable, and that they have succeeded in business the great demand for their organs fully attests. For price list and illustrated catalogue address as above, or call in person.

Whitehill Sewing-Machine Co.

Agency of E. E. Packard, 28 North Clark Street.

At this depot are found the Singer, Whitehill, New Home, Wheeler & Wilson, Domestic, Eldridge, in fact, all the prominent machines manufactured, both new and second-hand. Parties can here obtain machines of all varieties and grades, either for cash or on the installment plan. A specialty is made of the popular light-running Whitehill, a cut of which is given below.

The Whitehill machines are now manufactured in the best equipped factory in the country, and for simplicity, durability, ease, quietness and rapidity of motion, a perfect stitch and a large arm, they are peerless.

The Whitehill is the first and only shuttle machine constructed wherein the needle-bar is operated by a crank motion, forming a loop, entirely superseding the noisy and irregular cam motion. The wood-work is handsome and artistic in design, combining strength with durability, and fine finish with utility. It is built up in sections, to prevent warping and splitting. As a family machine it excels all others.

Examinations are requested, and a person will not only be amply repaid by a visit to this prominent machine depot, but surprised at the low prices charged for so fine a machine. They are wholesale as well as retail dealers, and all orders meet with prompt and satisfactory attention. Anything in the way of household furniture, pianos, organs, horses, taken in exchange for sewing-machines, pianos or organs. They are prepared to sell second-hand machines (perfect satisfaction guaranteed) at from $5 upwards.

T. W. Eaton.

Manufacturer of Hand, Foot and Power Circular Sawing Machines, 62 and 64 West Lake Street.

As a practical machinist Mr. T. W. Eaton, of Nos. 62 and 64 West Lake street, has few equals. He manufactures all kinds of hand, foot and power machines for circular saws, etc., and one of his specialties is the making of hair-pickers for mattress-makers. He has been at his present stand for four years, and his factory is fitted up with all necessary machinery and appliances for the successful carrying on of his trade. He employs from five to ten men, and is at present largely engaged in manufacturing a patent wood saw for two local firms. He turns out from one hundred and fifty to two hundred of these machines annually. Mr. Eaton is an old veteran, having served his country for four years and two months in the civil war. He was a member of the 9th Illinois cavalry. He saw much active service during that time, and has some very lively and interesting recollections of those stirring times.

A. B. Gehman & Co.

Publishers of Standard Subscription Books, 177 and 179 La Salle Street.

In writing an authentic exposition commemorative of the semi-centennial anniversary of the foundation of the city, forming thus a valuable hand-book of business facts and statistics, thereby spreading the fame of the Garden City far and wide over this and many other lands. In preparing the semi-centennial review of Chicago, a few houses in each branch of business will be represented as being typical of the city's progress. In the subscription book business, A. B. Gehman & Co. occupy, in their relations to the literary world, a position of the highest prominence and one which it would be difficult to fill. They publish a number of leading works on general subjects, among which "The History of the Grand Army of the Republic," also "The Great Cry of Labor," are of late issue. while such is the popularity of their standard publications and liberality of terms, that agents have found a connection with this house to redound greatly to their profit financially. Mr. Gehman is a native of Ohio, and established his business in Chicago in January 1886, which he has since conducted upon the most honorable commercial principles, thereby gaining the confidence and esteem of the community and placing his house upon a substantial and reliable basis.

M. Straus.

Artist, Rooms 79 and 80, Japanese Building, Corner Jackson and State Streets.

In the æsthetic arts, the productions of the landscape painter never fail to arrest the attention of even the most superficial observer, while true merit seldom fails to receive recognition and just reward. The colony of artists in Chicago, though not large when compared to European cities, yet possesses some of the brightest ornaments of the profession, among whom the citizens of Chicago pride themselves in numbering Mr. M. Straus, who for the past three years has permanently resided in our midst. A native of Bavaria, Germany, Mr. Straus came to America at the age of fourteen, and has practiced his profession for the last quarter of a century in different portions of this country, and has achieved a national reputation, standing today in the front rank of our most accomplished American artists; and when we add to this the fact that he is a self-made man in his calling, we but add honor to his achievements and luster to his career. Mr. Straus has spent many years traveling, and has thus studied extensively in all parts of this country from Massachusetts to Puget sound, and notably twelve years in California, where he doubtless caught that exquisite coloring, and which some who have never seen the gorgeous scenery of that country are apt to think overdrawn. Several of Mr. Straus' productions were exhibited at the New Orleans exposition, his noted masterpiece, the "Swamp Monarch," being owned in London, England, where it excites universal admiration; thus his fame is transatlantic. Mr. T. F. Oakes, vice-president and general manager of the Northern Pacific R. R., is the fortunate possessor of "Mount Tacoma," by many considered the equal of the "Swamp Monarch," while the Rev. D. M. Cooper, of Detroit, is also the owner of "Mount Tamalpais," "Montery Bay," several smaller gems, among them a view of the Golden Gate. The most expert critics have pronounced high encomiums upon the works of Mr. Straus, while among his brother artists who are the most eminent in their calling they are highly spoken of. Mr. Straus' style may be safely put down as a modification of the French school. In conclusion we can heartily say, as a lover of the productions of the *real*, innate artist, the artist who is one perforce and because he cannot help being one, if anyone wishes a continual feast for the soul, go and visit Mr. Straus' studio and become the possessor of one of his inimitable productions.

Liverpool & London & Globe Insurance Company.

Office, 124 La Salle Street.

There is no part of the civilized world where the Liverpool & London & Globe Insurance company is not known. Chicago has good reason to remember this company, for when most of smaller companies were in a dilemma and could not pay claims in full after the great fire of '71, this was one of the very few that met all just claims, paying 100 cents to the dollar. No less a sum than $3,272,782 was paid out in losses at that time, and the great fire in Boston in the fall of the succeeding year brought up the total claims paid for these two fires alone to $4,500,000.

This company was incorporated in 1836, and has its main offices at Liverpool, England, with branch offices and agents in all parts of the world. This branch was opened in 1875 as an office, though long prior to that agencies had been established here. The other branch offices in the United States are at New York, San Francisco and New Orleans. The yearly business done by this, the largest fire insurance company in the world, in the United States branch alone, amounted in 1885 to a receipt of $3,583,500 in net cash premiums, while the losses paid were $2,035,033. The shareholders are personally responsible in an unlimited liability, while losses are payable in cash without discount. The Chicago board of directors are John Crerar, of the firm of Crerar, Adams & Co., chairman; L. Z. Leiter, late of Field, Leiter & Co., and Ezra J. Warner, of the firm of Sprague, Warner & Co. The resident secretary for this district and as far west as the Rockies is Mr. Wm. Warren, to whom all communications should be addressed.

John O. Boesch.

Manufacturer of Center and Telegraph Tables, Cabinet-Makers' Tools, Etc., 29 and 31 North Jefferson Street.

The wood-workers of Chicago are recognized as an important factor in the commercial greatness of this city. Mr. John O. Boesch is a manufacturer of center and telegraph tables, general novelties and cabinet-makers' tools. He has a very extensive connection in the city and does a general jobbing trade. Mr. Boesch is a native of Switzerland, and came to this country in 1865. He started in business at No. 54 West Indiana street in 1880, but he latterly removed to his present location at Nos. 29 and 31 North Jefferson street. Here he is more centrally situated, and the premises are more extensive and better suited to the requirements of his ever-increasing trade. Mr. Boesch is a thoroughly reliable workman and is much respected in the trade. He has succeeded in building up a very fine business, which is rapidly increasing, as his goods become better known on the market.

Foster, Roe & Crone.

Printers, 170 Clark Street.

Were anyone required to state what has contributed the most to the enlightenment of the human race, the response unhesitatingly would be, the printing press, an art properly denominated "the preservative of all arts." Modern invention has contributed greatly to the improvement and development of printing, and at the present time its price has been so reduced by labor-saving machinery that books, pamphlets, and that great educator, the newspaper, and, indeed, all printed matter, are within the reach of all. One of the most complete and reliable printing establishments in Chicago is that of Messrs. Foster, Roe & Crone, equipped as it is with all kinds of the latest and most improved printing machinery, including rotary and job presses, large quantities of clear-faced book and job type, in all styles, and to which fonts are constantly being added as new designs are issued; in short, their facilities enable them to execute, at reasonable prices, promptly, all contracts for book and job work, the mechanical execution of which is unsurpassed by any printing house in the city. The house was established by Messrs. F. C. Foster and M. A. Roe in March, 1884. Mr. C. E. Crone becoming a member of the firm two years later, and have always commanded a liberal patronage and held a leading position in the trade. The firm employ none but the most experienced type-setters, pressmen, and other employes, and many of their specimens of work are masterpieces of this important industry.

H. H. Gardner & Co.

No. 241 South Water Street.

Chicago, by reason of her immediate contiguity to the lumber-producing regions of the great northwest, together with her unsurpassed railway connections, water routes and terminal facilities, affords the chief point in America, as well as the largest in the world, for the receipt and handling of lumber of all kinds, but the factors of paramount importance in building up her enormous trade in this line are the ample resources and distinguished energy and enterprise of her leading merchants. Besides being one of the largest, the house of H. H. Gardner & Co. is also one of the oldest in that line in Chicago, Mr. Gardner having been engaged in it continuously for the past twenty years. This house is doing an exclusively wholesale business, nothing less than cargo lots being sold. They manufacture at Muskegon, Whitehall and Escanaba, Mich., and at Ashland, Wis., and during the past winter cut and logged nearly forty million feet of their own timber. They are large owners of pine lands, and are continually buying more, purchasing only the best quality. This latter fact has become so well known to the trade that two-thirds of this season's cut of lumber was sold to eastern dealers before a log was sawed, the reputation of their high-grade stock being the principal factor of the sale. During the past winter they also sold large bills of heavy bridge and car timber, for spring and summer delivery, this material being cut from their coarse logs. The present firm is composed of Messrs. H. H. Gardner and C. J. Wood, and is one of the successors to the old Gardner & Spry company. With ample resources and plenty of energy, pluck and experience, they are destined to hold their place among the leaders of the great lumber industry.

J. A. Shepard.

Portrait Copying House, 289 Wabash Avenue.

Under the bright light of the nineteenth century, the arts, professions and sciences have advanced to such a degree of perfection that it seems hardly possible for future generations to improve upon them, and in no other thing has the progress of improvement left such indubitable marks as in the perfected processes at present in vogue in the copying and enlargement of pictures. The largest and leading copying house in the west is that so ably conducted by Mr. J. A. Shepard, of this city, whose corps of artists embraces the highest order of talent obtainable, and who, since inaugurating his business five years ago, has obtained both a liberal and influential patronage, and also an enviable reputation for fine work at moderate prices. All kinds of small pictures are copied and enlarged to any desired size, and finished in crayon, india ink, water colors, oil or pastel, the correctness of which is in all cases guaranteed, and canvassers will find it largely to their pecuniary interests to place their orders with this house, whose business reputation is not only of the best, but which possesses every necessary facility for enabling it to execute all commissions with promptness, and of the highest artistic merit.

Fyfe & Campbell.

Printers and Publishers, 128 and 130 South Clark Street.

The firm of Fyfe & Campbell, printers and publishers, of Nos. 128 and 130 South Clark street, has been established seven years. This firm does a general line of book and job work, commercial printing, etc. Their two watchwords are "expeditious" and "reliable," and they are very aptly chosen. The class of work this establishment turns out is standard, society printing being a specialty. A very large variety of type, borders, and electrotype cuts and emblems are to be seen here. The printing machinery consists of five Gordon presses, cutting and perforating machines, etc. The bulk of the trade is local, though orders are at times received from firms and houses as far distant as Colorado. Their aim is to treat a customer so that he shall return to them whenever he requires more work. In this way they have succeeded in establishing a good reputation in this city and vicinity. They are also publishers of the Scottish Clansman, a semi-monthly paper, devoted to the interests of the Scottish clans all over the United States. Although it is only established since September, 1880, it has grown much in favor, and increased its circulation greatly. The terms are $1 per year. For further information address Fyfe & Campbell, No. 128 South Clark street.

Strauss, Goodman, Yondorf & Co.

Manufacturers of Men's, Youths' and Boys' Clothing, Monroe Street and Fifth Avenue.

The great clothing interest of this city is one of its proudest triumphs, and it argues well to know that the semi-centennial of Chicago's history finds its strength unabated and the grip of its manufacturers and jobbers on the trade of the country in no sense relaxed. The house of Strauss, Goodman, Yondorf & Co. may fitly be considered the representative of the wholesale manufacturing clothing trade of Chicago, while their business has developed with the growth of commerce throughout the west. The original house, Mayer, Strauss, Goodman & Co., was founded in 1870, and actively conducted until its dissolution, some three years ago, resulted in the formation of the present firm, composed of Messrs. Abr. Strauss, Hugo Goodman, Simon Yondorf and Edward Rose. Their immense trade necessitates the occupation of their present very spacious five-story and basement building, 100 x 225 feet in dimensions, at the corner of Monroe street and Fifth avenue, and forms one of the finest wholesale manufacturing clothing houses in the United States. The firm devote special care to the selection of their woolens and suitings, manufacturing all grades of goods, which, as regards cut, workmanship and finish, have earned a reputation in the market strictly upon their merits. The building throughout is provided with all the modern facilities which science has devised as regards machinery for manufacturing purposes, as well as electric alarms, elevators, etc., for expediting the business, in which some five hundred operatives are employed, together with a large force of scientific cutters. The members of the firm are widely known, both in and out of trade, while their close application to business, and liberal dealings, combined with a strict adherence to the most rigid code of mercantile ethics, have wrought out a success in every respect typical of Chicago's remarkable development.

Illinois Terra Cotta Lumber Co.

Office, 42 and 43, 118 Dearborn Street. Works at Pullman.

The offices of this company are at 118 Dearborn street, rooms 42 and 43. We gained much information by our visit here concerning this new building material. This is a newly invented building material made of clay and sawdust, and when burned the sawdust is consumed, leaving the material porous or cellular, yet capable of bearing immense crushing strain, and it is only one-third the weight of brick.

It is absolutely fireproof and is suitable for all interior architecture. For sheathing columns, boilers, beams, girders, pipes, etc., it is peculiarly adapted, as it can be shaped with edged tools, sawn like a piece of timber or have nails driven into its substance. It costs less and can be set in place more readily than any recognized fireproofing. If a slab one and one-half inches thick be heated to a full red heat on one side, the other is so cool as not to scorch paper or white pine touching it.

The works are at Pullman. Samples only are kept at the office before named. The president of the company is Mr. Jas. Stinson; Quintin Johnston, secretary; and C. W. Brega, vice-president. For partitions this article is in special favor on account of its sound-proof qualities, also because changes in apartments can be readily made by sawing out doors or other openings therein.

The company has the sole rights for making and selling in this State. From fifty to sixty hands are employed at the factory and kilns.

J. Frank Waldo.

Artist, Room 34, 225 Dearborn Street.

It is natural in every man to wish for distinction, and whether in the domain of letters, art, science or trade, the struggle to obtain it is praiseworthy and should be applauded when won. To few has fame been more lavish in her favors than to Mr. J. Frank Waldo, the author of "Pike's Peak at Sundown," a masterpiece well known in the art galleries of America and to connoisseurs all over the world; also, "The Sacred Grove," of historic interest, near Taos, New Mexico.

Mr. Waldo is a native of Vermont, where he was born May 16, 1835, in the town of Newbury. His residence is a little more difficult to speak of with any certainty, his nomadic disposition having taken him all over this country and Mexico in search of subjects. In 1871-2 he was in Chicago, and again in 1876, and even for the past three years has been stationary here, and on the whole, perhaps, Chicago can justly claim his residence; at least, her citizens pride themselves in that belief. Mr. Waldo has exhibited at several of the Chicago expositions, at Milwaukee, at Minneapolis in 1886, and at both New Orleans expositions, where among the many artistic productions his merits received fitting recognition. Mr. Waldo makes a specialty of marine views, in which he excels, and he is no follower or imitator of anyone. A born artist, he seeks inspiration from nature, and interprets her with a faithfulness equaled by very few.

Salisbury & Cline.

Dealers in Rubber and Leather Belting, Hose, All Kinds of Rubber Goods, Etc., 109 Madison Street.

The oldest established house in the city in rubber and leather belting, hose and all kinds of rubber goods, is that of Salisbury & Cline, who opened this business in 1855. This firm have a large and extensive business, both in the city and all parts of the country. They represent the Boston Belting Co., Boston Woven Hose Co., Goodyear I. R. Glove Co., Gossamer Rubber Clothing Co., and James Davis Belting Co. They were located on Lake street in 1871, when the fire destroyed the whole of this part of the city, and have occupied their present commodious premises for the last five years. The business occupies the basement and first floor, each twenty-five by two hundred feet, at No. 109 East Madison street. Their specialty is wire-wound rubber hose, packing hose and belting, though a full line in all other branches is kept. Buying direct and in such large quantities from the manufacturers, and doing all their trade on a cash basis, they are enabled to quote as low prices as can be obtained from any firm in the trade, while the names of the firms and companies they represent are sufficient guarantee of the quality of the goods supplied and the enormous stock carried from which to select.

Muchmore & Muchmore.

Cylinder and Lubricating Oils, Naphtha, Gasoline, Turpentine, Axle Grease, Rosin, Waste, Etc., 31 Market Street.

When a house has enjoyed a liberal patronage and popularity for a long term of years, the conclusion is irresistible that its management has been characterized by integrity, ability and good judgment. Such are the circumstances connected with the establishment of Messrs. Muchmore & Muchmore, which was founded in 1878, and has since held a prominent position in the trade. The firm has been continuously located in this immediate vicinity, and for the past three years have occupied their present spacious premises, where a full and complete stock of cylinder and lubricating oils, naphtha, gasoline, turpentine, axle grease, rosin, waste, etc., is carried, embracing the products of the most reputable manufacturers in the country. The command of ample capital enables them to purchase direct, and in large quantities, for cash, thereby placing the firm in a position to quote prices difficult to be obtained elsewhere, and which have been largely instrumental in building up their widespread western trade, in addition to their flourishing local patronage. The brands carried are well known for their uniform reliability, and those desiring oils of a high grade, free from all alkalis or acids which so soon work irreparable injury to machinery, may safely avail themselves of the opportunity offered by this house to procure such supplies at reasonable prices. Messrs. J. E. Muchmore, Sr., and J. F. Muchmore, the gentlemen composing this firm, have resided in this city the greater part of their lives, where they are so well known and highly esteemed.

T. D. Randall & Co.

Fruit and Produce Commission, 219 South Water Street.

No exposition of the produce commission trade of our great city, now celebrating her semi-centennial anniversary, would be complete without prominent reference to the firm of T. D. Randall & Co., who are successfully conducting, under its pristine aggressive policy, the oldest fruit and produce commission house in Chicago, as it is also one of the largest. The history of this house in its struggles overcoming difficulties and drawbacks, on this face apparently insurmountable, is, in fact, the history of the trade itself, which it has so long honorably represented. Mr. Randall is emphatically an old-timer, having established this business in 1852, and is thus one of the pioneers in the produce trade, which he was destined to see grow and expand into its present colossal proportions, in the development of which his house played a most important part, and was always able to command fully its share of patronage. Of his then competitors none remain, death and financial reverses having claimed them all. Only once during the entire thirty-five years has this house failed to open its doors on every business morning; for upon that memorable 9th of October, 1871, nothing remained but a heap of smoldering ashes of his once stately and spacious building, while indeed its very site could not be positively determined for several days. Although the loss was severe, it was not crushing, and within a very short time the house was conducting business regularly upon a grander scale than ever before, and has since enjoyed an uninterrupted career of public favor and prosperity. His daughter, now Mrs. Geo. S. Bridge, creditably discharges the duties of cashier and bookkeeper, yet could and frequently does take charge of the entire concern. Fruit and produce of all kinds, hay, flour, feed and grain are handled. A board of trade membership belongs to the firm. The house being thoroughly well equipped with every facility for doing business promptly and satisfactorily, with ample capital, large experience, and an established reputation, shippers can make no mistake in entrusting their consignments to this old, energetic and reliable firm.

Ph. L. Raphael & Co.

179 Madison Street.

The largest wine and spirit houses in the world are represented by this firm, including the Harris Distilling Co., of Philadelphia, Pa.; the well-known house of Gonzalez Byass & Co., Jerez, Spain; Cook & Bernheimer, New York; Isidor Bush & Co., St. Louis, Mo.; and they are sole agents for the Parkland Distilling Co., Louisville, Ky.

Mr. Raphael, for twenty-five years, has been known throughout the United States to the wholesale trade. Their trade, which is rapidly extending, reaches from the Alleghenies to the Pacific and from Canada to the Gulf.

This house enjoys a large city trade, but the bulk of business is done through the entire country. Besides ably representing these large houses, this firm also sells on commission; and as they are well known to all the trade, some idea of the immense business enjoyed by Ph. L. Raphael & Co. may be gleaned from the fact that from one company alone (the Parkland Distilling Co.) from 8,000 to 10,000 barrels of whisky are sold yearly. A branch office for the sale of sherries from Gonzalez Byass & Co., of Spain, is located at 39 Broadway, New York. A limited supply of wines, etc., is kept in the customhouse at New York, for immediate orders, but the large bulks are supplied direct from Cadiz, Spain.

Cass F. Maurer.

Dealer in Cigars and Tobacco, 113 Adams Street.

There is so much that is palpably vile that passes for cigars that positive pleasure is afforded to refer to the well and favorably known Club House Cigar Factory, Cass F. Maurer, proprietor, whose products maintain such a high reputation for quality, flavor and finish, and for which there is everywhere such an increasing demand. Mr. Maurer is the successor of the old firm of Heller & Maurer, which in 1869 was dissolved by the purchase of Mr. J. Heller's interest in the business. This house is the headquarters for the favorite staple and fancy brands of smoking and chewing tobaccos, cigars, and smokers' sundries. His customers belong to the better class of merchants, board of trade and railroad men, who know and appreciate a good cigar; and his prices are reasonable and fair, Mr. Maurer finds his trade all he can well attend to, and today better than ever before during the entire thirty-two years in which he has been engaged in the business. In the great fire of 1871, Mr. Maurer, while at No. 134 Clark street, suffered the entire loss of his stock, but with characteristic energy was soon firmly re-established, and now enjoys the distinction of being the proprietor of one of the handsomest and best appointed stores in this city. Mr. Maurer is also one of our war veterans, having served with the gallant battery A, attached to the army of the Tennessee, having left Chicago for the front on April 1, 1861, and was mustered out July, 1864, having given for the sake of liberty three of the most valuable years of his life.

Thos. S. Cruttenden.

Agent for the Sale of Garner & Co's Goods, 252 Monroe Street.

Mr. Thos. S. Cruttenden is the first commission dry goods man in Chicago who has made a success, and has for the past twelve years represented the well-known house of Garner & Co., of 12 to 16 Worth street, New York, the largest cotton manufacturers in the world, controlling the entire output of the following mills: Cotton Mills—Harmony mills, Nos. 1, 2, 3, 4 and 5, Ogden mills, Strong mills, Cohoes, N. Y.; Newburgh steam cotton mills, Newburgh, N. Y.; Rochester cotton mills, Rochester, N. Y.; Little Falls cotton mill, Little Falls, N. Y.; Pleasant Valley cotton mill, Pleasant Valley, N. Y.; Franklindale cotton mill, Wappinger's Falls, N. Y.; Reading cotton mill, Reading, Pa. Print Works—Dutchess company, Wappinger's Falls, N. Y.; Rockland print works, Haverstraw, N. Y.; Dutchess bleachery and dye works, Wappinger's Falls, N. Y. Thus they are the largest producers, either in this country or in Europe, of prints, lawns, linings, silesias and percales, and of a quality which for years past has been regarded as standard in the trade, while Mr. Cruttenden, being the direct agent, is enabled to name the very lowest manufacturers' prices.

A spacious five-story and basement building, 25 x 165 feet in dimensions, is occupied in this city, and a large stock carried, from which all orders are promptly filled for the entire west, throughout which the house is ably represented by a large number of commercial travelers.

Canada Fur Manufacturing Co.

Simon Minchrod & Co., Proprietors, 168 and 170 Market Street.

This firm makes a specialty of gents' fur coats, fur-lined coats, fur attachments and fur trimmings; also seal sacques, dolmans, robes, etc., the largest assortment in the west. One of the advantages of buying from a bona-fide manufacturer is that a perfectly fitting garment is obtained at a reasonable price, which is well-nigh impossible under other conditions. The skins handled by this reliable house are always procured direct from first hands, thus enabling Messrs. Minchrod & Co. to offer their goods at prices that will compare favorably with those of any contemporary house in the city, a fact that outside merchants dealing in these articles have not been slow to appreciate. The house dates its inception from the year 1876, when the organization was effected as the Canada Fur Manufacturing company, this style being still retained, Messrs. Simon Minchrod & Co. becoming sole proprietors January, 1886. Spacious premises are occupied, forty by one hundred and fifty feet in dimensions. and over one hundred skilled workmen are constantly engaged the year round in manufacturing fashionable seal garments, fur coats, fur trimmings, etc., which for quality and workmanship are absolutely unsurpassed, and which meet with ready sale all over the west, needing only to be introduced to have their merits fully recognized. As a firm they are active, enterprising and pushing, full of life, and are highly regarded in mercantile circles.

P. & H. Johnson.

Manufacturers of Extension Curtain Cornices, Furniture Made and Repaired. All Kinds of Carpenter Work Promptly Attended to. Cor. Green and Ohio Streets.

Messrs. Johnson have lately started in business as manufacturers of extension curtain cornices. They manufacture and repair all classes of furniture to order. Messrs. Johnson are natives of Norway, and learned their trade in the old country. They have been here in Chicago for five years, and started in business on their own account in May, 1886. They are hard-working and industrious young men, and are sure to command success in the near future. Although so lately started, they have already a considerable number of orders on their books.

Morper, Dernburg & Co.

Manufacturers of Ladies' and Children's Cloaks, Nos. 156 and 158 Market Street.

One of the leading houses engaged in this branch of manufacture, which was formerly monopolized by eastern houses, is that of Messrs. Morper, Dernburg & Co., composed of Messrs. Jno. C. Morper and Carl Dernburg, who, with Mr. Julius Stein, six years ago founded the business to which they have, January 1, 1887, become the sole successors. The premises occupied are spacious, comprising five entire floors, each fifty by one hundred and fifty feet in dimensions, devoted both to stock purposes and manufacturing, in the former department carrying one of the finest and best assorted stocks of ladies' and children's cloaks in the market, while the latter is provided with all modern machinery and appliances and employs some five hundred operatives. They select only such qualities of material as they can guarantee, and, employing only the most skilled cutters and expert boss tailors, their garments have attained a high reputation in the trade. Their business, which extends to all points north, west and south, has been built up strictly upon the merits of the goods, their reasonable prices and the honorable dealings characteristic of the house. Messrs. Morper and Dernburg are well-known Chicagoans, and have been closely allied with the wholesale cloak trade for many years past, and Chicago is to be congratulated upon having in her midst a house which has proved itself to be so thoroughly enterprising and progressive.

Purtell & Kienzle.

Manufacturers of and Dealers in Saddlery Hardware. Gold, Silver and Nickel Plating. Nos. 2 and 4 La Salle Avenue.

This firm are manufacturers of and dealers in saddlery hardware of all kinds, and gold, silver and nickel plating. From twelve to fifteen experienced workmen are employed in the various departments.

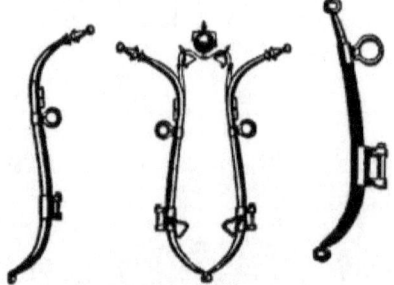

They are the exclusive manufacturers of a new and useful improvement in hames, of which the above cut gives a fair representation. This valuable invention is an improved means of securing the hame-tug to the hame-bar, as well as certain novel features in the construction and combination of parts. All the wear is confined to the metallic bearing, thus increasing the durability of the leather draft-strap. It also confines the wear to the sleeve and bolt, either of which may be removed when worn, and replaced by new ones. This is a great advantage, and one that is readily seen and appreciated by the trade. The firm consists of F. P. Purtell and W. F. Kienzle, young men of enterprise and energy, which, coupled with the long years of experience, enables them to give perfect satisfaction to all of their patrons.

H. Goettsche.

Cigars and Tobacco, Wholesale and Retail, 271 East Madison Street.

Among the numerous local manufacturers in this line, none are more widely known than Mr. H. Goettsche, whose establishment is at the corner of Market and Madison streets. A huge pipe over the entrance also shows that the proprietor does not confine his attention to cigars, but that pipes, briar and meerschaum, of all kinds, are dealt in.

Mr. Goettsche manufactures his own cigars, employing eight hands. The store is on the first floor, and is 20 x 45 feet in size. He opened this business in 1877 since which time it has steadily increased. The cigars manufactured by Mr Goettsche are standard goods, and the favorites appear to be "Lifespring" and "Toto" in the lower price, and "Pet" and "Bouquet" at the higher figure, and, besides his home-made goods, he also keeps a fine line of imported goods, and a business of some $15,000 is done. Mr. Goettsche was born in Germany (province of Hanover), and came direct to this city in 1866.

Western Furniture Co.

Wholesale and Retail Furniture, Carpets, Stoves, Etc., 87 Fifth Avenue.

On this street stores of this class were first opened when the city was but a village, and contained not a single brick or stone erection, and it still continues one of the chief streets for that class of stores. Amongst the largest of them may be named the Western Furniture company, managed by Mr. F. W. C. Macdonald. The building this company occupies is opposite the "Times" building (No. 87 Fifth avenue), and has been a furniture store for the past twenty years. The first, second and third floors, each 35 x 175 feet, are occupied in store and sales rooms. Offices and residences are furnished throughout. The bulk of the trade is for cash, though a small portion is on time. The country trade of this house is very extensive, goods being sent as far as western Nebraska, Kansas and Montana. These orders are from customers who have paid a visit to the city, and have given in their order from observations then made. A specialty is made of desks, which any intending purchaser should call and examine before deciding on the article.

C. Mears & Co.

Manufacturers of and Dealers in Lumber and Brick. Office, 242½ South Water Street.

This house is one of the oldest, not in this business alone, but in any branch of industry in the west, having been established in 1838, and lacks but one year of being co-existent with the foundation of Chicago—the city now celebrating its semi-centennial—in the development of whose commerce Mr. Mears has taken such a prominent and influential part. For years the house confined itself to lumber largely, and in which it also yet deals, with mills at Duck Lake, Lincoln and Mears, Michigan. At the same time Mr. Mears was interested in general merchandising and lumber manufacturing. Observing the prevailing tendency in all building operations toward brick, some four years ago the house, being the principal stockholder in the Middlesex Brick and Tile company, began the manufacture of these staples at Pentwater, Michigan, where it owns an unusually fine quality of brick-making clay, in apparently inexhaustible quantities. Cutting their own lumber and manufacturing brick by the aid of the latest devised machinery, the house is in a position both to fill orders promptly, and to quote bottom figures, while both commodities may be relied on as being the best obtainable for the money in the city.

Delta Transportation Co's

Cheboygan, Mackinaw and Sault Ste. Marie Line of Steamers. Office, 210 South Water Street.

The very name of this company brings before us the pleasures of a steamboat ride among the many beautiful islands which lie between the three great lakes of the north, Superior, Michigan and Huron. We refer to the Delta Transportation company's Cheboygan, Mackinaw & Sault Ste. Marie line of steamers, which ply between the grandest summer resorts to be found in the north. The company's general offices are located in this city, at 210 South Water street, corner Fifth avenue. The company was organized in 1884, and they now run a daily line of steamers between the points named above. The officers of the company are Ira H. Owen, president; F. H. Van Cleve, secretary, and W. R. Owen, treasurer. The latter gentleman is also the manager and looks personally to every feature of the company's business, and largely to his energy and perseverance is due the great success of the company. Their beautiful steamers, "Minnie M." and "Ossifrage," are among the finest on the lakes, fitted up in the most modern style and noted for their speed. Everything is done for the comfort, safety and happiness of the passengers. Some of our readers may have taken this trip, but as there are many of our friends who may wish to do so, we will describe the beauties along the route as seen by C. F. Crosby, who makes the trip every summer, and always sees some new points of beauty and interest. "After days of hot and dusty railroad travel, we reach, at break of day, our point of embarkation, Cheboygan. We soon go on board the company's beautiful and swift-running steamer, "Minnie M.," and, at six o'clock, start out on our pleasure trip towards Lake Superior. Already we catch something of the spirit of the beauty of the scene about us, the systematic beauty of any landscape and water view, while all around us is the clear, bracing, stimulating morning air, every breath of which fills us with new life and vigor. Our first stop is at Mackinaw City, then across the straits to St. Ignace. Backward we turn our course to the well-known and historic Mackinac island, the most beautiful and finest summer resort and home to be found among the lakes. Half the morning is now gone by, and our journey has scarcely begun. Onward we go, on Lake Huron, through the Detour pass, up between St. Joseph and Lime islands. Here and there beautiful scenes pass before our eyes like the ever-changing kaleidoscope. To our left is the beautiful little Round island, then we enter, to the right of Sugar island, the noted St. Mary's river, for we are on our way up; coming down, we pass on the other side, through Hay lake.

One feature of interest is the government canal, the improvements of which cost over $3,000,000, and here are the finest set of locks, docks, etc., to be found in the world. Another pleasant sight is that of St. Mary's falls, and then at 6 o'clock P. M., refreshed instead of fatigued by our journey, we enter Sault Ste. Marie, at our journey's end."

One feature of importance to a tourist is, that this company give moonlight excursions through this region, and anyone who is fortunate enough to take one of these delightful rides will never forget it. Their beautiful steamers can also be chartered by parties who wish to make an excursion alone.

All we can say to our many readers is to follow our friend Crosby's example, and not let the summer go by without taking a trip in the Delta company's beautiful steamer. For all information address Mr. W. R. Owen, 210 South Water street, Chicago, Ill.

J. F. Carse.

Stained-Glass Works, 19 and 21 South Canal Street.

This is one of the oldest businesses of this kind in Chicago, having been founded over thirty years ago by Robert Carse, father of the present proprietor. Every description of stained glass for use in private houses, churches, public buildings, halls, stairways, etc., is manufactured. Mr. Carse makes a specialty of stained-glass work for ecclesiastical purposes, and many of his designs are very elaborate and give evidence of great artistic merit. Mr. Carse has business pluck, which, combined with the excellence of the work he produces, has established for him a large and increasing trade. Lovers of art should not lose the opportunity when in Chicago of paying a visit to these works and inspecting the various designs and specimens on exhibition. Original designs are furnished on application, and prompt attention is given to all orders.

Phil. N. Marks & Co.

Wholesale Hosiery, Fancy and Staple Notions, Laces, Linens, Etc., 175 and 177 East Madison Street

This prosperous firm was established two years ago, and their stock is not only full and complete, but embraces the best quality from importers and manufacturers. They also import laces, etc., themselves, thus enabling them to give their customers the benefit of buying their goods at the lowest possible prices. The extent of this firm's trade embraces all parts of the west and northwest, as well as large city patronage. This firm makes specialties of all the prominent and popular novelties of the day. One of the features of this firm is their orders by mail, to which special attention is given. Prompt, reliable and close personal attention to all branches of their large and increasing trade insures satisfaction in every respect. Full information, samples, price lists, sent on application to the above address. They have in addition to their regular stock a great many job lots, which they receive daily from New York commission houses, consisting of hosiery of all kinds, jerseys, silk handkerchiefs, corsets, etc.

Brown & James Heating Co.

Manufacturers and Dealers in Brown's Water Heaters and Furnaces. Office and Salesroom, 2131 Wabash Avenue.

Our next visit was to the establishment of The Brown & James Heating Company, manufacturers and dealers in Brown's water heaters and hot-air furnaces. Their office and salesroom is located at No. 2131 Wabash avenue, where are exhibited their heaters, furnaces and a variety of ornamental screens, registers, etc. The works are located at No. 2126 Wabash avenue, and are fitted with all the approved machinery of the latest pattern. From twenty-five to thirty skilled workmen are employed making the construction of these furnaces and heaters first-class in every respect. See cut. There has been for years a growing dissatisfaction on the part of the public with the imperfect methods of heating buildings and dwellings. This led Mr. Brown (the president of this company) to give much thought, time and attention to the problem of heating by hot-water circulation. After years of toil he has been able to present to the public a means by which a delightful, healthful and uniform temperature may be maintained at all times, and under all conditions. He has incorporated in this plan those qualities which a life-long experience in the business have proven most desirable. In the perfecting of this system the company have spared no expense that could add to the success of the undertaking, and after thorough demonstration and many successful tests they are able to give to the public the best and most satisfactory heater in the market.

Their plan of ventilation, in connection with their hot-water circulation, makes the whole system complete and unsurpassed by any other way of heating, while it costs about the same as steam to put it in, but is much cheaper to operate, both in the consumption of fuel and the care and attention it requires. Any servant can operate it without any possible chance of its exploding. No safety valves are used, but the expansion tank is left open all the time, thus insuring against any possible accident. Mr. Brown began business in 1867. He was then located on State street near Madison. Mr. Brown is a native of Maine, and has been a resident of Chicago since 1861. An illustrated catalogue and price list, together with any information desired, can be obtained free on application to the company. Telephone 8303.

Mrs. E. T. Walsh.

Fine Millinery, 111 Twenty-second Street.

These parlors are finely fitted and filled with a fine stock of goods, in the latest and most fashionable styles, and orders are promptly executed for hats, trimmings, ribbons, etc. The business was established eight years ago, and has been successful from the day of its inception. Her qualifications are of a superior order, and she devotes particular attention to the wants of her customers. She employs about a dozen able and efficient assistants to help her with the business. All who deal at the New York millinery store meet with the best of satisfaction.

Lewis Brothers & Co.

Wholesale Dry Goods, 160 and 162 Market Street.

Among the various commercial interests for which Chicago is so celebrated, no branch occupies a more conspicuous position than that of the dry goods trade, in which Messrs. Lewis Brothers & Co., of New York, Philadelphia, Boston, Baltimore and Chicago, are admittedly among the representative exponents. The firm is one of the oldest in the United States, and eight years ago, recognizing Chicago's claims, opened a branch house here, which is under the efficient management of Mr. Noble A. Hamilton, a native of the Empire State. They occupy spacious premises and carry a large stock here, handling dry goods of various kinds, which includes prints, cotton goods, dress goods, woolen goods, etc., and possessing every facility for conducting operations under the most favorable auspices. They number among their permanent customers all of the leading jobbers and many of the large retailers, not only of Chicago, but all over the United States, while their resources have expanded with the lapse of years, and are now such as can only belong to those thoroughly conversant with the wants of the trade, and enterprising enough to take advantage of every means whereby all orders may be promptly filled to the satisfaction of the trade. The house is to be commended as one capable of meeting all requirements, and those entering into business relations with it may be assured of treatment and advantages in keeping with a just and progressive policy.

Enterprise Nickel-Plating Works.

Nos. 13, 15 and 17 South Canal Street.

The Enterprise Nickel-Plating Works, of Nos. 13, 15 and 17 South Canal street, is one of the few houses engaged in the silver-plating business. This is an incorporated company, of which Mr. J. G. Shuler is manager. Their factory is fitted out in the most approved style with all the known appliances for successfully carrying on this business, and they do a large and ever-extending trade in every description of nickel and silver plating, bronzing, dipping and lacquering, polishing and grinding. They employ a large staff of skilled workmen, and they are prepared to execute all orders entrusted to them on the shortest notice. Their manager, Mr. Shuler, is a very estimable gentleman, and spares no pains to give satisfaction and to attract business to the firm, and he is highly respected by everyone who comes in contact with him, either in his business capacity or as a private citizen.

H. M. Garlick.

Dealer in City, Suburban and Country Real Estate, Room 39, 118 Dearborn Street.

Nothing shows the rapid growth and importance of the city more than the increase in the value of real estate, and few investments have proved more profitable than those in this kind of property. Amongst the real estate dealers none are able to give better advice or offer greater inducements than Mr. H. M. Garlick, a veteran of many years' experience. He has been doing business on his own account for the last fifteen years. A general business is done in city and suburbs, special attention being paid to property in the western and southwestern portion of the city and suburbs, in lots vacant and improved. In acre property and farm land, he offers many very great inducements to purchasers, who can pay on time or easy payments, as they desire. He attends to purchase, sale and exchange of real estate, either near or distant, manages property, collects rents, provide tenants, pays taxes, attends to repairs, etc. He also negotiates loans on real-estate security, and is well known in business circles as a most reliable and experienced man. His city office is at 116 and 118 Dearborn street, room 39, where all communications should be addressed.

Adam Siebert.

Practical Carriage, Wagon and Sign Painting, 95 and 97 East Indiana Street.

Mr. Siebert is a practical carriage, wagon and sign painter, and has been in the business here since January 1st, 1887. He is well conversant with every branch of this business, as it is his life trade. His premises are eligible and commodious, occupying the top floors. He generally employs half a dozen experienced hands to assist him with the work, which is entirely local, but quite large. His patrons are among the most influential business men in the city. Mr. Siebert makes a specialty of fine work, and sees to it that none but first-class work is turned out. He is a native Chicagoan, and learned his trade right here in Chicago.

Brown, Pettibone & Co.

Blank-Book Makers, Stationers and Printers, 80 and 82 Adams Street.

In its special line this house is essentially a leader, whether its extended connection or the deservedly high reputation of its goods be considered. The premises occupied are unusually spacious, the offices and salesrooms comprising Nos. 80 and 82 Adams street, perfectly equipped with every modern appliance for the speedy and economical conduct of the business. In addition to office stationery a specialty is made of county records and large blank-books of similar character, with patent flexible backs, which allows them, however large, to lie open flat at any page, and of which Messrs. Brown, Pettibone & Co. are the sole licensed manufacturers for the States of Illinois and Iowa. The members of the firm are thoroughly practical and experienced gentlemen, who spare no pains to render satisfaction in every instance, and their house occupies an eminently representative and substantial position in the commercial world.

F. L. Raymond Co.

Manufacturers and Wholesale Dealers in Gummed Labels, Tags, Perforated Gummed Labels, Etc., 195 La Salle Street.

The day of small things is not to be despised, nor is the manufacture of small articles either, for some of the smallest are of the highest importance to our comfort and convenience. The articles made by F. L. Raymond Co., whose office and factory is at No. 195 La Salle street, are gummed labels, tags, pin and clothing tickets, stationery specialties, etc. They are now busily employed getting out a clothing tag, or ticket, which is the most simple and efficient ever introduced. It is fastened on in a moment to the cloth, will not scratch, tear nor become loose, and is cheap. Mr. Raymond commenced work here in August, 1885, and the business has steadily increased till the present time. They carry a good stock and supply chiefly jobbers and the large retailers. Mr. Raymond is essentially a practical man, and does his work in the soundest and most thorough manner. All goods supplied by him never fail to give satisfaction and insure a continuation of custom.

Victor D. Gowan & Co.

Tailors' Trimmings, 154 Fifth Avenue.

In this advanced stage of the tailors' art, the requirements in the line of trimmings are of the most exacting character, to supply which few houses are equally capable with that of Messrs. Victor D. Gowan & Co., a house of fifteen years' standing in the trade, and one noted for the good taste and sound judgment displayed in the selection of stock. Their connections in Europe are unsurpassed, enabling them to be foremost among American houses in displaying the latest novelties in silk and satin linings, facings, braids, buttons, etc. They not only import largely, but also handle full lines of staple and fancy trimmings of domestic manufacture, while their trade is very extensive among merchant tailors all over the country, not to speak of those of our own city. Messrs. Victor D. Gowan & Co. are merchants of the highest standing, and recognized authorities in their line of trade, while the policy upon which their business is conducted is characterized by liberality and the careful fostering of the interests of all patrons, so that transactions once commenced with this responsible firm may be made not only pleasant for the time being, but of such a nature as to become permanent and profitable to all concerned.

J. L. Hathaway.

Anthracite and Bituminous Coal, 38 Market Street.

One of the oldest established and best known men in the coal trade is Mr. J. L. Hathaway, who for twenty-two years has been in the coal business in this city. His office is connected by telephone with all the business offices and houses in the city, as well as with his dock yards at 68 Kingsbury street, 2423 South Halsted street, Clybourn place bridge, and the railroad yard at 94 North Wood street. He sells both at wholesale and retail, his rates comparing most favorably with those of any other house in the trade. He deals both in hard and soft coal, obtaining the bulk of his supplies from Pennsylvania and Ohio. When the great fire of 1871 destroyed all this part of the city, this coal yard was burning for a long time, but the fire was finally extinguished, and much stock saved. The fact that this yard and the river offered so little ground for the flames to spread from contributed more than anything else to save the adjoining block, between Randolph and Lake streets and west of Market street. From fifty to one hundred and fifty hands are employed in the trade of this house, according to the season. The trade is largely city. The yearly sales average from 75,000 to 100,000 tons. A large stock is always on hand, and orders are promptly executed.

The Hat Palace.

Gentlemen's Fine Hats, Northwest Corner Madison and La Salle Streets, Fred. S. C. Nichols, Manager.

All have observed the gilded horseshoe which serves as an arch through which to pass to the "Hat Palace," which occupies the basement of the building at this location. Here may be found at all times a very complete and fine stock of goods in this line. A large trade is done here, mostly local. Mr. Fred. S. C. Nichols, the manager, is fully occupied in attending to the wants of his patrons. This business was established in 1881 at 131 Madison street, and was removed to its present more commodious and central location last May. The proprietor is sole agent for Nickerson's silk hat, Philadelphia; also, for Judd and Dunning's flexible light-weight hats. Most of the trade is local, to meet the demands of which a large stock is kept on hand. Orders are constantly being received from all parts of the western States, as far distant as Omaha. The quality of goods is such as can be relied on for wear, and the prices are so low as to defy competition. The consequence is that the house does as large a retail trade as any in the city.

The Plano Mfg. Co.

Plano, Ill.

This company was organized in 1881 by Messrs. E. H. Gammon, W. H. Jones and G. W. Chamberlin who had been for many years prominently know to the farming public in and around Plano, Ill. in connection with their Marsh harvester. The success of the company from its inception to the present day has been phenomenal. This wonderful growth of business is rightly attributable to the general excellence of their machines. Among the numerous advantages claimed for their harvester and binder are excellence of material and workmanship, perfect adaption of parts, and great simplicity. It is a complete model of successful working in the field, and it is long lived and made for hard and thorough work. The parts of the machine which are most liable to wear and tear are interchangeable, and can be readily duplicated, and fixed by the farmer himself, without the necessity of removing the machine to a machineshop for repairs. The works at Plano cover five acres of ground, and give employment to six hundred men. They have a capacity of 12,000 binders and 6,000 mowers annually. Their harvesters and mowers are well known all over the world, and they ship large numbers to South America, France, Spain and Russia. The company is incorporated under the State laws of Illinois, and Mr. W. H. Jones is the president; E. H. Gammon, vice-president; G. W. Chamberlin, secretary; and L. B. Wood, treasurer. The company has agents in all the principal towns and cities in the Union, and Mr. A. J. McCormick is superintendent of agencies. Their Chicago office is situated at 81 and 83 West Monroe street, and is under the personal supervision of Mr. G. W. Chamberlin. The Plano Manufacturing company claims to be the third in point of size and importance of all the agricultural implement makers in the world.

W. L. Roseboom & Co.

Commission Merchants, Dealers in Broom-Corn and Broom Manufacturers' Supplies, Corner of Kinzie and State Streets.

One of the largest and most prominent broom-corn establishments in Chicago is the house of W. L. Roseboom & Co., at the northwest corner of State and Kinzie streets. Mr. Roseboom occupies seven floors, 40 x 100 feet in dimensions, which enables him to handle promptly the large consignments received from all parts of the United States. Besides broom-corn he also deals in broom manufacturers' supplies. All kinds of machinery pertaining to this line are kept on hand, besides wire, handles, etc. Mr. Roseboom is also proprietor of the Alba Broom-Handle factory, which is located at Alba, Michigan. It occupies two acres of ground, and turns out four million of handles per annum. Mr. Roseboom began the commission business in 1876. He employs from sixteen to twenty hands to assist with the various features of the trade, which extends to all parts of the Union, and aggregates a quarter of a million or more of dollars annually. He is a native of New York, and has been a resident of Chicago for the past fifteen years.

Northwestern Boiler Works.

Chris. Pfeiffer, Proprietor, Manufacturer of Steam Boilers, Tanks, Smoke Stacks, Etc., 64 Michigan Street.

The Northwestern Boiler Works are under the proprietorship and management of Mr. Chris. Pfeiffer. In this large establishment is manufactured steam boilers, tanks, smoke stacks, etc., which are shipped all over the northwest. Besides the large outside trade, they have performed many jobs for important firms in this city. The material used in these works is procured from the east and this city, and is the best the market affords. Upwards of fifty hands find employment with Mr. Pfeiffer. The work turned out by them is celebrated for excellent and careful workmanship, as well as great durability and strength. The business aggregates about $80,000 annually. All kinds of repairing in this line meets with prompt attention, satisfaction being given in all cases. Mr. Pfeiffer was born in Germany, and came to Chicago in 1849. This is his life trade, every department of which he is thoroughly familiar with. He has had charge of the business he now represents since 1877.

Wm. T. Feld.

Artist, 369 North State Street.

An interesting visit is to the studio of Mr. Wm. T. Feld, located at 369 North State street. Mr. Feld has made the study of painting and art a lifelong pursuit. After learning the rudiments here he studied for four years in Europe, visiting all the important art centers and copying from the old masters, and wandering in the finest old galleries of art and sculpture. Three years ago he returned and commenced for himself as a portrait artist, devoting his time closely thereto. A fine portrait executed by Mr. Feld is the one done for Archbishop Feehan, of this city. Many others in this line prove Mr. Feld's skill in this direction, both in oils and crayons. Some of his notable works are "Christ on the Cross," "Chicago," taken from the studio window, "A Gypsy Encampment," "The Old Monastery," "Van Dyke" and others. Mr. Feld also gives lessons in the art, either in mornings or afternoons, to suit his pupils. His rates are moderate, and the instructions personal and of the highest character.

J. B. Hassett.

Wholesale and Retail Dealer in Groceries and Jobber in Fine Teas and Coffee, 9 North Clark Street.

Mr. Hassett is a prominent wholesale and retail dealer in choice and staple groceries, and jobber in fine teas and coffees. He came to Chicago in 1870 and soon after entered the employment of a large grocer in the neighborhood, and, although working for a nominal salary, succeeded in saving enough to enter into business for himself, in company with Geo. H. Brown, in 1881. Two years later he bought out his partner and has since successfully conducted the business alone. He is liberal in all his transactions, and prompt with all orders. His long years of experience enable him to make the best of selections, and the finest the market affords can be found in his store. Being careful for the wants of his patrons, and reasonable in all his prices, he has won a trade which extends to every part of the city. Mr. Hassett has always been recognized as an active, reliable and enterprising business man, whose affairs are conducted upon a sound commercial policy.

A. D. Ferry & Co.

Commission Dealers in Broom-Corn and Broom Material, 225 and 227 Kinzie Street.

The representative establishment in the broom-corn and broom material line in Chicago is the house of A. D. Ferry & Co., at Nos. 225 and 227 Kinzie street. They occupy four floors and basement, each having a dimension of forty by one hundred feet. These are stocked with a large and varied supply of choice broom-corn, handles, wire, etc. The business was begun by Mr. Ferry in 1869, and, by close application and an enterprise worthy of emulation, he has established a trade which extends all over the States and Canada, and amounts to nearly a quarter of a million dollars annually. He buys the broom-corn in large quantities from all the States in which it is raised.

Gay & Culloton.

Plumbers and Gas-Fitters. Sanitary Plumbing a Specialty. 50 North Clark Street.

This business was established in 1877 by William Gay. In 1884 Mr. Culloton was received as a partner. They are thorough masters of their profession, and are experienced in every variety of work, and perform all their operations in a complete and faultless manner. They are amply provided with machinery and tools, and they employ a working force of fifteen skilled mechanics. Their specialty is in sanitary plumbing and gas-fitting, for which they carry a complete stock, for the fitting up of residences, flats, stores, factories, and public buildings. They undertake jobbing of all kinds in their line, and they have established a large trade, amounting to over $30,000 annually. For honesty, proficiency, and absolute reliability, they rank second to no other firm in this business. Their telephone number is 3182.

Gunderson & Lindberg.

Private Livery and Boarding Stables, Rear 385 and 387 East Superior Street; Branch Office, 222 Illinois Street.

This firm are proprietors of the North side livery, board and sale stables. Their main stables are located at Nos. 385 and 387 East Superior street. Both premises occupied are very central and convenient for business men who either wish to leave their horse for care, or hire a rig for a drive. The stables contain upwards of fifty horses, and a large and varied assortment of vehicles of every description. The business was begun five years ago on Superior street, and last year the branch was established on Illinois street. Twelve assistants are employed, and the best of care is given to both horse and vehicle that is boarded at these stables. Both members of the firm give their close personal attention to every detail of their large business, sparing no pains to maintain the high reputation always held by these stables. They are both experienced men in this line of business, and see to it that not only the best of order prevails, but that all orders by telephone No. 3337, mail, or personal, meet with prompt and satisfactory attention.

W. Hall.

Cigars, Confectionery and Specialties, 70 Fifth Avenue.

Among the many establishments that are doing a good trade in this line may be mentioned that of Mr. W. Hall, No. 70 Fifth avenue. He deals at retail in a standard line of cigars, all kinds of confectionery and specialties, to which he has lately added the manufacture of chewing-gum and flypapers. The cigars are obtained specially from St. Louis, and are a superior brand, while the confectionery is made by city houses. The trade is chiefly local, though goods are occasionally sent out as far as Colorado and Dakota. The business was established here in 1882, but has only been in its present form, under Mr. Hall, since 1885. A good trade is being done, and the chewing-gum is sold in all parts of the States.

Frank L. Allen Co.

Manufacturers of Shirts to Order, 152 and 154 Lake Street.

The house of Frank L. Allen Co. are manufacturers of shirts to order, and importers and dealers in gents' furnishing goods. They are centrally located at Nos. 152 and 154 Lake street, where they constantly require the services of a large number of employes in producing a variety of goods, which, for excellence of material, elegance of style and superior workmanship, are unsurpassed, only the best of material being used in the manufacture of their fine shirts, collars, etc. The growth and prosperity of this flourishing establishment is only commensurate with the energy and enterprise of its proprietors, who are W. P. Tuttle, president, and Frank L. Allen, secretary and treasurer. Not only a large and influential city trade has been built up, but one which extends throughout the States of Illinois, Iowa, Nebraska, Minnesota and Wisconsin. This is one of the old shirt companies of Chicago; in fact, from its small beginning have grown four large establishments besides the one represented above. This company has the full confidence of its numerous customers, and the community in general.

Hamburg House.

184 and 186 Randolph Street, M. Marks, Proprietor.

This city is well provided with hotel accommodations, but the only Jewish hotel is located at 184 and 186 East Randolph street. It was first opened in 1870, but was purchased by the present proprietor, Mr. M. Marks, only three years ago, when it was all newly fitted throughout and remodeled. It

contains thirty sleeping rooms, a restaurant, reading room supplied with all the leading daily papers, reception room, parlor and laundry for the accommodation of guests. The rates are very low considering the accommodations, only $1.50 to $2.00 per day. Special rates and arrangements are made for families, or visitors by the week. The rooms are all well lighted and ventilated, and the house throughout is remarkably warm in winter and cool in summer.

The cut represents a front view of the house as seen from Randolph street. Mr. M. Marks, the proprietor, will supply any further information to intending visitors, upon application.

J. Leland Fogg.

Successor to Western Seed Co., Garden Seeds, 31 Michigan Avenue.

The well-known establishment of J. Leland Fogg is successor to the Western Seed Co., and deals in all kinds of garden seeds. The business was established at Rochester, N. Y., in 1843, by the father of the present proprietor, who moved to this city in 1863. The premises occupied consist of four floors and basement, twenty-five by one hundred and twenty-five feet in dimensions, which are arranged in the best possible manner for the storage and shipment of all kinds of seeds. Mr. Fogg makes a specialty of garden seeds in boxes. His practice is to put nothing but fresh and perfect seeds upon the market, and it is this fact above all others that has won for him the confidence of the public, and established so large a trade. Mr. Fogg is a native of New York State and came to Chicago with his father in 1863. He took charge of the business Jan. 1, 1886, and has done much to extend and further the interest of his large trade.

Jacob Koehler.

Sale and Exchange Stable, 61 and 63 Wells Street.

The extensive sale and exchange stable of Jacob Koehler is one the most complete in the city. The stables consist of two stories and basement, and

cover an area of sixty-one by three hundred feet. He also occupies large premises on Illinois street. He has every facility for the buying and selling of horses and mules, and keeps constantly on hand a fine stock of horses suitable for all purposes. He has the reputation of being the most extensive dealer in mules in this city, and in this line possesses as fine a lot of animals as can be found in the country. A score or more of hands are employed to help with the business, and everything is done for the accommodation of his many patrons. Business was begun by Mr. Koehler in 1872, and all his transactions have been marked by fair dealing, which have won the confidence and the liberal patronage from the many business men of this and other large cities.

Close Bros. & Co.

Dealers in Western Lands, 84 La Salle Street.

This firm was established eight years ago, and has continued since, buying vast tracts of the finest western lands and selling out in small lots for farmers and others. At the present time they own about 1,000,000 acres in Kansas, Iowa and Minnesota. The aim of the firm is to settle the country and not to deal with speculators. For this purpose they divide up their land into lots of eighty acres and upwards, to about six hundred acres, according to the purchasers' wants; they also sell on easy payments, and charge a low rate for their lands, and interest on the balance of payments. The wild lands are sold with a deposit of $1 per acre, and balance to suit purchasers, extending over eight or ten years. The lands in Iowa consist of 100,000 acres of the choicest and best farming land in the State. They are situated in the counties of O'Brien, Dickinson, Osceola, Lyon and Plymouth. This State is generally conceded to be one of the most fertile of the Union, the soil being a rich, black inexhaustible loam from three to six feet deep. The price of this land is $10 to $15 per acre. In Minnesota the lands for sale are chiefly located in Pipestone, Rock and Noble counties, the best stock-raising country in the world. Land here is sold at from $8 to $10 per acre. Five hundred thousand acres are here for selection, and those who come first get the choicest lots, for every intending purchaser is invited to go and choose out for himself his farm, and on all sales of one hundred and sixty acres and upwards the railway fare is allowed. This region is rapidly developing and becoming settled. In Kansas this firm have about 500,000 acres of rich, fertile land, chiefly in Trego, Graham, Gray, Kearney, Finney, and Hamilton counties. This land, which is selling very rapidly, is charged for at the rate of from $5 to $8 per acre. In all their sales, this firm's terms are very easy, long time being allowed on deferred payments.

Racine Wagon and Carriage Co.

19 and 21 South Canal Street.

Undoubtedly one of the largest houses in this country engaged in the manufacture of omnibuses, carriages and wagons is the Racine Wagon and

Carriage company, of Racine, Wis. Their factory employs three hundred and fifty men, and is engaged in the manufacture of every description of spring wagon known in this country. They make everything from the largest omnibus to the lightest spring wagon, and their goods find their way to every part of the States. It is an incorporated company, with M. B. Erskine as president; H. E. Miles, secretary and treasurer, and Charles Comstock, superintendent and general agent. They have been in business eleven years, and during that time their business has increased so rapidly that it has taxed their ingenuity to the utmost to keep pace with the requirements of the public. Their Chicago business is cared for by their esteemed manager, Mr. D. J. Morey, at their repository, Nos. 19 and 21 South Canal street. The company has lately filled an order for the Fifth Avenue Transportation company, of New York city, for fifty buses to run on their line. They are the best constructed and finest finished vehicles ever offered to the public, and give the best satisfaction of any bus in the market. The Racine Wagon and Carriage company also have large repositories at Nos. 1524 and 1526 Broadway, New York, and on Market street, Philadelphia, for their eastern trade.

Remington Type-Writer.

196 La Salle Street.

About contemporary with the telephone in point of practical demonstration of fitness, and close upon the greatest discovery of the century, the telegraph, came the Remington type-writer. Probably as great difficulties had to be surmounted in its beginnings as with the telegraph or telephone; certainly it cost as much to demonstrate its utility, and only are the public fortunate today in possessing this admirable writing instrument by the indomitable pluck and perseverance of its inventors and proprietors.

It was an inspiration, no doubt, that put the principles, the simplest possible, in the minds of the inventors, Sholes and Glidden, of Milwaukee; those basic principles, the second order of levers and type-bars and separate type, are more than ever today demonstrated to be the only really successful way, so far as discovered, at least, of solving the writing-machine problem.

Unlike the sewing-machine industry, which saw spring up spontaneously, as it were, all over the country numerous devices for sewing by machinery, the Remington standard type-writer, possessing the "philosophers' stone" to the exclusion of all others, has seen no strong competitor. It is true that important improvements have been made, but more, perhaps, carrying out the original ideas, certainly in the line of greater simplicity. More than 30,000 are already in the hands of users, and the present output is upwards of 1,000 per month, and the sales double yearly.

It is handled exclusively by Wyckoff, Seamans & Benedict, home office, 339 Broadway, New York city, with ten branches in the large cities of the United States, and one at London, England. They have dealers in all important places in the world. The Chicago house or branch is located at 196 La Salle street.

Metcalf's Dancing Academies.

South Side, 137 and 139 Twenty-second Street; West Side, 188 Blue Island Avenue.

Prof. Metcalf is a dancing-teacher of standard reputation, having been engaged in the business for almost a quarter of a century. He took lessons for years under Profs. Allen and Dodge, of New York city, and has also received instruction from Prof. Wedgewood, of this city. He leaves nothing undone, sparing neither time nor money in keeping up with the times, in fact, ahead of them, as the popularity of his academics attests. During an absence of six years from Chicago, Prof. Metcalf was instructing in eastern cities and acquiring every new idea in his art, and returned here with increased knowledge in all branches.

He became proprietor of the West side academy, at 188 Blue Island avenue, four years ago, and two years later became the proprietor of the South side academy, formerly known as Sullivan's. It has been newly refitted, decorated, and arranged with all modern conveniences. The parlors, reception rooms and main hall present facilities second to none in the west. The main hall has a surface of fifty by seventy feet and as smooth a floor as can be found in Chicago. Those desiring to learn to dance correctly, and in a short time, should become members of Prof. Metcalf's classes, as his system of instruction is the most rapid and thorough. He is ably assisted with the classes by his wife, who has done much in making the academies what they are. Prof. Metcalf also gives private lessons, and has suburban classes. The dancing season is from September 1 to May 1, and each term is composed of twelve lessons. The classes are not open to the public, as none but parents of the pupils are admitted. Prof. Metcalf's orchestra, which furnishes all kinds of music for parties, clubs, socials, etc., is composed of some of the best musical talent in the city.

J. R. Alcock.

Plumber and Gas-Fitter, 120 Twenty-second Street.

Among the active and enterprising business men in this portion of Chicago engaged in the plumbing trade, none are more popular or do a better class of work than Mr. J. R. Alcock, located at No. 120 Twenty-second street. He has been in the business for the past fifteen years, first locating on Indiana avenue, coming to his present quarters about six years ago. Having thus a business of long standing, he is known to all classes on the South side and in Hyde Park. Mr. Alcock gives particular attention to plumbing in all its branches, as well as to gas-fitting, and as a sanitary plumber he is equal to any in the city, and his work is done to remain for years. He selects his plumbing goods with great care and sees that they are well adapted to secure both the health and comfort of his patrons. This is his life trade, and he studies carefully every feature of it. He believes in the establishment of a rule for all plumbers to work up to a certain standard, thereby increasing the honor of the trade.

J. S. Haskins.

Florist and Decorator, and Dealer in Plants, Flowers, Etc., 144 Twenty-second Street.

Mr. J. S. Haskins is one of the pioneer florists and decorators of Chicago. He opened the first flower store in the city nearly a quarter of a century ago, at No. 104 Madison street. After the big fire of 1871, he moved to this section of the city, and is now located at No. 144 Twenty-second street. His nursery is located several miles from the city, from which he receives fresh flowers daily. He is dealer in all kinds of plants, flowers, designs, etc. His trade not only embraces all parts of the city, but orders are received from all over the Union, and it would not be presuming too much to say that he is one of the widest known and most popular florists of the Garden City. Designs of all kinds, suitable for weddings, funerals, parties, etc., are arranged on shortest notice and in the most satisfactory manner. Mr. Haskins is a native of Vermont, and has been a resident of this city for many years.

E. S. Hobert.

Dentist, 163 Twenty-second Street, Corner Wabash Avenue.

Dr. E. S. Hobert's dental rooms are located at this point, which is very central for the residents of the South side. His rooms are finely fitted for the use to which they are applied, and he brings to his aid all the modern appliances of his profession. Gas is administered if desired, so that one-half the pain of the operation is thus done away with. In the operating department, Dr. Hobert is very proficient; in fact, his technical training and practical experience have peculiarly fitted him for his profession. His work is all first-class, which reputation has won for him a large practice. He has attained to a very prominent position, and his offices are the resort of the best classes of the community. He is a native of New York State and came to Chicago five years ago, when he established himself in business.

School of Art Embroidery.

Mrs. E. D. Hodge, Proprietor, 151 Twenty-second Street.

This business has been established for the past ten years, under the successful management of Mrs. E. D. Hodge. Both public and private lessons are given at all hours of the day. A full line of materials are constantly kept on hand, while two of the best teachers in this line in the city are employed for instructing. The large store in front of the schoolroom contains a fine stock of worsted and knit goods. Stamping is a specialty, and a great deal of work is done in this department. Specimens of the school work are also on exhibition here, and last year a pair of curtains, valued at over $500 was to be seen here. Some idea may be had of the extent of this school, when it is stated that upwards of 1,000 lessons are given each year. Every facility for the rapid progress of the student is to be found here, and all those contemplating learning the art will do well to call on Mrs. Hodge or any of her assistants.

Chas. E. Gifford & Co.

Commission Grain and Provisions, Rooms 62 and 63, 238 and 240 La Salle Street.

The Chicago markets dominate those of the world as to all dealings in grain and provisions, a creditable state of affairs largely due to the influence exerted abroad by such representative houses as that of Messrs. Chas. E. Gifford & Co. This business was established eleven years ago by Mr. C. E. Gifford, who has since admitted Messrs. I. Cushman and Chas. E. Gifford, Jr., into partnership. Mr. C. E. Gifford, the senior partner, was born in Albany, N. Y., and early in life embarked on a successful mercantile career, and in 1876 became a member of our Board of Trade. The firm are also members of the Milwaukee and Duluth boards of trade, and consequently every facility is enjoyed for watching the grain and provision markets and taking prompt advantage of the ever-varying prices. The firm carry on an extensive commission business in grain and provisions, all transactions executed through this responsible house being bona-fide purchases or sales made on 'change and in accordance with the strict rules which govern its members. With ample means, they are noted in our leading financial circles for their responsibility and honorable, prompt business methods.

Roundy & Son.

Manufacturers of Lodge Supplies, Regalia and Uniforms for All Societies, 188 and 190 South Clark Street.

Standing among the foremost of regalia manufacturers of the United States is the well-known house of Messrs. Roundy & Son, of this city. The extensive business so ably conducted by them is the very oldest established, in all probability, of those now in successful operation, having been originally founded in New York city in 1857. In 1861 Wadhams Bros. became the proprietors, upon the dissolution of which firm in 1873 Mr. D. C. Roundy entered the firm, the name and style of which being that of Wadhams & Roundy. About 1880, Mr. Wadhams retired, and Mr. Roundy associated with himself in partnership his son, Mr. F. C. Roundy, thus establishing the present firm. Their establishment has long been recognized as headquarters for lodge supplies of every kind, inclusive of regalia and uniforms, banners and flags for all societies, national, secret, masonic, benevolent, temperance and social. Military and theatrical goods form an important feature in the business, and they have the necessary experience, skill and facilities to promptly furnish any kind of military goods. Our amateur and professional actors alike find this establishment a complete repository for everything needed on the theatrical stage, the firm promptly fitting and making any required costume within a few hours' notice, which are absolutely correct historically and chronologically. As in Knights Templar uniforms, so in all lodge regalia the firm excel in careful attention to detail as well as to the superior quality of materials used, preferring to make only the best at reasonable prices, and leaving the so-called cheap houses to demonstrate their own unfitness—a course of procedure which has long ago placed their house upon its present substantial basis.

Ginn & Co.

Publishers of School and College Text-Books, W. S. Smyth, General Western Manager, 180 Wabash Avenue.

In American educational circles the firm name of Messrs. Ginn & Co., successors of Messrs. Ginn, Heath & Co., have justly become both familiar and respected. The business was first established in 1871, at 56 Madison street, whence the steady growth of their trade compelled the firm, in 1880, to remove to their present very eligible and central location at No. 180 Wabash avenue. Here they are actively engaged in the publication of school-books and educational works upon an extensive scale. Their publications include school and college text-books, besides books of reference that form a large miscellaneous collection of educational literature. Their catalogue embraces all the standard Latin and Greek text-books, music readers and manuals, and a comprehensive course under the head of English literature, including the works of such classic authors as Shakespeare, Coleridge, Burns, Burke, Webster, Bacon and others. Members of school boards and college faculties will find it to their interest to write Messrs. Ginn & Co. for their full descriptive catalogue, while correspondence in reference thereto will receive prompt attention. Mr. Edwin Ginn, the esteemed senior partner, is a native of Maine, and a publisher of much experience, whose long and honorable career in this field of enterprise renders him an acceptable authority. Mr. George A. Plimpton, the junior partner, is a popular and hard-working member of the firm, having full charge of the New York branch, while Mr. F. B. Ginn, the remaining partner, is also well known to the trade. The firm's general offices are at 9 to 13 Tremont place, Boston; 743 Broadway, New York; 180 Wabash avenue, Chicago; and 752 Ninth street, Oakland, Cal.; with branch houses in charge of managers at 13 Tremont place, Boston; 180 Wabash avenue, Chicago, W. S. Smyth, manager; 41 South High street, Columbus, Ohio; 743 Broadway, New York; and a Pacific coast depository, Cunningham, Curtiss & Welch, San Francisco, Cal.

Simonds Manufacturing Co.

Works at Fitchburg, Mass., and Corner Canal and Washington Streets, Chicago.

The Simonds Manufacturing Co., of Fitchburg, Mass., was established in 1832, re-organized in 1864, and incorporated into the present company in 1868. Six years ago they opened a branch establishment on Canal street at the corner of Washington. They manufacture a complete line of circular saws, solid; circular saws, inserted point; crescent ground cross-cut saws; gang, mill, mulay, drag and band saws; also planing-machine knives, paper-cutting and leather-splitting knives, etc. They carry a large and well-assorted stock and do an extensive business in all parts of the country. It is an incorporated company, of which Mr. Geo. F. Simonds is president, Daniel Simonds vice-president and treasurer, and E. F. Simonds the manager of the Chicago branch. Mr. E. F. Simonds is a most courteous and obliging gentleman, who has no notion of letting any business go by him for want of attention on his part, and it is mainly due to his exertions here that the trade of the company has taken such rapid strides through the western and northwestern States.

E. Earnshaw & Son.

Masons, Contractors and Builders, Room 73, Exchange Building, Pacific Avenue and Van Buren Street.

Since establishing business in 1865 upon his own account, Mr. E. Earnshaw, the head of the firm, has developed a large and permanent connection of a strictly first-class character, among both our leading architects and property-owners, for whom he has erected many of the substantial business blocks and elegant private residences which adorn the Garden City. He is still in the prime of life and a hard worker, with well-organized arrangements and facilities for the prompt completion of any contract undertaken, his staff of employes averaging 50 to 75 men in the busy season. Mr. Earnshaw is a native of England, and has been a permanent and honored resident of Chicago for the past thirty years. A close figurer and an active competitor for business, he has made it a practice from the very outset to decline contracts at prices which would compel him to do inferior work. On the contrary, Mr. Earnshaw having a reputation to sustain, and relying upon the merits of past work to secure continued favorable recognition, he is ready and willing to enter into contracts of any magnitude, however large, upon reasonable terms. The business thus stands upon the solid basis of commercial integrity, and is typical of the building interests of Chicago, whose industries are now being reviewed in her semi-centennial year.

W. W. Lazear, D. D. S.

Dentist, 2208 Wabash Avenue.

Dr. W. W. Lazear has been established in practice in this neighborhood since 1882, and has now a large patronage, embracing the best families on the South side. His office is finely and attractively fitted, and contains every modern appliance in the dental line, and patients who consult him can rely on prompt and thoroughly efficient work. Dr. Lazear is a graduate of the Philadelphia Dental college, of the class of 1882. Among the specialties used by Dr. Lazear is the perfection tooth crown, and teeth without plates, and he has been very successful in the treatment of his patients with those modern helps. He is a native of New Jersey, and came to Chicago fifteen years ago.

Wm. Frech.

Manufacturer of Metal-Working and Experimental Machinery, 68 and 70 West Monroe Street.

One of the best fitted machine shops in Chicago is that of Mr. Wm. Frech, at 68 and 70 West Monroe street. He is engaged in the manufacture of metal-working machinery and tools, experimental machinery, etc. The machines manufactured by Mr. Frech are his own inventions, and are the fruits of long years' study and practical experience. They comprise drill presses, screw, foot and power punching presses, dies and special tools, turret lathes, engine lathes, speed lathes, slide rests, and special machinery in general. His machines are noted for their simple and accurate construction, beautiful and studious design, and excellent workmanship. His celebrated power punching presses, of which he makes at present six different sizes, are substantially and accurately built. The adjustment of the slide is the most ingenious, simple and durable device in existence, and they possess numerous other advan-

tages. Gentlemen who are interested in this class of machinery would do well to call on Mr. Frech, or write for his catalogues. They will find him ever ready to give any information with reference to the numerous machines manufactured by him. Mr. Frech is a native of Rhenish Bavaria, Germany. He has been in this country seventeen years, and is engaged in the machine business for the last twenty-two years.

Baumann & Lotz.

Architects and Engineers, Rooms 59, 68 and 70, Metropolitan Block.

Chicago has proved to be the most important field in the United States for architectural enterprise, and in no sphere of the practice of the profession has more substantial progress been made than in that of the designing and erection of grain elevators and warehouses, wherein Chicago leads the world, both as regards number, capacity and perfection of equipment and arrangement. The representative of the favorite style of architecture embodied in these vast structures is the well-known firm of Baumann &

Lotz, who have long held a leading position in America as grain-elevator architects and builders. The combination of talent exhibited in this firm would be difficult to find elsewhere. Mr. Edward Baumann is an associate member of the American Society of Civil Engineers, having been closely identified with the architectural profession from an early period of his life. He has for years past made the designing of grain elevators a special study, while the improvements which he has embodied have proved to be of the most practical and acceptable character, as witness many of the most important elevators, among others, Armour, Dole & Co's, Munger, Wheeler & Co's and the C., R. I. & P. R. R. Co's, that form such striking landmarks. On the other hand, Mr. Wm. H. Lotz is one of the leading mechanical engineers of the country, a member of both the American Society of Civil Engineers and the Western Society of Engineers, with a national reputation for his skill and ability. Mr. Lotz was born in 1838, and received his education in Germany, his native land, and has been actively engaged in the practice of his profession in Chicago since 1865, with which he has combined the other natural branch of the profession, viz., the solicitation of American and foreign patents, having a large practice in patent cases, in which he is an expert, having been engaged therein since 1865. The firm are patentees of some very important inventions of their own, embodying improvements in grain elevators, breweries, malt-houses, etc., and are fully prepared with every facility to promptly fill all commissions in their line with that intelligent comprehension of the objects and requirements to which the structure is to be put, which has contributed so greatly to render them the representative exponents of this branch of the profession.

R. P. Layton.

Real Estate, Room 25, 182 Dearborn Street.

The great demand for choice suburban residence properties, together with the steady increase in value of such holdings, affords the best evidence of Chicago's growing wealth and prosperity. Experience shows that to the thrifty artisan, the salaried clerk and the moderate business man, these suburban offerings have proved of inestimable value in permitting them to acquire at reasonable cost a pleasant home in a healthful location apart from the turmoil of city life. In speaking of suburban properties reference is made to the beautiful suburb of Tracy, one of the finest building sites in the neighborhood of Chicago, and which offers superior inducements, both to those desiring permanent homes or an investment for speculation. Since being put upon the market only three years ago, several hundred lots have been sold, many for immediate improvement. Tracy is immediately accessible to the city via the Rock Island railroad, upon which it is situated, twelve miles from the depot, on ground from eighty-five to one hundred feet higher than Lake Michigan, and in a beautiful grove of forest trees, where all the conveniences of schools, churches, stores, post office and express office are enjoyed. The lots are large size, and offered upon unusually favorable terms, by Mr. R. P. Layton, who resides there and is interested in the property. The finest depot on the road has been built at this point, and new houses are going up in every direction. Mr. Layton, formerly of the well-known firm of Clark, Layton & Co., and more recently the successor of Layton, Thayer & Co., is a native of New York State, and has resided in this city over twenty years.

McNamara & Dick.

Manufacturers and Dealers in All Kinds of Trunks and Traveling Bags, 62 West Madison Street.

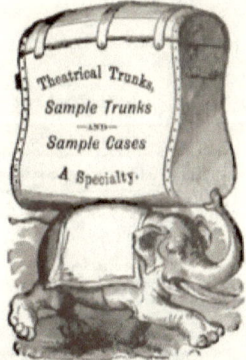

To a class of people who travel so often and so far as Americans do, good serviceable trunks and traveling bags are articles of prime necessity. A reliable house, which makes a business of supplying these articles, is that of Messrs. McNamara & Dick, of No. 62 West Madison street, near the Union depot, manufacturers and dealers in all kinds of trunks and traveling bags. They make a specialty of theatrical and sample trunks, great care being taken to make them strong and durable, while for lightness and beauty of construction they are unexcelled. They have a large trade, which is steadily increasing. They make goods to order, and give attention to all kinds of repairing. All orders meet with prompt and satisfactory attention. The members of this firm are both citizens of Chicago, and have only been associated in business for two years, although they have individually been connected with this trade for a much longer period.

The Holbrook Mfg. Co.

Office, 173 Madison Street.

The Holbrook Manufacturing Co. are widely known in connection with their chemical specialties, among which is the great Russian corn and bunion exterminator, automatic shading, writing and coloring inks, Lock's gelatine starch, toilet and tooth powders. The office and stockrooms are at 171 East Madison street, second floor.

The business was established on Clark street in 1870, and two years later removed to its present address, where the trade has maintained a steady increase. The business is exclusively wholesale. Their customers are city wholesale houses, while a considerable trade has also grown up in the country districts and the neighboring States.

All colors of fine rubber-stamp inks are also made to order by this company. A new thing just brought out is a very fine face powder, named "Queen of Lilies," which is experiencing a rapid sale.

A. D. Hewitt.

Fire Insurance, Successor to E. S. Hewitt, 147 La Salle Street.

The fire insurance business conducted by A. D. Hewitt, at No. 147 La Salle street, was established in 1873 by Mr. E. S. Hewitt. After a successful career of thirteen years it was taken in charge by the present proprietor, who has placed it in the prominent position held among companies of the first class. The companies represented by evidence the estimation in which the agency is regarded in this special line. Among them are the Sun, California; Dwelling House Insurance company Boston, Mass.; New Hampshire Fire, New Hampshire; Traders, Chicago; and Fire Insurance Association, England. These companies are known for their worth and stability wherever fire insurance exists, or a policy drawn, and the fact of A. D. Hewitt holding the Chicago agency for these different interests in Chicago and vicinity shows his fidelity to their interests and his popularity among the policy-holders. The present manager of the office business, Mr. Wm. A. Graham, assumed the position in August, 1886, and has already proven his adaptability for so responsible a position.

Rogers, Brown & Co.

Pig Iron Commission, W. W. Backman, Manager, 98 Dearborn Street.

One of the largest firms in this city doing exclusive business in southern and Ohio brands of pig iron is that of Rogers, Brown & Co. The offices are located at 98 Dearborn street, and are in charge of Mr. W. W. Backman as manager. The headquarters are at Cincinnati, southeast corner Third and Walnut streets, and branch offices have also been opened in St. Louis and Louisville. Orders only are received here. Iron is shipped direct from the various furnaces this firm represents. This firm supplies all the west and northwestern States as far as Dakota, 9,000 tons being supplied by this branch alone last month.

This firm are exclusive agents for eighteen of the largest furnaces in Ohio, Tennessee and Georgia. The brands are celebrated as being of excellent quality, and for many purposes the best to be obtained. This firm are the largest suppliers of the soft and coke pig iron in the district, and one well known by all iron manufacturers in this part of the country.

H. C. Hoffman & Co.

Manufacturers, Dealers, and Contractors for Granite Monuments, Vaults, Headstones, Etc., 12 and 14 Van Buren Street, Near Michigan Avenue.

The State of Vermont has long been noted for its extensive quarries of the finest marble and granite, the most noted granite quarries being located at Barre, about eight miles from Montpelier, the State capital.

One of the largest and most complete plants in the country for the manufacture of the finest grades of marble and granite work is that owned and operated by the Burlington Manufacturing company, of Burlington, Vt., on Lake Champlain. They use the latest improved machinery for sawing, cutting and polishing marble and granite, employing a large force of skilled workmen, and in the last ten years have erected some of the finest monuments and buildings in the country.

In the spring of 1886 the firm of H. C. Hoffman & Co. succeeded to the extensive monumental and granite business of the above mentioned establishment, Mr. Hoffman having been associated with the old company for many years.

Within the past year H. C. Hoffman & Co. have erected some very fine monuments in the cemeteries of Chicago and other cities of the northwest. Among the most noted are the Perkins shaft, the Mason and the Chambers-Farwell sarcophagus at Rosehill, and the Ayres monument in Graceland cemetery, in Chicago; the Nisbet monument at Evansville, Ind.; the Beebee monument at Denver, Colorado; the Blossom sarcophagus at Kansas City, Mo., and a fine monument purchased by General John A. Logan, erected at Murphysborough, Ill.

This firm is using in its work granite from the celebrated Westerly, R. I., quarries, the dark Quincy quarries of Quincy, Mass., and the dark blue quarries of Barre, Vt. They are the agents in this city of the red syenite granite from the quarries of Cohn & Robertson, Wausau, Wis., which is undoubtedly one of the best red granites in the world, being very hard and durable and susceptible of a high polish, and showing a strong contrast between the polished and hammered surfaces, which shows lettering or carving very plainly, making inscriptions more legible than on any granite in the market. These quarries are practically inexhaustible, the ledge being about two miles long. The granite is entirely free from iron blotches, checks or other imperfections and is uniform in color.

A fine stock of monumental work in all the best granites and marble may be seen at the wareroom of H. C. Hoffman & Co.

This firm has a high reputation for first-class work at low prices, and for the faithful performance of their contracts and for always endeavoring to please and satisfy their customers. They are practical men in the business, H. C. Hoffman and Dorrell McGowan constituting the firm, the senior member being a designer of no mean ability, having had a long experience in the business. They are prepared to furnish designs and estimates on all kinds of monumental and building granite work, and they invite all persons requiring anything in their line to call at their wareroom at 12 and 14 E. Van Buren street, near Michigan avenue, Chicago, Ill.

F. A. Lindstrand.

Jeweler and Optician, 179 Twenty-second Street.

Mr. Lindstrand established this business over 12 years ago. His stock of goods is of the finest in his line, consisting of diamonds, gold and silver watches, all kinds of clocks, lockets, bracelets, rings and other articles too numerous to mention. All kinds of jewelry of the latest designs and styles are selected with great care. Popular prices prevail in this establishment, and all goods are warranted in every particular. He employs from three to five competent and skilled workmen, and repairs of all kinds are executed with dispatch and neatness. Mr. Lindstrand was born in Sweden, where he learned his trade of jeweler, and came to Chicago in 1871, and has become one of Chicago's prominent business men and popular jewelers.

A. Lorenz & Co.

Designers and Engravers on Wood, 84 and 86 La Salle Street.

Amongst the leading firms in this city which produce the finer kinds of wood engraving mention is made of the house of A. Lorenz & Co., who have been established here about ten years, and who have earned the reputation of producing only good and reliable work. Perhaps the most difficult branch of this art is that of portrait engraving. This the firm have a name for excelling in, though the bulk of the work is for catalogue illustrations and book publishers' orders. The firm is known all over the States, and orders are constantly being received from all parts, from New York to California. From four to twelve hands are employed, according to the state of trade. The firm have lately removed from the corner of Madison and Clark street to their present more commodious premises at 84 and 86 La Salle street, where all orders and communications should be addressed.

Wm. Seydel.

Contractor, Carpenter and Cabinet Maker; Office and Shop, 153 Twenty-first Street.

Wm. Seydel, contractor, carpenter and cabinet maker, whose office and shop is located at No. 153 Twenty-first street, is prominent in this line of business. His business career was begun twenty-five years ago, in Germany although he has been working at his trade here in Chicago, for only about five years. In the short space of time he has been in business in Chicago he has won a very large and lucrative patronage. He is a practical and experienced workman himself, having learned this trade in his native country. He employs only good workmen, and does all kinds of repairing neatly and satisfactorily. As a contractor and carpenter his job work is unsurpassed. He came from Germany in 1881 and after sojourning for half a year in Philadelphia, he came to this city.

Peter Wehle.

Merchant Tailor, 2135 Wabash Avenue.

Peter Wehle occupies at this point elegantly fitted apartments, where is displayed a fine stock of goods. He always keeps on hand a full and complete line of piece goods from which to make selections, embracing all the novelties in French and English cassimeres and seasonable goods for gentlemen's wear. He began business in 1873, in this same neighborhood, and by good work has built up a large and lucrative trade, embracing some of the leading and influential citizens of Chicago. From five to eight competent and reliable workmen are employed. Perfect fits and reasonable rates for all work, combined with his thorough knowledge of the business, place this establishment in the front ranks of the tailoring business in this city. Mr. Wehle is a native of Germany and has been a resident of Chicago for the past fifteen years.

C. T. Boal.

Wholesale Stoves and Hollow-Ware, 247 and 249 Kinzie Street.

The large wholesale stove and hollow-ware establishment of C. T. Boal, at Nos. 247 and 249 Kinzie street, occupies a building 40 x 100 feet in dimensions, five stories in height, with a large basement. It is thoroughly stocked with all varieties of heating and cooking stoves and hollow-ware, equal to anything of the kind in the northwest. Mr. Boal is also representative of the house of Orr, Painter & Co., of Reading, Pa., and Jas. Bell & Co., of Wheeling, W. Va., and the Highland Foundry Co., Boston, Mass., three prominent establishments of stoves and hollow-ware. Mr. Boal has had long years of experience in this line, although he has only established the present business about two years ago. Eighteen to twenty hands are employed in the various departments, and all orders are promptly attended to. Mr. Boal is a native of Ohio, and came to Chicago in 1854, and for many years has been engaged in the manufacture and jobbing of stoves in this city. He was an officer in the 88th Illinois second Board of Trade regiment, which served in the army of the Cumberland.

Headen & McAuley.

**Manufacturers of Beer Stills, Railroad Tanks, Etc.,
112 to 118 East Indiana Street.**

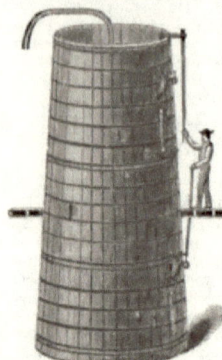

This firm are prominent manufacturers of beer stills, railroad tanks, and all kinds of distillers', brewers' and vinegar tubs, etc. They have spacious and commodious quarters, fitted up with all conveniences, latest machinery, and everything for the rapid prosecution of their work. An engine of eighty horse-power is used, while from fifteen to twenty-five men are employed. One large ground floor, forty-nine by one hundred feet in dimensions, consists of their workshop. We would especially call attention to the bevel croze made by this firm in all their work. The crozing machine is their patent (April 24th, 1883), and is the best of the kind in the market. The business dates back to 1868, when it was begun under the firm name of Hemingway & Headen, being changed in 1875 to the present firm. The business has grown very large, and the trade extends throughout the city, south and west. Both members of the firm are natives of Canada, and have been residents of the Garden City since 1867.

J. Regan.

Fine Confectioner and Baker, 63 North State Street.

The fine confectionery store and bakery of J. Regan, at No. 63 North State street, is a first-class one in every respect. Mr. Regan does all his own manufacturing and uses nothing but pure material. His candies may be relied upon as being entirely free from all adulterations. This fact alone has built up a large trade. His bread and rolls are fresh twice a day and are much sought after by the families in the neighborhood. During the summer months Mr. Regan keeps a force of six hands employed to facilitate prompt attention to his business. He also makes a specialty of manufacturing fine ice-cream of all flavors, twelve varieties, which is served in his parlors, and orders taken from outside parties. He is a native of this city and for years has been represented in the business interests of the Garden City.

Richard Truppel.

Pharmacist, 96 Wells Street.

This finely appointed establishment was begun fifteen years ago, but Mr. Truppel has only had charge for the past three years. He has three assistants, and careful attention is given to all orders received, while prescriptions are carefully compounded at all hours, day or night. The business, although entirely local, is quite large, which attests to the popularity and efficiency of Mr. Truppel as a first-class druggist. He is a German, and came to Chicago three years ago, when he bought out this business. He is a graduate of the university of Jena, at Thuringia, Germany, and a licentiate of this city, and will give entire satisfaction to all requiring his services as a druggist.

The John J. Crooke Co.

Manufacturers of Plain, Colored and Embossed Tinfoil and Metallic Capsules, 84 Franklin Street.

The John J. Crooke Co. occupy the large, four-story building at Nos. 84 to 88 Franklin street. They also have offices in New York, 186 Grand street, where the business was begun thirty years ago. They moved to Chicago in 1881 and have succeeded in building up a large western trade. They are the largest and most popular manufacturers of plain, colored and embossed tinfoil in the Union, being the pioneers in this business. They also manufacture metallic capsules, over twenty-five thousand dozen being turned out weekly. This company possess every facility for good and rapid work, and are among the enterprising firms of the Garden City.

W. H. Montgomery.

Manufacturer of Artificial Limbs, 73 Clark Street, Corner of Randolph.

Amongst the various artificial-limb makers of the city none deservedly occupy a higher place than Mr. W. H. Montgomery, who is located at 73 South Clark street, corner of Randolph. Mr. Montgomery has been connected with the business here for eleven years, succeeding Mr. Foster, on his decease in 1881, as sole proprietor of the trade and owner of the patent known all over the country as Foster's patent union limb. For twenty-four years he has been connected with the business, and is therefore no novice, but thoroughly understands the business and has brought out several improvements of his own. From the old single stick or peg-leg, so long in vogue, to the finely moulded and well finished pieces of mechanism now made, there have been many improvements, but nothing has ever been introduced to compare with the Foster patent union limb for ease, gracefulness or durability. These limbs are made upon a foundation of white willow, which is light, tough and durable; upon this, a covering of strong rawhide, made expressly for the purpose, and upon this is a delicately tinted, waterproof enamel or cement, colored to closely imitate nature. These limbs are models of lightness, strength, simplicity of construction, durability, naturalness of motion and anatomical beauty. The trade is large and steady, no dull season is experienced, and having gained the reputation he has, Mr. Montgomery is kept pretty busy with his assistants in supplying orders. Catalogues and all further information will be sent upon application.

Bliss & Tracy.

Iron and Steel Shafting, Steel-Rim Pulleys, Friction-Clutch Pulleys, Etc., 51 South Canal Street.

Any person coming to Chicago with the intention of buying machinery of any description would naturally go straight to South Canal street, where he would be sure to meet with everything he required. Among the numerous wholesale houses there located, Messrs. Bliss & Tracy carry on an extensive business at No. 51 South Canal street as dealers in iron and steel shafting, steel-rim pulleys, friction-clutch pulleys, hangers, and power-transmitting machinery of every description. They carry a large stock, and have a very old established connection in the western and northwestern States. Messrs. S. E. Bliss and E. C. Tracy, the individual members of the firm, are well known in engineering circles and are duly appreciated in the business world.

The Living Church.

Rev. C. W. Leffingwell, D. D., Editor and Proprietor, 162 Washington Street.

The Living Church is an ably written, well-edited weekly journal devoted to church news. It has the largest circulation of any Protestant Episcopal paper in America, and is sent to all parts of the States and Territories, as well as to the Canadian provinces. The editor and proprietor is the Rev. C. W. Leffingwell, D. D. The journal was founded by the Right Reverend Samuel Smith Harris, LL. D., second bishop of Michigan, in 1878, in connection with the Rev. John Fulton, D. D. They retained the editorship for six months only, and then sold the paper to its present owner. The circulation is rapidly increasing and is very large already, especially in the eastern States and Canada. The rate of subscription is $1 in advance. Each copy contains sixteen pages, well printed, on good paper, in magazine form. From the central location of the office, and as Chicago is the inland metropolis of this growing country, the Living Church is able to collect and disseminate more promptly church news than any other periodical. By an experience of many years the publisher has learned the wants of the people and secured the means to meet them. The following are some of the popular features of this work: News and notes, articles on the church season, church history and biography, the revision of the Prayer-book, independent editorials, opinions of the press, pastoral work, the household, notes of current literature, political contributions and correspondence.

J. B. Devlin.

Dentist, 127 Twenty-second Street, Corner Michigan Avenue.

Dr. Devlin is a graduate of the Toronto Dental college, and came to Chicago in 1869, when he began practice for himself, in the same neighborhood in which he is now located. His parlors are fitted up in the most attractive manner and contain all the latest devices in the dental line for the furtherance of the business. All work turned out is done by Dr. Devlin, and he sees to it that everything is satisfactory. It is his superior work which has won for him so large and extended a practice among the leading families of the South side.

Wm. Schmitz.

Importer and Dealer in Musical Instruments, 185 Twenty-second Street, Chicago.

These premises are finely arranged for the storing of the various kinds of instruments which Mr. Schmitz handles. Although but recently established, he is doing a very fair business. He is one of the leading importers and dealers in musical instruments on the South side, and imports direct from the old country violins, accordions, flutes, etc., of the finest quality and best grade. He carries on business with the leading musical houses of Europe, thus guaranteeing a genuine article. He is a native of Germany, and has been living in Chicago for the past twelve years, where he is highly esteemed by all.

John Davison & Son.

Ship Chandlers, Sail Makers, Riggers, Etc., 282 and 284 South Water Street.

There are few of the many sailing vessels on Lake Michigan but come into business relations with the ship chandlers announced at the head of this article, and it would be exceptional if the majority of them did not require an outfit at the commencement of navigation, and require refitting during the season. The owners or captains of such vessels usually call upon John Davison & Son to procure their outfits or to have repairs attended to. This firm has been following the ship chandlery business for a quarter of a century, and as sail makers and riggers there cannot be much for them to learn as to what is needed to make a vessel perfect in her sea-going equipments. Occupying four floors in the building at 282 and 284 South Water street, there is plenty of room and every convenience for supplying the wants of maritime traffic, not only the room and conveniences, but a large and complete stock of ship chandler's and sail maker's goods from which to select. The varied assortment kept in stock makes the house of John Davison & Son a popular one.

G. F. Charles.

Photographer, 2029 Wabash Avenue.

G. F. Charles is one of the most practical photo artists in the city whose love for the picturesque and beautiful exhibits itself in every detail of his business. His parlors and studio are models of elegance and comfort, and are conveniently arranged, everything being on the first floor. The large gallery is immediately in the rear of the studio and salesroom. Mr. Charles has had long years of practical experience, and has carefully studied every branch of his profession, and by good work and close application, has now a liberal and influential patronage from the best classes of Chicago. His elegantly fitted studio contains a splendid array of specimens of Mr. Charles' work and skill. Besides being a talented photographer, he excels as an artist, his crayon, india-ink, water colors, and pastel work being equal to the best in the city. His fidelity to detail, brilliancy of touch, and ability to preserve every feature, prove that he is an artist of true genius and animated with but one aim, namely, to excel in his chosen profession. Mr. Charles is a native of Kingston, Canada, and has resided in Chicago since 1881.

The Chalcedony Company.

Manufacturers of Saxolin and Chalcedony Soaps, 93 Dearborn Street.

The high character and reputation of Chicago's products are every day becoming more widely known throughout the civilized world, while the facilities it enjoys enables its persevering and energetic manufacturers to compete with any of the older establishments situated elsewhere. Although established the present year, the honorable manner in which its products have been introduced to the public, assisted by the recognized standing of its managers in the commercial world, have already made a place for saxolin and chalcedony soaps upon the market. The factory embraces every modern improvement and facility known to the business, while they employ a large amount of skilled labor, the majority of whom must obviously be proficient and well versed in chemistry. Saxolin is a new and valuable compound for cleaning, scouring, polishing and household purposes generally. Chalcedony soap, in several grades, is designed for cleaning purposes, and for general toilet use; each of these kinds of chalcedony soaps is unique in its action and particularly adapted for removing the most obstinate substances from the hands and skin. The business of this corporation is all under the general supervision of its secretary, Mr. W. T. Blair. All of the soaps and compounds of this company are of the best quality made, and instead of being perfumed by the base and rancid extracts of the common butyric acid in such general use by less scrupulous manufacturers, nothing but the cleanest and purest essential oils are used. Yet, owing to their improved process, the price compares favorably with any. Most of their manufactures are specialties, and their like are not attempted by any other manufacturers. This house enjoys a solid reputation among the business men of the city, while its products are worthily assisting in maintaining its fair fame abroad.

Robins & Talcott.

Building Specialties, Room 11, 115 Monroe Street.

Among the various extensive and growing commercial interests of Chicago which exert an important influence on our general trade and bear the marks of continued increase and prosperity, none, perhaps, occupies a more useful position than the trade in building specialties, which is so satisfactorily represented by Messrs. Richard Robins and Ed. N. Kirk Talcott. These gentlemen have for years past been so prominent in the building fraternity that from the very outset in 1886 the success of their house was guaranteed. The firm represent the Hecla Architectural Bronze and Iron works of New York and Brooklyn, the Magneso Calcite Fireproofing company, Boston Terra Cotta works of Boston, and several stone producers; and they successfully cover the entire field of ornamental ironwork, terra cotta, granite, marble, sandstone and fireproofing, orders for which Messrs. Robins & Talcott are prepared to promptly fill on terms which cannot be duplicated elsewhere. Their trade, already of great magnitude, is steadily increasing, and is reaching out rapidly into the far west. Architects and builders, as well as owners and those needing representation in the west, are now fully appreciating the advantages to be derived through this house.

J. D. Marshall.

Manufacturer of Chicago Slaughter Sole Leather; Office, 72 to 86 Hawthorn Avenue.

One of the largest and most complete tanneries of the Garden City is that of J. D. Marshall, located at Nos. 72 to 86 Hawthorn avenue. The tanbark yard covers an area of 250 x 300 feet, while the tannery proper is 150 x 275 feet in dimensions, and the buildings are all arranged in the most convenient manner for the transaction of business. Only sole leather is tanned, and in this special line it is one of the most extensive tanneries in the Union. Over

4,000 cords of tanbark are used, and 50,000 sides are tanned annually. Twenty-five hands are employed, and an engine of sixty horse power is used. The business was established in 1861, under the firm name of Grey, Marshall & Co., but ten years later Mr. Marshall took entire control and has built up a trade which covers all the States in the Union. He came from New York to this city near thirty-six years ago and has been closely related with the business interests of Chicago ever since.

Germania Fire Insurance Co.

E. G. Halle, 153 and 155 La Salle Street.

One of the first fire insurance companies of the Union is the "Germania," with head offices at 179 Broadway, New York. The branch in this city is located at 124 La Salle street. This company was incorporated in 1851, while the branch was opened in 1880. This Chicago branch is managed by Mr. E. G. Halle, and the rapid strides made during the past few years bespeak his zeal and activity in the work. At the last audit the company's total assets amounted to the large figure of $2,700,075.63. As showing the careful and sure manner in which the business is carried on, of this sum no less than $1,672,000 is invested in U. S. bonds, and $510,000 in real estate. The bulk of the assets are thus absolutely secure, while it should also be remembered, as an additional safeguard to policy-holders, that this company has accumulated a surplus of $567,341. The rates of premium are very reasonable, and this fact, together with its stability and security, is the reason why it is preferred to many others of a like kind, and why this office is doing one of the finest insurance businesses in the city. Mr. Carl Huncke is the local agent for this city.

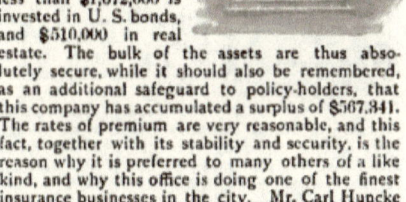

Freiberg's Music Hall.

Henry Freiberg, Proprietor, Nos. 180-182 Twenty-second Street.

One of the interesting features of Chicago is Freiberg's Music hall, at Nos. 180 and 182 Twenty-second street, between State street and Wabash avenue. It is situated on the main floor and has a space of 50 x 115 feet, with a stage 22 x 50 feet in dimensions. The Freiberg block was erected in 1885, but the opera house has just been remodeled and refitted in the latest and most approved style at a cost of $15,000. The stage is fitted with new and fine scenery, and all appliances and machinery necessary for a first-class theater. The fourth floor of the building is fitted up as a large lodge hall for the use of secret societies. It covers an area of 50 x 70 feet. Just across the hallway of this lodge room a gymnasium is being fitted for the use of the S. S. Turners. All the apparatus used by this society is found here, and it is one of the finest arranged halls of the kind in Chicago. The large music hall not only contains fine stage, scenery, and gallery, but also a large dining room, ladies and gentlemen's dressing rooms, etc. It is for rent for balls, concerts, theatricals and other entertainments. The hall is owned by Messrs. Fred and Julius Freiberg, and managed by their brother Henry, who resides in the building, and to whom all communications should be addressed. The Freiberg brothers' orchestra consists of from thirty to fifty pieces and furnishes first-class music for all occasions at reasonable rates. String and brass instruments are used, and some of the best talent in the city is found among its members. The office of the orchestra is at No. 85 Washington street, room 8. They are all natives of Germany and came to Chicago in 1857; later Mr. Fred Freiberg went to New York, and when the war broke out became a member of the famous 7th regiment band. He remained with it for several months at Washington, D. C., and returning joined the 45th New York regiment band. After the war he was for years a member of the renowned Gilmore's New York band.

H. J. Smith & Co.

Publishers, 161 and 163 La Salle Street.

In preparing a reliable exposition, commemorative of the semi-centennial anniversary of the foundation of the city, mention is made of the prominent house in the subscription book business, H. J. Smith & Co., formerly Smith & Miller, who occupy in their relation to the literary world a position of prominence. They also have an office at 249 South Sixth street, Philadelphia, and publish a number of leading works, mostly on theological, medical, historical and biographical subjects, but confine themselves to no particular branch or specialty. Coming here from Wisconsin three years ago, Mr. Smith established his business and has already gained the confidence and esteem of the community and placed his house upon a substantial basis. The prominent subscription books of this firm consist of the "Crown Book of the Beautiful, the Wonderful and the Wise," presenting in attractive form some of the most notable things found in poetic and prose literature, in the works of man and in the works of nature, in history and in biography, in philosophy and in music; "Brave Men and Women, Their Struggles, Failures

and Triumphs," by O. E. Fuller, A. M., author of "The Year of Christ," "Ideals of Life," etc., illustrated; "Wife and Mother, or Information for Every Woman," adapted from the writings of Pye Henry Chavasse, M. D., together with an introduction by Sarah Hackett Stevenson, M. D., of Chicago. The object of this book is to teach a physical redemption for woman, and that she need no longer go down to death's door in giving birth to children. The knowledge contained in it will be a boon to every woman in all stages of life, and we understand the book is having a remarkable sale. "Our World's Great Benefactors;" this work, containing about seven hundred pages, gives brief biographies of nearly one hundred people, both men and women, who have accomplished anything in literature, art, science, discovery, invention, philosophy or philanthropy, that has entitled them to be considered benefactors of the whole world. It aims in this way to give an epitome of the world's work since the introduction of the art of printing and is an invaluable work in any library. Each biography is accompanied by a full-page illustration made expressly for this book at large expense, thus making it doubly interesting and instructive.

The latest work of H. J. Smith & Co. is "Pleasant Hours for Home and School," by Prof. Robert Graham, State Superintendent of Public Instruction for Wisconsin. It consists of four departments. The first three are choice selections for readings and recitations, suitable for all ages and classes. The fourth is for home amusements, and consists of charades, shadow pantomimes, mock trials, etc. It is a work to be desired by every home circle, and will add much to the enjoyment and profit of every individual of the home.

Besides this, we believe, the firm handle an extensive line of juvenile books, bibles and albums, and also supply their customers with any of the standard or trade books, so that their large force of agents throughout the United States and Canada find a business connection with this wide-awake house both pleasant and profitable.

J. N. Hostetter.

Dealer in Coal, Coke, Wood, Hay and Feed, 1136 West Madison Street.

Just across the Chicago, St. Louis and Pittsburgh R. R. tracks on West Madison street is located the office of J. N. Hostetter, a prominent dealer in this neighborhood in all kinds of hard and soft coal, wood and coke, with a side line of hay and feed. The business was established four years ago under the firm name of Hostetter & Townsend, which was dissolved about two years ago, and Mr. Hostetter continued the business alone. He has a force of from three to five men to assist him with the business, and patrons may rely upon having their orders filled promptly. Trade is done with the suburbs as well as city, and a large patronage has been won by fair and honorable methods. Mr. Hostetter is a native of Pennsylvania, and came to Chicago four years ago, although he has been in the State for the past six years.

B. Van Buren.

Druggist and Pharmacist, 1249 Madison Street.

This fine establishment is under the proprietorship of B. Van Buren, a prominent pharmacist of over thirty years' experience. He is a native of New York State, and attended the medical department of the Cooper institute, of New York city. He settled in this city in 1872, and for six or seven years prior to this he was a resident of Lemont, this State. He opened up his present store about eleven years ago, and has established a large and influential trade with this part of the city. He is a dealer in pure drugs, medicines, perfumery, paints, oils, glass, brushes, calcimining and artists' materials, etc. Special attention is given to the prescription department, which is well patronized by the medical fraternity of the West side. Special attention is called to Van Buren's rheumatic compound, being a positive cure for rheumatism and all disorders of the blood or nervous system, especially neuralgia, headache, gout, etc. It contains no minerals, and is not injurious to the system. This article is warranted to cure rheumatism in all its forms, no matter how long standing or the age of the patient. It is purely vegetable. Being already so well known, it needs no comments here. The price is fifty cents and $1 per bottle.

His other noted preparations are malarial globules, dyspeptic elixir, imperial liniment, and diarrhœa and cholera killer. These medicines, especially the compound, are shipped to all parts of the United States, and have relieved and cured thousands, as some of the most flattering testimonials in the possession of the doctor will attest. Mr. Van Buren is proprietor of the large and beautiful opera hall which bears his name. (See cut above.) It is the largest and finest structure of the kind in this section of the city, being fifty by ninety feet in dimensions, and the height of ceiling is twenty-two feet. It is well arranged in the most modern style and has a large and handsomely fitted stage. It is rented at a nominal price for parties and entertainments. Many creditable performances have been given during the past season. On the second floor is a large and finely fitted lodge room, which is in use by the various clubs and societies every night in the week. For further information address the Central Park Pharmacy, 1240 West Madison street, telephone 7007.

Byron A. Baldwin & Co.

Real Estate and Loan Agents, 154 Washington Street.

To certainly attain the greatest measure of security in real-estate investments and the best results, the services of an experienced and reliable agent are always necessary. Prominent among the members of the real-estate fraternity in Chicago is the firm of Byron A. Baldwin & Co., whose offices are located at 154 Washington street, telephone 800. Although the firm has only been in existence since January 1, '86, yet the members of it have been residents of Chicago for years. Their knowledge of property in this city and vicinity is thorough, and investors can in all cases rely on their sound judgment in such matters. The firm consists of Byron A. Baldwin, a member of the Chicago Real-Estate board, and his son Walter S. Baldwin, a notary public, both well-known and influential business men. Their connections are first-class, and include many leading capitalists, and property owners. They make a specialty of negotiating loans on bonds and mortgages, and give the utmost satisfaction in this important branch.

The management and care of estates is another special feature of their business. Rents are collected and remitted promptly, taxes paid, investments made, property sold, and repairs economically attended to at reasonable rates. They are prominent builders and have considerable property on Central Park boulevard, and on Humboldt Park boulevard. Mr. Byron A. Baldwin is a native of Pennsylvania and came to the Garden City in 1864. He is director in the Peoples' Building and Loan association, and is also prominently connected with the R. A. and A. L. of H., of this city. Mr. Walter S. Baldwin was born in Milwaukee, Wis. He graduated from Yale college with honors in the class of '85. He is secretary of the Calumet Council of A. L. of H.

J. H. Hogey.

Pharmacist, 3038 Cottage Grove Avenue.

One of the finest stores in any part of the outside districts of the city is that of Mr. J. H. Hogey, on the corner of Thirty-first street and Cottage Grove avenue. Here a full stock of chemicals and drugs, absolutely pure and fresh, can be obtained. Mr. Hogey manufactures the cologne and cough syrups so largely known and widely used in this neighborhood. His stock includes all well-known preparations of fine toilet and fancy articles, perfumery, nursery goods, mineral waters, etc. Mr. Hogey has been in the business twenty-five years, being thirteen years in business for himself.

The business, which is very extensive, is of a superior class, and the largest in this part of Chicago. The trade is local and suburban, many coming in from Hyde Park, Normal Park and Englewood to trade here. The cable-cars running past the front of the store, and the horse-cars past the side on Thirty-first street, make it readily accessible from all parts. Mr. Hogey has the U. S. postal agency for the accommodation of the public. He is a licentiate in pharmacy for New York city and State, and also for Illinois, and a member of the American and Illinois pharmaceutical associations.

Ed. L. Fowler.

Photographer, 3105 Prairie Avenue.

Mr. Ed. L. Fowler is an artistic photographer of the first order of merit, who is destined to make his mark and achieve high distinction in the photographic art. Mr. Fowler studied under Mr. Barker, the well-known photographic artist, who carried off the first prize at the last photographers' convention at St. Louis, against over one thousand competitors. Mr. Fowler is rapidly achieving distinction, and Mr. Barker himself writes of his work, concerning a portrait made of himself, "I am greatly pleased, would not ask for anything better." He has had eight years' experience in the largest cities of the central and western States, and has lately set up on his own account. His studio occupies the whole second floor of 3105 Prairie avenue, corner of Thirty-first street. The samples of his work seen at his studio bear comparison with any to be found in the city or this country. Mr. Fowler makes a specialty of high artistic finish and re-touching. His photographs are real works of art, and will bear the most minute inspection. Mr. Fowler uses the finest instruments made and best materials, and guarantees all work. The business is large and rapidly increasing, being of the better class. To be properly understood and appreciated, no article would give a correct idea. The work is simply perfect in shading, expression and general finish.

Hollingsworth & Coughlan.

Old Pioneer Contractors, Office 159 La Salle Street, Room 73.

This house are beyond doubt the pioneers in their important avocation in the west, in which it has attained a reputation for skill, care and reliability conceded to but few firms in the country, while their record of thirty years' experience in handling the heaviest and most costly buildings without accident or damage affords their best indorsement. Their specialty is in raising, lowering and moving brick, stone and iron buildings, and for this purpose they have provided a perfect plant of improved machinery, devices and appliances, and spare no pains, time or expense to insure the successful accomplishment of all contracts undertaken. The origin of the house was in 1857, and one year later the firm of Brown & Hollingsworth was organized, which continued until 1860, when Mr. Brown retired, and Mr. Coughlan came in. Mr. Jas. Hollingsworth is a native of Delaware, and Mr. John Coughlan, of Ireland, both of whom are too well known in this community to require any personal mention at our hands, but for the benefit of those who are unacquainted with them, it may not be inappropriate to state that there is no firm in this country better prepared to execute contracts promptly or at more reasonable and just prices.

S A. Kean & Co.

Bankers, Successors to Preston, Kean & Co., 100 Washington Street.

One of the oldest private banking establishments in the city, and withal one of the most sound and reliable, is that of S. A. Kean & Co., of 100 Washington street. The business has been conducted for twenty-five years and has passed most triumphantly through some great commercial crises without its credit having been impaired. It was founded and carried on for many years as the firm of Preston, Kean & Co. A branch office has lately been opened at 205 La Salle street as an adjunct of the Home safety deposit vaults there, of which Mr. Kean is president. A general banking business in all its branches is transacted, such as the receiving of deposit accounts of merchants, bankers, and others; handling government bonds, municipal bonds; discounting commercial paper; foreign exchange, letters of credit, United States land warrants, etc. It is ably superintended by Mr. Kean, who has had direct personal management of both this and the preceding firm. Mr. John Farson, also an able banker, is one of the present firm. He managed the bond department for the old house.

The bank occupies a central position, in a fine stone structure having a frontage on Washington street of forty feet and a depth of eighty feet. It is commodiously and handsomely fitted up in the interior and possesses vaults of remarkable size and strength. The bank is backed up by the highest class of business men and authorities as one of the soundest and most reliable in the city.

Harroun Manufacturing Co.

Manufacturers, Jobbers, and Dealers in Sewing Machine Supplies, 248 Wabash Avenue.

In the city of Chicago no house occupies a greater field of usefulness than the Harroun Manufacturing company, possessing, as they do, every facility for supplying owners of sewing machines and sewing machine agents and dealers with all the many parts of any and every machine made, attachments, oils, needles, etc. They also deal in all varieties and grades of sewing machines, their terms and inducements being, however, unusually favorable to purchasers. Their spacious establishment, occupying the entire second floor at No. 248 Wabash avenue, contains a very large stock of sewing machine supplies, the completeness of which has long since caused this to be regarded as the emporium and supply store for the west. The business dates its origin to the year 1867, when it was established by Mr. H. C. Goodrich, who was succeeded in 1879 by John H. Grant & Co., the latter retiring Jan. 24, 1885, in favor of Messrs. W. S. Harroun & Co., while in 1886 the business had increased so largely as to render an incorporation advisable, which was accordingly effected, Messrs. G. Wallace Smith being president, and John E. Lewis secretary and treasurer. They are both highly regarded in commercial circles, while the enormous volume of their annual sales, which extend all over the country, affords the amplest evidence of the popularity of this useful business which they are successfully conducting.

Jones' City Express & Transfer Co.

Office, 2225 Cottage Grove Avenue.

The majority of our readers, especially on the South side, have no doubt heard of Jones' City Express and Transfer Co., whose office is located at No. 2225 Cottage Grove Avenue. Mr. Theodore W. Jones established the business some score of years ago and by his energy and particular attention to the performance of good work has built up a large and influential patronage among the first families of the city. He employs from twelve to fifteen competent workmen, and is prepared at a moment's notice to supply any number of trucks and express wagons desired. Furniture is moved by a new and improved system, adopted only by this company. Pianos are packed, shipped and removed in a careful manner. All work is done at reasonable rates, while his express-age and parcel-delivery is very cheap, trunks being received from and delivered to all parts of the city, depots, hotels, steamboat wharves, etc., at the nominal price of twenty-five cents, parcels and packages ten cents. Arrangements are also made for the storage of furniture at moderate rates. Mr. Jones is very systematic in all his transactions, the best of order being maintained in all departments of his business. Mr. Jones is a native of Hamilton, Canada, and has been a resident of Chicago for almost a quarter of a century. His telephone number is 8416.

S. E. Cleveland & Son.

Livery, Boarding and Sale Stables, 962 and 964 West Madison Street.

This is one of the oldest stables in the neighborhood, having been established ten years ago, although the present firm has only had charge since May 1, 1886. They have enlarged it to double its original size, it now covering an area of 50 x 200 feet, with upper and lower stabling. It is undoubtedly the largest and finest livery stable on the West side. In the livery department the stock of horses and vehicles kept for hire is among the best to be found in the city, for balls, parties, funerals, and pleasure driving. In the winter the sleighs turned out from these stables are noted for their beautiful appearance and fine finish. We wish to call special attention to their boarding department. They have box stalls—single and double—fitted up for 125 horses, a few being of clay bottom, a specialty which none of the other stables enjoy. They also have a large lot 75 x 100 feet as exercise room. All horses left in their charge receive the strictest care and attention at reasonable prices. Satisfaction is guaranteed in every particular. The telephone number is 7207, and persons coming to the city can have carriages meet them at the depot.

J. Parsons.

Dispensing Chemist and Perfumer, 194 Thirty-first Street, Corner of Prairie Avenue.

One of the largest and finest drug-stores in this neighborhood is that of Mr. J. Parsons. He has had a long experience in the city in this line of business, having been established twenty-three years. He has lately removed to his present fine and commodious store from 1409 Wabash avenue. He has a new and extensive stock of the finest chemicals, drugs, toilet perfumery, patent medicines, etc. He also manufactures largely Parsons' inimitable cologne, which is sold in all parts of the country, and is superior to any other kind in use by the public. Mr. Parsons with his long experience is eminently qualified to make up prescriptions, which he does with care and exactness. The business is large and steadily increasing with the growth of the neighborhood. The residents, being all of the upper class, require only the best quality of supplies, and it is Mr. Parsons' aim to secure the first quality only. He is widely patronized, and has facilities equal to any retail druggist's in the city. His premises include the first floor, 25 x 60 feet, and basement. He employs only experienced help, and may be relied on to give every satisfaction in his power, while the quality of his goods is not to be surpassed.

S. Stein & Co.

Woolens, 197 Madison Street.

One of the largest houses in the woolen goods trade in the United States is that of S. Stein & Co., of Nos. 446, 448 and 450 Broadway, New York. They are directly connected with a large manufacturing firm at Bradford, England, and import large quantities of the finest English broadcloth. They also obtain large supplies from the eastern mills. That such a house should have an agency office in this city is not to be wondered at. The firm long enjoyed a large western trade, but since the opening of this office in October, 1885, this has very considerably increased. This office is located at 197 Madison street, room 2. At present no stock is kept, merely patterns of goods, the orders being supplied direct from the New York house. The old established firm to which this office belongs has long had the reputation of supplying goods of a superior quality and at the most liberal rates. The fact that this business has increased at a most rapid rate in this neighborhood since the opening of this branch proves the wisdom of the step, and the need that existed for the direct representation of so renowned a firm.

J. H. Haake.

Dealer in Staple and Fancy Groceries, 74 Wells Street.

If you enter the above finely appointed grocery store you will find all parties busy as bees filling orders and waiting on the crowd of customers. While waiting our turn we took a survey of the commodious quarters and choice lot of goods displayed. We took note of the prices attached to a number of these articles and were surprised at their low figure, and more so when we came to examine the fine brands of canned goods and the fine quality of the staple and fancy groceries. Mr. Haake receives his butter and eggs direct from the country daily, and all his goods of every description are fresh and pure. His motto is, and always has been, "Good goods at the lowest prices for cash." This, with his honest dealing, has made his business a standard one, and rendered him the most popular grocer on the North side. The business was established in 1853 by Mr. J. D. Haake, father of the present proprietor. He sold out to Wm. Barmuth in 1868, who disposed of it to J. H. Haake in 1877. A competent and polite corps of assistants aid him with the business, which aggregates over $50,000 annually. Mr. Haake is a native of this city, a thorough business man, honorable, fair and liberal in all of his transactions, and richly merits the large and prosperous trade he has helped to establish.

George A. Arnold & Co.

Carpenters and Builders, Rear 82 Dearborn Street, Court Place.

This business is owned by the firm of George A. Arnold & Co., who employ from twenty to fifty hands. Mr. Arnold has been in business in the city since 1856, and has an extensive trade in all branches of carpentering and building, both in the city and suburbs. The firm are ready to undertake any class of work, either jobbing work or by contract, for which they furnish estimates free, and as low as any firm in the city. They employ only skilled workmen upon whom they can rely, and have in their employ cabinet-makers, upholsterers, painters and locksmiths. Mr. Arnold, being a thoroughly practical and experienced man, supervises all the work personally, and is thus able to guarantee perfect satisfaction. Mr. Arnold is well known and esteemed for his thorough business qualities and reliability.

The Guarantee Company of North America.

Chicago Branch, 175 La Salle Street, James Grant, Secretary and Attorney.

The province of the Guarantee Company of North America is to obviate the frequent financial loss consequent upon the defalcation of salaried employes of financial and commercial corporations. It issues bonds of suretyship upon such risks exclusively, maintaining equitable rates, such as will enable it to perform a proper and satisfactory service. At the close of its fifteenth year the position of the company is stronger than at any time in its existence, and far in advance financially of that of any other similar corporation, its resources for the security of policyholders reaching the enormous sum of $896,917, the deposit in the United States for the special and sole security of United States patrons being $240,000. The company was organized Aug. 2, 1871, at Montreal, Canada, where its principal offices and headquarters are situated, and began its United States business in April, 1882, and has now eleven branch offices therein, each with its separate board of directors, besides having agencies in all the principal cities in this country. The Chicago board of directors comprise the following well-known gentlemen: Lyman J. Gage, vice president First National bank; R. R. Cable, president C., R. I. & P. railroad; the Hon. J. Russell Jones, president C. W. D. railway; C. T. Wheeler, president Continental National bank; and E. Nelson Blake, ex-president Board of Trade; Mr. H. P. Collins being inspector, and James Grant secretary and attorney. The company have issued 81,181 bonds, and rejected 7,495 applications, and the records in each case being preserved enables it also to protect employers against undesirable persons. This is the only company that confines its business exclusively to salaried employes, studiously declining to issue bonds for trustees, administrators, guardians, contractors, and similar extra hazardous risks, while the readiness with which its bonds are accepted by the leading banks, railways and commercial institutions is an evidence that its principles are approved.

The Bowman Dairy Co.

Purveyors of a Safe Supply of Pure Country Milk, 68 and 70 North State Street.

This company, who succed M. A. Devine, have recently completed the largest milk house in the west, with a storage room, the sanitary condition of which is perfect in every way. They also have commodious offices, and a fully equipped

laboratory in charge of a practical chemist, C. E. Peck, M. D., graduate of the medical departments of the University of Buffalo and Bellevue Hospital college. It has been their principle and practice through all their business experience to serve their customers honestly. Feeling the necessity of protecting themselves and to be able to guarantee a safe and perfect milk supply to them, they have established a laboratory, and their chemist will analyze samples of the milk from each farm as it is received. By this means they will know not only that the milk has not been skimmed, watered or adulterated, but that the cows have been fed proper food in proper quantities, thus securing a milk supply not only as pure as it is shipped from the country, but fully up to the standard as established by leading experts of England and America, and perfect in its qualities. Then to ascertain that the milk has been received by their customers in perfect condition, their inspector will call on them from time to time to learn of and correct any fault in the service, and bring back to the laboratory samples to be analyzed as often as necessary.

Kuh, Nathan & Fischer.

Manufacturers of Clothing and Jobbers of Woolens, Tailor Trimmings and Cloth, 126, 128, 130, 132 Market Street.

As manufacturers of clothing and jobbers of woolens there is no name in the western metropolis more highly esteemed or widely known than Messrs Kuh, Nathan & Fischer, which since their organization six years ago have always commanded a liberal and influential patronage not of Chicago only, but of the entire great west. The individual members of this co-partnership, Messrs. Abrm. Kuh, Adolph Nathan, and S. M. Fischer, have had long practical experience and a keen appreciation of the requirements of their first-class trade, which have placed them in the highest position in their specialties as manufacturers of men's boys' youths' and children's clothing and jobbers in woolens, cloths and tailors' trimmings. Besides full lines of domestic goods, the firm import direct from the most famous manufacturers of Europe the finest broadcloths, cassimeres, suitings, piece goods, and trimmings, which are absolutely unexcelled in this market, while some idea of the magnitude of the business annually transacted may be drawn from the fact that five entire floors are occupied, each 100 x 150 feet in dimensions, the factory, equipped with the latest improved machinery and appliances, employing over five hundred operatives in the building, not to mention the thousands who take work out to be finished at their own homes. The direct connections of this house with Parisian and London centers of fashion and its facilities for arriving at reliable decisions as to the prevailing modes for any season have made their patterns of clothing as popular in the trade as they are eagerly sought after by the public for their artistic cut, finish and workmanship and reasonableness in price.

H. C. Fisher.

Importer and Jobber in Teas, Cigars, Spices, Baking Powders, Etc., 33 Michigan Avenue.

The commercial metropolis of the west, a proud position attained by the Garden City, although the first half-century has only elapsed since its foundation, has also become the recognized center of the trade in teas, cigars, spices, baking powders, etc., and the interests thus actively identified with Chicago have grown to proportions of the greatest magnitude, in which men of acknowledged ability find profitable employment both for their time and capital. The present well-known house in this line of Mr. H. C. Fisher was established in 1886, removing hither from St. Joe, Mo., where the business was established in 1874, and the advent of a few more such houses cannot fail to add materially to the importance of Chicago as a trade center. Mr. Fisher imports largely of teas from China and Japan, and also cigars direct from Havana, the stock carried requiring the occupation of the entire five-story and basement building, 33 Michigan avenue. The fine quality and reasonable price of these goods have induced a trade extending over the entire west, and as permanent as it is extensive. The activity and enterprise of this house need not be recounted here, since its merit is fully recognized in the trade, and Chicago may well be congratulated on the possession of such an energetic business man as Mr. Fisher is known to be.

The Farm, Field and Stockman.

156 and 158 Washington Street.

The Farm, Field and Stockman is a weekly publication, issued by Howard & Wilson Publishing Co., of 156 and 158 Washington street. It was first issued in 1877 as a monthly publication, but in October, 1885, it was bought by the present company, who changed it to a weekly. It is intended to treat practically the great variety of subjects related to agriculture, stock-raising and fruit-growing, and to afford entertaining and newsy reading for the family. It has a large circulation in every part of the United States and teritories and also in the British provinces, averaging weekly 52,000 copies. The editor is Gen. Charles H. Howard; associate editor, Prof. J. Periam; and business manager, James W. Wilson. This paper is sent to 20,571 post offices, and no State but has its circulation of the Farm, Field and Stockman. Over 25,000 new subscribers have been added since the new management took the paper. The subscription is only $1.50 yearly. Advertising rates were reduced by the present firm from sixty cents to thirty cents per agate line, with discount according to number of lines during the year. Sample copies mailed free on application.

C. B. Allen.

Druggist and Pharmacist, 61 North State Street.

This business was begun six years ago at the same location by the present proprietor, C. B. Allen. He is the only druggist on this street who keeps his store open at all hours, day and night. His quarters are attractively and conveniently arranged, and he enjoys a large and influential patronage. He carries a full stock of drugs, medicines, chemicals, fancy and toilet articles, sponges, brushes, perfumes, etc. A fine assortment of patent medicines and a full line of mineral waters are also found here. Dr. Allen worked for years with Tolman & King, the popular wholesale druggists, before he began business for himself. His long experience enables him to present some of the best compounds ever introduced to the public. They have proven by continued use to be very efficacious in curing the diseases for which they are recommended, and are prepared from absolutely pure materials. The following are among the most prominent: Allen's tonic bitters, liver-wort kidney cure, popular liver invigorator, compound syrup of sarsaparilla with iodide of potassium, concentrated essence of Jamaica ginger, cough balsam, compound laxative elixir, jonquil cologne and a dozen other prominent and reliable medicines.

128   A BUSINESS TOUR OF CHICAGO.

Douglas Club Stables.

**Livery and Boarding, 116 and 118 Thirty-fifth Street,
H. Mather, Proprietor.**

A large and important establishment in this line in the neighborhood of Thirty-fifth street and Rhodes avenue is that conducted by Mr. Mather. It occupies Nos. 116 and 118, having a frontage of fifty feet. The stables afford excellent accommodation for eighty-five horses, and are fitted up in the latest and most approved style, with every convenience. The sanitary arrangements and ventilation are as perfect as can be, and the horses placed in their care are well cared for by experienced hostlers. They have also the best accommodations for boarders' rigs, carriages, buggies, etc. The proprietor, Mr. H. Mather, has also for hire carriages, buggies and surreys, with twenty horses, at the usual rates, making special terms by arrangement. These stables are well patronized, and may be relied upon for the best and most careful attention to the patrons' wants and interests. The business has been in existence over a year, and is a great boon to the inhabitants of this neighborhood. An inspection of the stables and carriage rooms is invited, after which few persons in the district will care to "go further and fare worse."

C. Koehnke.

Music Dealer, 126 Dearborn Street, Room 25.

A most musical race are the Germans. What city or town of importance is there but has its German band? A full supply of music for bands and orchestras especially is imported direct from Germany by Mr. C. Koehnke, of 126 Dearborn street. He carries a good stock of all the latest airs and compositions. He has been established here for the last two years, and is the only house in the city importing direct this class of music. He is the sole agent in the United States for Ed. Kiesler's band and orchestra music. He is well known by the largest music publishers and dealers in this city, and is doing a large and increasing business.

Albert A. Lee.

Manufacturer of Men's, Boys' and Youths' Boots and Shoes, 11 and 13 Dearborn Street.

In 1877 Lee & Runnion established themselves in the business of manufacturing boots and shoes on Franklin street near Lake, the latter, however, only remaining in the firm six months, since which time Mr. Albert A. Lee has been sole proprietor. Mr. Lee is a careful manager, and, himself being a practical workman, employs only those who approach his standard, and he has thus won a strong position among the manufacturers of the city, while trade once secured has been invariably retained. His spacious factory is fitted up with steam-power and the best appliances for the speedy and economical manufacture of men's, boys' and youths' boots and shoes, pegged, screw-nailed and machine-sewed, which, on account both of their durability and reasonable prices, are popular with the public as well as among dealers. Mr. Lee is a Canadian by birth and has resided in Chicago since 1865, and is fully imbued with that push characteristic of our successful business men. He has founded a business that is a monument to his own perseverance, integrity and keen foresight and a credit to this city whose industrial resources are now being reviewed.

L. Dietmann.

Manufacturer of Meerschaum and Amber Goods, 73 South Clark Street.

The finest meerschaum imported from Europe, and obtained from the mines in Asia Minor, is used by Mr. Dietmann in the manufacture of his goods. Amber and jet too are imported, and these products are used up in mouth-pieces, etc., with remarkably good effect. Mr. Dietmann is very skillful and executes some very elaborate modeling and carving in this line, one pipe with a group of horses and horsemen being valued at $35. This work is mostly made to order for the large firms of tobacco and pipe dealers, but the public only have to know that such a clever workman is here to give him their patronage direct. He learnt the trade in Austria, of which country he is a native, and for several years worked in Vienna, coming to Chicago in 1882.

Acme Engraving Co.

L. H. Crumb, Manager, 89 Randolph Street.

Few lines of commercial industry in Chicago are of greater importance than that so ably represented by the well-known house conducted under the title of the Acme Engraving company, whose manager, Mr. L. H. Crumb, a native of New York, is himself a highly skilled artist. He executes the greater part of the finer work with his own deft and cunning hand, leaving the cruder and easier parts to his staff of skilled assistants. All kinds of engraving, wood, photo, etc., are executed for newspapers, publishers and catalogue work, many of the productions being masterpieces of artistic excellence. Their rooms are always a scene of activity, and their patronage, by no means confined to the city, is increasing with rapid strides. Established in 1882, the company was incorporated in the following year, while the continuous success which has followed may be ascribed to their good business methods.

H. F. Orvis & Co.

Grain and Produce Commission Merchants, No. 231 South Water Street.

No exposition of the business interests of Chicago would be complete without mention of the house of H. F. Orvis & Co., one of the conceded representatives of the produce commission business, and whose head and founder is also the esteemed treasurer of the Produce exchange. Mr. Orvis is an old-timer, and has been identified with the trade on the street even prior to establishing business for himself in 1871, at a time when the trade in produce was almost in its infancy, and when, compared with its present colossal proportions, it was utterly insignificant. Mr. Orvis gives his business close personal supervision, the firm handling large consignments of grain and produce of all kinds, upon which liberal advances are made. Shippers and growers can make no mistake in intrusting their business to this energetic and reliable house.

Jacob Boser.

Dealer in Hard and Soft Coal, Office and Yard, 1 to 17 West North Avenue.

To gain an idea of the magnitude of the coal trade of Chicago one has only to enter the large yard of Jacob Boser at Nos. 1 to 17 West North avenue. Here we found a covering over the entire plant, 100 by 300 feet in dimensions, whereby all the coal is kept dry during the entire year. He keeps constantly on hand the best grades of hard and soft coal, and delivers promptly to all parts of the city. He began business in a small way in 1864 on Hawthorn avenue, and has been very successful in establishing a large and growing trade of over 30,000 tons per annum. He moved to his present quarters two years ago, and has the best facilities for the receiving and delivering coal, having a dockage of about 200 feet. Mr. Boser is a native of Germany, and came to Chicago in 1847, and has become one of the successful and representative coal merchants of the Garden City.

Oscar Goes & Co.

Manufacturers of Saws and Knives, All Kinds of Wood-Workers' Tools, Etc., 41 and 43 South Canal Street.

Messrs. Oscar Goes & Co., of 41 and 43 South Canal street, manufacturers of saws, knives, woodworkers' tools, etc., take a prominent place in supplying the numerous houses engaged in the woodworking and furniture manufacturing industries with suitable and necessary tools. They manufacture a full line of saws, making a specialty of fret saws and band saws to meet the requirements of those houses which are engaged in the finer branches of the trade. Mr. Goes was associated at first with Mr. Sweet for eight years; two years ago Mr. Goes dissolved partnership with Mr. Sweet and associated himself with Mr. Albert Brabets, and the premises were changed from 61 to 41 South Canal street. These gentlemen are well known throughout the trade, and the gentlemen engaged in the woodworking business could not do better than call and inspect the factory at 41 South Canal street.

D. W. Ryan.

Manufacturer of All Kinds of Cooperage, 19 to 27 Coventry Street.

This is one of the largest steam cooperage shops in the northwest. It is owned by D. W. Ryan, and has a frontage of one hundred and thirty feet, and extends back to the C. & N. W. railway. The building is three stories in height and fitted up with all the latest improved machinery for this work. In fact, a barrel can be made from the rough oak timber inside of a few minutes by machinery, no hand work being employed upon it. All kinds of cooperage are turned out from this establishment, but the specialty is whisky barrels, kegs and half-barrels. Nearly one hundred men are employed in the shop alone. A large engine of seventy-five horse-power is used to run the vast machinery. Some of the noted machinery consists of the barrel hooper, howel and crozing machine and large stave planers. His oak woods are received from Indiana, Wisconsin and Tennessee, while his iron is received from Cleveland. His trade is altogether local and so great that he turns out 1,500 packages every week.

The old Romans prided themselves on the marble floors of their dwellings, and the proof of their knowledge of its durability is demonstrated by the recent discoveries made in Roman ruins, where the marble mosaic pavement retains its original designs and colors. Of late years, an Italian artist, Mr. Caretti, has introduced this work in some of our new fashioned residences. In his establishment can be found the finest and most beautiful designs of Roman mosaic marble flooring. He has done more towards advancing and rendering popular this style of flooring than any other person in the United States. His workmanship is perfect, and the best of satisfaction is guaranteed. Orders by mail meet with prompt and careful attention. Specimens of his work can be found, not only in many of the fine residences of the prominent men of this city, but in various parts of the northwest. He is his own designer and has nothing but the latest styles, and he sees to it that they are perfectly executed by skilled workmen. He also does all kinds of fresco painting and interior decoration for residences and in this line has done work in some of the finest residences in the west. Mr. John Carretti is a native of Italy and has been a resident of Chicago for the past sixteen years, and we are glad to have such an artist in our midst.

Geo. Rounsavell.

Manufacturer of Cooperage, Office and Factory, 68 to 76 Clybourn Place.

It has been said that machinery can work wonders, but to fully understand the truth of this saying, one has only to visit the noted cooper establishment of Geo. Rounsavell, at Nos. 68 to 70 Clybourn place. Here all parts of a barrel are prepared, put together, and finished by machinery in just one minute's time. When completed they are as perfect as if made by hand. The machinery used is the latest, and is run by an engine of forty horsepower. Although all kinds of cooperage are manufactured, still the specialty is patent white barrels, for which this establishment became noted. The plant occupied and owned by Mr. R. is 125 by 325 feet, while the building is 60 by 110 feet in dimensions and three stories in height. The business was begun in a very small way over a quarter of a century ago, only three men being employed; now eighty men find employment, and over 300,000 barrels, kegs and casks are turned out annually.

Wm. Evers & Co.

General Commission Merchants, 215 South Water Street.

The semi-centennial of Chicago's birth finds the trade in produce one of the most important of her industries, in which the western metropolis is well represented by a large number of responsible and reliable houses, none of whom have achieved either a trade or reputation superior to that of Messrs. Wm. Evers & Co. They have been established since 1882, and from a comparatively small beginning, their business has steadily grown, until now it ranks among the largest in the trade, with a widespread connection among producers all over the west. They possess first-class facilities for the prompt disposal of the largest consignments of country produce of all kinds, and makes a prominent specialty of the choicest creamery butter, taking the entire production of some of our most noted creameries. Mr. Wm. Evers, the head of the house, is one of our war veterans. He is a native of Germany, and came to the United States about twenty-seven years ago. Mr. Evers is a thorough judge of all kinds of produce. This house, as may be inferred, is widely known in the trade, the high estimation in which it is held being solely due to a long course of honorable and liberal dealings with its customers. He has been connected with the commission trade on South Water street since 1870.

Tiffany Pressed Brick Co,

Office, 175 Dearborn Street, Commercial National Bank Building.

The Tiffany Pressed Brick Co. was incorporated in September, 1884, upon a paid-up capital of $150,000, which has since been increased to a quarter of a million dollars. The following are the officers: President (resident of Chicago since 1854), J. Van Inwagen; vice president, Joel Tiffany, the inventor of the celebrated Tiffany refrigerator car; secretary, F. Van Inwagen; business manager, Solomon Snow; superintendent of works, Wm. Alsip. The company have large works at Momence, this State, fifty miles south of Chicago, on the C. & E. I. railway, whose sidetracks run directly to the works, and the line of production consists of the finest pressed brick, both plain and ornamental, made by an entirely new method known as the "Tiffany" process,

by which pressed brick, equal if not superior in quality, color and finish to any produced elsewhere, is being manufactured. The company is a Chicago concern, its headquarters being located here, its officers and stockholders being well-known business men of the city. The works employ a large force of skilled artisans. The intrinsic merit of the "Tiffany" pressed brick has attracted the attention of the leading architects and builders throughout the country, who are unanimous in its commendation.

The following testimonials from representative architects have been shown us by this company: William W. Clay, architect, of Chicago, says: Since the Tiffany Pressed Brick Co. commenced to supply our market. I have used many thousands of their fine pressed bricks, and they have given me great satisfaction. I prefer them to any other red pressed bricks that I know of. Their compactness of texture, and perfection of surface, and beauty of color, all combine to make them a building material of the highest order.

M. L. Beers, architect, of Chicago, says: I have used the Tiffany pressed brick in several buildings that have been under my supervision as architect, and I am highly pleased with them. I take pleasure in recommending them.

Col. Arthur Crooks, architect, of New York, says: I consider the "Tiffany" one of the best bricks I have ever examined, and I feel confident that a ready market would be found here for such a perfect material.

D. Adler, architect, of Chicago, says: The Tiffany bricks that I have seen as samples in your office, and in use as facing bricks on many buildings in this city, are so remarkable for regularity of shape, smoothness of finish, firmness and uniformity of texture, and richness of color, that I must recognize them as the equals of any and the superiors of most of the high-grade facing bricks manufactured in this country.

The certificate submitted from the Chicago Forge and Bolt Co. below shows a strength of material in the Tiffany brick that has never been paralleled:

CHICAGO, ILL., Feb. 21, 1887.
TIFFANY PRESSED BRICK CO.,
175 Dearborn Street, Chicago.

GENTLEMEN: The following is result of tests on brick, by express from Momence, Ill.:

Mark.	Ultimate Crushing Strength.
Hard Building	402,000 pounds.
No. 12 Stock	516,000 "
Ornamental, No. 52	480,000 "
No. 50	648,000 "

Yours Respectfully,
CHICAGO FORGE AND BOLT CO.,
C. Weatherson, Supt.

The Blake Patent Spring Doubletree.

O. D. White & Co., Proprietors.

This doubletree is an improvement in a new direction as redounding to the welfare and comfort of the beast, and appealing also to the idea that a merciful man will be merciful to his beast. This is

the most complete doubletree in use, and is guaranteed to last one-third longer than any other kind, thus making it a cheap article, although it costs a little more in the beginning. As a spring seat is easier to ride on than a common board, so a spring on the doubletree is equally saving on the horse's neck, who can only rely upon the humanity of his owner to provide for his comfort. This spring doubletree makes the load start easy and takes off all the strain and jar from the horse's shoulders, and the load is said to pull one-fourth easier on the team and prevents crippling horses, and prolongs their lives and usefulness, and is thus profitable as well as humane. In starting it allows the horses to firmly set themselves in the harness, and as they pull on the spring it yields gradually until the tension is strong enough to start the load, and when under way it is easily understood how the spring will relieve the jarring or pounding of the shoulders when striking an obstruction and easing off the shock by its elasticity.

The elliptic spring is used, which is the only reliable spring that can be used where great strength, durability and fine action are required. It is made of the very best English spring steel, oil tempered. No coil spring can ever be successfully adapted for this purpose, for reason that the shape and thickness of the steel is such that they cannot be tempered entirely through, consequently they lose their elasticity in a very short time. If you already have a good doubletree the spring and attachments can be furnished, and they can easily be fitted on your doubletree simply by boring two small holes. They are made to fit any size doubletree. These spring doubletrees are especially adapted for farmers on their wagons, plows, mowers and reapers, as it not only prevents the usual shock and strain on the horses' shoulders when the wagon, plow, or machine strikes a stump, stone, or other obstruction, but saves the machine and harness from being broken.

A. L. Campfield.

Commercial Printer, 73 Clark Street.

Amongst all the facilities existing for getting printing done in this city, none offer lower rates for card printing than Mr. A. L. Campfield. He is located at 73 South Clark street, rooms 9 and 11, and here with his four presses and assistants he executes large orders for this class of work. His charge for 1,000 business cards of the ordinary size is $1.00. He is ready to execute other orders for general commercial and jobbing work at equally low rates, but his specialty is card printing. He has been established five years, and is well known as a reliable printer. His customers reside in all parts of the surrounding country, and he as well enjoys a large city trade. He even executes orders for customers residing in Texas and other equally distant States.

John Zengeler.

New York Steam Dye Works, 2323 Cottage Grove Avenue, Corner Prairie Avenue.

Mr. John Zengeler is proprietor of this popular house, and begun the business almost a quarter of a century ago, locating first on Clark street, near Adams. After the big fire of '71, in which he was a heavy loser, he moved to his present large and commodious quarters. He does dyeing and cleaning in all its branches, and has by good work established a large and influential trade throughout all parts of the city and State. Garments are cleaned without ripping or removing trimmings, and the best of care is taken with all articles received, and strict attention given to all work performed. Fifteen competent and efficient hands are employed in the various departments of the business. Mr. Zengeler was born in Bonn, Germany, and came to Chicago thirty-three years ago. This is his life trade, and he has followed it most successfully, and has built up one of the finest houses in this line in Chicago.

J. H. Pank & Co.

Maltsters, Clybourn Place Bridge.

The plant of this large malting establishment covers a whole block, 375 by 450 feet, just east of Clybourn place bridge, and contains buildings four stories in height, which are well arranged with the latest appliances for this business. They have a total capacity of 300,000 bushels of grain. A Corliss engine of twenty-five horse-power is in use, and over 300,000 bushels of malt is produced from this house annually, and is distributed over all parts of the United States. A force of twenty hands are employed to assist with the business. The business was begun about twenty years ago, and has changed hands several times since then. Mr. Pank, who is an old resident of Louisville, Ky., purchased the plant three years ago, and under his able management the business is increasing year by year. He has been interested in the Kentucky Malting company for over seven years, and is now its honored secretary and treasurer.

Fred. P. Rosback.

Manufacturer of Planers, Presses, Light Machinery, Dies, Etc., 224 East Washington Street.

This firm established business six years ago. Repairs to machinery was all the firm attempted till three years ago, when the more important work of manufacturing was undertaken. The class of goods made here is that of presses, planers, jewelers' and tinners' tools, perforating, beveling and slitting machines, bookbinders' machinery and all kinds of special tools and machinery to order. Mr. Rosback is also an inventor, having produced a planer and a knot-tyer, the latter having been purchased by Mr. McCormick and inserted in his great reaping machine.

Mr. Rosback's life is one of interest. Born in Germany, he came to this country in 1851, and resided in Springfield, Ill. In February, 1864, he joined the 7th Illinois regiment and took part under General Sherman in many actions. He obtained an honorable discharge in July, 1866, and went back to Springfield till 1881, when he came and took up his residence in this city. He is a musician, and during the campaign was detailed as leader of the band. Being a thoroughly practical man, and thoroughly understanding the business he is now conducting, it is no wonder that it has met with a large and growing amount of success.

Adolph Kurz.

Carriage, Sign and Ornamental Painter, 582 and 584 North Halsted Street.

At the carriage, sign and ornamental paint shop of Adolph Kurz about a score of men are employed lettering and preparing wagons for dealers of all kinds, and they will be used by the various owners to advertise their trade by their ornamental sides as well as to serve for conveyance. Mr. Kurz has a reputation for good work, which is well attested by the large amount of work constantly on hand. His shop consists of two stories, forty by sixty feet in dimensions. The best of material is always used in his work, and the latest designs and illuminations placed upon trade wagons. Mr. Kurz founded the business twelve years ago at the corner of Blackhawk and North Halsted streets, removing to his present location three years ago. He has resided in Chicago for over twenty-two years and by close attention to business and good work has built up a very large trade.

Robert Stevenson & Co.

Wholesale Druggists, 92 and 94 Lake Street.

Affording an example of a long, honorable and prosperous mercantile career, the house of Messrs. Robert Stevenson & Co., known as "The Old Corner Drug House," justly portrays the present status of the wholesale drug trade in Chicago, in commemoration of whose semi-centennial anniversary these pages are dedicated. Mr. Stevenson, the head and founder of the house, has been continuously engaged in business since 1853 in the present building, with the exception of the short time necessarily occupied in rebuilding the premises after the great fire of 1871. The firm is composed, besides himself, of Messrs. I. Giles Lewis and Arthur Dawson. The house is widely known throughout the west, its extended and influential trade constituting the best indorsement of its methods, occupying, as it does, a place in the commercial world only accorded to the most substantial and reliable concerns. Of the stock but little need be said, other than that it embraces full lines of drugs, chemicals and druggists' sundries, while that the goods are what they should be, and the prices correct, are amply attested in the liberal patronage the firm have always been able to command.

Heinold Bros.

Manufacturers of Fishing, Sporting and Sign Nets, Hammocks, Etc., 15 and 17 Market Street.

Messrs. C. and J. Heinold compose the firm of Heinold Bros., with office at Nos. 15 and 17 Market street. They are manufacturers of fishing, sporting and sign nets. So extensive has the business of this house become that their fishing and sporting nets are used wherever their purposes are indicated. Not only are the brothers manufacturers of these nets for capturing animals, but with dextrous movement they weave a net for protection to the brute creation, as shown in the widely-known fly nets for horses. In addition to being extensively engaged in knitting, they afford ease and pleasure in the hammocks produced at their establishment. In addition to this they are known as dealers in cordage and twines of all kinds, sizes and weights.

H. D. Casteel.

Manufacturer of Havana Cigars and Dealer in Leaf Tobacco, 95 and 97 Adams Street.

The extent and importance to which the cigar trade has attained in Chicago can scarcely be understood by those not actually engaged therein. Conspicuous among the foremost establishments engaged in this line in Chicago is the well-known and extensive concern conducted by H. D. Casteel, manufacturer of Havana cigars and dealer in leaf tobacco, Nos. 95 and 97 Adams street, established originally in Indianapolis, Indiana. After a prosperous business for eight years he was burned out in 1873, suffering a total loss of his business. He then moved to Chicago, settling on the West side, where again, in 1884, after having established a good trade, he was once more burned out and lost all he had. Since locating in his present premises he has suffered two heavy robberies, sustaining total loss each time. Through all his adversity he has been undaunted, and has now a fine trade. Mr. Casteel is one of our war veterans, going to the front in 1861, where he served the full period of his enlistment—three years —and, upon its expiration, re-enlisting, serving till its close, two years later, with the fall of Richmond and the surrender at Apomattox, and though made a prisoner three separate times, was so fortunate as to escape each time with less than four months' detention in rebel prisons, in which the records show that fully as many Union soldiers perished as laid down their lives on the field of battle in the cause of liberty.

Geo. W. Hoyt & Co.

Dry Goods Commission, 241 to 245 Monroe Street.

Among the representative houses in the dry goods commission business in Chicago the firm of Geo. W. Hoyt hold a conspicuous position, both as regards the volume of trade done and the standard grades of goods handled. The house was established in 1871, the year memorable of the great fire. The transactions of the firm extend to all points usually reached by the proverbial enterprise of Chicago business concerns. The house are really the pioneers in the special branch of staple notions, braids, etc., and in this line they are always prepared to offer special inducements to the trade, and of a quality and standard excellence which is characteristic of this house.

Geo. W. Hoyt, the head of the firm, is a gentleman of much and varied experience in this branch of trade, which valuable experience is available to patrons in relying upon his judgment as to quality of goods sold to them, the good faith of which has never been abused by such reposed confidence.

Merchant & Co.

Importers of Tinplate, Metals, Etc., 202 Lake Street.

In that important branch of industry, the tinplate and metal trade, Messrs. Merchant & Co. do a very large and growing trade, their operations extending throughout the western States, and many of the goods of their handling finding their way even to the Pacific slope. Their spacious salesrooms contain a very large stock of tinplate, sheet copper and brass, seamless brass and copper tubes, seamless copper house boilers, Russia, galvanized and black iron, sheet zinc, reservoir metal, brass, copper and iron wire, "Gilbertson's Old Method" and "Camaret" guaranteed roofing plates. Root's spiral formed pipe and pumps, together with tinners' tools and machines, and also the tin and roofing plates in both regular and odd sizes. The exceptional advantages to be derived through purchasing here will thus at once be recognized by manufacturers and jobbers, especially when they realize the extent, character and variety of metals and specialties carried by this enterprising firm. The house is an old Philadelphia one, their headquarters being in that city at Nos. 525 Arch and 520 Cherry streets, their New York branch being at No. 9 Burling slip. They also established a branch house in London, England, on January 1, 1887.

H. J. Nagle.

Ornamental Confectioner and General Caterer, 175 Twenty-second Street.

The fine establishment of H. J. Nagle is located at No. 175 Twenty-second street, where he carries on an extensive trade as an ornamental confectioner and general caterer, fine creams being a specialty. His store is fitted up in the most attractive manner, with a view to securing absolute cleanliness and comfort. His Ice-cream parlor is tastefully arranged and decorated, and obliging attendants look after the wants of the patrons. In the manufacturing department Mr. Nagle brings a life of practical experience to bear upon the fine production of creams, ices, cakes and confectionery of all kinds. His reputation in this line is attested from the fact that he receives the highest prices for his goods, and is being constantly called upon to serve wedding occasions, parties and receptions, balls, birthday aniversaries, etc., with his productions. He makes to order and delivers the choicest plain French and fancy creams of all varieties, also frozen fruits, souffles and waterices of all desirable flavors. The very choicest ingredients only are used, the sugar being the best refined, the cream pure, rich and fresh, and the fruits the best in the market. Mr. Nagle has been in business here since 1882, when he came from his native place, Jeffersonville, Indiana. Besides his Twenty-second street establishment, Mr. Nagle has a beautiful little

caravansery near South Park station, known as the Rosalie cafe, which is largely patronized by visitors to that delightful suburban place of recreation. At this place he does a large business in the season, and many visitors to the Garden City as well as dwellers therein can testify as to the character of the delicacies provided, and the pleasure of a visit to the Rosalie cafe. Taken altogether Mr. Nagle is probably one of the most prominent and successful caterers of Chicago, and is popular with all classes and rapidly building up a flourishing business.

Alfred Payne.

Portrait and Landscape Painter, Lakeside Building, Southwest Corner Clark and Adams Streets.

To lovers of the beautiful in art the handsomely appointed studio of Mr. Alfred Payne, to which visitors and pupils are admitted from 1 to 5 P. M., presents many attractions, as upon its walls are to be found many pictures that bear the indubitable stamp of originality of conception and marked artistic ability. Mr. Payne is a native of England, and has been permanently located in Chicago for the past fourteen years, and is well known in her leading art and social circles. In his specialty, portrait and landscape painting, he is prepared to execute commissions, and in addition has on exhibition a choice collection of works, the products of his own facile brush, which he offers at remarkably reasonable prices. He has profited by a thorough, practical training, which, coupled with his natural adaptability to his profession, has enabled him to attain to his present enviable position as a portrait and landscape artist.

A. J. Cameron & Co.

Worsted and Woolen Yarns, 77 Market Street.

One of the chief branch businesses carried on in this city is that of A. J. Cameron & Co., manufacturers of worsted and woolen yarns, with store and offices at 77 Market street. This firm manufactures the worsteds extensively known as the "Thistle" brand worsteds, so successfully handled by jobbers throughout the country. Their long experience and thorough knowledge of all the details of the business enable them to supply manufacturers with all kinds of yarns suited to the various purposes of knitting, weaving, crocheting, etc. Wool is the only staple they use in the manufacture of their goods.

The firm consists of Messrs. Alex. J. Cameron, Alpin J. Cameron and William P. Denegre, and the chief office is at 85 Walker street, New York, with mills in Massachusetts and Philadelphia. The business is an old established and substantial concern. The branch office was opened in Chicago by Mr. Denegre, and has been established for years on Market street, and consists of first floor and basements, together with warehouse. The business is solely with manufacturers and jobbers, and the firm has a large city and country trade. Their present manager Mr. Ayers has been with them some time, and devotes his energies particularly to the wants of manufacturers and knitters in general.

The yearly sales are large and increasing. The firm invite and defy competition in the matter of price and quality for anything in their specialty of worsted and woolen yarns. The business tourist will find other firms in this line of business in this city, but none possessing more stability or higher business qualities than this we have visited and described.

Charles E. Rand.

189 La Salle Street, Manufacturing Sites on the Calumet River.

Within the past few years a number of large manufacturing industries have sought the Calumet region (fifteen miles south of Chicago) as the place best fitted, by reason of its unexcelled railway and water facilities, for conducting such business. Added to this inducement was of course the low price at which the land could at that time be bought or leased. Ten years ago property at the mouth of the Calumet river was worth a few hundred dollars per acre; now it is worth as many thousands, and within a few months one piece of ten acres was transferred for $100,000.

The village of Hegewisch, the site of the United States Rolling Stock company, is situated at the forks of the Calumet, and the railways projected, added to those already in operation at the point (seven in number), will probably make the locality one of the greatest railroad crossings in this part of the country. The government will soon begin widening and deepening the river to admit of the passage of vessels drawing fifteen feet of water.

Splendid manufacturing sites, dock property, or acres for subdivision into lots can be purchased at low prices today. Mr. Rand will be happy to send maps and information and to accompany investors to the locality at any time.

Val. Blatz.

Chicago Branch, Corner Union and Erie Streets, Henry Leeb, Manager.

The reputation of Milwaukee beer is co-extensive with the country. Whatever be the reason therefor, careful management, judicious brewing, using only pure and select ingredients, or larger experience, it matters not, the fact still remains that Milwaukee beer ranks at the head of all American beers, not in Milwaukee alone, but all over the continent, and the sales are growing more extensive every year. In the manufacture of his beer, Mr. Blatz uses none but selected and pure ingredients; nothing but hops and barley malt enter into its manufacture. As a tonic for invalids it is incomparable, as an invigorating, nourishing and pleasant beverage it is unsurpassed. Realizing that his extending trade necessitated careful management and depot facilities at this point, where the consumption was rapidly growing, and the facilities for transportation were so favorable, he in 1865 established his Chicago branch.

At the Philadelphia exposition the Val. Blatz beer was awarded a gold medal, the highest premium, for its excellent qualities and because it excelled in point of body, flavor and purity. The fact remains that the beer has won an international reputation for its unsurpassed quality, and in order to satisfy the demands of the trade, agencies have been established in all of the leading cities in the United States and elsewhere. During the recent exhibition held at New Orleans, a wonderfully unique and well-adapted exhibit was displayed, representing Mr. Blatz's manufacture, which has been described at length in the daily papers, owing to its grandeur, and which no visitor passed by unnoticed. The grounds and buildings at the corner of Union and Erie streets cover eight city lots. Mr. Leeb, the manager, has the ability and experience in a high degree to fill his responsible position. Courteous, obliging and strictly honorable, he is extending the reputation and trade of the Blatz brewery.

Henry T. Nichols & Co.

General Agents for Bass & Co., and Pale and Burton Ales, 214 and 216 Washington Street.

Nothing does the average Englishman miss so much on coming to this country as his ale. This city possesses a branch of the house of H. T. Nichols & Co., 58 Broad street, New York, importers of Bass & Co's pale Burton ales, so well known all over England, also of their extra and imperial stout. They also import Guinness & Co's Dublin extra stout. Nothing can be too enterprising for a go-ahead city like Chicago, and accordingly we find a branch office which will deliver at our very doors these luxuries so well known the other side the water. The first floor and basement of 214 and 216 Washington street are occupied with these goods. Since this branch was opened, three years ago, the trade has increased fourfold, being chiefly done with city firms and residents, but also with the country towns as far distant as Dakota, Denver, Kansas, St. Paul and Minneapolis coming in for a good share. Supplies are obtained by direct shipment from England and also from the New York house. A large stock is kept, and the yearly sale already amounts to $70,000. The manager of this branch is Mr. J. Murphy, who has been very active in forwarding the business at this point.

George B. Whitman.

Commission Dealer in Pine Lumber, 196 La Salle Street, Room 16.

Of such houses as that of Mr. George B. Whitman, their very existence is the most emphatic evidence of the honorable position they occupy and the long course of faithful dealing they have pursued, whose business character it is a pleasure to record. Mr. Whitman was for years engaged in the lumber trade in Michigan, and since establishing his business in Chicago some ten years ago has developed a trade of such magnitude as to become a most important addition to the industries of this great city, the admitted lumber market of the United States. He handles exclusively on commission pine lumber, lath and shingles, and enjoys an extended connection which enables him to promptly dispose of the largest consignments, upon which liberal advances are made when desired. Mr. Whitman also handles largely white and yellow pine lands, in which he is prepared to offer such inducements as prudent lumbermen cannot afford to ignore, dealing as he does only in such as he can personally guarantee, and of whose soundness of title in his principal, indubitable evidence is in his possession.

Red Star Line.

Wasmansdorff & Heinemann, Western Passenger Agents, Southwest Corner Randolph and La Salle Streets.

An imposing shipping office is that on the southwest corner of Randolph and La Salle streets. Here the Red Star line is ably represented by Messrs. Wasmansdorff & Heinemann, bankers, etc., this company, of which Peter Wright & Son are general agents, having their main offices at New York, Philadelphia, Boston, Antwerp and this city. The line consists of ten large steel and iron built full-powered steamers, which carry neither sheep, horses, cattle nor pigs, but which are fitted throughout in the latest and most perfect manner for the transportation of passengers. The tonnage ranges from 3,000 to 6,000. Six of the vessels run between Antwerp and New York, and the other four between Antwerp and Philadelphia, leaving Antwerp and New York every Saturday. This line carries the mails of Belgium and the United States. They run in connection with the Pennsylvania railroad. The accommodations on these vessels are unsurpassed, and the second cabin rates have just been reduced to

$45. The rates are as low as by any other first-class line, and it is a fact that this line has run its steamers with unprecedented regularity and punctuality without the loss of a single life. All further information, rates, time of sailing, etc., will be readily furnished on application to this office.

A. L. Luetgert.

Summer Sausage Works, 69 and 71 North Avenue.

Almost everything in the line of work in this establishment is done by hand, over fifty men being employed in the various departments. A large steam boiler of fifteen horse-power is used. Everything is scrupulously clean and kept in the best of

order. The factory is of brick, four stories in height, and covers an area of 40 by 48 feet. It is only run from the 1st of October to the 1st of April. Not one pound of these goods is sold in the city, but find a ready market all over this country, and some is shipped to Germany. The business was begun in a small way at Nos. 105 and 107 North avenue, in 1880, but it grew so rapidly that the present large quarters were obtained a few years ago to increase the facilities demanded by the trade. A stock worth from $30,000 to $50,000 is constantly kept on hand, while the sales reach upwards of $100,000 per annum. Mr. Luetgert is a native of Germany and came to Chicago in 1866 and has become one of the representative men in his line of trade. He is not only owner, but fills the position of manager and overseer of his factory, every detail coming under his personal notice, thereby assuring success in all the departments of his large and rapidly increasing business.

Alburger, Stoer & Co.

Manufacturers and Importers Tailors' Trimmings, 228 and 230 Fifth Avenue.

A branch of industry of growing importance in the west, and more especially in Chicago, is that denominated under the head of tailors' trimmings, while one of the most enterprising houses in this line is that of Messrs. Alburger, Stoer & Co. The house is an old Philadelphia concern, and one of the oldest in the country, naving a purchasing agency at Bradford, England, and a branch in this city, opened three years ago, under the efficient management of Mr. J. R. Terhune, a gentleman well known in mercantile circles, and who brings a wide range of practical experience to bear. Spacious premises are occupied, and a large and well-selected stock of tailors' trimmings carried, mainly of their own manufacture and importation. Their facilities for the transaction of business are of an unusually complete character, enabling them to place the latest novelties in the market, and to fill all orders promptly at lowest market rates. The firm are noted for their liberality in business transactions, and Mr. Terhune, being an enterprising, pushing business man, is achieving a well-merited success, and largely advancing the interests of his house in the west.

Wasmansdorff & Heinemann.

Bankers, 66 La Salle Street, Southwest Corner of Randolph Street.

The firm of Wasmansdorff & Heinemann has long been known in business communities of this city as one of the most reliable and honorable houses engaged in the banking business. They occupy commodious offices, centrally located, on the corner of Randolph and La Salle streets, where they have been located since 1883. The business consists chiefly in the investment of moneys in good securities, especially in real estate. This kind of property is also bought and sold extensively by this firm in all parts of the city and suburbs. Loans are made on the most liberal rates, but are confined to this county. A large deposit business is done with this firm, for they enjoy to a large extent the confidence of the business part of the community, and deservedly so, for they have made it their object to act fairly and honorably in all transactions. On certificate deposits, that is, deposits that will not be withdrawn for a specified time of twelve months or over, interest of four per cent. is allowed.

Chas. Stattmann & Co.

Manufacturers and Importers of Sealskin Garments, Fine Furs, Etc., 216 and 218 Monroe Street.

An active experience of over a quarter of a century as a practical furrier has eminently fitted Mr. Chas. Stattmann, the head of the responsible house of Chas. Stattman & Co., and given to his house a special degree of prominence in the manufacturing fur trade. Becoming a resident of this city some thirty years, ago Mr. Stattmann established himself in business in 1876 at No. 314 West Madison street, removing two years later to No. 85 Madison street, and by May 1, 1885, his business had so largely increased as to compel him to seek his present commodious quarters at that time. The premises are fifty by one hundred feet in dimensions, and over fifty skilled workmen find here remunerative employment the year round in the manufacture of sealskin garments, fine furs, caps, gloves, muffs, trimmings, robes and coats, that embody the choicest furs that are found on this continent or imported from Europe, and made up under his personal supervision in the highest style of workmanship. Mr. Stattmann is an acknowledged authority on furs, and handles skins only that are procured from first hands direct, and is thus enabled to offer his handsome goods at prices difficult to duplicate elsewhere.

August Schwarz.

Boston Fancy Steam Dye House; Store, Office and Works, 156 and 158 Illinois Street.

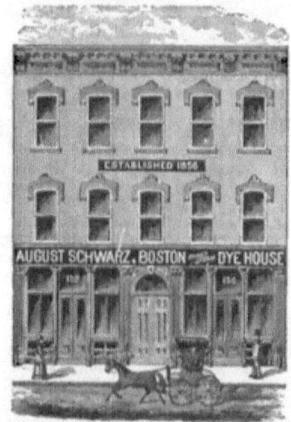

The store, office and works of this prominent establishment are located at Nos. 156 and 158 Illinois street, while the branch offices are at No. 190 South Clark street and No. 505 West Madison street. Every description of silks, satins, velvets, crapes, ribbons, woolen or mixed goods, shawls, cloaks, clothes, alpacas, reps, curtains, fringes, trimmings, hosiery, gloves, etc., are cleaned, dyed and finished in the most perfect manner. All kinds of merchant's goods also receive prompt attention. Gentlemen's coats, pants and vests are cleaned, dyed and repaired promptly and in the latest and best style. Crape veils are beautifully cleaned. Ladies' suits, in silk, pongee, woolen and mixed goods, also embroidered sacques, wrappers, etc., cleaned by the dry-cleaning process. This process is acknowledged superior to any method ever introduced in this country. It does not necessitate the ripping of the garment, or the removal of even the most delicate trimmings. The goods are not shrunk; the luster and finish are preserved; the most delicate colors are not injured; all expense of making up is saved. This applies to velvet trimmings as well. All kinds of carpets are cleaned, plumes are cleaned, dyed or curled, kid gloves are cleaned and dyed black. All articles received are carefully inspected, and an stains are taken out before dyeing. The business was established in a small way, in 1856, on the site where it now stands, and by good work, prompt and liberal business policy, Mr. Schwarz has built up a large and rapidly increasing trade extending over all parts of the Union. He employs from thirty to forty hands in the various departments. He is a native of Germany, was born in Wurtemburg in 1824. This is his life trade, which he learned in his native country, and followed throughout various portions of the empire. He was foreman for a long time in one of the largest establishments in Germany. He has been a resident of Chicago for the past thirty years, and has done much to build up its industry and add to its fame.

A. Goodrich.

Attorney and Counselor at Law and Loan Broker, 124 Dearborn Street, Room 1.

Perhaps one of the best known of Chicago lawyers is Mr. A. Goodrich, attorney and counselor at law, notary public and loan broker.

He has been established at 124 Dearborn street for twenty-one years. He was in the same place before the fire and only removed for a few months during the close of 1871, till the buildings were erected. He does a business in real estate, handling only his own property, which lies in most advantageous positions on the West and South sides of the city. He also makes loans on real estate, bonds and collaterals. He is, however, chiefly known in connection with his legal practice, which is very extensive and lucrative. His office is central, and he is generally looked upon as one of the most able and reliable legal advisers and attorneys in the States.

J. B. Rogan & Co.

Commission Merchants, Grain, Seeds and Provisions, Insurance Exchange, 218 La Salle Street.

The course of the grain trade westward has been rapid and steady. Thirty years ago Buffalo commanded the entire trade of the country; a few years afterward Toledo received the greater portion of the wheat and corn of the west. Eventually, however, the center of production changed to the Mississippi valley, and Chicago, lying on the shortest railway lines and water-ways to the eastern seaports, became the natural market for the world. The unrivaled facilities and resources of the western metropolis have been greatly developed by the energy and enterprise of such representative members of the board of trade as Messrs. J. B. Rogan and Thomas Gregg, whose house, J. B. Rogan & Co., was established in 1865. The firm transact a general business in grain and provisions and are highly esteemed on the floor for their excellent business methods and inflexible integrity and have ever given a conscientious support to all measures conducive to the benefit and permanent welfare of this national institution. In every respect this house may be considered a representative one, all its operations being conducted strictly in accordance with the rules of the board, and with a single eye to the interest of their patrons, so that business relations entered into with them are sure to prove pleasant for the time being and satisfactory to all concerned.

Washington Foundry & Machine Shop.

13 North Jefferson Street, Holmes, Pyott & Co., Proprietors.

Visitors to Chicago who have been in the vicinity of new building operations of late years will have been struck with the quantity of iron that is now introduced into the work, both to strengthen and beautify the structures. Messrs. Holmes, Pyott & Co., of the Washington Foundry and Machine Shop, No. 13 North Jefferson street, do a very large business in this particular line. They commenced on the South side twenty-four years ago, but after remaining there three years they removed to their present location. They have a perfectly equipped foundry and machine shop and employ seventy-five men. All kinds of shaftings and pulleys are manufactured by them, and they do a large trade in printing-presses, notably the Chicago stop-cylinder press. They have business in every large city in the country, and their work gives universal satisfaction. Messrs. Holmes, Pyott & Co. are the owners of the very extensive block in which their own works are situated, and they supply the motive power to fifteen other manufacturing concerns from a large two hundred horse-power engine, which is of their own manufacture, this, by the way, being the fourth large engine that they have turned out for themselves. The Messrs. J. M. and D. Pyott are Scotchmen, and they are well supplied with that native foresight and perseverance for which their countrymen are proverbial. The other member of the firm, Mr. E. B. Holmes, is an American-born citizen. Between them these gentlemen have organized and successfully built up a most extensive connection, and their name is a synonym for strict honesty and integrity in all commercial transactions.

Lafrentz & Karstens.

Kinzie Street Feed Mill, 259 East Kinzie Street, Telephone 3029.

A tour through the Kinzie Street Feed Mill will convince anyone of the extensive business of Messrs. Lafrentz & Karstens, which, although entirely local, amounts to upwards of $200,000 per annum. They are wholesale and retail dealers in grain, hay and all kinds of mill feed. They occupy three floors, twenty five by one hundred feet in dimensions. Besides the firm, there are six hands and four teams employed in all departments of the business. Smith & Lafrentz was the name of the firm that begun the business eighteen years ago, but about ten years ago the present firm took charge, and by energy and first-class stock of goods, have established their large and growing trade. Mr. Lafrentz is an honored member of the board of trade. The firm are both natives of Germany, and for years have resided in Chicago, and been connected with its interests and commercial advancement.

Mikkelsen & Bendtsen

Manufacturers of Store and Office Furniture, Tables, Counters, Signs, Etc., 74 and 76 West Washington Street.

Prominent in this branch of business we mention the popular and important firm of Mikkelsen & Bendtsen, of Nos. 74 and 76 West Washington street. These gentlemen do a large manufacturing business and a general jobbing trade in office and store furniture, tables counters, signs, etc. Their factory is replete with every modern improvement in the way of wood-working machinery, and they employ ten skilled workmen. Their principal patrons are among the wholesale furniture houses, but they make a specialty of contract work in fitting up stores, etc., in all styles of hard and soft wood furniture. The members of the firm are both Danes by birth and have been associated in their present undertaking for the last six years. They have established a very enviable reputation for good workmanship and liberality in their business dealings. They are very obliging and courteous, and are much esteemed by their large circle of friends and patrons.

H. Philippi.

Bar Glassware and Bar Utensils Generally, 276 State Street.

In the line of bar glassware and bar utensils generally, the most prominent position in the community is indisputably held by Mr. H. Philippi, who, since embarking in business in 1878, has been successful beyond his most sanguine expectations. He occupies two entire floors, each 25 by 125 feet in dimensions, the whole being admirably lighted, well appointed and neatly and tastefully arranged. His trade is largely retail, although he enjoys an extensive wholesale patronage, extending for hundreds of miles in every direction, while many of the first-class hotels, restaurants and saloons obtain all their glassware, chinaware and utensils from this house, well knowing that everything needed, from the finest imported glassware to the goods of American manufacture, may here be obtained without delay, and at reasonable prices. Of the stock, but an inadequate idea can be conveyed. Suffice it to say that it embraces every desirable article comprehended under the generic headings of bar, hotel and restaurant glassware, chinaware and utensils, and the fact that the goods and prices are what they should be is fully attested by the extensive trade which this reliable house has always been enabled to do.

The Troy Steam Laundry Co.

147 Twenty-second Street.

This business was begun by the present proprietor, H. W. Howe, three years ago. It is systematically conducted in the several different departments, each being in the hands of skilled workmen, assisted by labor-saving machinery of the most approved style and designs. They have all the facilities for rapid and first-class work. From twelve to fifteen hands find employment here. Particular attention is devoted to shirts, collars, cuffs and ladies' fine underwear. Orders by mail are promptly attended to, and goods are called for and delivered in all parts of the city. The trade, although entirely local, is quite large, and gives evidence of still greater increase. Mr. Howe is a native of the State of Massachusetts, and has been a resident of this city for the past sixteen years. He entered the war of the rebellion as a soldier in the 10th Massachusetts volunteers. In conclusion, we cheerfully commend the Troy steam laundry to our many readers, feeling assured that all business relations with them will be pleasant and satisfactory.

Frederick Baumann.

Architect, Room 32, Metropolitan Block, Randolph and La Salle Streets.

The profession of an architect is a very difficult one, requiring constant study, and, in addition, a practical training in active service and a thorough scientific and mechanical education, and it does seem a little remarkable, since the architect, equally with the chemist, holds our lives and health in his power, that the one profession should be surrounded with stringent regulations by law, inclusive of a severe examination, and the other by none. The essential requisites for a competent and skillful architect are found in a marked degree in Mr. Frederick Baumann, who has been engaged in the practice of his profession in Chicago since 1853, and is the first of German architects in the city. Proofs of his skill are very numerous throughout the western metropolis as embodied in the many splendid buildings he has designed, and which have been erected under his supervision during the past thirty-four years. He employs a full force of competent draughtsmen, and bases his estimates upon the most practical and comprehensive knowledge of quantities and value. Born in Germany in 1820, he received his education in Berlin, and in 1850 came to Chicago, where in business circles generally he is regarded as one of our most solid men.

Eureka Foundry.

Kolben Johnson, Proprietor, Manufacturer of Light and Heavy Castings, 122, 124 and 126 South Jefferson Street.

Mr. Johnson is engaged in the manufacture of light and heavy castings of every description, and he makes a specialty of printing-press work. The foundry is well equipped with all the necessary ma-

chinery and gives employment to a full force of workmen. Mr. Johnson does a large and increasing trade, exclusively in the city. He has been at his present undertaking for the last eight years, although his connection with this business extends back to a much longer time. Mr. Johnson is a native of Norway, and has been in this country for nineteen years. His energy and perseverance have been rewarded, and he is now at the head of a most prosperous and thriving business. The above cut gives a good idea of this establishment.

Cook, Hallock & Gammon.

Dealers in Lumber, Sash, Doors, Blinds, Etc.; Planing Mill, 53 to 63 North Avenue.

The establishment of Cook, Hallock & Gammon is one of the representative, live business houses of the city of Chicago. Their planing-mill is one of the most complete in the city, while their yard is full of the choicest lumber in the market. They are located at Nos. 53 to 63 North avenue, with one hundred and sixty feet front and a depth of one hundred and twenty-five feet. The business was begun in 1871 under the firm name of Cook & Hallock, but four years ago was changed to the present firm. In their planing-mill the specialty is sash, doors and blinds, while re-sawing and carpenter job-work is done to order in the most satisfactory manner. From fifty to eighty skilled workmen find employment here, and their trade, which extends throughout all parts of the city, amounts to from $150,000 to $200,000 annually, and is rapidly increasing. Their planing-mill contains the latest improved machinery, which is run by an engine of eighty horse-power. They enjoy a liberal patronage in every branch of their business, which is accounted for by the good management and fair dealings of the firm.

J. F. Freitag.

Manufacturer of Carriage and Cab Lamps, 4 La Salle Avenue.

Mr. Freitag is a prominent manufacturer of carriage lamps, hook and ladder truck and hose cart lamps, fire engine signals and trumpets, hub caps, curtain rollers and carriage candles of all sizes. Mr. Freitag is a thorough and experienced workman in this line of trade, having filled the position of foreman for the house of A. H. Heyner for years. The premises occupied are convenient and well arranged for the business. None but the best workmen are employed, and he gives his close personal attention to every department of his large business, which extends throughout all parts of the city and the country generally. Re-plating and repairing is a specialty and no more reliable house can be found with which to do business. Mr. Freitag is a native Chicagoan and well known in business circles.

Heer & Seelig.

Manufacturers of Engineers' and Surveyors' Instruments, 192 and 194 East Madison Street.

The most prominent house engaged in the manufacture of these goods in the west is that of which Messrs. Peter Heer and Roman Seelig are the proprietors. Both are German by nativity and highly skilled workmen, and have, since organizing their firm as successors of R. L. Strassberger four years ago, built up a business throughout the country, which fully entitles them to be classed as among the most enterprising engaged in this line. The machinery used at their factory for the manufacture of these goods is the most exact and accurate made, and, employing only highly skilled artisans, the firm have been able to successfully defy competition both as to excellence and price. They make rules and other measures to any fraction of an inch desired, their output being universally regarded by engineers and others as the best now offered either in this country or Europe. Their spacious store contains a large stock of all those many useful instruments used by the architect, draughtsman and surveyor, including the many varieties of chains, rods, tapes, rules and measures, as well as transits, levels and compasses arranged in handsome cases and boxes, or singly, as may be desired, especial attention being also given to repairing and adjusting, and all goods are put to the severest tests before being offered for sale.

La Verne W. Noyes.

Manufacturer of Dictionary Holders, 99 and 101 West Monroe Street.

One of the most useful inventions of recent issue is the dictionary holder, and its manufacture is carried on in Chicago by Mr. La Verne W. Noyes, at 99 and 101 West Monroe street. Mr. Noyes has been engaged in this business since 1879, and has established a very large connection among the principal wholesale booksellers in the country. The dictionary holder is an article that has taken a great hold on the public, and the demand for it is steadily increasing. Mr. Noyes is equal to the occasion, however, and keeps pace with the times. He employs a staff of skilled workmen, and himself personally superintends all the details of the factory. Mr. Noyes is an American, and has been long and closely connected with the rise and progress of our great city.

B. W. Eisendrath & Co.

Importers and Dealers in Window and Plate Glass, 117 and 119 Lake Street.

The house of B. W. Eisendrath & Co. may be fitly considered among the representative firms of its kind in Chicago, their business having developed apace with the growth of commerce throughout the west. They have neglected no opening which presented itself nor failed to retain the trade which the unsurpassed quality of their goods and liberal terms have secured, the patrons of the house being found in every portion of the United States. The house was founded in 1881, and occupies spacious premises, carrying the largest stock in the west of enameled and colored glass, cathedral glass, car, coach and picture glass, French and German mirror and plate glass and American window glass. The success of the house has been brought about by the exercise of

ability and enterprise, coupled with a strict adherence to mercantile integrity, and in every respect is typical of Chicago's remarkable progress, whose semi-centennial anniversary is now at hand.

Sears & Sears.

Designers and Engravers, 126 Dearborn Street.

This is one of the most reliable and skillful firms of wood engravers in the west. Their office is at

126 Dearborn street, where a number of skilled artists and workmen are employed. Their long experience enables them not only to make drawings from nature or manuscript, but also to engrave, print and bind a complete book ready for the public, and could, if called upon, furnish the manuscript on any given subject. They graduated from the firm of Messrs. Harper Brothers under their father, and have since executed work for Scribners, United States Sanitary commission, etc., and were the pioneers to send an artist into the Black hills for the purpose of making sketches to illustrate a book written by Edwin Curley. If you should wish any wood or photo engraving or printing don't fail to call upon Sears & Sears, for they can turn out expensive or cheap work at a figure as reasonable as any house in the city.

W. Buckley & Co.

1307 West Van Buren Street.

In this model house are found the best goods pertaining to a first-class market, and a great reduction in prices. In fact, a visit to this admirable new market will save consumers upwards of twenty-five per cent. on all purchases. In Mr. Buckley's own words, "We intend to sell the best quality of goods at the very lowest prices for cash." Besides fresh and salt meats and fish, he keeps oysters and game in season, and all kinds of provisions and country produce. A specialty is made in fresh country butter and eggs, in which line he does a large business. All orders receive the closest attention, and prompt deliveries are made. Mr. Buckley is a practical and experienced butcher, this being his life trade, and all customers may rely upon receiving the best of satisfaction. He has been located in this part of the city for the past ten years, coming here from his native city, Philadelphia. Mr. Buckley served during the war in the 1st Delaware zouaves and acquitted himself nobly in his country's cause. Mr. Buckley has been prominently identified for years with the leading secret organizations of this country, and has held important offices in the same. He has succeeded in establishing a large family trade, and special inducements are offered to boarding-houses and restaurants.

The Continental.

C. Collins, Proprietor, Southeast Corner Wabash Avenue and Madison Street.

The Continental is one of the oldest and most popular hotels in the city. At the beginning of this year a change in proprietorship was made, and the entire house was remodeled, thoroughly cleaned, refitted and furnished complete. It contains all the modern conveniences, and no pains or expense has been spared in making it the most comfortable and attractive house in Chicago. It is located in the business center, convenient to all the large wholesale houses, theaters and railroad depots in the city, and is in fact the best $2 per day hotel on the South side. It is under the proprietorship of the former management of the St. Denis hotel—C. Collins—which fact alone bespeaks success, and already everything around the house betokens an air of comfort and substantial hospitality, which makes it so homelike and pleasant for strangers visiting our city. Merchants and travelers will always find clean, pleasant rooms and a first-class table. One feature of this hotel is the large, fine merchants' sample rooms on the office floor. Every attention is given to the guest, whose comfort and safety is closely looked after, and those who visit the Continental are likely to become regular patrons.

C. W. Ternand & Co.

Manufacturing Jewelers, 113 East Madison Street.

The goods of this well-known house are not surpassed for finish and design by any in the market. Mr. Ternand has been in the business fifteen years and is a thoroughly practical and experienced working jeweler. He started for himself nearly two years ago as head of the firm above named. Most of the work is to order, and he executes private orders promptly and at lowest rates. Most of the material he furnishes himself, except the stones, when such are required. The rates for setting stones, etc., charged by this firm are extremely low, and the work of the highest and most reliable order. The bulk of the trade is of a light nature, though all kinds of orders are undertaken and executed promptly and satisfactorily.

Berger Bros.

Wholesale and Retail Dealers in Michigan and Indiana Charcoal, Office, 170 Michigan Street.

The firm of Berger Bros. are wholesale and retail dealers in Michigan and Indiana charcoal. They make a specialty of large contracts, and in this line they can offer as good inducements as any firm in Chicago. They not only have a large city patronage, but their trade extends all over the country. Their telephone number is 3182, and all orders received in this manner or by mail meet with as prompt attention as though given personally. The brothers have been in business for eight years, and, by honest dealing and prompt attention to the wants of their patrons, have built up a trade equaling 30,000 bushels monthly. They have been residents of Chicago for over fifteen years and are well acquainted with every department of the trade which they represent.

L. L. Wadsworth.

Manufacturer of Spring Trucks and Wagons, 252 Michigan Street.

The construction work at Mr. Wadsworth's place is as fine as can be found in the city, while repairing is promptly and neatly done, in fact, for wagon work and general blacksmithing Mr. Wadsworth has few equals and no superiors. He has been established in the business since the great fire, and his large trade, which is entirely local, attests to the reliability of his work. Mr. Wadsworth designed and executed the large, fancy truck wagon of Jas. S. Kirk & Co's, which for beauty and finish has no equal in the city. We noticed some large iron letters in this establishment, four feet four inches in height, and on inquiring found that they were for the new Sibley block on North Clark street and the river, and are placed in position on the roof of that building. Mr. Wadsworth was born in Detroit, Mich., and came to Chicago in 1865, and is therefore a comparatively old resident.

Johnson & Metzler.

Manufacturers of Carriages, Buggies, Etc., 260 and 262 Michigan Street.

Those of our business men who desire a first-class wagon or truck are referred to the old and reliable establishment of Johnson & Metzler, at Nos. 260 and 262 Michigan street. They are manufacturers of carriages, buggies, spring trucks and wagons. Their shops are 25 by 100 feet in dimensions, and two stories in height, with a large basement. The business was begun by Mr. Johnson in 1871, but three and a half years ago Mr. Metzler was received as a partner. Their trade is large and extends all over the city. The superiority of the trucks manufactured by this firm has caused them to be much sought after by the trade in general. Not only are all orders filled promptly, but all kinds of repairing, painting and trimming is done, quickly and satisfactorily. They have done work for the following concerns in this city: James S. Kirk & Co., Blomgren Bros., City Transfer Co., Procter & Gamble, Allen Paper Car Wheel Co., and many others.

C. H. Julius & Son.

Merchant Tailors, 16 East Jackson Street.

Among the many enterprises that have contributed to make Chicago one of the leading centers of fashion, that of the merchant tailor is one of the most important. Among the fashionable merchant tailors in this city, none can claim a more liberal patronage, or a more steady and growing trade among the better class of citizens, than Messrs. C.

H. Julius & Son, whose success has been largely the reward of perseverance in the face of almost insurmountable difficulties. The house was founded in 1860 by Mr. C. H. Julius, in a very humble way, at his home, at No. 102 West Polk street, which nine years later was removed to No. 50 Wells street, now Fifth avenue. At the same time, his brother John becoming his partner, another store was opened at No. 186 Lake street. Both were doing a prosperous business when the great fire of 1871 destroyed both stores, which, the insurance failing, ultimately proved a total loss. The partnership was at this time dissolved, and Mr. Julius began life again, re-opening at his home on West Polk street, whither his old patrons followed him, and, enjoying unimpaired credit, he soon had a good stock of the best cloths and suitings. In January, 1882, after his son, Mr. C. H. Julius, Jr., had been admitted to participation, the business was removed to its present eligible location in the Leland hotel, where the firm take a justifiable pride in showing their large stock of cloths, cassimeres and suitings, which include the latest fabrics of both European and domestic manufacture, specially selected by reason of their durability, fast colors and fashionable pattern. Being artistic cutters themselves, Messrs. C. H. Julius & Son employ none but first-class workmen, and that their garments are faultless in fit, finish and workmanship, is best evidenced in the fashionable trade they have not only been able to attract, but permanently to retain.

Ames & Frost.

Manufacturers of and Dealers in Woven Wire Mattresses, Spring Beds, Etc., 45 South Desplaines Street.

As manufacturers of woven wire mattresses, the firm of Ames & Frost stands unrivaled in Chicago. They manufacture and deal in every description of spring beds, cots, hospital and asylum beds, etc. They also deal extensively in hard maple lumber, making a specialty of the higher grades. At their mill at Blackhawk and Cherry streets, they have the most perfect facilities for kiln-drying and dressing maple flooring, etc. They employ 130 workmen and do a large business among the principal furniture dealers in Chicago and throughout the country. Messrs. Ames and Frost are both American-born citizens and have been associated together in business for the last nineteen years. Mr. Ames, who manages the Desplaines street office, is from Maine. The resources of the firm are such that all orders can be promptly filled, and in this way they have succeeded in winning the confidence of the public. Mr. Frost is located at present at Muskegon, Mich., where they have a factory employing a hundred hands in the manufacture of curtain rollers.

Gale & Blocki.

Druggists, 111 Randolph Street, Branches, 44 and 46 Monroe Street and 126 North Clark Street.

This firm form what is undoubtedly the representative retail drug house in Chicago, and, as such, is worthy of permanent record in reviewing her leading industries upon the occasion of her semi-centennial celebration. Their business was established in 1847, and besides their main store at No. 111 Randolph street, branches at Nos. 44 and 46 Monroe street and 126 North Clark street are conducted, all of which are spacious and elegantly appointed, while they contain the finest and most complete stock in the city, embracing a full assortment of drugs and medicines of every description, approved proprietary remedies and fancy and toilet articles. The firm are proprietors of the White Rock springs and western agents for Ridge's food, and are also large dealers in artificial eyes and Swedish leeches. Many of our leading physicians indorse this firm on account of the reliability and purity of its drugs and scientific service in the prescription department. The individual members of the firm, Messrs. E. O. Gale, W. F. Blocki, J. M. Baker and W. H. Gale, are all old residents of this city, whose career is in every respect a credit to themselves and to the profession with which they are identified.

George Salvesen.

Practical Carriage Trimmer, Carriages Neatly Trimmed and Repaired, 95 and 97 East Indiana Street.

Mr. Salvesen is one of the most practical and experienced carriage trimmers in Chicago, and, although only established in business for the past two years, has succeeded, by fine work, in building up a large trade all over the city. This is his life trade, with every feature of which he is thoroughly conversant. Before starting in business for himself he worked for ten years for the large firm of Henry Willets. He makes all styles of buggy-tops, cushions, etc. Special attention is given to private orders, and work of all kinds is turned out with perfect satisfaction to all. In his repairing department, everything is turned out with promptness. Mr. Salvesen superintends all orders, and sees to it that none but efficient and experienced workmen are employed. Satisfaction is guaranteed, and orders solicited from the trade.

National Tobacco Review.

Franklin S. Anderson, Publisher, 166 Randolph Street.

The National Tobacco Review is a monthly journal devoted to the interests of tobacco and its manufactured products. It has as large a circulation (6,000) as any tobacco trade paper in America, and is sent to every State in the Union. It also has subscribers in all parts of Europe, Sandwich islands and Cuba. The Review consists of twenty pages, double column, printed in large, attractive type, composed of the latest and most interesting events pertaining to the tobacco trade. Subscription price is one dollar per annum. Advertisers will find the National Tobacco Review an excellent medium through which to reach the entire tobacco trade. In the Review's job printing department are very complete facilities for the execution of all classes of printing at the lowest rates. The Review was founded in 1885, and its enterprising proprietor and publisher, Mr. Franklin S. Anderson, has spared no pains in making it the best paper of its kind in the Union.

Walter M. Jackson.

Real Estate and Loans, 80 Dearborn Street.

Mr. Jackson has proved himself to be a responsible and reliable operator in this line during the decade in which he has been actively engaged in business, having developed a connection of the highest order among capitalists and operators in realty. A lawyer by profession, Mr. Jackson devotes his entire attention to real estate, bringing to bear a class of knowledge peculiarly serviceable in such transactions, and possesses ample facilities for conducting operations under the most favorable auspices, while his books contain long lists of eligible properties, either acres for subdivision or residence, business and manufacturing sites. A general business is transacted, buying, selling, exchanging and renting property, loaning money on bond and mortgage, and taking entire charge of estates, many properties of non-residents being in his charge. A specialty of the office is in fine residence properties on the boulevards, avenues and desirable locations. The opinion among his many permanent patrons is that none are better qualified to conserve their best interests than Mr. Jackson, because of his ability and integrity in promptly executing any commissions intrusted to his care.

U. E. Atwater.

Real-Estate and Furnished-House Agency, Room 9, Adams Express Building.

The development of the real-estate interests of this city has resulted in no small degree from the energy and enterprise of our leading brokers, among whom Mr. U. E. Atwater, since establishing business in 1885, has obtained a sound reputation. Besides conducting a general real-estate business, buying, selling and renting on commission, making a specialty of the furnished-house business, wherein he is prepared to show a larger and more desirable list than any other office in the city, Mr. Atwater also deals in real-estate securities and chattel mortgage loans, which his connections among capitalists enable him to place without any unnecessary delay, while his terms cannot be duplicated elsewhere. His room-renting and boarding-house directory is another prominent feature and one of peculiar service to all desiring such accommodations. Mr. Atwater became a permanent resident of Chicago in 1884, coming hither from Homer, N. Y., his native State, and is both popular and respected in business circles, while in his policy and methods he is a thoroughgoing exponent of the great cardinal principles which form the only basis of enduring prosperity.

W. S. Thurber.

Importer and Dealer in Fine Arts, 210 Wabash Avenue.

The advance of science and art now permits even those in very moderate circumstances to adorn their homes with the productions of the most celebrated American and European artists, and fac-similes of pictures that can be seen only in the most renowned public and private galleries. In this city are many establishments devoted to the fine arts, but none more satisfactory to the connoisseurs in art than that of Mr. W. S. Thurber, No. 210 Wabash avenue, which since its inception, in 1880, has obtained a high reputation for its beautiful paintings, engravings, etchings, and other artistic treasures. The premises occupied are very spacious, handsome and attractive, and fitted up in a style unsurpassed by the most celebrated art galleries of New York, Paris or London, and pictures from the most eminent modern artists are always on sale here. A specialty is made of artistic picture framing, in which original and artistic designs are displayed. Mr. Thurber is a native of Ogdensburgh, N. Y., and is eminently fitted by education, natural taste and ability for this business, in which the signal success achieved highly reflects his own enterprise and indefatigable zeal in its promotion.

Chas. Raiser.

Manufacturer of Children's Carriages, 62 and 64 Clybourn Avenue.

As an illustration of the results of energy, enterprise and honorable dealing, the success which has attended the business career of Mr. Charles Raiser is especially noticeable, rendering him a representative of his industry in this review of Chicago's commerce in her semi-centennial year. Mr. Raiser manufactures every style of children's carriage, upon whose merits alone his reputation has been won, his house today being by far the most extensive on the North side, and one of the first in its line in the city. He occupies commodious premises, carrying a very fine and large assortment, and is at all times prepared to quote bottom prices and to extend every legitimate accommodation to buyers. He is himself a practical workman, many of his carriages being the productions of his own hands; in fact, his skill and experience were on the start his main capital in trade, through which he has reared an eminently prosperous business, himself standing high in general esteem as an honorable business man. Mr. Raiser makes a specialty of selling his carriages direct to private parties, and buyers can see the advantage to them in this plan. He sends carriages to all points within 500 miles of Chicago free of charge. A catalogue will be sent to anyone free on application.

City of London Fire Insurance Co., Limited, of London, England.

Western Office, 153 La Salle Street, Edwin A. Simonds, General Agent.

The agency in Chicago for this company has been established since 1881, and Mr. E. A. Simonds, being an old insurance man, has been a prominent factor in increasing its business throughout the extent of his territory, which is a large one, and where his managing capabilities have become thoroughly known. A statement of the United States branch, January 1, 1887, shows the company to be in an excellent financial condition. The following figures are condensed from the statement: Assets, $746,-186.25, of which $624,500.00 are U. S. bonds, 3 and 4 per cent., market value, while other items of the assets are correspondingly secure. The liabilities are light, being but $390,577.82, leaving a net surplus over all of $355,608.43. The names of the officers of the United States branch are men eminently sound in their respective avocations, the trustees, in Boston, Mass., for the United States being Chas. F. Choate, president Old Colony R. R. Co., and Old Colony Steamboat Co., Oliver Ames, of Oliver Ames & Son, and Reuben E. Demmon, president Howard National bank. The head offices in the United States are at 20 Kilby street, Boston, Mass., with John C. Paige, resident manager.

Henry C. Jacobs.

Real Estate and Loans, 57 Calumet Building, 189 La Salle Street.

The vast interests centered in real estate in Chicago render this branch of commercial activity by far the most important in the western metropolis, and it is little wonder, therefore, that its representatives include many of our leading citizens, among whom none have attained a better recognized position in their chosen occupation than Mr. Henry C. Jacobs. He came to Chicago in 1861, and was formerly engaged in the produce commission business, from which, however, he retired in 1873, to engage in real estate traffic. Though transacting a general business in real estate and loans, his specialty is in subdividing suitable acre property, and he has now on the market several of the most promising subdivisions in our suburbs, which are rapidly filling up with improvements of a substantial and desirable character, attracted alike by the favorable location and the unusually generous terms upon which the property is offered. Mr. Jacobs is highly esteemed in the leading financial circles of the city, as being a thoroughgoing exponent of those enduring principles of equity and honor which alone form the sure basis of permanent prosperity in every department of business activity.

Snyder & Rathbone.

Wholesale Fruit and Produce Commission, 217 South Water Street.

As a branch of industry peculiarly successful in Chicago few excel in enterprise those engaged in the wholesale fruit and produce commission trade, while it is such houses as Snyder & Rathbone who are the recognized exponents of Chicago's commerce, whose prominence has been honestly attained by years of fair and liberal dealing. They receive large shipments of country produce from Illinois, Wisconsin and Iowa, making specialties of butter, eggs and poultry, and also handle largely all kinds of early vegetables and domestic fruits in their season. Their connection among both producers and the leading dealers is of an highly influential character. The house was established by Mr. J. Snyder in 1878. Two years later, Mr. P. D. Rathbone becoming his partner, the present firm was organized. They refer to the First National bank, Chicago, Ill.; First National bank, South Haven, Mich.; German bank, Sheboygan, Wis.; Steele, Wedeles & Co., wholesale grocers, Chicago, Ill.; while the policy on which the business is conducted is such as to have met with the hearty commendations of the trade.

I. C. Rogers & Son.

Commission Merchants, 267 South Water Street.

The produce commission trade in 1886 received an important accession to its ranks when I. C. and B. E. Rogers organized the house of I. C. Rogers & Son, which has since developed a large and permanent patronage of a strictly first-class character. These gentlemen have well organized arrangements and are large receivers of produce from a vast extent of the surrounding country, making a prominent specialty of green fruit and vegetables, butter, eggs and poultry. They handle extensive consignments of these staples, effecting quick sales at current rates and remitting promptly to shippers and growers. They occupy one of the finest establishments of the kind in the city, centrally located at No. 267 South Water street, where buyers are always sure of finding a large and choice stock of produce of every description. The house is a recognized authority on butter and is building up a fine shipping trade to New York and other eastern points, while their financial standing is of the highest character. The specialty of this firm is the packing of their own fruit from orchards all over the country, and in this line they have an extended trade.

Finney & Channon.

Ship Chandlers and Sail Makers, 270 and 272 South Water Street.

Few industries have exerted an equal influence over the destinies of Chicago with that of our maritime interests. The shipping interests being thus extensive the supplying of their wants constitutes a trade the sum total of which is a material item in her industrial resources. As ship chandlers and sail makers, Messrs. Finney & Channon occupy a most prominent position, carrying as they do an unusually large and complete stock of ship supplies at their spacious salesrooms Nos. 270 and 272 South Water street, while as sail makers they have obtained an enviable reputation for the excellence of their workmanship. The firm is composed of Messrs. George C. Finney and J. Channon, the latter an old lake captain and well known in every port throughout the entire chain of lakes, while Mr. Finney was formerly a resident of Oswego, though permanently located here for the past twenty-five years. These men stand at the very front of their useful and important industry, and are prepared to furnish promptly anything in their line at bottom prices.

Henry A. Fitch.

Prescription Druggist, 884 West Madison Street, Corner of Leavitt, Telephone 7176.

The well-arranged and finely-fitted drug store of Mr. Henry A. Fitch is located at the above location. The store has lately been refitted and furnished, presenting a fine appearance, with its large plate-glass windows and fine corner entrance. Mr. Fitch possesses every requisite necessary for the first-class trade he has established. He is a practical druggist, and keeps only the most reliable chemicals and the best and purest of drugs. His other articles of stock, perfumes, toilet and fancy goods, etc., are strictly first-class in every respect. Special attention is called to his prescription department, which he personally superintends, and the utmost precaution is taken in compounding medicines of all kinds. His telephone number is 7176, and all orders given meet with prompt and satisfactory attention.

Shields & Brown Co.

Manufacturers of Sectional Insulated Air Coverings, 78 and 80 Lake Street.

Among those firms who manufacture sectional insulated air coverings for steam, gas and water pipes, boilers, drums, heaters, etc., is that of the Shields & Brown Co. of this city, whose goods in the severest competitive tests have invariably proved their superiority, while they have likewise received the cordial indorsement of all the leading fire insurance companies in the country, yet in price they compare favorably with any. Their western office and factory is located in this city, with eastern office and depot at No. 143 Worth street, New York, thus being in a position to promptly supply the steadily increasing demand from all parts of the country. The Shields & Brown Co. refer with just pride to the largest houses and finest office buildings in Chicago as among their customers, and of the many places where their insulated air coverings can be seen in large quantities we mention the Pullman building, First National bank, Chicago Opera house, Union League club, Chicago City Railway Co. cable plant, Brother Jonathan building, H. M. Kinsley's restaurant, Grand Pacific hotel, Elgin National Watch Co. works at Elgin, Pullman Palace Car Co. works at Pullman, McCormick Harvesting Machine Co. works, McCormick building, Reaper block.

Chicago Herald Company.

120 and 122 Fifth Avenue.

Among our prominent daily papers is the Herald, the office of which is at Nos. 120 and 122 Fifth avenue. This paper has the largest circulation of any strictly morning paper in the city. It was established in 1881, the first copy being issued on May 10th of that year. The circulation commenced with a daily sale of 3,000 copies, from which it has steadily advanced to 35,000. This paper is owned by a corporation under the name of the Chicago Herald Co. The publisher is Mr. James W. Scott, and Mr. Martin J. Russell is the editor. The business occupies the whole building of four floors and basement, twenty-five by eighty-four feet. In the different departments not less than one hundred hands are employed, and the printing is performed by three presses, manufactured by C. Potter, Jr., & Co. These presses are worked by a twenty-five horse-power engine, and are each capable of turning out 30,000 copies per hour. The Sunday Herald is one of the most complete and interesting papers published in the west, and, besides the general news, contains first-class serial stories. A weekly paper is also issued, which is unsurpassed as a journal of general information.

B. Garcia & Co

Spanish Cigar Manufacturers, Importers and Dealers in Havana Leaf, 44 and 46 La Salle Street.

The natural and acquired advantages that have contributed to make the city of Chicago a commercial center have also induced here the establishment of enterprises which for magnitude and character have become celebrated throughout the United States. Such an one is that of Messrs. B. Garcia & Co., which was established by the present proprietors in 1879, since which time they have obtained a large patronage in consequence of the excellence of the pure Havana cigars emanating from their factory. Mr. Garcia is a native of the province of Asturias, Spain, and early in life went to the island of Cuba, where he became practically conversant with every detail of the Havana tobacco trade, from the culture of the leaf in the Vuelta Abajos and other favorite districts up to the manufacture of the choicest Cuban cigars. He removed from Havana to the United States about fourteen years ago, for a time being engaged in business in New York city. In 1879 he came to Chicago, and has since been a permanent and respected resident. From small beginnings his factory has steadily grown to its present satisfactory proportions, employing in the ordinary course of business sixty skilled cigarmakers, while the trade, in addition to that derived from the city, embraces all the neighboring States. This house purposes to maintain the character of their famous cigars, in which none but the best grades of Havana tobacco, of his own direct importation, is used. Further comment is unnecessary, the well-known character of the house placing it above criticism and affording, as it does, an example of an honorable and prosperous mercantile career.

Griswold, Palmer & Co.

Successors to J. W. Griswold & Co., Manufacturers and Importers of Cloaks, Cloakings and Trimmings, 236 and 238 Monroe Street.

A house closely identified with the growth of Chicago's commerce, and one which is also admittedly one of its leading representatives, is that of Griswold, Palmer & Co. Established upon a very modest beginning in 1857, four entire floors, each 40x170 feet in area are now required for the transaction of their business, extending from Ohio to California, some idea of the magnitude of which may be gathered from the fact that during the busy season the firm have daily in process of manufacture fully 2000 garments. The factory is provided with all the most improved modern machinery and appliances; all the operations of cutting, sewing and pressing being conducted by steam-power, while upwards of 800 skilled operatives find remunerative employment here. An endless variety of cloaks and suits in all the prevailing styles are carried, while the firm have always been noted for their liberality and reasonableness in price, which they are enabled to do profitably by reason of their perfect manufacturing facilities, and importing direct their own cloakings and trimmings. Messrs. Griswold are natives of Hartford, Conn., and came to Chicago many years ago, where their interests have since been centered.

Ira Brown.

Real-Estate Dealer and Private Banker, 177 La Salle Street, Room 9.

The steady ratio of development observable in the Chicago real-estate market, and the universally high reputation that investments therein have attained, reflect the greatest credit upon our leading real-estate agents and dealers. Among the most enterprising members of the profession, Mr. Ira Brown occupies a recognized position; while being also one of our leading capitalists, his resources permit operations on a scale of magnitude attained by few others. Mr. Brown is a native of Ohio, and, after having received an excellent education, early in life embarked in a financial career with great success. In 1858 he commenced business in Chicago at No. 24 N. Clark street, and eventually, in 1872, removed to his present eligible location, 177 La Salle street. His specialty is in the purchase of large tracts in an available location, and the subdivision of the same to suit the wants of customers, for whom also he builds houses to order and accepts monthly installments in payment. At present he has large amounts of property for sale at Evanston, Norwood Park, Desplaines, Glencoe, La Grange, Wheaton, Park Ridge, and other equally desirable suburbs. Though Chicago realty claims his principal attention, he also deals largely in western properties, and particularly at San Diego, California, where he has an office with a resident agent in charge. Mr. Brown also conducts a private banking business in all its departments, and likewise makes liberal advances on government, State, municipal and railroad securities. His widely extended and varied experience, keen appreciation of values, together with his wide acquaintance with business men, render his services peculiarly valuable to parties dealing in realty.

Eagle Carriage Works.

James B. Thomas, Proprietor; Manufacturer of All Kinds of Children's Carriages, Sleighs, Etc., 114 North Peoria Street, Corner Kinzie Street.

So soon as a child can walk, or even sit alone, he should be supplied with useful and amusing toys. It is surprising how soon a little one will amuse itself with a score or two of little cubes of light wood. How soon these can be made a source, not only of amusement, but of instruction. When tired of these, what an acquisition is a little wheelbarrow, and when this gets rusty and worn, with what delight he lays hold of a little cart or wagon. With a very little pleasant oversight and instruction he amuses himself, learns to love home and annoys nobody. The "Eagle Carriage Works" of Mr. James B. Thomas are at Nos. 114 to 120 North Peoria street, corner Kinzie street. The various articles turned out from this factory are baby carriages, baby jumpers, chairs, rockers, sleds, girl's sleighs, rocking-horses, velocipedes, etc. They are all of the most modern pattern, and noted for fine finish, durability and beauty of construction. The factory occupies one hundred and twenty-five feet on Peoria street, and as many on Kinzie, and each of its three stories is well arranged to turn out neatly and quickly these useful and interesting articles for children. All the work is executed under the eye of Mr. Thomas, who had eight years' experience in New York before he opened his factory here in 1859. This experience, together with the unsurpassed facilities at his command, enables Mr. Thomas to furnish, as he has in the past, the best carriage that can be found in the market, at the most reasonable prices. Merchants would do well to examine his goods before purchasing elsewhere, as he buys in large quantities for cash and sells for a very small profit. The large and successful trade he has established shows the merit of his goods and the demand that is made for them all over the United States.

Townsend & Yale.

Commission Merchants, 160 and 162 Market Street, G. L. Forman, Manager.

The time has long since gone by when any argument was needed with the trade to convince them of the utility of placing their orders directly with the commission houses—a system which is daily becoming more and more the order and method of trade; the connecting link, as it were, between producer and consumer, enabling the former to directly reach the market, and the latter to procure their goods at manufacturers' prices without the trouble and expense heretofore incident thereto. One of the oldest and largest as well as the most prominent houses thus engaged in the United States is that of Townsend & Yale, of New York, Boston, Philadelphia and Chicago. The branch in this city is under the management of Mr. G. L. Forman, having been established in 1871, and was for many years located at Nos. 213 and 215 Fifth avenue, from whence, in 1885, the press of business necessitated a removal to their present spacious premises at Nos. 160 and 162 Market street, where they are prepared to show the largest and most complete line of knit goods, hosiery, cotton piece goods, etc., to be found anywhere in the country, representing as they do many of the leading manufacturers of these goods both at home and abroad. Mr. Forman, the manager, is a native of Scotland, and is a gentleman both esteemed and liked in business circles, and it is due very largely to his persistent efforts that the trade of the house has been so widely developed over the western country. They have lately become the sole agents for the Lawrence Manufacturing Co. and the Boston Manufacturing Co.

A F. Seeberger & Co

Wholesale Hardware, 38 and 40 Lake Street, Chicago.

As a branch of industry peculiarly successful in Chicago, and forming an important factor in the commercial greatness of the Garden City, the hardware trade is entitled to much consideration in a work the compilation of which has for its main object a review of the mercantile and industrial resources of the city commemorative of her semi-centennial anniversary. Chicago has every reason to be proud of her many concerns identified with this industry, as they are as a class thoroughly reliable and conducted upon sound business principles, and none are more representative of the hardware trade than the house of A. F. Seeberger & Co., who have been engaged therein since 1864, and whereof, taken in any respect, whether as to the character and extent of the stock, or the volume and scope of their business, or the liberal policy upon which it is conducted, their house fully typifies their branch of commerce. The firm occupy the spacious five-story building, Nos. 38 and 40 Lake street, and carry a complete stock of hardware in all its departments, making a prominent specialty of cutlery, tinplate, metals, nails, etc., which, purchased direct from first hands, they are enabled to place upon the market at prices which have secured liberal recognition, both in the local trade and that of points west and northwest. Of the individual members of the firm, Messrs. A. F. and Chas. D. Seeberger, comment is superfluous, their reputation extending over many years, while the business which they have built up speaks in the most expressive language of the confidence with which their house is so widely and justly regarded.

Wells & Nellegar Co.

Wholesale Hardware and Cutlery, 72, 74 and 76 Lake Street.

The Garden City of the west has in more ways than one seriously affected the commercial supremacy of New York city, her only rival, but in no branch of trade has more rapid and substantial progress been made than in that of hardware and cutlery. Typical of the remarkable development of the city itself, has been the success attained by the Wells & Nellegar Co., organized nine years ago, and which now occupies such a prominent position among the industrial resources of Chicago, the celebration of whose semi-centennial anniversary these pages are designed to perpetuate. They are extensive dealers in all kinds of hardware, cutlery, tinners' stock, etc., and in the prosecution of the business occupy a spacious five-story and basement building, one hundred by one hundred and fifty feet in area, giving employment to a large force of men, while their trade, expanding rapidly with each succeeding year, covers all points reached by our complex railroad system and magnificent water routes. Throughout our leading financial circles, the officers of the company, Messrs. J. B. Nellegar, president, R. M. Wells, vice president and treasurer, and J. B. Battles, secretary, are known for their honorable and liberal business methods.

Suburban Homes.

One of Chicago's Latest Additions.

Eggleston, with its finely macadamized and stone-curbed roadways and alleys, its rows of shade trees, its large urns filled with flowers, and lastly its handsome new residences, which in beauty of architecture surpass those of any other suburb around Chicago, make it the most desirable place for a suburban home. The projectors have seen the wisdom of making all public improvements, such as water supply, gas mains, macadamized roads and alleys, in advance of sale of property, for there is nothing so annoying to a house and lot owner as to have these things done after occupancy. A year ago people used to inquire, where is Eggleston? Now it is as familiar as Englewood or Normal Park, which it joins on the south, Seventy-first street being the north boundary line; it has the same railroad facilities afforded these suburbs. This property is in the hands of and is being managed by the firm of J. P. Mallette & Co., who have offices at room 518 Royal Insurance building, Chicago, and 2 and 3 Central block, Englewood.

J. K. Russell.

Planing-Mill, 82 to 96 Fulton Street, Chicago; Mouldings, Dressed Lumber, Sash, Doors and Blinds, Resawing, Kiln-Drying, Box Factory, All Kinds of Mill Work, Hauling.

One of the largest and oldest planing-mills on the West side is that of J. K. Russell, at Nos. 82 to 96 Fulton street. It occupies a site of 170 by 170 feet, which contains a large building four stories high, with basement. The business was begun in 1850, under the firm name of Cleveland & Russell, but in 1857 Mr. Cleveland withdrew, since which time Mr. Russell has had complete charge of the business. His large factory is fitted up with all the latest improved machinery for this business; his trade extends throughout all parts of the west and northwest, and aggregates upwards of $200,000 annually, and 125 workmen are employed in the various departments. He manufactures all kinds of mouldings, dressed lumber, sash, doors, blinds, hardwood flooring and resawing. One feature of his business is that of kiln-drying on a large scale, having facilities for 100,000 feet at one time. Mr. Russell has always been closely identified with the lumber interests of Chicago, and is one of the representative mill men.

The G. M. Jarvis Co.

39 North State Street.

The foundation of this company was laid in 1800 by Mr. G. M. Jarvis, the senior member and president of the company, when he planted the famous Vine Hill vineyard. This property, of about two hundred and forty acres, is located on the Santa Cruz mountains, at an elevation of nearly two thousand feet above the beautiful bay of Monterey, and nearly twenty miles from the city of San Jose. Much of this vineyard was set out in early days to the grape known as the Oporto wine grape, and from it a most excellent article of port wine was made, rivaling the foreign wines, as early as 1870. This port took the first prize at the Centennial at Philadelphia. It also took first prize at the New Orleans World's fair, over both foreign and domestic wines, and it has taken all the first prizes at the State, district and mechanics' fairs in the Golden State. Prof. Peirce, of Harvard university, says, "It is not only a pure wine, but is the finest I have ever known made in this country." This wine is now fifteen years old and is pronounced by chemists and connoisseurs the finest and best in the United States. Besides this the company has almost all ages of port wine, sherry, muscatelle, angelica, reisling, hock, white wine, chasselas, sauterne, clarets, burgundy, blackberry wine, blackberry brandy, peach and apple brandy, and the famous Jarvis reisling grape brandy, vintage of 1877. Their trade now extends over most of the northwest, while east it reaches into Pennsylvania and New York. Prof. J. H. Long, analytical and assaying chemist, of the Chicago Medical college, says, "Gentlemen, I have analyzed your wines and your brandies. These tests show me that they are not only perfectly pure, but that they contain all the essential elements so much admired by leading wine chemists." Twenty-five years producing grapes, making wine and distilling brandy, gives this company many advantages over new firms, who have to buy their products from other new beginners, that often spoil the market with their new and half-made productions. A quarter of a century in making and aging wines and brandies ought to make a good nucleus for a prosperous business. For samples, price lists, etc., address the G. M. Jarvis Co., corner of State and Michigan streets.

Wm. Garnett & Co.

Real-Estate Brokers, 77 Clark Street, Room 1.

The rapid rise in the value of real estate in and near this city has given a great impetus to investing in that kind of security. Foremost amongst this body of men is the firm of Wm. Garnett & Co., consisting of father and son. Mr. Garnett has had twenty-four years' experience in this city, and has been engaged in the real-estate business for the last eighteen years, doing a steadily increasing business in selling, managing property, collecting, renting, etc. Special attention is given to non-residents' estates, loans are negotiated, and all business of this nature is honorably and reliably transacted. Mr. Garnett has besides vacant lot property in large variety, also acre property for disposal at Cragin, near Humboldt park, seven miles from the center of the city. This property, at $500 per acre, will in a few years be worth a large advance over present value. Knowing so much of real estate interests, Mr. Garnett's advice and opinions are in constant demand.

The D. F. Bremner Baking Co

Manufacturers of Crackers and Fine Biscuit, Office and Factory, 76, 78 and 80 O'Brien Street, Branch Office, 19 Market Street.

In Chicago there are many enterprising houses thus engaged in this branch of business, but among them few have attained a more merited distinction than Mr. D. F. Bremner, whose business, since its organization in 1872, has constantly grown in magnitude and importance, until now it is one of the largest in the west, employing over 150 hands, at the spacious factory on O'Brien street, where every facility has been provided so as to meet the demands of the trade, including the latest improved labor-saving machinery, and every device calculated to advance the work in hand in the interest of economy and cleanliness. The celebrated Eureka bread is made by Mr. Bremner, a bread which these many years has obtained a firm foothold in public esteem, the demand for which is so great. In addition to the Eureka bread, a full line of plain and fancy crackers and fine biscuit are made, and this is the only house in the west that makes a full line of such goods. They are in all respects equal to the finest eastern or imported goods, and are taking their place rapidly, being much fresher and nicer. Since May 1, 1888, Mr. Bremner has occupied the spacious building at Nos. 19 and 21 Market street, fifty by two hundred feet in dimensions, as a branch depot, removing thence from Nos. 46 and 48 Michigan avenue, on account of its specially central location as a distributing point. Mr. Bremner is of Scotch descent, and in his business life presents the type of the enterprising, self-made and successful merchant and manufacturer, who, while winning the patronage of the public, has also retained the confidence and esteem of all with whom he has been brought in contact.

O. W. Richardson & Co

Carpets, Mattings, Oilcloths, Etc., 261 and 263 State Street.

With the rapid strides made in recent years in the manufacture of carpets, as regards improved machinery, beautiful, brilliant and durable new colors, coupled with the skill of expert designers, has come the welcome fact of great reductions in price, rendered still lower by the enterprise of such houses as that of Messrs. O. W. Richardson & Co. of this city, at 261 and 263 State street. Their business, though rather a novel departure in the trade, has proved both popular and successful, and since its inception in 1875, they have developed a widespread and influential patronage throughout the entire west. This firm are jobbers of cut carpets, mattings, oilcloths, linoleums, and smyrna rugs, with a system whereby dealers are enabled, by merely carrying their samples, to exhibit to their customers the assortment of one of the largest jobbing houses in this metropolitan market at least 5 per cent. cheaper than if they were obliged to carry a stock. The carpets are ordered from the samples, and Messrs. Richardson & Co. do the cutting, matching and sewing. They are cutting over one hundred of their choicest patterns without waste. The advantage of their system needs only once to be understood to effect an entire revolution in the carpet trade. The firm occupy spacious premises, and carry a completely assorted stock of the finest imported and domestic carpetings, including all the leading novelties and seasonable designs in wiltons, moquettes, velvets, brussels, choice tapestries, ingrains, druggets and art squares in vast variety, while their connections among manufacturers enable them to name prices that defy competition. The house also own the patents for the northwest for Richardson's patent carpet exhibitor, whereby their samples are displayed to as good an effect as if the whole roll was on the floor. Messrs. O. W. and E. C. Richardson and M. M. Curry compose this reliable firm, which has built up its business by dealing honestly and justly with the trade.

One of the most pleasing indications of higher culture in Chicago is found in the artistic interior decorations now considered indispensable in homes of refinement and wealth, the science of interior decorating having attracted into its ranks in this city some of the most skilled artists of the old world, and among whom Mr. Wm. Phillipson, a native of Holstein, Germany, takes high rank. The Phillipson Decorative Co. is the result of the business originally founded by Mr. Phillipson in 1882, and of which he is still the head. Their specialty is decoration in all its branches, and they have painted many of the beautiful frescos that are so much admired in the churches and public buildings, and notably in our city, in the Board of Trade building, also the State Capitol, at Springfield. The house carries in stock a large line of imported dados, friezes, elaborate wall papers, leather hangings, lincrusta walton, tapestries and papier mache. the latter being peculiarly adapted for household and theatrical decorations, this house being the sole importers into the United States of these papier-mache decorations. Mr. Phillipson is a thorough artist, and possesses the happy faculty of originating designs and harmoniously blending shades and colors to produce pleasing effects, and patrons desiring really artistic work may confidently place their orders with this house, and rely upon having their commissions executed promptly, at reasonable prices, and to their entire satisfaction.

Star Chemical Works.

Manufacturer of Landell's Products, No. 6 Dearborn Street, John E. Landell, Proprietor.

Among those houses which have risen to deserved prominence in Chicago, by virtue of enterprise and industry, must be classed that of the Star Chemical Works, manufacturers of grocers' shelf goods. Although founded, in 1870, on a scale far from extensive, the energy and discernment with which the business has been conducted have been effective in building up a trade of the most satisfactory character. The premises occupied comprise the spacious three-story and basement building, No. 6 Dearborn street, and the factory at corner of Bowery and Tilden avenue, on West side, where heaviest goods are made, admirably arranged and fitted with all the modern appliances and conveniences for the prosecution of the business, employment being given to a large force of skilled operatives, who are engaged in the manufacture of the celebrated Landell's baking powder, true extracts of fruit, lemon and vanilla, essence of peppermint, cinnamon and wintergreen, indigo liquid bluing, mucilage, school inks, cold drawn castor oil, sewing machine oil, hair oil, ground spices, mixed birdseed, bird gravel, diamond bath brick pulverized, washed whiting, toilet soaps, pepper box bluing, improved French shoe blacking, shoe dressing, stove polish, lye, potash, licorice, mustard, etc., while the enterprise of the house is well illustrated in the high grade of goods which Mr. John E. Landell, the proprietor, places upon the market at prices difficult to duplicate elsewhere.

G. L. Beck.

Publisher and Bookseller, 26 North Clark Street.

G. L. Beck, the prominent publisher and bookseller of Chicago, began business in 1874, in a small way, on Clybourn avenue, but trade increased so rapidly that he moved to more central quarters in 1876, and in 1884 located at his present eligible quarters. He has periodicals, papers and books in all languages and at reasonable rates. He sells on subscription, and has twenty-five or more assistants. His sales amount to over $25,000 annually, and his patronage extends all over the northwestern States. Mr. Beck is also interested in Dr. C. Bernhard's Glorious Discovery, Johanniter oil, salve, tea and drops, which have become so noted throughout the United States. The oil is a never-failing remedy. It is an internal and external remedy, is incomparably better than all contemporary medicines, and of wonderfully rapid and strong action, although at the same time totally harmless, even for the most delicate constitutions, and sells for fifty cents per bottle. The Johanniter salve is a popular remedy, and is sold at twenty-five cents per box. The Johanniter drops are blood-purifying, cathartic and strengthening. These drops are the very best remedy of modern times, and should be found in every household.

For further particulars address G. L. Beck, No. 26 North Clark street, room 16.

Dauchy & Co.

Manufacturers of Patent Vault and Sidewalk Lights, Etc., 125 and 127 Indiana Street.

his firm are noted manufacturers of patent vault and sidewalk lights, and their premises are well arranged and fitted with all the appliances and conveniences necessary for this business. Besides a variety of vault and coal-hole covers, they are putting in a great number of forms and shapes of roof and floor lights, and with different colors make very handsome and ornamental work for both ceilings and floors. They call especial attention to Ross' patent light for vaults, which this firm uses. This is by far the greatest improvement made in vault light work for a long time, being one whereby they are able to greatly increase the light, and thus make deep basements more valuable. The plate is cast with shoulders in the hole where the glass is inserted, whereby the glass, with corresponding shoulders, can be inserted from below, and then being partly turned around is thereby fastened in so secure a manner when cemented that it cannot be got out without breaking it to pieces, nor can it be jarred loose. The Ross patent has many other advantages, which will be fully explained on application to this firm.

Acme Laundry.

James Donnellan, Proprietor, 1035 West Madison Street.

The Acme laundry has been established for over six years, but the present proprietor, James Donnellan, has only had charge of it for the past four years. The specialty is hand-work, every article being handled in the most thorough manner, and without any injury to the garment, as is often the case where machinery is used. The best of order prevails in the receipt and delivery of all goods, which shows the good system of management of this laundry. Goods are called for and delivered free of charge. The price of family washing is from 75 cents to $1.50 per dozen, and rough-dry from forty to fifty cents per dozen. Mr. Donnellan is a native of Ireland and has been a resident of Chicago for the past thirty-five years. He is one of the energetic and live business men of the West side and well merits the large trade he has won for the Acme laundry.

Edwards & Fitzgerald.

Family Market, 55 North State Street.

This house of Edwards & Fitzgerald is not only in name but reality a "Family Market," and enjoys the patronage of some of the best citizens in all parts of Chicago. Meats of every variety and description can be had here at reasonable prices. Choice poultry, game, fish and oysters, as well as all kinds of vegetables and fruits in their season, constitute part of their fine stock. The finest cutlets, steaks, roasts etc., are always in stock here, and prompt attention in delivery is the rule in the place. Both members of the firm are old and experienced butchers, and have followed this business in Chicago for a long term of years.

Great Western Wire Works.

198 East Madison Street, Theo. Spangenberg, Proprietor.

Theo. Spangenberg, the proprietor of the Great Western Wire works, since inaugurating his business in 1868, has continuously retained his lead in the manufacture of all kinds of wire goods, store and window fixtures, milliners' and hatters' trees, wire show and advertising signs, stands, brackets and an infinite variety of other wire goods, making a specialty of papier maché and wax forms. A handsomely illustrated catalogue of the goods actually manufactured by this house is published and mailed free on application to those interested, and which those desiring anything of this character will do well to consult before placing their orders elsewhere. Mr. Spangenberg is a native of Germany and has been a resident of Chicago since 1807.

Keller & Co.

Manufacturers of Bouquet Stands, Tables, Pedestals, Etc., Corner Lake and Jefferson Streets.

One of the prominent furniture manufacturers of this city is the firm of Keller & Co., corner of Lake and Jefferson streets. They are manufacturers of bouquet stands, tables and pedestals, easels, music stands, etc. They turn out some very elegant work at this factory, their designs being artistic. They do a very extensive city jobbing trade, and their goods are in great demand among the large wholesale houses in the city. Their factory is fitted up with all the most modern wood-working machinery, where they employ fifteen workmen. The business has been established since 1883. Mr. Edward A. Keller is a designer and wood-carver, and has been a prominent business man in this line of trade for many years. Mr. J. G. Wartenweiler is partner in the business, and has done much to advance the business to its present high standing. He is a native of Switzerland, learning his trade (wood and bone turning) in that country. After learning his trade, he traveled through all the large cities, gaining new points and perfecting himself in all the branches of turning. He came to Chicago in 1867, and has always been recognized as one of the most experienced and skillful members of his trade in the city.

Augustus Burke.

Successor to Burke Bros., Practical Felt, Composition and Gravel Roofers, Office and Warehouse, 15 West Superior Street.

One of the greatest considerations in building a house is how to get a substantial roof. This question has been practically solved by Mr. Augustus Burke, of 15 West Superior street, near North Halsted. He is a practical felt, composition and gravel roofer, and dealer in roofing material. This gentleman has made this class of work his study for the last eight years, and during that time has executed work on many large buildings in this city, and always with the greatest satisfaction. He has an extensive connection with the principal builders, carpenters, masons and architects of the city and suburbs, and is always open to take contracts for the execution of any amount of this kind of work. He has excellent facilities and accommodations, the plant being ample, and a staff of efficient workmen are always employed. Parties who are connected with the building trade would do well to consult Mr. Burke at his office. They will find him ready to give any information that lies in his power. The notable jobs performed by Mr. Burke were for the city police and fire departments, for the West Division Railway company, the Chicago and Northwestern railway, Cribben & Sexton, Brunswick & Balke, Washingtonian home, etc.

M. T. Coughlin.

Manufacturer and Dealer in Oils and Engineers' Supplies, 49 North Market Street.

Continuing our tour of the city, we entered the establishment of M. T. Coughlin, at No. 49 North Market street. He is manufacturer and dealer in all kinds of oils and engineers' supplies. One of the important special brands of this firm is "Old Gold" cylinder and machine oil, which is so popular and much sought after by the trade. Mr. Coughlin has been in the business for the past seven years and during that time has built up a trade extending throughout all parts of the south, west and northwest, and aggregates nearly $30,000 annually. He is a marine engineer of life-long experience, which enables him to supply the best articles for this trade. Entire satisfaction is guaranteed, and those wishing supplies in this line will do well to give him a call before going elsewhere.

D. Needham's Sons.

Red Clover Blossom Preparations, 11 and 118 Dearborn Street.

The simple and common red clover blossom has been found to be one of Nature's great remedies for whooping cough, catarrh, inflammatory rheumatism, erysipelas, etc., and has cured many cases of cancer. It is not a patent medicine, but simply what it is called red clover blossoms, and the extract of the blossoms. It is conceded by thousands of sufferers in all parts of the country who have used it, and by many of the leading physicians, to be the best blood purifier known, and as a regulator of the bowels the solid extract has no equal. It is pure simple, harmless and efficacious. Great care is taken by this house in picking the blossoms to get only the pure red clover, and to exclude leaves and stems, and their red clover preparations now have a world-wide reputation as being pure and unadulterated. They do not advertise extensively, but effect many sales through customers who have seen or known persons benefited by the use of the clover blossom remedy.

The Great Atlantic & Pacific Tea Co.

John L. Crist, Manager, Chicago Main House and Western Headquarters, 160 State Street.

The representative concern in its line and the largest importers and retailers in the world are recognized to be the Great Atlantic and Pacific Tea Co. This great company was organized a quarter of a century ago, with headquarters at 35 and 37 Vesey street, New York. The company began operations in 1861 with ample resources and facilities, that have never since been rivaled by any other house on either hemisphere. There, today, in the company's counting-rooms, is conducted the business which has grown to magnitudinous proportions. The company have 172 retail stores throughout the United States, and are the heaviest importers of fine teas and coffees brought to this country. Having connections in Europe, India, China and Japan, their resources for securing the choicest goods are unlimited, and they deal today with millions of people on the basis of pure teas and coffees. No rubbish or doctored goods can be found in their stock. The oldest and most practical tea men are at the head of this vast business, and by judicious use of enormous capital, the members of the company have long held the lead, and must necessarily continue to do so. Special agents are kept by them in the tea-growing districts of China and Japan, who secure the finest yield of this fragrant plant, and no second-grade or last season's teas, such as is usually foisted on the public by small and inexperienced dealers.

The company is entitled to the credit of breaking up the high prices which teas and coffees were sold at some twenty years ago. The gross outgo of coffee in their vast business is simply stupendous, and it does not seem credible that one concern can handle and consume at retail the enormous amount of five hundred tons of coffee per month, or one million pounds. The coffee-roasting department has in operation forty roasters, and they are taxed to their utmost, being obliged to roast night and day in order to supply the great demands made on them from their branch houses. The first retail store was established in Chicago in 1871, and now six large establishments, all in flourishing operation, are located as follows: 160 State street, 91 North Clark street, 245 West Madison street, 148 Twenty-second street, 428 Milwaukee avenue and 240 North avenue.

Revere House.

Corner Clark and Michigan Streets, J. D. Fanning, Proprietor.

This is one of the finely appointed and newly fitted hotels of Chicago. It is also conveniently located for trains and boats, and the pleasure resorts, places of amusement, parks, etc., can be readily reached by street-cars from this hotel. It is six stories in height with a large basement, and is entirely fire-proof, and from basement to roof everything is arranged after the most improved modern plans. Upwards of $100,000 were expended last year alone for improvements and furnishing. The house has a frontage on North Clark street of 150 feet and 100 feet on Michigan street. Thus it receives plenty of light, while fresh breezes from the lake pass through every room in the house. This standard house has been in existence for over a quarter of a century, and although razed to the ground by the fire of 1871, it has arisen, phœnix-like, from its ashes in grander proportion and increased magnificence. A finely fitted cafe, news stand, telegraph office, barber shop and billiard room are located on the office floor. The Corinthian hall is a prominent annex to this hotel, a covered tin bridge uniting the two. The hall is 100 x 100 feet and is used for public and private balls, receptions, etc. The present proprietor, Mr. J. D. Fanning, has had charge of this house for the past three years, and it is to his efficient management and energy that the improvements spoken of were made and the present high standing has been reached. Both the American and European plans are followed; the rates for the former are two dollars per day, while at the latter rooms can be had from seventy-five cents to one dollar per day and meals fifty cents each. Mr. Fanning is a native of New York, and brings with him a great practical experience in this business, in which he is popularly known throughout this country.

Henry J. Frieman.

Fancy Bakery, Coffee House and Restaurant, 91 Washington Street.

One of the most convenient and pleasant places to get a meal, in the neighborhood of Washington street and Clark, is that of Henry J. Frieman, at 91 Washington street. This house has been for nine years a well-known, reliable restaurant. All kinds of fancy baking is made on the premises, and everything is as clean and inviting as possible. The room—20 x 150 feet—is fitted with twenty tables, is well ventilated, and kept at a uniform heat of about sixty degrees, both in summer and winter. Meals are served up on the European plan, according to the menu card. Thus everyone gets just what they prefer, at a moderate cost. About twenty hands are employed, and about one hundred can be seated at one time, and on an average from six hundred to seven hundred are fed here every day. The business is steadily increasing, and is as prosperous as that of any establishment of the kind in the city.

H. C. Nelson.

Maker of Fine Parlor and Professional Banjos, 716 Dania Ave.

Mr. H. C. Nelson makes the finest and handsomest banjos in the market, and a more skillful workman is not to be found in the country. He has lately made and sent a fine instrument of this kind to H. R. H. the Prince of Wales. One lately made for a prominent citizen is simply perfect in construction, the finger-board and neck being of ebony, the tuning keys of ivory, body of silver and silver plate worked on a base of rosewood, inlaid with tulipwood and ebony. The material alone cost about $60, and the instrument was to be disposed of for $125. Such an one could not be purchased in any retail music warehouse for less than $200. Mr. Nelson makes solely to order, both for private individuals and for the trade. He has been in the business for six years, the last five of which have been spent at his present location. The tone of his instruments is very fine, and not to be excelled and very rarely equaled. His prices are from $15 upward.

Dr. L. O. Gibbs.

125 South Clark Street, Room 79.

Amongst the various remedial agents in cases of disease, blood impurities, and especially in the case of throat and lung affections, none is receiving more attention than the oxygen treatment. The inhalation of oxygen compound has been productive of good results in many cases, and is indorsed by many of the leading physicians of the day. Dr. L. O. Gibbs has made this treatment a specialty, and also uses, as aid, electricity and herbal remedies. He has been established in this building and locality for the past fifteen years, and is well known. He graduated at Bennett Medical college in this city, and has continued here since, having a large and increasing practice. He gives his treatment direct, at his office, 125 South Clark street, room 79, and charges nothing for consultation. His charges are moderate, and he gives one trial treatment free. His office hours are from 10 A. M. to 5:30 P. M.

Phil. Henrici.

Cafe and Fancy Bakery, 175 and 177 East Madison Street.

This house was established in 1869, burned out in 1871, re-established in 1872, and has continued in the same block ever since. About one hundred and fifty guests can be accommodated at one time, and about a thousand a day patronize this establishment. The rates are based on the European plan—what is ordered is charged for, the price being plainly marked on the menu card. The provisions are of the best quality, well prepared, and served up in a thoroughly clean and pleasing manner. It is, however, more for the fine pastry and coffee that this house has become noted, and as such we can cordially ask any visitor, whether on business or pleasure, to give it their patronage.

Henry Schoellkopf.

Importer and Wholesale Dealer in Groceries and Foreign Produce, 232 and 234 East Randolph Street.

Amongst the oldest and best known mercantile houses in the city, and a leading one in the grocery and fruit line, is that of Mr. H. Schoellkopf, of 232 and 234 East Randolph street. This gentleman came to this country from Germany when not more than twenty years of age, and settled for four years at Buffalo. He came to this city in 1851, and when but twenty-four years of age opened this business. The trade, which is both wholesale and retail, is very large, extending to all parts of the city and embracing a large country business. The goods are sent out as far as Dakota, Colorado, etc., and are of the best quality, and low in price. Mr. Schoellkopf sends out no agents, advertising in the local papers in preference. He keeps a large stock, and makes a specialty of foreign cheese, canned fish, dried fruits, and imports both direct and obtains through importing houses. The bulk of his other supplies are obtained from New York houses of the largest kind. Mr. Schoellkopf has just erected some fine residences on North Clark street and North Park avenue, near Lincoln park. They are models of architectural beauty, and among the finest residences of the North side.

John Snitzer.

Tailoring, Dyeing and Scouring, 125 Dearborn Street.

One of the oldest established and most reliable houses where cleaning, dyeing, scouring and repairing is made a specialty, is located at 125 Dearborn street, on the second floor; also at 1824 Dearborn street, at his residence. The proprietor, Mr. John Snitzer, has been connected with the business all his life, and succeeded to this established trade years ago. This house has been established here since 1852, and is well known throughout the city. It suffered with the rest in the great fire of 1871, but speedily built up again, and has a name for careful and thorough work, and customers come, some from long distances, to avail themselves of its advantages. From six to eight hands are constantly employed, and as the expenses are low, the charges will be found to be as moderate as at any similar establishment.

A. Lipman.

Diamond Broker and Loan Agent, 99 East Madison Street.

A standard and reliable establishment in its line is that of A. Lipman, of 99 East Madison street. Here the passer-by is attracted to the most beautiful and costly collection of jewelry, diamonds, etc., while inside a more varied assortment still is displayed. Mr. Lipman has been long established, having commenced in this business a quarter of a century ago, and has won the confidence and esteem of all who have had dealings with him. He is well known to all the hotel proprietors and is recommended by them to any who may need temporary help. He is fair dealing and can be depended upon for honest and upright treatment. His stock of diamond jewelry is very fine, many beautiful designs being shown, some single stones being worth close upon $1,000. All in all, Lipman's is a standard place.

Mrs. E. M. Hoyt.

Artist, 1239 West Jackson Street.

The city of Chicago is possessed of a large number of first-class artists, who, by close application to study, have gained not only a local, but national reputation, and none are more worthy of special mention than the lady whose name heads this sketch. She has had over fifteen years' experience in portrait and landscape painting, and has received instruction from prominent European artists, and been a pupil of Mrs. Fassett and Prof. Carling. She is known not only as an able artist, but as an excellent and proficient teacher, having pupils and receiving work from all parts of the city, suburbs, and the States of Illinois and Wisconsin. She does all kinds of artist work, such as crayon, india-ink, pastels, water colors and oil. Special attention is given to portrait painting and enlarging and finishing old pictures. She is most thorough in the course of instruction given to her pupils, and does everything in her power to perfect them in their work. Her studio is located at her residence, 1239 West Jackson street, where she can be addressed or visited at any time. All orders received by mail meet with prompt and careful attention.

La Pierre House.

European Plan, Corner Washington Boulevard and Halsted Street.

The West side hotels are proverbial for comfort, and they are most extensively patronized by a large class of people when they make a visit to our important city. The La Pierre house, at the corner of Washington boulevard and Halsted street, is a notable example of what we mean. The popular proprietor has been in this business for eleven years, and understands it thoroughly in all its branches. There are fifty rooms, and accommodation for eighty guests. This hotel is a fine brick structure, and is considered one of the safest in the city, as regards the construction and general internal arrangements. Every precaution is taken to insure the safety and comfort of the patrons of this house. The house is very conveniently situated with regard to easy access to the business portions of the city, as the street-cars pass by the door, and the Union depot can be reached by a person walking in five minutes. The idea of the management is to make it a home hotel, and in this regard a great success has been achieved.

Henry Newgard.

Practical Locksmith, Bell-Hanger and Brass-Finisher, 167 East Madison Street.

Mr. Newgard is a thoroughly practical and experienced workman. His trade is that of locksmith, bell-hanger, brass finisher and erector of speaking tubes, electric bells, burglar alarms and gas-lighting apparatus. His work may be relied upon, and an order is promptly attended to. His trade has been steadily growing since 1883, when he first commenced in business for himself. He keeps a stock mostly of materials for his use, which he obtains from city houses. His premises on Madison street comprise office, work-shop and stock room in one, and here the proprietor may be found when not superintending work in the city or surrounding districts. All the work and material

are of the first quality and are guaranteed to give satisfaction. Mr. Henry Newgard is an energetic and practical workman, and the information may not be out of place in a work which, like this, is intended to be a thorough guide to the business man.

Lucke Bros.

Merchant Tailors, 121 Fifth Avenue.

One of the most reliable houses in this branch of trade is that of Lucke Bros., of No. 121 Fifth avenue, who have long been established and known as first-class merchant tailors. They deal only in the best goods (all cloths being imported), make up in the latest styles and with the best workmanship. The effort made by this firm is to produce as perfect an article as can be made, and the giving of satisfaction is more sought for by them than the amount of profit gained by the transaction. Eleven years ago they opened this business on Washington street (84), and removed to their present premises only this year. They are centrally located, in the very center of the business part of the city, and their premises are admirably suited to their requirements. The bulk of the trade is local, but orders are constantly being received from all parts of the State, chiefly from their old customers, who cannot find another firm to suit them so well in their new place of abode.

R. Ernesti.

Artist, Studio, 77 South Clark Street.

Mr. R. Ernesti is an artist of fine reputation and of sixteen years' experience in his profession, and can be said to stand today among the leaders in this line. His $10 crayon and india-ink pictures which he makes with good frame complete for $10, are clever reproductions. Mr. Ernesti is very rapid, and his work is indeed a marvel at the price, and orders come in faster than they can be executed. Mr. Ernesti takes his copy either from life or from a photograph, as may be desired. Those taken from life, however, are always the most satisfactory. All who desire to get a valuable and good portrait of themselves or their friends should avail themselves of this unexampled offer. Visitors are welcome to inspect the work and specimens, and for the $10 they can choose their own style of frame.

Wm. Casler.

Dress Plaiting and Button Hole Bazar, 99 East Madison Street.

A very important item in the expenditure of ladies is the making of their dresses. This in many cases exceeds the cost of the material, and many would make their common dresses were it not that they find such difficulty in making the plaiting, kilting, etc. For the benefit of such, we venture to cite the establishment of Mr. Casler, known as the Dress Plaiting and Button Hole Bazar, 99 East Madison street. Here all the difficult portions of the work can be brought, and skilled hands will overcome the difficulty and make any kind of plaiting desired, at low rate of charge. Mr. Casler has lately added a branch to his line of business in the button hole line, making the finest button hole that was ever yet produced. It is different from all others, and has the appearance of hand-made work, and is just as durable. The kilting of skirts is a specialty, and contracts are made with dressmakers for this class of work, some of which cannot be done with ordinary machines. Mr. Casler has been in the business nine years in the same location, his business having steadily increased since the commencement. He employs six skilled hands, and uses steam power for the sewing machines.

Lansing & Sickler.

Restaurant, 122 to 126 South Clark Street.

The vast improvements lately completed here place this restaurant the equal of anything of the kind in

the city. The ladies' department is elaborately furnished and fitted, and reserved especially for them. The house has been established ever since the big fire, and has obtained a wide reputation and patronage. The place is fitted up with the latest mosaic tiling for the floors, lincrusta walton for the ceilings, and fine mirrors for the walls. Philip Best's and imported beers are served, and lunch counter and tables are fitted up with all that goes to supply the inner man, while from thirty to fifty obliging waiters look after the interests of all. About fifteen hundred to two thousand persons are served daily at this model restaurant.

Mrs. L. Kehl.

Masquerade Costumer, 62 North Clark Street.

At No. 62 North Clark street are the parlors of Mrs. L. Kehl, the popular masquerade costumer of Chicago. She keeps constantly on hand a full and varied supply of all make-ups, and patrons can be fitted out with any style on short notice. Although established only four years in Chicago, she has a large and growing patronage, extending over all parts of the United States. Upwards of twenty hands are employed to assist in manufacturing and fitting, and all orders meet with prompt and careful attention. Costumes for large parties can be furnished on short notice, and all prices are reasonable. Mrs. Kehl has had long experience in this business, and is able to please the most fastidious masquerader as to a suit and trimmings. Her proficiency in this line has won for her all the theatrical trade—German and English—in the city. Letters of the highest testimonials are in her possession, showing the satisfaction of her work to clubs, societies and individuals.

Adam Breuer.

Manufacturer of Fine Brands of Hand-Made Cigars, and Dealer in Tobacco and Smokers' Articles, 14 Rush Street.

Mr. Breuer is not only a dealer in tobacco and smokers' articles, but makes a specialty of manufacturing fine brands of hand-made, unadulterated cigars, prominent among which is the Henry Clay and La Rosa Conchas. In this line he is not surpassed by anyone in Chicago, and many of his customers walk blocks out of their way to procure one of his desirable brands. On account of this merited reputation his trade is very large, and amounts to over a quarter of a million cigars annually. Mr. Breuer began business in 1860, at No. 355 Superior street. Although a heavy loser by the big fire, his energy and will were too great to be thus downed, so he made another start, which has resulted in his present large trade. He moved to his present quarters in 1880, and has six skilled workmen employed in the factory.

James Ball.

Ladies' and Gentlemen's Fine Boot and Shoe Maker, Avondale.

One of the very finest custom boot and shoe makers in the city is Mr. James Ball. Mr. Ball uses imported leather and only the best materials of all kinds, and employs skilled hands only. He makes exclusively to measure in the latest styles, and guarantees satisfaction, and your measure can be taken at your residence by sending a postal card. For thirty years he has been in the trade, ten of which he has been foreman in some of the largest Chicago houses. He is a Cornishman and left England when twenty-six years of age. He came to this city twelve years ago, and early in 1885 commenced making on his own account. He employs from six to ten hands, and has a large local trade. He buys his material from local importers, and is well known as a thoroughly reliable and hard-working tradesman.

McEwan's

Temperance European Hotel and Coffee House, 93 and 95 West Madison Street.

One of the finest establishments of this kind in the city is McEwan's Temperance European hotel and coffee house of 93 to 95 West Madison street. The hotel is a handsome fire-proof structure, containing one hundred and thirty rooms, which are all well furnished in a style superior to the general run of hotels of this description. The interior arrangements are admirable, and the strictest attention is paid to cleanliness and comfort. Mr. McEwan also runs a restaurant in connection with the hotel. It has a spacious, well-lighted dining-room, and is well patronized, as many as 1,200 meals a day being served. Mr. McEwan is an old resident of Chicago, having been settled here since 1855. Visitors to Chicago will find this a very comfortable and convenient hotel, as it is very centrally located and within easy access of the Union depot and all the principal business houses and places of amusement.

Fred. J. Wallis.

Artist, Room 75, Japanese Building.

There are few artists in whom the innate qualities essential to success more strongly predominate than in Fred. J. Wallis, now permanently located in Chicago. He is widely known as a portrait painter, and is patronized by many of our best families. Mr. Wallis' work gives evidence of marked natural ability, thorough technical training and originality of conception, while the careful attention he pays to the minutest details insures the utmost perfection in his treatment of a subject. Mr. Wallis is a native of Germany, but has resided in Chicago since 1857, and in his specialty, oil and crayon portraits, has become widely known, both at home and abroad, his productions embellishing the walls of many of our own palatial mansions, while as a public-spirited and representative citizen he also occupies a prominent position.

Sandberg & Co.

Dealers in Engravers' Wood and Engravers' Tools, Factory 86 and 88 Dearborn Street.

This firm is engaged in the production of engravers' woods (bolted blocks being a specialty), tools and requisites for wood engraving. Their boxwood is imported from Turkey, while maple, pine, etc., are obtained from domestic sources. These latter woods are used for common engraving, but the better class are all executed on boxwood. The boxwood does not reach a circumference of more than about eight or ten inches, and of this the center contains knots and the outside cracks, so that blocks can only be cut of about four inches square. When larger are required they are made by "bolting" together two or more of these smaller blocks. Some of the largest engravings are executed on bolted blocks, of great size, and containing a hundred or more separate blocks. The fitting of these together, smoothing them off, etc., is a delicate process, and requires much skill. This business has been established twelve years, and has steadily increased until at present about fifteen hands are employed, and the blocks are supplied to engravers in all parts of the United States, and are also sent in considerable quantities to Canada. The quality of the work cannot be surpassed, while having every facility for the prompt execution of orders, they are able to work for as low rates as any firm in the country.

A. R. Ohlman.

Glass Engraver, 113 Madison Street.

Mr. A. R. Ohlman, glass engraver, is thoroughly skilled and experienced in all kinds of glass engraving, having been established since 1869. He has been a large loser by fire; first in 1871 he lost all, and nearly all, except his tools, in the spring of 1886, on Dearborn street. The tools cannot be bought, and have to be made specially for the work, generally by the engraver himself. It is astonishing with what speed a skilled workman will execute a piece of engraving. In about four minutes, while watching the proprietor, he took up a glass bottle, fixed his tools and engraved first a name, in old English, then an ornamental top and bottom figure of leaves, work that apparently would take ten times as long to perform. He also has specimens of some of the finest and most delicate engravings to be anywhere seen. Monograms, especially, and initials are executed most skillfully and accurately by him or his skilled workmen. Most of his orders are from firms, but he is open to execute orders for private individuals, etc., at very low rates.

Anna House.

102 and 104 North Clark Street, A. B. Young, Proprietor.

This house was opened ten years ago especially for hotel purposes, and is six stories high. The offices, parlors and large dining hall are located on the second floor, while the rest of the building is given to sleeping apartments, of which there are over fifty. The house is furnished throughout in the most elegant and latest style, while all modern conveniences and appliances are used. The rooms are large and airy, and everything is done for the comfort and safety of the guests. The standard of the Anna house is so well known that it is constantly crowded. It is more of a home hotel than any one in the city. The rates are $1.50 and $2.00 per day, according to location of room. Special attention is given to family patronage, and in this line a large trade has been established. Mrs. A. B. Young has been proprietor of the hotel for nearly two years, and under her efficient management its patronage has greatly increased.

United States Home Mfg. Co.

Inventors and Manufacturers of Specialties in Ladies' and Children's Underwear, 37 Lakeside Building.
N. B. Little, Manager.

There is probably no line of manufacture in which has been made greater progress in the last few years than in the manufacture of specialties in connection with the ladies' furnishing goods trade, while no house in the business has attained an equal reputation with that built up by the U. S. Home Manufacturing company, in the five years which have elapsed since its organization. In the sale of their rubber underwear for ladies and misses, an entirely new thing, the invention of Mrs. H. F. Little, thousands of lady agents all over the country have found remunerative and easy employment, as this article needs only to be introduced to insure a certain sale. Besides ingenious machinery, there are hundreds of operatives steadily engaged in the manufacture of these goods. The manager, Mr. N. B. Little, gives his close personal supervision to the business, thereby insuring that only articles of first-class quality shall leave the premises. The enterprise of this concern has been fully illustrated by the superior character of the articles placed on the market.

J. H. Purdy & Co.

Watch Materials, Tools, Etc., Room 4, 170 State Street.

Among the wonders of a great city, the magnitude attained by seemingly unimportant lines of business is not the least. A notable illustration is in the line of watch materials, jewelers' supplies, jewelers' and watchmakers' tools, etc. A prominent representative of this branch of trade in Chicago is the house of J. H. Purdy & Co., noted for completeness of stock and thorough knowledge of this special business. Beginning as a watchmaker's apprentice, Mr. Purdy's experience covers nearly one-third of this century. When the U. S. Jewelers' Guild, an association of retail jewelers represented in nearly all the States, determined to supply themselves and patrons with reliable stamped goods, they found it necessary to entrust their interests and stamp to some one of undoubted integrity, who should act as their representative in obtaining and distributing this supply, and Mr. Purdy was the first choice. Mr. Purdy is a native of Bath, N. Y. He came west in 1859, settling at Des Moines, Iowa. In 1865 he traveled for a large jewelry house of this city, and in 1875 commenced selling on commission, in his own name. He opened a regular jobbing business in 1880, soon after which he took charge of the Guild jewelry. He has invented many important tools and articles pertaining to the trade, that have met with large sales in this and other countries.

North Side Restaurant.

53 North Clark Street, Mrs. Williams, Proprietor.

This orderly establishment is conducted by Mrs. Williams, who has had charge of it for the past six years. Everything of the best the market affords can be had here, at very reasonable rates. Mrs. Williams gives every feature of the business her close personal attention. She has nine efficient assistants to help her with the work. The restaurant is well patronized, and commutation tickets are sold for $3.00, on which $3.50 worth of meals can be procured. Lunches and suppers are prepared on short notice and at reasonable terms. It is also an all-night restaurant, and meals can be had at all hours.

P. H. Bolten & Co.

General Commission Merchants, 223 South Water Street.

A thoroughgoing exponent of the commission business in Chicago is to be found in the reliable house of Messrs. P. H. Bolten & Co. They do a general commission business in country produce, making a specialty of butter and eggs, in which their extensive acquaintance among the trade enables them to effect quick sales and immediate returns, thus tending greatly to the advantage of those placing consignments with them. Mr. Bolten has been in the commission business since 1871, and is fully acquainted with every feature of the trade. The gentlemen at the head of this house, Messrs. P. H. Bolten and J. William Johnston, are held in high esteem and bring long experience and marked ability to the conduct of their enterprise. They are doing an extensive business, honestly earned by the fairness of their methods and the promptness with which is executed all orders entrusted to their house.

Stephen Paddon & Co.

Chemical and Drug Importers, 156 Washington Street.

A very important firm is that of Stephen Paddon & Co., chemical and drug importers, glass-makers', soap-makers' and paper-makers' supplies, and manufacturers of glass bottles, located on the first floor No. 156 Washington street. This firm was established in 1875, the office having been located here ever since. The chemicals and drugs are imported direct from Europe, while the sales are chiefly in the country, west and north, from Cincinnati and Ohio to the Pacific. The manufacture of glassware was added in 1881. The factory is located at

La Salle, Ill., and employs about 180 hands, all kinds of bottles, chiefly those required by bottlers of wine, ales, cider, etc., being the article of manufacture. Samples only are kept here, orders being supplied direct from the factory and warehouses in the city. The trade is large and steadily increasing, numbering amongst its patrons many important and well-known firms.

J. Jerusalem.

562 and 564 North Halsted Street.

The large Weiss Beer brewery of Mr. J. Jerusalem is at the corner of North Halsted and Rees streets. He is one of the old residents of this city, and suffered heavily from the big fire in 1871, having his entire establishment, which was then located on Rush street, burned out, but with energy and perseverance he began again, and his business has steadily increased ever since. He owns the large building in which his brewery is located, although he only occupies one-half of it, 30x126 feet, three floors and a basement. A large force of men is employed, and several teams run to accommodate his many customers. Mr. Jerusalem is a native of Germany, and came to Chicago in 1865.

Charles W. Rose.

Merchant Tailor, 168 East Washington Street.

In the merchant tailoring trade there are none who have a better name for turning out superior goods than Mr. Charles W. Rose, successor to L. Wunderle. This business was first established in 1854, and was carried on by Mr. Wunderle till the 6th of March, 1883, when the present proprietor bought the business, since which time the trade has rapidly improved, and employs thirteen hands in the making-up department alone. The second floor of No. 168 and basement of the next door building are occupied by this business. Mr. Rose only deals in best imported cloth, Italian, and other materials. Suits are furnished complete on short notice from $35 upwards, and this, considering the quality of the goods and the workmanship, is extremely reasonable. The yearly sales amount to $25,000, and have more than doubled in the last two years.

W. H. Horn.

Commission Merchant and Dealer in Lumber, Shingles, Etc., 238 South Water Street.

Prominent among the old established business concerns of Chicago stands the well and favorably known house of W. H. Horn, lumber commission and dealer in shingles, railroad ties, wood, bark, cedar posts and telegraph poles. The business was established upwards of twenty years ago, and has been carried on continuously and successfully ever since. Mr. Horn handles all kinds of lumber, lath and shingles on commission, in car and cargo lots, having old established connections with the largest mills in the northwest, and cuts from his own lands railroad ties, cedar posts, telegraph poles, wood and bark, and is therefore in a position to promptly fill the largest orders at the lowest market quotations. Besides his other business ventures, he is the proprietor of Horn's Pier, Door county, Wis., from which millions of railroad ties, cedar posts and poles are annually loaded, being one of the best piers on the lakes. During his long and active business career, Mr. Horn has displayed large business capacity, shrewd foresight, and is well and favorably known in business circles.

John Clottu & Son.

Dealers in Wringers, Carpet Sweepers, and Manufacturers of the Banner Washing Machine, 277 East Madison Street.

Mr. John Clottu and his son Victor are successors to Calkin Brothers and P. H. Weber & Co. in this business, which consists of the manufacture of the "Banner Washing Machine" and the sale and repair of all kinds of wringers and carpet sweepers. This firm occupy the first floor and basement, the former being the store, and the latter the place of manufacture. Three skilled and six unskilled workmen are constantly employed. Mr. John Clottu came to this country in 1849, and for many years traveled through the States representing various commercial interests. His son was born in Minnesota in 1861, and came to this city in 1865. They have a good local trade, and also export to Australia to a considerable extent. In Chicago, where washing and laundry work is so dear, every family should possess one of the "Banner Washers," which are the best in the market, and very reasonable in price. And Mr. J. Clottu & Son make it a point never to sell an article they cannot guarantee.

F. Gustorf.

Agent, Lumber Commission, 242 South Water Street, Room 16.

The enormous amount of capital invested in the lumber trade of the United States, and the general interests involved give to this branch of business an importance that does not attach to many of the other leading lines of commerce. Among the old established and best known houses engaged in this line in this city is the deservedly popular and highly successful one of which Mr. Gustorf is the proprietor, lumber commission, than which none maintain a higher standing in the trade or enjoy a larger share of public favor and patronage. He handles all kinds of lumber in car and cargo lots, received direct from the chief producing regions of Michigan,

Wisconsin and the northwest, upon consignment of which liberal advances are made when requested. Mr. Gustorf, who has conducted the business with success for twenty years, is a gentleman of unmistakable ability and of the highest integrity, and the large measure of prosperity he now enjoys affords the amplest evidence of the general satisfaction he renders to those entrusting consignments to his care.

S. F. Wright & Co.

Livery and Boarding Stables, 248, 250 and 252 Kinzie St.

Those desiring to see the much talked of boulevards and parks of Chicago will always find good facilities at the fine livery and boarding stables of S. F. Wright

& Co., at 248 to 252 Kinzie street. The business was established in 1857 by Mr. A. J. Wright, at the corner of Madison and Clark streets. In 1864 S. F. Wright united with his brother, and two years later large and commodious stables were erected on the present site, but were burned out in the fire of 1871. They moved to the West side, where they remained until 1873, when the partnership was severed, and S. F. Wright returned to the present site and erected the large three-story brick stable now used by him. In 1880 his nephew, George N Wright, was admitted to the business, and has don much to promote their large trade. The stables cover an area of 100x150 feet, and are as finely fitted and arranged as any livery in Chicago. For ventilation, light and care given to all horses left in their care, these stables are unexcelled. Some of the finest turn-outs in the city can be procured here, and the trade consists of patrons from all the leading clubs and families of Chicago. A force of twenty-five men are constantly employed, and nothing is left undone to keep up the reputation of the stables for prompt attention to orders and first-class equipages. For further information call up telephone No. 3065.

Potter & Kisselburg.

Dealers in Hay, Straw and Grain, 1073 West Madison St.

This firm deals extensively in hay, straw and grain of all kinds, besides feed. Their trade is quite large, especially among the various stockmen of the city and suburbs, and since the State fair has been held in this city, this firm has had the contract for furnishing forage for the association, and also for the fat stock show for the past four years. They began the business in 1878 at No. 622 West Madison street, and after several changes moved to their present quarters three years ago. Their premises are fitted up in such a manner as to insure the prompt handling of all stock, so as to fill orders in the quickest and most satisfactory manner. They make selections of the best that can be procured, and their prices for such goods are very reasonable. Mr. Potter has been a resident of Chicago since 1876, and Mr. Kisselburg came to this city twenty years ago.

W. M. Paine.

Dealer in Fresh and Salt Meats, Poultry, Game, Etc., 1066 West Madison Street.

The enterprising establishment of Mr. W. M. Paine is at this location. Here is kept all kinds of fresh and salt meats, together with poultry, game, fish, vegetables, etc., which at once indicates the first-class character of this market, and conducted by a man experienced in this branch of trade. Mr. Paine has been located at his present quarters for the past three years, although he was in business for himself five years ago, at No. 75 West Adams street. He gives all his attention to his present market, and by bringing his life experience to bear upon the business has won a fine reputation and gained a large patronage from the best class of citizens in this part of the city. Mr. Paine is a native of this State, and has spent most of his life in this city. He was among the first to answer the country's call during the war, and enlisted in the 52d Illinois volunteers. He is an honored member of Custer post, No. 40.

Western Patent Agency.

H. P. Crawford & Co., Proprietors, 125 South Clark Street, H. C. Pockman, Attorney.

When an inventor brings out a patent, the next difficulty is to dispose of it to the best advantage. Several means are offered of doing this, but none have so great a merit as that system pursued by the "Western Patent Agency." The manner in which this is done is by judiciously advertising and placing the merits of the invention before the manufacturers and merchants dealing with that line of goods. This is done by publishing a journal, "The Inventors' Review," and mailing this to all such persons, in all parts of the country. The proprietors of this agency are H. P. Crawford & Co., Mr. H. C. Pockman being the associate in the business and the attorney for the company. The terms for disposal are as moderate as any other reliable agency, and depend largely upon commission, from ten to thirty per cent being charged upon the sale, according to the merits of the invention. The firm also obtain estimates for the manufacture of inventions for all inventors who place their business with them. They also obtain United States and foreign patents on the most reasonable terms. Satisfactory references are given, and satisfaction guaranteed. Engraving, printing, etc., is done on the lowest terms; estimates given on application. This business was carried on for five years in San Francisco, at which city a branch office still exists.

Meath Bros.

Wholesale and Retail Dealers in Furniture, Carpets, Etc., 265 and 267 West Madison Street.

At Nos. 265 and 267 West Madison street will be found the commodious store of Messrs. Meath Bros. These gentlemen are wholesale and retail dealers in furniture, carpets, stoves, oil cloth, curtains and everything in the house-furnishing line. This firm are very liberal with their customers, and are advocates of the easy payment system. They manufacture a considerable quantity of parlor furniture for their own trade, and have a well-fitted factory to carry on this branch of their business. They carry a large stock, and are prepared to furnish any sized house at the shortest notice. The firm is a new one in this locality, having only started in business here on the 1st of July, 1886. But they succeeded to an established business, and are gentlemen of experience in the furniture trade, and know how to give satisfaction to their customers, and to keep the trade together.

Charles Racine.

Pattern-Maker and Millwright, 86 and 88 West Randolph Street.

Mr. Charles Racine, of 86 and 88 West Randolph street, is extensively engaged as a pattern-maker and millwright. He gives special attention to putting up shafting and setting machinery, a branch of business in which he has had a long and varied experience. Mr. Racine makes a specialty of the manufacture of metal signs for shop doors, windows, etc. He has a large trade through the west and northwestern States, and his goods give universal satisfaction. Mr. Racine was born in London, England, and served his apprenticeship at the Millwall shops. He came to this country in 1857. In 1865 he started in business for himself, and by his energy and perseverance has succeeded in establishing a very snug business.

Svenska Tribunen

(The Swedish Tribune) Published Every Saturday at Corner Clark and Kinzie Streets, Room 23.

This is a liberal political weekly journal, published every Saturday by the Swedish Publishing Co. The Swedish Tribune is devoted to the interests of the Swedish people, not only of Chicago, but throughout the United States. Its popularity is attested by the large circulation of over twenty-five thousand copies. It is liberal in its politics, and upholds that which is right and just, no matter what the party name may be. Its columns are full, not only of the news of the day, but contain choice and interesting reading for the household. As a medium through which to advertise to reach the notice of this people, there is none better, and business men will do well to give it a trial. The price of the paper is $2.25 yearly, and $1.15 for six months. A large subscription list of over fifteen hundred is sent to Sweden every week. The officers of the company are A. Chaiser, president and manager; C. G. Linderborg, secretary and treasurer; and F. E. Jocknick, assistant treasurer. The paper was begun in 1869, and has met with great success. The most prominent Swedish writers of this and the old country contribute to it. Mr. C. O. Carlson is advertising manager, and all communications should be addressed to him.

E. T. Marsh.

Manufacturer of and Dealer in Harness, Collars, Whips, Robes, Etc., 1055 West Madison Street.

This business was established over seven years ago, and Mr. Marsh has had charge of it since March, 1886. He is manufacturer of and dealer in all kinds of harness, horse-collars, whips, robes, horse-clothing, etc. He employs the most competent workmen, and uses only the best of material. Mr. Marsh has a large and lucrative trade, and satisfaction is given in every case. He has had a life-long experience in this trade, which enables him to make the best of selections for his patrons, and to produce his manufactured goods at most reasonable prices, and also does all kinds of carriage trimming and repairing. Mr. Marsh has lived in Chicago for the past fifteen years. He served in the war of the rebellion in the 3d Wisconsin cavalry, where he did valiant service.

Charles T. Brown.

Attorney-at-Law and Counselor in Patent Causes, and Solicitor of American and Foreign Patents, Offices, No. 225 Dearborn Street.

However learned and intelligent an inventor may be, however skilled in his profession or business, ignorant alike of the letter of the patent laws as passed by congress, and of their meaning as construed in the many decisions made in litigated cases in the United States courts, the difficulties and delays experienced in properly preparing an application and in presenting it to the rigid examination necessarily required in the patent office are almost insurmountable by an inventor, and he has but little chance of obtaining his just rights, unless aided by an able and experienced patent solicitor. The importance, in litigation concerning patents, of securing the assistance of an attorney specially trained in the patent law and skilled in the analysis of mechanical devices is recognized by all litigants. It is universally admitted that many of the patent attorneys and solicitors of Chicago, located, as they are, in the very center of a large manufacturing district, and upon whom the demands from the factory, the machine shop and the field are almost unlimited, are specially fitted for and exceptionally successful in their chosen profession; and especially is this true of Mr. Charles T. Brown, of No. 225 Dearborn street. Mr. Brown has the best facilities for making exhaustive examination of all official documents of American and foreign patents, and since his admission to the bar of Illinois, his success has been phenomenal, both in the soliciting of important patents and in patent suits before the United States circuit and supreme courts. We recommend all interested in inventions to call upon or correspond with Mr. Brown and obtain his advice and opinion concerning their patentability and cost of obtaining American or foreign patents.

A. W. Heggie & Co.

Wholesale and Retail Dealers in Imported and Domestic Cigars and Tobaccos, 74 Washington Street.

One of the largest businesses in cigars and tobacco is that of A. W. Heggie & Co. The retail store, well stocked and fitted up, is located at 74 Washington street. Here lovers of the fragrant weed can obtain all the leading brands of both imported and domestic cigars. Mr. Heggie has had many years' connection with the trade as jobber, manufacturers' agent, etc. He deals in good, reliable brands only, and does a considerable trade with country retailers. His retail trade is large and steadily increasing; the box trade especially is growing, as special inducements and reductions are made to such customers. A full line of smoking and plug tobacco is also kept, of qualities not to be surpassed and at the lowest market price. Mr. Heggie is well known to the trade, his connections with them having been long and always of an honorable character.

M. Schwalbach.

Manufacturer of Church and Tower Clocks, 426 Ninth Street, Milwaukee, Wisconsin.

The construction of this clock is so simple that anybody can easily understand its working, take care of it and keep it in good order. The pendulum, having vibrated free one-half-minute, one minute receives a new impetus by a light spring, to keep it vibrating; the small wheel at the top of the pendulum counts the number of vibrations and loosens the clock. The weight pushes the clockwork and the hands ahead one half-minute, or every minute, and braces the little spring, which then follows the pendulum and communicates to it a light pressure, the clockwork thereafter again resting thirty seconds. The fan at the front of the pendulum serves to detain the weight. Behind the fan is the escapement-wheel with three rollers. Inside of the escapement-wheel is the little spring, which on one end is fastened to the shaft and on the other to the escapement-wheel. The first shaft revolves around one-third every half-minute, making a full rotation in one and one-half minutes. The second shaft turns every quarter of an hour and starts the quarter-striking, while the quarter-striking, having struck the four quarters, starts the hour striking, this being done on the largest bell. The third shaft makes one full rotation every hour, indicating the time on a small dial at front of the clock; the third shaft, by means of a rod running upwards in the rear of the clock, also moves the hands on the dials of the tower.

C. M. Barnes.

Wholesale Books and Stationery, 75 and 77 Wabash Ave.

Of the various commercial enterprises that have made Chicago one of the great trade centers of the nation, it is easy to perceive that the book trade has exerted an important influence. Prominent among the leading and representative houses engaged in this trade is that of Mr. C. M. Barnes, a gentleman both by education and taste peculiarly adapted to the book business. Mr. Barnes was for fifteen years a minister of the Congregational church, but failing health necessitated a change to other pursuits, and after three years spent in the government service, he established his present business in 1876, and soon thereafter, through judicious management, attained to his present prominence in the trade. Though devoting himself to no particular class of literature, his prominent specialty is in second-hand and shop-worn school-books, in which his facilities permit of his offering the most advantageous terms. His line of new school-books is also very extensive. The house was formerly located at Nos. 151 and 153 Wabash avenue, but more enlarged accommodations were long since demanded to properly transact the business, and on May 1, 1887, the present spacious premises were occupied. Mr. Barnes is a native of Canton, Ill., and is highly appreciated by all know him, while in his relation to the educational world, he occupies a place which it would be difficult to fill. In addition to the school department, he has so largely increased the miscellaneous and stationery departments as to require an entire floor for these two departments alone.

Tuckhorn & Co

Manufacturers of Billiard and Pool Tables, 92 Fifth Ave.

As manufacturers of billiard and pool tables and dealers in supplies, Messrs. Tuckhorn & Co. have for years occupied a position of the highest prominence, their tables being regarded as standard among

players, while their reasonableness in price places them within the reach of all. The house was established in 1850, a branch also being conducted at No. 28 Mifflin street, Madison, Wis., while in addition to the manufacture and repair of billiard and pool tables, for which every facility is enjoyed, the firm are extensive importers and dealers in materials of all kinds, inclusive of cloths, balls, marbles, pool-pins, bottles, chalk, cue-tips, cue-wafers, cement, glue, brushes, court plaster, dice and cups, cue-cutters, triangles, pool-pockets, pool-checks, poker-chips, pocket-irons, playing-cards, chess, dominoes and dealing-boxes. Second-hand tables are also purchased, and balls re-turned and colored. Their trade is co-extensive with the Union, rendering further comment superfluous, their business furnishing as it does an example of an honorable and prosperous career.

H. F. Vehmeyer.

Dealer in Broom Corn and Broom Manufacturers' Supplies, 204, 206, 208 and 210 Michigan Street.

As Chicago will ever continue to retain its prestige as a great food supply center, its importance

augment in other commercial pursuits as This is clearly demonstrated in the industry of broom corn, which within recent years has assumed proportions not equaled by any other city in the United States, and is fast developing itself into an enormous trade specialty. The heaviest dealer the west in this line is Mr. H. F. Vehmeyer, his warehouse comprising 204, 206, 208 and 210 Michigan street Chicago. He was formerly located No. 190 East Kinzie street, he has been engaged in the business at this about six years. His trade increased rapidly that he was forced to carry heavy stocks of goods. In order to accommodate them he erected the structure occupied by him at his own expense and from designs originated by himself, his long-continued experience told him were It is a very strong and well-proportioned building with cut stone trimmings, five stories and basement in height, and 80 x 100 feet in The facilities now enjoyed by Mr. Vehmeyer enable him to handle more promptly his growing business, while the structure put up by him will as a monument to his business enterprise, and feature of adornment to the locality in which stands. He is well known in trade circles, where has the record and reputation of an honorable fair-dealing merchant and successful operator sides broom corn Mr. Vehmeyer handles all kinds broom-makers' supplies, and in this line of trade as well as in broom corn, he sells at the smallest possible margin consistent with a fair and profit.

Hotel Brevoort.

European Plan, 143 and 145 East Madison Street.

The new Brevoort house has lately undergone an entire change, so marked that, but for the location, none of the old patrons would recognize in this beautiful, modern, palace hotel the old home of days gone by. It is now the best European hotel in the city, with all modern improvements and accommodations for her many guests. Entering from Madison street the spectator finds himself in a brilliantly lighted office on the ground floor, with marble tiling, marble sideboards, beautiful frescoed walls, solid brass chandeliers suspended from the ceiling, superbly grand in finish and design, shooting out a dozen or more gas-jets, which seem to be enviously vying with their more powerful and brilliant competitors, the electric arc lights, the whole combining to make the most cheerful and inviting hotel office in the city. The furnishing of the new Brevoort house was left entirely to Mrs. Field, and to her excellent judgment in selecting and arranging is due the rich and home-like air which pervades every part of this beautiful hotel. No two rooms are furnished with exactly the same pattern of carpets. The curtains and draperies are all of the very latest patterns, rich in design, texture and finish. The furniture is all in antique oak and mahogany finish with marble tops throughout.

The new dining-room in rear of the office is fitted up in elegant style, with private stairway for ladies leading to the parlors of the hotel. The restaurant will be open to the general public as well as to the guests of the hotel, the main entrance way facing the old board of trade court. It is the purpose to make this the model restaurant of the city, and to make the prices as reasonable as first-class accommodations will allow. The dining-room is the handsomest and best furnished of its kind in the city. The new Brevoort is under the proprietorship of Mr. George M. Hubbard and Mr. Rush H. Field,

166   A BUSINESS TOUR OF CHICAGO.

both experienced hotel men, while Mr. Martin Burke, late of McCoy's hotel, will preside as head clerk. This will comprise a strong trio, as they are all men who have individually made hosts of friends in their past connections. Mr. Field was for many years the proprietor of the Wiler house, of Mansfield, Ohio, while Mr. Hubbard has been connected with the Palmer, McCoy's and Brevoort of this city.

Henry Sievert.

Dealer in Imported and Domestic Cigars, Tobacco and Smokers' Articles, 41 North Clark Street.

One of the oldest cigar stores in Chicago is at No. 41 North Clark street, opposite the Casino. This store is kept by Mr. Henry Sievert, dealer in imported and domestic cigars, tobacco and smokers' articles. He is doing a flourishing business, and keeps one of the finest stocks in this line in the city. He began business in June, 1885, at his present central and eligible quarters. Cigars by the box is a specialty. While he keeps on hand all the principal brands, "No. 41" is his special brand, and meets with great favor from the public. Mr. Sievert is a native of Germany, and came to Chicago in 1880.

The Jewish Occident.

155 and 157 Washington Street, Chicago, Julius Silversmith, Editor and Secretary.

The Jewish community in this city numbers 85,000. These have a newspaper devoted to their interests issued weekly, entitled the Occident, which has an extensive circulation of over 31,000. This is the only Jewish paper in the western States with

such a circulation, and the only one printed and published in the city. The offices are at 155 and 157 Washington street. This journal is generally recognized as the radical reform Jewish newspaper, edited by Julius Silversmith, M. A., and printed and published in Chicago since 1872. It has had or now numbers among its contributors the following most eminent writers in this country and abroad: B. Felsenthal, Ph. D., Dr. E. G. Hirsch, Dr. Samuel Sale, Liebman Alder, Julius Rosenthal, Esq., Henry Greenebaum, J. O. M. Hewitt, D. D., Rev. Dr. Max Heller, Rev. Dr. H. M. Bien, Vicksburg, Miss., Rabbi Joseph Krauskopf, Kansas City, Mo., Dr. E. Schreiber, California, Adolph Moses, Esq., Chicago, A. E. Frankland, A. E. Laing, N. J., Dr. Ed. Rosen-

thal, Paris, France, and many others. This is the only Jewish reform organ in the United States, and numbers amongst its patrons many of the leading and influential Israelites of the city and vicinity. It contains general news, literature, science, art and is devoted to the interests of Judaism generally, being the official organ of congregations, societies and orders, and is a fine advertising medium. The subscription price is $3.00 per annum, and same rates for six or three months.

Francis W. Holbrook.

Expert Accountant, Room 4, 171-173 East Madison Street.

Many who are trying hard to make money "have a kind of a suspicion," or an "ill-defined intuition that something must be wrong with their books," and yet, "don't quite—in fact, don't want to suspect the one making or directing the entries therein of being dishonest or incompetent," and therefore, spend much of the valuable time which their business demands in trying to explain away from their own thoughts the idea that they are being wronged by their confidential man, their book-keeper or cashier, because neither seems to be that kind of a man —their habits, industry, and general deportment are all against such an idea. Nothing but an examination of your books and methods of calculating profit, either thoroughly or in a general way, by one disinterested and competent, can relieve your suspicions or fears. The ordinarily good book-keeper cannot do this for you. An expert accountant (not "lightning calculator"), one who has trained himself by long and exacting hours, for years, to be able to detect errors and erroneous entries, alone knows where to look for them, and determine their significance. There is no accountant more skilled or experienced than the subject of this sketch, Mr. Francis W. Holbrook. His practical experience covers a period of over thirty years, viz., twelve years in Albany City bank, twenty years jobbing business in New York city, in credit and financial departments, holding full power of attorney from late firm of A. T. Stewart & Co. If any of our readers desire at any time special service for examination or investigation of commercial or estate accounts, bank reports, business ledgers, trial balances, or any matter of a financial or mercantile nature, conducted in strict confidence, either in the city or out of it, he is at your service. Chicago references: Mr. H. N. Higinbotham, Mr. Henry W. King, Mr. Benjamin Douglass, Mr. J. McGregor Adams, Mr. James H. Walker, Mr. Cyrus H. McCormick, Mr. Robert Hill, of Storm & Hill; Mr. James M. Horton, of Wm. Blair & Co.; Mr. S. A. Kean, banker, Messrs. H. G. Foreman & Bro., bankers; Mr. A. M. Henderson, director Board of Trade.

The Catholic Normal School.

Of the Holy Family and Pio Nono College, St. Francis, Wis.

This institution was founded by the Rev. Dr. Salzmann in the year 1870, and opened on the 2d of January in the following year. In appreciation of such a praiseworthy and beneficial project, the gen-

erous Louis I., king of Bavaria, before all others, donated the sum of $1,704 towards the erection and completion of this institution, the first and only Catholic normal school in America. Beautifully located two miles south of the city limits of Milwaukee, near Lake Michigan, on the Chicago & Northwestern railroad, the building presents an aspect at once grand and inviting. Elegant in its proportions, it is constructed and arranged with the utmost care and regard for the comfort and convenience of pupils. The house is thoroughly supplied with water from an artesian well, lighted by gas, heated by steam, and amply provided with all modern improvements. As special care is taken to promote the health and vigor of mind and body, the spacious grounds around the institution are intersected by pleasant, shady walks, and in bad weather a large hall is provided for healthful exercises and youthful recreation. The entire building comprises two departments, viz., the Catholic normal school and the Pio Nono college. In the former, Catholic young men are educated, trained and prepared for the profession of teaching. In the latter department, Catholic youths are grounded in the principles of Christian faith and educated for the various branches of literary and commercial life. The united effort for the restoration of Cecilian music to its pristine purity and grandeur had its origin in this institution, under Dr. Salzmann, in the year 1873, when a society known as "The Cecilian Society" was established under the presidency of Sir John Singenberger, graduate of the musical school at Regensburg, Bavaria, and professor of music at the normal school. The members of this society, extending, as it does, over the whole United States, now number almost five thousand (5,000), amongst whom are many priests, bishops and archbishops. Sir John Singenberger, who is yet president of the society, edits "The Cecilia," a beautiful literary organ of church music, published at the Normal school. The faculty of the institution are Rev. Chas. Fessler, rector and professor of exegesis, pedagogy and German; Rev. Aug. B. Salick, master of discipline, professor of Christian doctrine and German; Rev. J. F. McMullen, professor of Christian doctrine and English; Chevalier J. Singenberger, professor of vocal and instrumental music; Mr. J. T. Kelly, professor of English, geography, history and penmanship; Mr. Dominic Schuler, B. S., professor of natural science, mathematics and bookkeeping. The course of studies in the normal school comprises four years. The programme of studies embraces Christian doctrine, exegesis, liturgy, church history, pedagogy, music (vocal and instrumental), English, German, Latin, arithmetic, algebra, geometry, natural science, geography (political and physical), United States history and government, penmanship and drawing. In the college department, the course of studies comprises religious instruction, English, arithmetic, algebra, geometry, geography, commercial law, book-keeping, United States history and government, penmanship, drawing and the optional studies, viz., German, Latin, music and natural science. Connected with this institution is the St. John's Deaf-Mute asylum, under the direction of Rev. Chas. Fessler. It was founded in the year 1875 by the Rev. Theo. Bruener, now rector of St. Boniface church, Quincy, Ill. Every care and attention is paid towards promoting the knowledge and advancement of these pupils. The boys are instructed by Mr. Lewis Mihm, and the girls are taught by the good Sisters of St. Francis.

James P. Smith & Co

Wholesale and Retail Dealers in Ice, Offices, 145 East Monroe Street and 1522 Indiana Avenue.

That a trade should be prosperous whose productions are an actual necessity and to be found in universal use, is a natural sequence, and hence there are no more flourishing establishments in the United States, and particularly in the western metropolis, than those engaged in the ice trade, the representative exponent of which is the old established house of James P. Smith & Co., whose enterprise is well illustrated in the high quality of ice which they place upon the market, while their facilities are such as enable them to name prices which only the most thoroughly equipped houses can hope to compete with. A large trade in car lots is done with the south and west, as well as a fine retail business in the city, their ice-houses being located as follows: Crystal Lake station, M. C. R. R.; Cold Springs, M. C. R. R.; Riverside, Ill., C. B. & Q. R. R.; Batavia, Ill., C. & N. W. R. R.; Fond du Lac, Wis., C. & N. W. R. R.; Forty-first street and Ellis avenue, S. Y. R. R.; 1522 Indiana avenue, I. C. R. R.; thus affording ample storage of hundreds of thousands of tons. The house was originally established in 1848 by Hiram Joy, to whom Mr. James P. Smith succeeded in 1855, and ten years later the present firm was organized by Messrs. Homer

A BUSINESS TOUR OF CHICAGO.

E. and John S. Sargent, becoming his co-partners, all of whom are also members of the Board of Trade. The test of time has shown that no house is better qualified to supply the trade as well as that few are equally desirable with whom to establish business relations, while in its development there are aptly typified the elements that have made Chicago the most progressive city in the world.

Joshua Smith.

Dentist, 2139 Wabash Avenue, Northeast Corner Twenty-Second Street.

The dental parlors of Dr. Joshua Smith, on the northeast corner of Wabash avenue and Twenty-second street, are well arranged and handsomely furnished. The rooms are light and airy and possess all those desirable and complete appointments which bespeak more emphatically than anything else, first-class work. Able assistants are employed and every endeavor is made to not only do good work at moderate prices, but to be patient and careful, and give satisfaction in all cases. Dr. Smith is a practical self-made man in his profession from many years' practical experience. In 1871 he opened parlors for himself at No. 2244 Indiana Av., but in Nov., '85, moved to his present fine quarters. He has produced a dentifrice known as "Dentaline," which has become popular among the trade, and is much sought after wherever introduced. It is an unrivaled preparation for cleansing, beautifying and preserving the teeth, inducing a healthy action of the gums, and imparting a natural sweetness and fragrance to the breath. Children as well as adults are delighted with it. It contributes to health and comfort, thoroughly cleanses and preserves the teeth, keeps the mouth free from injurious accumulations, renders it fresh and agreeable, and is, in fact, one of the finest toilet luxuries of the age. Its superiority and worth is attested by high testimonials from Prof. Walter S. Haines, professor of chemistry, pharmacy and toxicology in Rush Medical college, from Chas. Krusemarck, M. D., Ph.G., 175 Twenty-second street, Chicago, Ill., and from the late Dr. J. S. Swartley, surgeon-dentist, southwest corner Wabash avenue

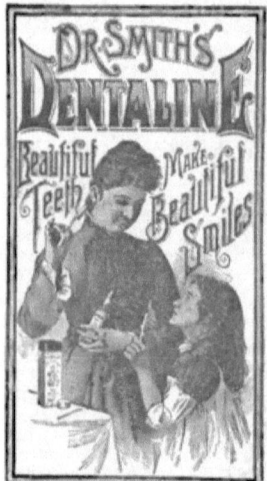

and Twenty-second street, Chicago, Ill. It is kept in stock by all the large wholesale druggists of every city, and being rapidly introduced throughout the whole country. One trial will insure its constant use.

James B. Goodman & Co.

Real Estate, Room 17, No. 105 Dearborn Street, Chicago.

One of the oldest and best known firms of real-estate dealers is that of James B. Goodman & Co., composed of James B. Goodman and Marion A. Farr. They do a very extensive business in suburban property and pine and timber lands in Michigan and Wisconsin. This firm are also agents for all classes of city property, vacant and improved. They specially deal in houses, lots and blocks on Madison street, Washington, Randolph, Lake, Fulton, Kinzie, Park avenue, Carroll avenue and other streets between West Fortieth and Forty-eighth streets, near Garfield park. This is embraced in one of the largest subdivisions about Chicago, is owned by the West Chicago Land company, and is managed by Mr. Farr in person. This property is developing rapidly, and during the next five years the probability is that it will double in value. James B. Goodman & Co. take the entire management of property for non-residents renting. Their spacious offices are centrally located at 68 Washington street.

J. B. Hall & Co

Tailors and Men's Furnishing Goods, 128 Dearborn Street.

Our next visit was to the establishment of J. B. Hall & Co. at 128 Dearborn street. There are two departments here, a tailoring, where best suits are made to order from finest imported or domestic materials, and a men's furnishing department, a specialty being made of neckwear and custom-made shirts. The tailoring department occupies from twenty-five to thirty hands during the season, the suits being made in the latest styles, and in a manner and of material not to be surpassed. The first floor and basement, 18x80 feet, are occupied by this firm. The business has steadily increased, and is now one of the largest of its kind in the city. The firm buy largely, and a long time ahead, thus, catching the markets when at their lowest point, they are enabled to undersell many of their competitors. All their business is conducted on cash principles, and to this in no small measure is due their success. They are thoroughly experienced themselves and employ only skilled hands on their work.

Phrenological Institute.

Prof. Thayer, Proprietor, 113 East Madison Street.

Professor Thayer has made this specialty a lifelong study, having become deeply interested in the science at the early age of sixteen, being employed at that time as a "frame spinner" in a cotton mill, in Uxbridge, Massachusetts, at $4 per week; the working hours at that time being from 6 A. M. to 7:30 P. M. with thirty minutes out for dinner; yet he managed under these circumstances to pay board at $1.75 per week, to dress fairly well, to pay for a seat in church, to supply himself with works on phrenology, anatomy, physiology, a phrenological bust, and to take "Life Illustrated," the first monthly published by Fowler & Wells, to take one weekly paper, and to devote from one to three hours to study nearly every night. In a few months he commenced a gratuitous practice among friends and acquaintances, soon acquiring quite a local reputation as a phrenologist. He practiced for a long time in Rhode Island, and came to Chicago nine years ago, since which time, by industrious application, honesty of purpose and accuracy in all character delineations, he has established a reputation second to none in the field of his profession. His examinations of children, to whom he gives special attention, are said to be of a very interesting character, always reliable, practical and beneficial to a high degree, giving perfect satisfaction in all cases. A visit to his institute, which we most cordially recommend, cannot fail to be interesting and profitable to all.

C. W. Flint.

Manufacturer of Picture Frames in Every Variety, 133 Clark Street, Room 16.

Mr. Flint has been in this line of business since 1860. He with many hundreds of our business men was a victim of the disastrous conflagration of '71, but very soon afterwards launched forth with his accustomed energy, and the result we see in the successful business he has established. Mr. Flint is a practical artisan, and manufactures picture frames of all styles and designs, including the new styles of ash, oak, cherry, etc. He has no traveling agents, and employs none but the best of workmen. His gold work is of the finest kind, some specimens of which can be seen at his establishment. It is this superior work which has caused Mr. Flint to become so popular among the dealers and general public, and it will repay all those interested to call on him and see his work.

John Ruprecht.

Broadway Market, Fresh and Salt Meats, Sausages, Hams, Etc., 77, 79 and 81 West Randolph Street.

One of the largest concerns of the kind in this locality is the Broadway market, 77, 79 and 81 West Randolph street. The proprietor of this establishment, Mr. John Ruprecht, does a large wholesale and retail business as a dealer in fresh and salt meats, sausages, hams, etc. The market is very centrally situated, in a thickly populated district, and a very large business is transacted daily. Mr. Ruprecht has a perfect system of cooling and refrigerating rooms, and the greatest care is exercised in keeping the premises neat and clean, and imparting that wholesome appearance which does so much to encourage patronage in the eyes of a discriminating public. Mr. Ruprecht has been engaged in this business since 1850, and among his many customers he numbers several who have dealt with him continuously since that time.

The Sigwalt Manufacturing Co.

Manufacturers of Check Protectors, Seal Presses, Self-Inking Hand Stamps, Etc., 11 South Canal Street.

The business of this company extends to all parts of the Union, Canada, and South America. All descriptions of seal presses and engravers' supplies are turned out by them in the most perfect and rapid manner. They possess every facility in the shape of the latest improved machinery and experienced workmen. Besides the various seal presses, they call special attention to their Excelsior self-inker, the Little Gem self-inker, pen and pencil stamp, and the latest novelty in this line placed upon the market, the Garden City rubber stamp press. These presses are useful in all branches of business, especially so for the reason that any number of dies can be used with one press for printing letterheads, billheads, noteheads, statements, postal cards, business cards, etc., the same being quickly and easily adjusted. Each press is fitted with an improved movable gauge to hold any size paper in position while printing.

Wm. Cowan.

Wood Turner, 82 Fulton Street.

The business of the wood turner is one that requires constant care and attention as well as a natural aptitude that is only acquired after long practice and the closest application. Mr. William Cowan is a worthy exponent of this class of work, and carries on business at No. 82 Fulton street. Mr. Cowan is a Scotchman by birth, and has been in business on his own account for the last six years. He has a good jobbing trade with the principal builders, carpenters and furniture houses. He is a very expert workman and is kept constantly busy. His business connections are very extensive, and he is highly respected among them for his honest and straightforward work. He inherits all the shrewd common sense and patient energy for which his countrymen are proverbial the world over, and he owes his success in a great measure to these traits of character.

Peterson & Oveson.

Manufacturers of Center, Library and Parlor Tables and Flower Stands, 141 to 151 North Sangamon Street.

There is no class of naturalized citizens of America in Chicago who show such aptitude for steady hard work and patient perseverance as our citizens from

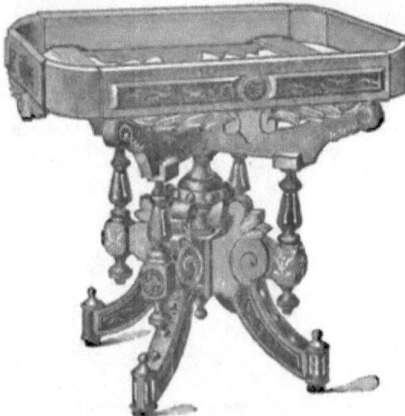

Norway. They are mostly engaged in the wood-working business, and generally bring a ripe experience with them from the old country. Among the number of these we may mention the firm of Peterson & Oveson, of 141 to 151 North Sangamon street, corner of Austin avenue. This firm are manufacturers of center, library and parlor tables and flower stands. They do a very large jobbing trade among the wholesale furniture houses in the city. Their light and handsome factory is well equipped with machinery, and they give employment to sixteen expert workmen. These gentlemen have only been associated in business for the last three years, and have been located at their present premises for one year. They exercise great care in selecting the lumber for the different articles they manufacture, and the factory is under the strict supervision of the head of the firm. They spare no pains to give satisfaction, and this is the great secret of their success.

J. P. Ellacott.

Mechanical Engineer, 194 Madison St., Corner Fifth Ave.

Mr. Ellacott has been a resident of Chicago since 1854, and established his present business as proprietor in 1872. He has been engaged as consulting engineer and mechanical expert by several of the largest concerns in the country. He was for a while the superintendent of the mechanical department of the Inter-State Industrial exposition. He laid out the plans and assigned the space as superintendent of the World's Exposition of Railway Appliances in 1883. Among his patrons are the American Press association, the Union Brass Manufacturing company, Rand, McNally & Co., the International Press association, the Chicago Newspaper union, the Bryant & Stratton Short-Hand Machine Co., the American Desk and Stool Co., for whom he invented and designed a number of opera chairs, of which they sold and placed in theaters over 25,000 in one year. Mr. Ellacott makes a specialty of assisting inventors, who, without the necessary mechanical skill or knowledge, are unable to put their ideas into practical shape. To such his assistance is invaluable. His reputation for skill, honesty, integrity and sterling worth as a man is one of which he may well feel justly proud, and anyone wanting a model made, or experimental machine work done, will never regret visiting Mr J. P. Ellacott, mechanical engineer, Nos. 192 and 194 Madison street, Chicago.

W. Levy & Son.

Butchers and Provision Dealers, 94 North Clark Street.

W. Levy & Son, 94 North Clark street, are the prominent and representative butchers and provision dealers of the North side. They carry a very large and choice assortment of all kinds of meats, including beef, lamb, veal, mutton, pork and everything in this line of business, besides all kinds of salt goods, and vegetables of all kinds. They are both experienced judges of meats, and have a deservedly high reputation among their customers for the superiority and fine quality of goods furnished. In their large and extensive premises are found everything pertaining to a first-class establishment of this kind, including large and ample refrigerators, while an air of cleanliness and neatness pervades the whole establishment. The business was established in 1856, on the corner of Madison and Clark streets, when Chicago was but a small town. In 1868 they moved to their present quarters. This firm has such a wide reputation and large patronage that all the principal hotels, restaurants and families have seen it to be to their advantage to get their provisions from them. Many of the large lake vessels also purchase supplies from them. Mr. Levy is a native of Germany, and has made his home in Chicago ever since he begun business in 1856. He and his son are both fine business men, prompt and honorable, and are highly regarded by all who know them.

F. Prussing.

Dealer in Foreign and Domestic Groceries, 51 and 53 North State Street.

One of the most complete and best appointed grocery stores in Chicago is the fine establishment of F. Prussing, at Nos. 51 and 53 North State street. He is an extensive dealer in all kinds of foreign and domestic groceries. His store is in one of the best sections of the city, and is commodious and well arranged, having an area of 40 by 150 feet. His staple and fancy groceries, including fine teas, fragrant coffees, best East India spices, sugars and syrups of standard grades, canned goods and other table luxuries, are fresh and first class in quality. He imports all his foreign goods direct from England, France and Germany. His large custom, which amounts to nearly $100,000 per annum, calls for the employment of ten hands and four delivery wagons. All orders meet with prompt attention, and customers may have the satisfaction of knowing that nothing inferior or adulterated will be sold to them. Mr. Prussing was born in Germany, and came to Chicago in 1874. He founded his present business nearly nine years ago, and during that time has built up a successful trade and established a highly honorable reputation.

Wm. H. Grubey.

Merchant Tailor, 113 South Clark Street.

One of the largest and most noteworthy tailoring establishments on South Clark street is that of Mr. Wm. H. Grubey. He is well known and widely patronized, his customers hailing from every State in the Union. He has been established in the city for twenty years, and during that time his trade has steadily increased, till now it probably ranks second to none in size, and is certainly unsurpassed by any in quality of the work turned out. Only the finest class of trade is catered for, and all material is imported goods. The establishment is centrally located, being readily accessible from all parts of the city. Three cutters are employed, and a force of about thirty-five hands. The finish and make throughout of the suits furnished by this house are such as to command, not satisfaction merely, but appreciation and recommendation. The proprietor is well known, and has many influential patrons. He keeps a large stock of material, and is able to furnish suits in the latest style at short notice. Three salesmen are constantly engaged, and the increase of business has been so great of late that even the large force employed has barely kept pace with it.

E. Norcott

Manufacturer of Tin and Copper Ware, Wholesale and Retail, Corner State and Illinois Streets.

Mr. Norcott is wholesale and retail manufacturer of tin and copper ware at the above location. From eight to ten practical and experienced workmen are employed, and special attention is given to the jobbing trade, and all orders are promptly and satisfactorily executed. Roofing and guttering also done in the most complete manner. Furnaces and stoves are put up and repaired, and all kinds of tin and copper specialties manufactured for the trade. Although the business was only established in August, 1885, connection has been established with the prominent jobbers of Chicago, and the trade is rapidly extending to all parts of the city and suburbs. His workshop is equipped with all the latest appliances and tools necessary for the rapid prosecution of business, and he aims to merit patronage by superior work. He is a native of New Jersey, and has had years of experience in this line of business, it being his life trade. Anyone can feel assured that any commercial relations entered into with Mr. Norcott will be agreeable and satisfactory.

Canfield & Co.

Manufacturers of Show Cases, Drug-Store Fixtures, and Wall Cases for All Purposes, 7, 9, 11 and 13 Wabash Avenue.

The offices of the large show-case establishment of Canfield & Co. are located as above, their factory being located on Curtis street, and fitted up with

every convenience for the prosecution of their extensive business. The inception of this firm dates back fifteen years, and during that time they have not only won a large city trade, but send their goods to all parts of the Union, and are now preparing to introduce them in the European and Australian markets. They have unsolicited testimonials from all over the country, as to the merit and fine workmanship of their cases. The fact that they have sold to one firm alone over 3,000 cases is a sufficient guarantee of the fine quality of their work. They manufacture every variety of show cases, drug-store fixtures and wall cases. They are the only manufacturers of druggists' sectional fixtures, which are the most complete, convenient and economical way of fitting up a drug store. The firm consists of Mr. H. S. Canfield and his son P. E. Canfield. They are both experts in this branch of industry, and practical and experienced business men.

Geehr & Gardner.

Hide Brokers, 178 Michigan Street.

Geehr & Gardner, at 178 Michigan street, are among the prominent hide brokers of this city, and have been associated in business since January 1, 1883, and in that short time have won the confidence of a host of patrons, and established a trade equaling a million of dollars annually. Their specialty is green salted hides for union cropped leather. They buy from all over the city, and make extensive shipments to the east and south. Their New York office is located at No. 91 Gold street. For references they have Stephen Kistler's Sons and Keck, Mosser & Co., both of New York city. Mr. Geehr was born in Pennsylvania, while Mr. Gardner is a native of Scotland, and both came to Chicago in 1883.

W. E. Blair.

Board and Glass Signs of Every Description, 171 and 173 Madison Street.

The visitor to this city can scarcely fail to notice the large number of signs which adorn the fronts of stores, factories, etc., and a special kind of wire open-work signs which surmount or depend from the roofs of many of our largest establishments. This kind of sign is almost exclusively the work of Mr. W. E. Blair, who occupies three floors, 30 x 85 feet, and employs ten hands in producing them. This was the first house which produced this class of goods, having the patent and control of sale in the whole of the western States. This business was begun in 1873, and has occupied its present premises ever since. Orders are shipped to all parts of the western States, as far as Denver and Kansas. Glass and board signs are also turned out, of the first quality, their aim being to please, and so extend their business.

W. W. Wyman.

Dealer in Fresh, Salt and Smoked Meats, Etc., 1004 West Madison Street.

To the careful buyer no establishment can be more highly favorable than that of Mr. W. W. Wyman. He is an extensive dealer in all kinds of fresh, salt and smoked meats, besides poultry, game, oysters in their season, vegetables, etc. He is located at No. 1004 West Madison street, corner Western avenue. The store is commodious, well fitted up, and possesses every requirement for the transaction of business. His trade is large and still growing, and the frequent depleting and replenishing of his stock insures to purchasers fresh goods, while prices are moderate. Mr. Wyman was born in Racine, Wis., and came to Chicago ten years ago, opening up business for himself on the South side, corner Thirty-fifth street and Indiana avenue, where he only remained three years, when he moved to his present desirable quarters. Mr. Wyman is an energetic and enterprising business man, wide-awake and progressive, and has made his market the most popular in this section of the city.

Ferdinand Schweitzer.

Jewelry Cases and Trays, Etc., 113 Madison and 133 Clark Streets, Room 28.

Mr. Ferdinand Schweitzer manufactures jewelry cases and trays, sample, medicine and silverware cases of every description. This business was commenced here by the present proprietor in 1882. The wood used (when covered) is white pine, or, if left exposed, walnut or some fancy wood. The linings are silk, satin, velvet or plush, according to order. He keeps a stock of samples, but makes all to order, supplying some of the largest firms in the city. He makes in his own original designs, and some of the patterns have great merit for beauty of workmanship and general appearance. His charges are very reasonable, as his expenses are light, and he buys his material very low. None of his patrons have ever yet had to complain of the goods he has furnished. He is known by all who deal with him as a deserving and reliable manufacturer.

Yerbury & Barry.

Steam Laundry, 2218 Wabash Avenue.

A business enterprise which by reason of able management and good work has attained proportions of great magnitude within a comparatively brief period is Yerbury & Barry's steam laundry, located at No. 2218 Wabash avenue (Seaverns' block). It has been established for the past two years, and is under the proprietorship of A. G. Yerbury and J. Barry, two experienced men in this line of trade. All the latest improvements are to be found in this first-class laundry, and the work turned out is satisfactory in every respect. A force of twelve or more hands are employed in the various departments of this business. The prices are reasonable, and the best of order prevails in the receiving and delivering of orders. Special attention is paid to family washing, in which line they have a large trade. One trial will convince a person of the fine quality of work done by this laundry, which is becoming a standard one.

N. D. Swansen.

Bakery, Confectionery and Ice Cream, 1047 West Madison Street.

A standard place to go for first-class ice cream, confectionery and bakery articles is to N. D. Swansen, at No. 1047 West Madison street. The premises occupied are fitted up in the most attractive and pleasing manner, while both Mr. and Mrs. Swansen are obliging in their attention to the wants of their many patrons. Mr. Swansen first established the business on the North side in 1877, and moved to his present location in 1882. All the articles kept by him are of the best quality. He deals exclusively in his own creams and ices, and not only serves it in his parlors, but takes orders for families at their houses. Mr. Swansen has won a large and lucrative patronage, which is steadily on the increase. He has been a resident of the Garden City for the past seventeen years, and by energy and thrift established his present business. He keeps all monthlies, illustrated papers and city dailies, and receives orders for all papers and magazines at as low rates as they can be procured from the publishers, thereby saving postage and exchange.

Wm. A. Gaw.

Bookseller and Bookbinder, 126 and 128 Dearborn Street.

Mr. Gaw is agent for several large New York houses, and handles solely subscription works, which he sells in parts, through sub-agents. The following are some of the chief of the works, which, it may be added, can be purchased only by subscription: "Treasury of Universal History," "History of the late Civil War," Zimmermann's "Popular History of Germany," Johnson's "Household Book of Nature," Spencer's "History of the United States," Lossing's "History of Our Own Country," "Lives and Portraits of the Presidents of United States," "Life and Times of Washington," "National Portrait Gallery of Eminent Americans," "Portrait Gallery of Eminent Men and Women of Europe and America," etc., Bibles, self-interpreting, etc. Fleetwood's "Life of Christ," poetical works of Lord Byron and Thomas Moore, "Living Thoughts of Leading Thinkers," etc. These works are all standard books, well written, and edited by some of the most able authors of the day. Mr. Gaw has been in this business nine years and is sole agent in the city for the works above mentioned. He also makes a specialty of binding these parts to order in the finest and most durable manner, in any style desired. This way of purchasing works, namely, in parts, enables everyone to become the purchaser and owner of a fine library, which otherwise he would never get.

Samuel Myers & Co.

268 and 270 Madison Street.

It would be difficult to name a house in their line of trade more prominent than that of Samuel Myers & Co., jobbers in fine Kentucky whiskies. When a house has enjoyed a liberal patronage and popularity for a long term of years, the evidence is conclusive that its management has been characterized by integrity, ability and liberality Such are the circumstances connected with this well-known house, which, since its foundation in 1847, has continuously held a prominent position in the trade, both at home and abroad, their patronage embracing the leading dealers throughout the entire western country. The firm occupy extensive premises in this city, covering two entire floors and basement, each 50 x 100 feet in dimensions, and carry a stock second to none in the country, embracing the choicest vintages of the old world, as well as the most celebrated distillations of our own country, a specialty being made of old rye and bourbon whiskies, among which their popular M. & Co. rye-malt whisky, a pure distillation from grain, deserves special mention, as well as their Monticello rye and Anderson's bourbon and rye. An unusually large stock is carried both of domestic and foreign goods, the latter being of their own direct importation, while the unrivaled reputation of the house has been won solely upon the merits of the goods. Both Messrs. S. G. Myers and H. Wilkinson have resided in Chicago the greater part of their lives and have achieved that success which is the usual result of strict adherence to a rigid code of mercantile honor.

MacLachlan & Co.

Dealers in Food Products, Etc., 104 and 106 Twenty-second Street.

The large grocery and market of MacLachlan & Co. is one of the most prosperous, and finely appointed places of business on this thoroughfare, and well deserves the name of being the leading establishment of this class of business on the South side. The business was established in 1867, under the firm name of MacLachlan, Campbell & Co., which so continued until 1881, when the present firm took charge. The premises occupied are large and convenient, and are arranged into two departments, one for groceries, and the other for meat and provisions. The patronage of the firm is very large and consists of city and suburban trade. The large refrigerators insure at all times a fine condition of meats, and excellent quality. Everything is a model of cleanliness and neatness, while strict supervision is given to every detail by the firm and their fifteen able and obliging assistants. Their staple and fancy groceries embrace as large and varied a stock as can be found in the city. Mr. MacLachlan was born in Scotland, and has lived in Chicago for the past twenty years.

Charles S. Wallace.

Sanitary Plumber, 362 Wabash Avenue.

There is no class of business or trade that is more intimately connected with the comfort and good health of the residents of a large city than that of the sanitary plumber. One of the leading and popular members of this important trade in Chicago is Mr. Chas. S. Wallace, whose office is located at No. 362 Wabash avenue, telephone 1448, where he has but recently moved. The business was under the firm name of White & Wallace until the 1st of July, 1886, when Mr. White withdrew. A force of from four to six competent hands are employed, and sometimes a much larger number is enrolled, according to the amount of job work on hand. Mr. Wallace gives special attention to sewer building and ventilating. Estimates on all kinds of contract work readily given. All job work is promptly attended to. Mr. Wallace was born in Buffalo, N. Y., and came to this city when a mere boy. He is corresponding secretary of the Chicago Master Plumbers' association.

174   A BUSINESS TOUR OF CHICAGO.

Tom. N. Donnelly & Co.

Loan and Diamond Brokers, 118 Dearborn Street.

This is one of the largest loan and diamond establishments of the city and is owned by Tom. N. Donnelly & Co. The business has been established six years and is known throughout the city as one of the most reliable and fair-dealing houses in Chicago. All kinds of jewelry, watches, old gold and silver, diamonds and precious stones are bought, or loans are advanced upon them. Bargains can always be had here, by a buyer. Most of the articles can be purchased for about half their original price, and a very large assortment is in stock. Some of the finest and rarest bracelets, pins, rings, etc., are to be seen here, and a fine stock of field and opera glasses, telescopes, etc., are always in stock. A visit will prove highly interesting, and to one who wishes to purchase, undoubted bargains are to be had. Their goods are both new and second-hand, and their customers hail from all parts of the United States.

English Bros.

Avenue Market, 112 and 114 Twenty-second Street.

English Brothers' Avenue market was established some fifteen years ago, although the present proprietors only took charge in March, 1886. This market has always enjoyed a most liberal and substantial patronage, and has won the reputation of being the representative market on the South side. The present proprietors have added to its popularity, by devoting close personal attention to the wants of the trade, and making careful study of the markets. In this way they are always able to supply their customers with the finest quality of goods that can be procured, and at reasonable prices. An extensive and finely assorted stock is carried to meet the steadily increasing demand. The premises occupied are spacious and commodious, having a frontage on Twenty-second street of fifty feet. A competent corps of efficient and obliging workmen are constantly employed, while four wagons are kept busy delivering to various parts of the city. The two brothers, W. P. and E. J., are natives of Wisconsin, and begun business years ago in Kenosha, where they still have a large establishment.

M. D. Coder & Co.

Real Estate and Loan Agents, 125 La Salle Street, Room 8.

Few real estate and loan agents do a wider or more general trade than the firm of M. D. Coder & Co. Special attention is paid to the sale of furnished houses, grocery stores, cigar stores, sample rooms, etc. Exchanges are made and partnerships formed. Good business chances are always on hand in all parts of the city. Anyone desiring business or opportunities to begin well in some paying trade should consult this firm. Another specialty is that of farm lands in this State and Indiana, both vacant and improved, and also in hotels. This firm has always a number of this class of investments in nearly all parts of the United States. No firm deals more fairly with its clients, nor has obtained a better class of customers than that of M. D. Coder & Co., and they are well known throughout business communities as being honorable and reliable in their transactions.

Wolf, Becker & Co.

Wool Commission, Pelts and Furs, 221, 223, 225 and 227 East Kinzie Street.

This firm has only been in existence since February, 1886, but it is composed of young business men of energy and determination, who in that brief time have won a large and highly creditable patronage. Wool is the specialty, although they handle largely pelts and furs. Their consignments are from all parts of the west, southwest and northwest, and besides their large city trade supply both eastern and western manufacturers with raw material. They occupy four floors at the above number, 40 by 100 feet in dimensions. This gives them ample facilities for the storage and handling of their large stock. The personnel of the firm is A. S. Wolf, S. M. and A. E. Becker, who look to the prompt and satisfactory filling of all orders. The attention of our merchants is called to the substantial advantages offered by this new firm, feeling assured that any relation which may be entered upon with them will be upon a basis of strict business integrity.

Diamond Palace.

Diamonds, Watches and Jewelry, 119 East Madison St.

One of the most attractive establishments, both on the exterior and inside, on Madison street is the "Diamond Palace," at No. 119. The firm, composed of L. Hirschberg and E. Driscoll, established the diamond, watch and jewelry business here in 1877. A fine stock of genuine diamonds, many of great beauty and brilliancy, precious stones, rock crystal, Waltham, Elgin and Springfield watches, and the latest novelties and designs in jewelry are to be seen here. The splendid cases outside attract the notice of passers by, while the windows and show-cases display to great advantage the valuable stock on sale therein. A very interesting sight also is a case of fine and accurate models of the largest crown diamonds of Europe, including the Great Mogul of Russia of 279 9/16 carat, the Kohinoor, blue diamond, etc. The firm import diamonds and some of the latest Parisian designs direct, the other articles being obtained from the large eastern manufacturers. The quality of all goods supplied by this house is of the highest order, and dependence can be placed implicitly on the goods being exactly what they are represented to be. A large and almost exclusive western trade is done by this house in the real Parisian diamonds, cut by the most skillful lapidaries from crystal quartz. Theatrical specialties are made up to order in the most perfect and gratifying manner.

Schreiber & Annas.

Manufacturers of Ornamental Cut Glass, Plain and Fancy Beveled Glass, 13 and 15 South Canal Street.

Of all the gorgeous decorations devised to ornament our homes and public buildings, nothing exceeds the brilliant effects of artistic cut glass in its different forms, such as cut and ground door, transom and office lights, plain and fancy beveled glass, etc. No other form of glass ornamentation can compare with this class of work. The firm of Schreiber & Annas, of 13 and 15 South Canal street, devote their sole attention to artistic glass cutting in its highest perfection, in all its branches. This concentration of their abilities makes it possible for them to furnish perfect work of the most difficult description, such as making jewels of any size to pattern or drawing, glass engraving, hammered beaded mitred, scored and fancy beveled glass. They have introduced many new and effective ideas in this line, and have established an extensive business. They are both ambitious and determined that no eastern concern shall lead Chicago in turning out artistic glass work. They will cheerfully give any information in regard to their business, and when desired will furnish designs and estimates on application, and will sustain their reputation for promptness and reliability by striving to oblige their patrons at all times and by turning out perfect work only.

Henry H. Hindshaw.

Scientific and Ornamental Taxidermist, 86 La Salle Street.

A most interesting visit is to the studio of the noted scientific and ornamental taxidermist, H. H. Hindshaw, at room 14, No. 86 La Salle street. He has for the past three years been located in this city. He is a native of England, and learned the art for which he has become famous at the noted schools of Manchester. When he first came to this city he was taxidermist for Col. Wood, of museum fame, but when he went out of the business, two years ago, Mr. Hindshaw began to do work for himself. His fame had become known, and his many friends soon gave him plenty of work to do. Birds and animals are mounted to order, and first-class work is guaranteed. His work consists mainly of large bird skins, animals, deer and elk heads, hat birds, fans, screens, etc.

S. A. Maxwell & Co.

Booksellers, Stationers and Wall Paper Dealers, Nos. 134 and 136 Wabash Avenue.

The name of "Maxwell" has been long and honorably identified with the bookselling interests of the country, and the business now conducted by Messrs. S. A. Maxwell & Co., Nos. 134 and 136 Wabash avenue, upon such an extensive scale, is the outcome of a steady adherence to the legitimate principles of trade. This house was originally founded in 1855 by Mr. J. W. Maxwell, in Lacon, Ill., and was conducted by him there with great success, but with several changes in the name of the firm till 1866, when Mr. S. A. Maxwell purchased an interest in the business. Eventually, after a very successful career Mr. J. W. Maxwell retired in favor of his sons, Messrs. E. E. and C. E. Maxwell, and son-in-law, H. C. Prevost, who now, with Mr. S. A. Maxwell are the co-partners. In 1882 Messrs. S. A. Maxwell & Co. established their house in Chicago, since which period they have obtained a liberal and influential patronage from all classes of society. The premises occupied are very extensive and commodious, and comprise a splendid five-story building with basement, which is fitted up with every convenience and facility for the accommodation and display of the large and valuable stock. The firm carry on the bookselling and stationery business in all its branches, and deal both wholesale and retail in books, blank books and stationery. They are the largest dealers in wall papers in the United States. Messrs. S. A. Maxwell & Co. may be justly considered as thoroughly identified with the best interests of the western metropolis, in this her fiftieth year.

Joseph Blakemore.

Manufacturer and Gilder of Gold and Metal Leaf Frames, Office and Manufactory, 234 East Lake Street.

The manufacture of picture frames has become an industry of no mean importance in Chicago, during the last few years. As an exponent of this branch of art, for art it may fairly be called, we may mention the well-known house of Joseph Blakemore, at No. 234 East Lake street, manufacturer and gilder of gold and metal leaf frames. His stock of patterns is replete with some of the most beautiful and elegant designs. Some we noticed in antique bronze were exquisite beyond anything we had ever seen of the kind before. If Mr. Blakemore keeps on perfecting his frames and mouldings, the picture itself will shortly be a matter of secondary importance, and all the admiration will center in the frame. Mr. Blakemore is an Englishman, and came to this country from Liverpool forty years ago. He has been in the picture-frame business all his life. He employs ten skilled assistants, and his articles are shipped all over the States. Mr. Blakemore is a genuine type of his countrymen, and has won himself a wide reputation for his bluff honesty and liberal business methods.

John Horn.

Clothes Cleaning and Repairing Rooms, 126 Dearborn St.

This business consists of cleaning and repairing all kinds of men's and boys' clothes. How many suits are laid aside before half worn out, because the bottoms have become frayed, or a tear has accidentally disfigured the articles. Then, too, alterations are sometimes needed, and unless the goods were purchased at some local tailor's, a difficulty is experienced. All this is avoided and a great saving made by patronizing Mr. Horn, who keeps a stock of material for mending, repairing, altering, etc. He occupies two rooms in the basement, and does his work extremely cheap. Mr. Horn has been in the tailoring business for twenty-three years, having worked for his brother until 1879, when he set up for himself.

E. F. Angell & Co.

Brass and Bronze Workers, 87 and 89 Franklin Street.

The hum of industry nowhere in Chicago plays a livelier tune than proceeds from the workshops of this firm. The long lines of shaftings, revolving pulleys and flying belts keep in motion the varied machinery, which under the control of able mechanics transforms the large rolls of brass, long lengths of tubing, and the rough, unpolished iron and steel into graceful and artistic patterns of fenders, frames, grates, brass tables, brass easels, office railings, wickets, grilles and every conceivable article the firm's patrons demand in ornamental brass, bronze and iron work. The many unique and original designs in fireplace trimmings, furniture trimmings, office fittings and ornamental metal work of all descriptions manufactured by this concern can but elicit the admiration of the visitor, and satisfy the various tastes of the most critical buyers. With years of practical experience, and their facilities for production, this firm is holding unchallenged its place among the manufacturers of fine metal work.

C. M. Staiger.

Printer and Publisher, 1 and 3 North Clark Street.

This business was established just after the great fire of 1871. Mr. Staiger employs fifteen hands to help him, and looks to it that every job that leaves the office is correctly and satisfactorily executed. It is this great care which has won for him so large a custom. His printing is in different languages, of which English is the principal one. The bulk of the trade is located in the city, and comprises all kinds of job, book and newspaper work. Mr. Staiger is thoroughly proficient in everything pertaining to this line of business, and is zealous and enterprising in the promotion of the art which has been his life work. He is a native of Germany, and came to Chicago in 1867.

Katholischer Jugend-Freund.

Catholic Juvenile Friend.

This paper was established in 1877. It is one of the best papers for the young found in the city of Chicago. Rev. A. J. Thiele, pastor of the St. Aloysius church, is editor, and has ably filled that position for ten years. It is published semi-monthly, in German and English. Its subscription list numbers over 10,000, and is rapidly increasing. Two traveling agents look after its interests throughout the country. For the past four years it has been published in the interest and for the benefit of the Rose Hill orphan asylum.

John Myers.

Palace of Pharmacy, 1002 West Madison Street, Corner Western Avenue.

The large and handsome premises of John Myers deserves its name "Palace of Pharmacy." A fine stock of drugs and chemicals, popular patent medicines, perfumeries, toilet articles, wines and liquors for medical use, in fact, everything to be desired in a first-class metropolitan establishment of this description is found here. The pharmacy was founded in 1866 by Dr. O. P. Hatheway, who in 1876 sold out to Mr. Myers, who had been with Dr. Hatheway since the inception of the business. The prescription department is presided over by Mr. Myers and competent and skilled assistants, who possess the confidence and esteem of the medical profession generally. Of the proprietary medicines of the Palace pharmacy the most important are Dr. O. P. Hatheway's hair tonic, which is now a standard article in the trade. His concentrated ferro-phosphorated elixir of calisaya bark and strychnine is a preparation which represents three very important remedial agents, namely, iron, phosphorus and calisaya bark. The bitter taste of the bark and the nauseous, inky taste of the iron are entirely concealed by aromatics, which renders it an agreeable elixir, adapted to the most delicate stomach. His concentrated essence of Jamaica ginger is a preparation made from the very best Jamaica ginger, especially for domestic uses, and the utmost pains have been taken to make it reliable in all respects. His improved cherry pectoral, for coughs, colds, asthma, croup, etc., is unsurpassed, and his glycerine cream is an exquisite article, superior to camphor ice, cold cream or anything in use for chapped hands, face, lips or rough skin without being sticky or greasy. These goods are shipped to all parts of the United States, and found upon the shelves of the principal druggists throughout the country. Mr. Myers is a native of Ireland and has been a resident of Chicago since 1865.

Wilson & Bayless.

General House Furnishers, 314 and 316 West Madison Street.

The firm of Wilson & Bayless, general house furnishers, although only established one year, have taken the lead on this live thoroughfare. This is the headquarters for the latest designs of fine furniture, the most modern and stylish patterns of carpets, folding beds and reclining chairs, that cannot be excelled in the city. The firm makes a specialty of the Windsor folding bed, being one of the five firms who are allowed to handle them on the West side. These beds are among the best in the market and combine beauty, strength, durability and fine finish in their construction. Wilson & Bayless are also manufacturers of the world-renowned "Wilson Adjustable Chairs." They consist of the adjustable chair, invalid propelling wheel chair, and Wilson's physicians', surgeons', and gynæcological chairs. These chairs are a combination of beauty, lightness, strength, compactness and simplicity, and for comfort in health or sickness are unsurpassed. Their reputation is world-wide, having received the highest awards from the following expositions: United States Centennial,

Philadelphia, 1876; International exposition at Paris, 1878; World's Industrial exposition at New Orleans, 1884-5; the Southern exposition at Lou-

isville; Cincinnati Industrial exposition, and many others of note throughout this country and Europe. It is economy to have one of these chairs in every home, as they will last a lifetime. Illustrated catalogue, price list and full information given free on application.

Messrs. Wilson & Bayless are well-known and reliable gentlemen and treat all their patrons with the utmost fairness, and it is not too much to assert that since entering the commercial field they have done as much as any other firm in Chicago to promote the welfare and general interests of the Garden City.

Lewis & Howard.

Wool, 184 and 186 Washington Street.

The firm of Lewis & Howard is a prominent one in this line. The premises, Nos. 184 and 186 Washington street, second, third and top floors, are occupied by the house for storage and office purposes. The firm are wool merchants, and are old residents and well-known citizens of this city, Mr. Lewis having resided here for the past thirty years, and his partner sixteen years. The business was established in 1850, and since that time, though temporarily checked by the disaster of 1871, which consumed the premises in South Water street which the firm then occupied, it has continued to increase, until this last year, when the trade has doubled that of the previous year, and the firm have added to their already extensive trade in domestic wool that of importing, so that their business now includes the following wools: American, Australian, Cape, Montevideo, East India, Levant, English and German nigwaste extracts, garnetted worsted, camel's hair, noils, English noils, Iceland noils, Russian hair, Cheverette and Louisville shoddy in all grades and colors. The firm, having had such a long and practical acquaintance with the business, are authorities in the market, while their trade extends to all parts of the States, a good business being done with

New England. The approximate yearly sales amount to 4,000,000 pounds, which, on an average of twenty-five cents per pound, means $1,000,000. This firm give steady employment to about thirty hands, and is one of those old established houses that have done much to build up the present commercial prosperity of the city.

Northwestern Parlor Suit Co.

687 to 701 Clybourn Avenue and 28 to 36 A Street.

The factory and office of this company are located at Nos. 687 to 701 Clybourn avenue and 28 to 36 A street. The main building is 40 x 212 feet in dimensions and four stories high. It is fitted up in the best manner, with all the facilities for the manu-

trade. This establishment is not only a representative one of the kind in this city, but one of the leading ones in the Union.

Leroy Payne.

Palmer House Stables, 169 to 173 Michigan Avenue, Telephones 5437 and 5462; Also, Southern Hotel Stables, 2021 and 2023 Wabash Avenue, Telephone 8532.

In the line of livery the fine establishment of which Mr. Leroy Payne is the proprietor is regarded on all hands as a representative one, while personally Mr. Payne affords an admirable example of the self-made man. At the early age of seventeen, with creditable self-reliance, he began in the livery business at Kankakee, Ill. with only one team, for which he paid

facture of parlor furniture frames. On the first floor are located the large engine of seventy-five horsepower, all the planers and heavy machinery. The second floor contains the mortise machines and polishers. On the third and fourth floors all the frames are put together and prepared for shipment. These frames are not only perfect in construction, but of the latest designs. One hundred and fifty men are employed in the various departments, to meet the demands of their large and growing trade, which extends throughout all parts of the Union. The woods used in the construction of these frames are well seasoned and of the best quality in the market. The mahogany is procured in large quantities from Cuba. The present company has only been in existence since 1884, but the business was established in 1877. The officers are Fred. Koropp, president; Joseph Doetsch, treasurer; and A. Hoffman, secretary. They are all representative business men of Chicago, and thoroughly acquainted with every feature of the cabinet and furniture

$200, $100 down, and the balance in installments, taking six months to liquidate the debt. To get his start in the world, Mr. Payne worked for $7 a month, and by great economy was able to save enough to make his first payment as above stated. He rapidly developed a fine business, and, to meet its growing demands, kept constantly adding to his stock, until a few years later found him the proprietor of a large establishment at Bloomington, Ill., where he also owned and operated the omnibus line. Eventually Mr. Payne sought a wider field for his energies, and, already recognized as one of the leading and most successful liverymen of the State, he removed to Chicago, and opened in November, 1875, at No. 145 Michigan avenue, with a stable of fine horses and the best made carriages in the market. In 1880 a removal was made to his present spacious stables, 120 x 180 feet in dimensions, two stories and basement in height, and perfect in all appointments and arrangements, a thorough system of organization being maintained, and a large staff of experienced hands assisting in every department. His stock includes some of the finest roadsters in this city, besides a large number of fine carriage horses, while his desire to excel is also seen in the excellence of his carriages, including coupes, coaches, victorias, buggies, road-wagons and sleighs in vast varieties. The guests of the Palmer house patronize this livery, which is fully in keeping with everything about that palatial hotel, from which it is only two blocks distant, and directly opposite the Exposition building on the lake front, while it is but one block from the Leland hotel, and convenient to the most fashionable sections of the city. To accommodate the residents and hotels of the southern part of the city, in 1886 Mr. Payne opened the "Southern hotel stables" at Nos. 2021 and 2023 Wabash avenue on a scale and in a style fully in keeping with the "Palmer house stables," and no city, not even New York itself, has more adequate livery accommodations than these two stables afford the citizens of Chicago. Besides his livery business, Mr. Payne is also the proprietor of the "Horse Home," situated at Chebanse, in Kankakee county, this state, on the Illinois Central railroad, sixty miles south of this city. This beautiful farm home for the raising, training and care of horses, consists of nearly 1000 acres. The entire farm is fenced in, and divided into twenty or more pastures. Mr. Payne established this horses' home in 1880, and it has for its objects, (1) a place where horses overworked in the city and foot-sore can be kept for less money than in the city, and, at the same time, imparting new life and energy, incident to the change, (2) for the training of all kinds of horses, and for the breaking of colts, and for conditioning of horses. The horses' home is looked upon by the business man as a refuge where he can seek a moment's relaxation; he enjoys the country, admires the horse, and dwells with eager delight upon the young stock. Harbored there, he finds himself poetized and lifted out of the rut of mercantile slavery, and gives himself up to the delightful enjoyment of freedom and rest; so we claim for the horses' home a high place in the tabernacle of human enjoyment, and so pray we for a long continuance of this farm, under Leroy Payne's careful eye and active mind, for he is truly a philanthropist. No visitor to the semi-centennial jubilee should fail to pay a visit to this "home," as he will not only be courteously received, but gain information and pleasure which will more than repay him for all expense and trouble incurred.

J. D. Roberts.

Glass Beveler and Silverer, 39 Canal Street.

A leading branch of commercial industry, and one that is fast assuming prominence in this city, is that technically known as glass beveling and silvering, a branch of trade so ably represented by Mr. J. D. Roberts, of No. 39 Canal street. Since establishing his business in December, 1885, it has developed into most prosperous proportions. Mr. Roberts is a native of Rutland county, Vermont, and has been a resident of Chicago for the past thirty-five years, having been engaged in the business of house and sign painting for some eighteen years prior to embarking in his present undertaking. At the outbreak of the great civil war, Mr. Roberts at once went to the front as a member of McAllister's battery, achieving a gallant record at the various engagements in which it participated, being assigned to Bolton's battery, after receiving his commission as second lieutenant for meritorious conduct in the face of the enemy. After three years' constant service sickness finally necessitated his discharge, upon which he returned to this city. His three brothers also served through the war, one in Col. Brackett's regiment, 9th Illinois cavalry, most remarkably passing through 160 of the great battles and skirmishes of the war without receiving a scratch. In commercial life Mr. Roberts has been as successful as he was gallant as a soldier.

Young, Gatzert & Co.

Successors to Andrew Young, Plumbers and Gas-Fitters, 965 West Madison Street.

The plumbing establishment of Young, Gatzert & Co. is a good representative of business improvements and scientific progress during the past fifty years of Chicago's history. Mr. Andrew Young founded this business in a small way in 1866, which has steadily advanced to its present large patronage. In May last he received as partners Milton Gatzert and Charles Cavanna, two practical and experienced plumbers and gas-fitters, who have spent a lifetime at this business, working for years at the large establishment of E. Baggot. Mr. Young has a national reputation as a thorough sanitary engineer and plumber. He has held the office of president and also vice-president of the National Plumbers' association at various times, and twice elected president of the local association, and was appointed on the committee on sanitary appliances to the World's Exposition at New Orleans in 1885. He believes in State legislation, and that examinations should be as rigidly made as for applications to any government position. Mr. Young is inventor of an automatic attachment for unhitching horses, which is just being placed upon the market. It is found to cause a revolution in getting horses from barns and stables during a fire. This firm make and execute contracts for the complete fitting up of buildings of all kinds, and in sanitary plumbing, which is their specialty.

The New York Central and Hudson River R. R.

THE ONLY FOUR-TRACK RAILROAD IN THE WORLD

THE BEST ROUTE FOR PLEASURE and BUSINESS TRAVEL.

Speed, Safety and Comfort is Assured the Patrons of this Line.

The only Line having a Depot in the City of New York, landing Passengers in the very heart of the Great Metropolis.

The New Passenger, Drawing-room, Sleeping, Buffet and Dining Cars, now in use on the New York Central and Hudson River R. R. and connections, are unequaled in elegance of finish and their modern appliances to promote the comfort of Passengers.

THROUGH CARS ARE RUN TO NEW YORK AND BOSTON WITHOUT CHANGE FROM THE FOLLOWING CITIES:

CHICAGO, CLEVELAND, INDIANAPOLIS, DETROIT, ST. LOUIS, COLUMBUS, TOLEDO, CINCINNATI, BUFFALO.

W. B. JEROME,
GENERAL WESTERN PASSENGER AGENT,
97 Clark Street, - CHICAGO.

E. J. RICHARDS,   HENRY MONETT,
ASS'T GENERAL PASSENGER AGENT,   General Passenger Agent,
Grand Central Depot, - NEW YORK.

A BUSINESS TOUR OF CHICAGO.

D. J. McNAMARA,   **J. H. DICK.**

McNAMARA & DICK,

Manufacturers and Dealers in all Kinds of

Trunks, Traveling Bags, &c., &c.

THEATRICAL AND SAMPLE TRUNKS A SPECIALTY.

62 West Madison Street,

Repairing of all kinds promptly attended to.   **CHICAGO.**

[See page 113.]

MICHENER BROS. & CO.,

Packers and Curers of the

Celebrated "Banana Brand" of Hams,

AND DEALERS IN PROVISIONS GENERALLY.

PACKING HOUSE,   OFFICE, ROOM 211,
UNION STOCK YARDS.   INSURANCE EXCHANGE BUILDING,
                216 La Salle St.

Telephone 9508.   **CHICAGO.**   [See page 83.]

J. F. CARSE,

Stained Glass Works.

ORIGINAL DESIGNS FURNISHED ON APPLICATION.

Artistic Stained Glass for Domestic and Ecclesiastical Purposes in Every Style. Antique, Opalescent, Venetian, and Cathedral Glass. Cut and Molded Jewels.

19 & 21 Canal St.,   **CHICAGO.**

[See page 104.]

Abrm. Kuh.   Adolph Nathan.   S. M. Fischer.

Kuh, Nathan & Fischer,

MANUFACTURERS OF

CLOTHING,

AND JOBBERS IN WOOLENS.

126, 128, 130 & 132 Market St., CHICAGO.

Telephone No. 710.   [See page 127.]

J. L. Hugee, President,   Geo. D. Kirkham, Secretary,
J. H. Wydeck, Vice-President.   A. G. Van Schaick, Treasurer.

VESSEL OWNERS TOWING CO.

240 SO. WATER ST.

ELEVEN TUGS.

A. G. Van Schaick, Protection, Rebel, Union, Satisfaction, M. Shields, Black Ball No. 2, A. A. Carpenter, E. P. Ferry, Thos. Hood, J. V. Taylor.

Geo. D. Kirkham, Supt.   **CHICAGO.**

[See page 94.]

J. E. Muchmore, Sr.   J. F. Muchmore.

MUCHMORE & MUCHMORE,

→LUBRICATING OILS←

Naphtha, Gasoline, Turpentine, Axle Grease, Rosin, Waste, Etc.

31 MARKET ST.,   **CHICAGO, ILL.**

TELEPHONE 903.   [See page 100.]

Abr. Strauss.   Hugo Goodman.   Simon Yondorf.   Edward Ross.

STRAUSS, GOODMAN, YONDORF & Co.,

Manufacturers of

→ **MEN'S, BOYS' AND YOUTHS'** ←

CLOTHING,

MONROE STREET & FIFTH AVENUE,

Telephone No. 1373.   **CHICAGO.**   [See page 99.]

Jesse Spalding, President.   R. H. McElwee, Treasurer.

Spalding Lumber Company,

LUMBER · MANUFACTURERS,

248 S. WATER STREET.

TELEPHONE 1508.   [See page 89.]

★ — DON'T FAIL TO PAY A VISIT TO THE — ★

Bee-Hive

STATE STREET, OPPOSITE PALMER HOUSE.

DRY GOODS, MILLINERY, CARPETS, Etc.

[See page 76.]

Alex. H. Revell & Co.

FURNITURE,

Carpets, Stoves, Desks, Show Cases, &c.

COR. FIFTH AVE. AND RANDOLPH ST.,

[See page 95.]   TELEPHONE 1029.   **CHICAGO.**

A BUSINESS TOUR OF CHICAGO.

RICHARD TRUPPEL,
PHARMACIST
No. 96 Wells St., Corner Indiana,
CHICAGO.
TELEPHONE NO. 3426.   [See page 118.]

Henry C. Jacobs,
Real ★ Estate ★ and ★ Loans
57 CALUMET BUILDING,
189 LA SALLE STREET.
Property bought and sold on commission. Special attention given to the care and management of real estate. Taxes paid, and rents collected. Interests of non-residents carefully looked after.
[See page 145.]

There is perhaps no place in our beautiful world half so charming as HOME, especially when one owns it. Do you own a home? If not come and see us. We have for years made a specialty of building and selling Residences in Chicago and vicinity, and we are all the time planning new and beautiful designs, in Cottages and Two-Story Houses, with bay-windows, plate and Cathedral Glass, Stone and Brick Cellars, Bath-rooms supplied with Hot and Cold Lake water, Marble Mantels, all built of elegant material. And we are prepared to sell, with small cash payment, balance monthly, or any way you prefer.
R. W. KESLER.   A. F. KESLER.
KESLER BROS.
REAL ESTATE DEALERS
146 LA SALLE STREET, 1st FLOOR, CHICAGO.
Residence: 3112 Michigan Ave.   [See page 79.]

J. SNYDER.   P. D. RATHBONE.
SNYDER & RATHBONE,
WHOLESALE FRUIT AND PRODUCE COMMISSION,
Butter, Eggs and Poultry Specialties,
217 S. WATER STREET,
REFERENCES:
First National Bank, Chicago, Ill.
First National Bank, South Haven, Mich.
German Bank, Sheboygan, Wis.
Steele, Wedeles & Co., Wholesale Grocers, Chicago.
Chicago.
[See page 146.]

J. H. WALLACE,
DEALER IN PINE AND
Hardwood Lumber,
242 SOUTH WATER ST.,
ROOM O.
City Telephone 1006.
Yard Telephone 4284.   CHICAGO.
YARD, NORTH BRANCH AND EASTMAN ST.   [See page 85.]

JNO. J. INKERSELL,
FINE
GROCERIES
1006 WEST MADISON STREET.
[See page 69.]

ESTABLISHED 1871.
H. F. ORVIS & CO.
GRAIN AND PRODUCE
Commission Merchants,
No. 231 South Water St., CHICAGO.
TELEPHONE NO. 836.   [See page 128.]

Richard Irwin,
DRAPER AND TAILOR,
No. 41 NORTH STATE STREET,
CHICAGO.
[See page 63.]

A. B. GEHMAN & Co.,
PUBLISHERS OF
Standard Subscription Books
— AND BIBLES —
NOS. 177 & 179 LA SALLE STREET,
[See page 97.]   CHICAGO.

I. JONAS,
MERCHANT TAILOR
22 RUSH STREET, CHICAGO.
Clothes Cleaned, Dyed and Repaired at Reasonable Prices. Good Fit and Workmanship Guaranteed.
[See page 70.]

T. D. RANDALL & CO.

ESTABLISHED 1852.

FRUIT AND PRODUCE

COMMISSION,

219 S. WATER ST., CHICAGO.

OLDEST FRUIT AND PRODUCE COMMISSION HOUSE IN CHICAGO. [See page 100.]

A. C. MATHER & CO.

IMPORTERS AND MANUFACTURERS

KID GLOVES,

122-124 MARKET ST.,

[See page 90.] CHICAGO, ILL.

G. T. BOAL,

WHOLESALE

STOVES AND HOLLOW WARE

247 & 249 KINZIE ST. [See page 117.]

RIES & CO.,

R. RIES. M. GUETTEL.

LADIES' AND GENTS'

Furnishing Goods,

251 TO 255 MONROE STREET,

[See page 90.] CHICAGO, ILL.

VICTOR D. COWAN & CO.,

Tailors' Trimmings,

134 FIFTH AVE.,

CHICAGO. [See page 106.]

SELZ, SCHWAB & CO.,

BOOTS AND SHOES,

192, 194, 196, 198 & 200 FRANKLIN ST.,

CHICAGO.

TELEPHONE No. 829. [See page 89.]

GEO. F. KIMBALL,

IMPORTER AND DEALER IN

Polished Plate and Window Glass

315 to 321 WABASH AVENUE,

[See page 85.] CHICAGO, ILL.

Albert Galloway,

STEAM HEATING AND VENTILATING

FOR PUBLIC BUILDINGS, RESIDENCES AND GREEN HOUSES.

By High and Low Pressure Steam and Hot Water.

NO. 198 JACKSON STREET,

Jobbing of All Kinds Promptly Attended to. CHICAGO.

Telephone No. 1048. [See page 94.]

SIMEON FARWELL & CO.,

MANUFACTURERS AND JOBBERS OF

Men's Furnishing Goods,

244-246 MONROE STREET,

[See page 90.] CHICAGO.

BARLY & CO.

Masquerade and Theatrical

COSTUMERS

3427 STATE ST., CHICAGO, ILL.

A Large Stock of Costumes, Wigs, Beards, Mustaches, Masks, Tableaus Fire, Etc., Constantly on Hand, For Sale or Rent.

JNO. SCHIPPERS,
Bakery and Confectionery,
222 So. CALIFORNIA AVENUE.

Fresh Baked Bread, Cakes, Pies, Etc., Etc.,
Always Kept on Hand.

I. C. ROGERS.   D. E. ROGERS.
I. C. ROGERS & SON,
GENERAL
Commission ✦ Merchants,
GREEN FRUITS AND VEGETABLES,
BUTTER, EGGS AND POULTRY,
267 South Water Street,
CHICAGO.
[See page 116.]

E. B. HOLMES.   J. M. PYOTT.   D. PYOTT.
WASHINGTON FOUNDRY & MACHINE SHOP,
No. 13 North Jefferson St., Chicago, Ill.
HOLMES, PYOTT & CO., Proprietors.
MANUFACTURERS OF
Iron Work of All Kinds for Buildings
SHAFTING, PULLEYS, STEAM ENGINES, CHICAGO
TAYLOR PRINTING PRESSES.
CASTINGS AND HEAVY MACHINERY.   [See page 138.]

JOHN G. BOESCH,
MANUFACTURER OF
Center and Telegraph Tables,
CABINET-MAKERS' TOOLS, Etc.
29 & 31 N. Jefferson St.,
[See page 94.]
CHICAGO

ABEL M. THOMSON, President.   J. R. TAYLOR, Vice-Pres't.   J. R. HARLEY   GEO. THOMSON, Sec'y and Treas.
THOMSON & TAYLOR SPICE CO.
IMPORTERS AND MANUFACTURERS OF
Roast and Ground Coffees, Whole and Ground
Spices, Mustards, Baking Powder, Flavoring Extracts, Indigos, Dry and Liquid
Bluing, Hops and Sage, Seeds.
34, 36, 38 & 40 South Water St.,   CHICAGO.
[See page 92.]

Whitchill Sewing Machine Co.
28 NORTH CLARK ST.
E. C. Packard, Man'gr.
[See page 96.]

GEO. W. HOYT & CO.,
Dry ✦ Goods ✦ Commission,
Nos. 241 to 245 MONROE ST.,
CHICAGO.
[See page 135.]

E. W. BLATCHFORD.   N. H. BLATCHFORD.
E. W. BLATCHFORD & CO.
70 NORTH CLINTON ST., CHICAGO.
Lead and Tin Pipe, Sheet and Bar Lead, Pig Lead
and Block Tin, Solder and Antimony, Antimonial Leads, Linseed Oil and Oil Cake,
Babbitt Metals, Stereotype, Electrotype, Type Metal, Copper, Spelter.
TELEPHONE 4221.   [See page 85.]

THE
SIMONDS SAWS AND KNIVES.
SIMONDS MANUFACTURING CO.
FITCHBURG—CHICAGO.
ESTABLISHED 1832.   RE-ORGANIZED 1864.
INCORPORATED 1868.   [See page 113.]

FRANK HEADEN.   FRANK McAULEY.
HEADEN & McAULEY,
MANUFACTURERS OF
Beer Stills, Railroad Tanks
AND ALL KINDS OF DISTILLERS', BREWERS' AND VINEGAR TUBS, CISTERNS, &c.
112 TO 118 E. INDIANA ST.,
(Cor. Franklin, North Side,)
Telephone No. 3144.   [See page 118.]   CHICAGO.

A BUSINESS TOUR OF CHICAGO.

The Hiram Sibley Fire-Proof Warehouses.
HIRAM SIBLEY & CO., PROP'RS.
2 to 18 NORTH CLARK STREET, - CHICAGO, ILL.
GENERAL DEALERS IN
AND BONDED STORAGE. GRASS AND FIELD SEEDS.
TELEPHONE No. 3269.

SHIPPING DIRECTIONS:
Consign Goods to The Hiram Sibley Fire-Proof Warehouses,
Care Chicago & North-Western R. R.
[See page 97 and 98.]

---

136 E. Wheeler St., 227 Broadway, 566 Canal St., 300 S. Fourth St.
Newark, N. J. New York. Cleveland, O. St. Louis, Mo.

Murphy & Company,
VARNISH MAKERS
262 WABASH AVENUE, CHICAGO.
F. H. TAYLOR,
RESIDENT MANAGER. *Hello 5546.* [See page 82.]

NATIONAL BOILER WORKS
J. DEE, Proprietor,
56, 58 & 60 Fulton St., CHICAGO, ILL.
(Between Clinton and Jefferson Streets.)
All Kinds of Marine, Locomotive and Stationary Boilers,
Sheet-Iron Work of All Kinds. Boiler Heads and Flue
Holes Flanged by Machinery.
☞ *Repairing Promptly Attended to at Reasonable Rates.*
ORDERS SOLICITED BY TELEPHONE No. 1272. [See page 90.]

E. EARNSHAW & SON,
Masons, Contractors and Builders,
Room 73, Exchange Building.
[See page 114.]

S BOOKWALTER. S G KELLEY. C. H. BARTLETT.
BOOKWALTER, KELLEY & CO.
General ⁎ Commission ⁎ Merchants,
SPECIAL ATTENTION GIVEN TO THE SALE OF FINE
BUTTER, CHEESE, EGGS AND POULTRY.
78 SOUTH WATER ST.,
REFERENCES:
Park National Bank, Chicago. *Chicago.*
People's Bank, West Liberty, Iowa.
First National Bank, Davenport, Iowa.
Merchants' Exchange Nat'l Bank, Muscatine, Ia. [See page 91.]

JOHN W. MASURY & SON,
New York——and——Chicago.
MANUFACTURERS OF
PAINTS AND VARNISHES.
NEW YORK OFFICE. CHICAGO OFFICE,
BENNETT BUILDING, M. J. ROSS, Manager,
Fulton Street, cor. Nassau. **MASURY BUILDING,**
190, 191, 192 Michigan Ave.
TELEPHONE NO. 5777. [See page 75.]

H. C. Hoffman. Darrell McGowan.
H. C. HOFFMAN & CO.
(Successors to Burlington Mfg. Co's Monumental and Granite Business)
MANUFACTURERS, DEALERS AND CONTRACTORS FOR
Granite Monuments, Vaults, Headstones
AND ALL KINDS OF CEMETERY WORK.
OFFICE AND SALESROOMS:
12 & 14 Van Buren Street, near Michigan Avenue,
CHICAGO.
Estimates given on Polished Granite Columns and other Granite
Building Work [See page 115.]

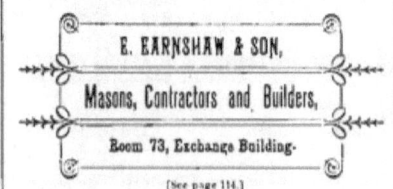

CLARK D. OSBORN. ALFRED L. GAYZER.
OSBORN & GAYZER
MANUFACTURERS OF
GLOVES AND MITTENS,
FINE GOODS A SPECIALTY.
238 & 240 ADAMS ST.,
FACTORY,
GLOVERSVILLE, N. Y. CHICAGO, ILL.

IMPORTER AND DEALER IN
FINE ARTS.
PAINTINGS,
ENGRAVINGS,
ETCHINGS, ETC.
ARTISTIC FRAMING.
210 WABASH AVENUE
[See page 145.]

Andrew Mullen. James Mullen. Charles Collin.
MULLEN BROS. & CO.
W·O·O·L·E·N·S
—AND—
TAILORS' TRIMMINGS,
264 & 266 MADISON ST.,
Corner Market St. [See page 97.] CHICAGO.

→J. H. HAAKE←
Dealer in Staple and Fancy
GROCERIES
74 North Wells Street, Chicago.

Our Motto—Good Goods at Lowest Prices for Cash.
[See page 125.]

HENRY A. FITCH,
864 W. Madison St., Chicago, Ill.
Telephone 7176.
DRUGS, MEDICINES, AND CHEMICALS,
FANCY AND TOILET ARTICLES,
Toilet Soaps, Sponges, Brushes, Combs, Perfumery, &c., &c.
Physicians' Prescriptions Carefully Compounded.
[See page 146.]

S. E. CLEVELAND & SON.
LIVERY, BOARDING & SALE STABLES
962 & 964 WEST MADISON STREET,
Between Oakley and Waters Ave. CHICAGO.

Carriages promptly furnished at all times for Weddings,
Telephone 7207. Parties, Theaters, Depots, etc. [See page 105.]

D. F. BREMNER, Pres. and Treas. J. P. DUNLAN, Sec'y.
THE
D. F. BREMNER BAKING CO.
MANUFACTURERS OF
Crackers & Fine Biscuit
OFFICE AND FACTORY, BRANCH OFFICE,
76, 78 & 80 O'BRIEN ST. | 19 MARKET STREET.
CHICAGO, ILL.
[See page 150.]

A. D. FERRY & CO.,
COMMISSION DEALERS IN
BROOM CORN
AND BROOM MATERIAL.
NOS. 225 & 227 KINZIE STREET,
CHICAGO. [See page 106.]

C. H. FARGO, C. E. FARGO, S. M. FARGO, F. M. FARGO.
C. H. FARGO & CO.,
Manufacturers and Jobbers of
BOOTS AND SHOES,
116, 118 and 120 Market Street,
CHICAGO.
[See page 65.]

T. W. EATON,
Manufacturer of Hand, Foot and Power
Circular Sawing Machines,
Also Hair Pickers for Mattress Makers,
62 and 64 WEST LAKE ST.,
[See page 96.] CHICAGO, ILL.

P. H. BOLTEN & CO.
General Produce Commission
AND WHOLESALE DEALERS IN
Butter, Cheese & Eggs,
223 SOUTH WATER STREET,
CHICAGO.
Reference: Hide and Leather National Bank, Chicago.
TELEPHONE NO. 925. [See page 150.]

GEORGE D. EDDY. ALBERT M. EDDY.
GLOBE FOUNDRY.
R. M. EDDY'S SONS,
Castings for
BOILER FRONTS,
Buildings, Machinery, Etc.
41 to 55 EAST INDIANA ST.,
(Telephone 3429.) CHICAGO, ILL.
Particular Attention Paid to Heavy Castings.
[See page 57.]

Established 1882. ACME Incorporated 1883.
ENGRAVING CO.
L. H. CRUMB, Manager.

81 Randolph Street, Cor. Dearborn,
Designs Furnished. → CHICAGO. ← Send for Samples.
TAKE ELEVATOR. [See page 126.]

THE CONTINENTAL
C. COLLINS, Proprietor.
S. E. Cor. Wabash Ave. and Madison St., CHICAGO.
$2.00 and $2.50 per Day.

Under New Management. Thoroughly Renovated and Re-furnished. In Business Center and Convenient to Principal R. R. Depots and Theaters. Eligible Rooms for Families and other Permanent Boarders. Day Boarders Accommodated.
[See page 142.]

NORTH ☩ WESTERN ☩ BOILER ☩ WORKS.
CHRIS. PFEIFFER, Prop.
— MANUFACTURER OF —
STEAM BOILERS, TANKS,
Smoke Stacks, Etc.
REPAIRS PROMPTLY ATTENDED TO.
64 Michigan Street, - CHICAGO, ILL.
Residence, 70 Lincoln Ave. Telephone 3100. [See page 107.]

STEVENS,
PHOTOGRAPHER,
McVicker's Theater Building,
CHICAGO.
[See page 77.]

GEO. SALVESEN,
PRACTICAL
CARRIAGE TRIMMER.
Landaus, Landaulettes, Coupes, Coupelettes, Broughams and All Other Carriages Neatly Trimmed and Repaired.
95 and 97 Indiana Street,
[See page 144.]   →→CHICAGO, ILLS.

H. PHILIPPI,
No. 276 State Street, Chicago,
HEADQUARTERS
For all the Late Styles of
BAR GLASSWARE
And BAR UTENSILS GENERALLY,
Hotel and Restaurant CHINA.   [See page 139.]

ENGRAVING
WOOD
CHICAGO ENGRAVING CO.
FINE WORK
85 RANDOLPH ST.

M. JOHNSON.   J. METZLER.
JOHNSON & METZLER,
— MANUFACTURERS OF —
Carriages, Buggies,
SPRING TRUCKS and WAGONS,
260 & 262 Michigan Street, near Rush,
All kinds of Painting and Trimming promptly attended to.   CHICAGO.
Telephone 3329.   [See page 144.]

H. C. FISHER,
IMPORTER and JOBBER.
Teas, Cigars,
SPICES, BAKING POWDERS, &c.
33 MICHIGAN AVENUE,
[See page 127.]   →→CHICAGO.

MILLS at DUCK LAKE, LINCOLN, and MEARS, Michigan.
ESTABLISHED IN 1888.
C. MEARS & CO.
Manufacturers and Dealers in
LUMBER AND BRICK,
Office, 242½ South Water Street,
201 Hawthorne Avenue, Red Office.
Brick Dock, East End Madison St. Bridge.   CHICAGO.
[See page 103.]

SERVOSS FURNACE CO.
Manufacturers and Dealers in
The Late Improved Servoss ELECTRIC HEATER,
AND THE CELEBRATED AUTOMATIC
FIRE REGULATOR,
The Servoss-Ekstrom Kitchen Ventilator
AND AIR RENOVATOR. HOT AIR FLUES, MANTELS, GRATES, &c.
135 & 137 Lake St., near Clark, CHICAGO.
Telephone 1579.   [See page 55.]

A BUSINESS TOUR OF CHICAGO.

FRANK ALSIP, PRES'T & GEN. MANAGER.   WILLIAM H. ALSIP, SEC'Y & TREAS.   FRANK B. ALSIP, SUPERINTENDENT.

ALSIP BRICK CO.
Office, 159 La Salle Street, Room 73,

CHICAGO.

YARDS:
43d St. West of Ashland Ave.
Chicago and Hamlin Avenues.

Telephones:
43d Street Yard, No. 9604.
Chicago Ave. Yard, No. 7266.
Office, No. 96.

[See page 86.]

F. R. JACKSON, Manager.

CHARLES CREAMERY CO.
68 & 70 N. State Street, CHICAGO,
MANUFACTURERS OF THE CELEBRATED
"CHARLES CREAMERY BUTTER,"
And Dealers in STRICTLY FRESH EGGS,
Delivered free, to all parts of the city, twice a week.
Orders by mail receive prompt attention. [See page 71.]

MORPER, DERNBURG & CO.
—— MANUFACTURERS OF ——

Ladies' AND Children's Cloaks,

156 & 158 Market Street,

[See page 102.]   **CHICAGO.**

WM. M. DALE,
MANUFACTURING and DISPENSING

——> CHEMIST <——

Corner Clark and Madison Streets,

CHICAGO. [See page 83.]

EDW. BAUMANN, Architect.
ASSO. M. AM. SOC'Y C. E.

WM. H. LOTZ, Mechanical Engineer.
M. AM. SOC'Y C. E.   M. WESTERN SOC'Y E.

BAUMANN & LOTZ,
ARCHITECTS AND ENGINEERS,

Rooms 59, 68 and 70 Metropolitan Block,

SPECIALTY.—The design and erection of Grain Elevators, Malt Houses and Breweries.

CHICAGO, ILL.
[See page 114.]

DAUCHY & CO.
MANUFACTURERS OF

Patent Vault and Sidewalk Lights.

Vault and Coal Hole Covers always on hand.

125 & 127 INDIANA STREET, NEAR WELLS,

TELEPHONE No. 2163. [See page 152.] **CHICAGO, ILL.**

BROWN & JAMES HEATING CO.,

Manufacturers and Dealers in

Brown's Water Heaters and Furnaces.

Office and Salesroom, 2131 Wabash Ave.,

[See page 104.]   **CHICAGO, ILL.**

HARROUN MANUFACTURING CO.

Manufacturers, Jobbers and Dealers in

Sewing Machine Supplies,

No. 248 WABASH AVENUE,

CHICAGO.

S. A. KEAN & CO.
Bankers,

(Successors to PRESTON, KEAN & CO.,)

100 WASHINGTON STREET,

CHICAGO.
[See page 124.]

THE JOHN J. CROOKE CO.
—— MANUFACTURERS OF ——

Plain, Colored and Embossed Tinfoil and Metallic Capsules,

84 FRANKLIN STREET,

[See page 118.]   **CHICAGO, ILL.**

A BUSINESS TOUR OF CHICAGO.

FOSTER, ROE & CRONE,

Fine Printers,

170 Clark Street, ♦ ♦ CHICAGO, ILL.

[See page 99.]

H. H. BOULTER, M. D., D. D. S.,

—◊Dentist,◊—

ROOM 29, CENTRAL MUSIC HALL,   S. E. Cor. Randolph and State Sts.

Hours, 9 to 4.   TAKE ELEVATOR.

F. GUSTORF,

Agent, ‡ Lumber ‡ Commission,

242 SOUTH WATER STREET,

ROOM 16.   [See page 165.]   CHICAGO, ILL.

J. SAUTTER.   J. APKING.

SAUTTER & APKING,

——MANUFACTURERS OF——

Men's, Boys' and Youths' Pegged, Nailed and Machine-Sewed

BOOTS AND SHOES,

Nos. 66, 68 and 70 W. Lake Street,

[See page 89.]   CHICAGO.

R. M. WEIR,

DRUGGIST ✦ AND ✦ APOTHECARY.

PURE GOODS OUR SPECIALTY.

TELEPHONE 7808.   1236 West Jackson St.,

N. W. COR. CALIFORNIA AVE.

Physicians' Prescriptions Accurately
Compounded, at all hours.   CHICAGO.

RECORD BROTHERS,

→Dry Goods←

Commission ‡ Merchants,

267 and 269 FRANKLIN ST.,

CHICAGO.

NELSON B. RECORD.   MILTON L. RECORD.

Alfred Payne,

PORTRAIT ✤ LANDSCAPE PAINTER,

Southwest Cor. Clark and Adams Sts.,

[See page 134.]   →CHICAGO, ILL.

Charles S. Wallace,

Sanitary Plumber,

TELEPHONE 1465.   362 Wabash Avenue,

Remodeling of Old Work a Specialty.   →CHICAGO.

[See page 173.]

CHAS. HOLMBERG,

NORTH-WESTERN

COPPER WORKS,

54 and 56 Wells St., CHICAGO.

☞ Manufacturer of Confectionery and Steamboat Work in all its Branches.

Henry B. Grier.   Albert Jack.

GRIER & JACK,

Wholesale

Lamps, Glassware and Fruit Jars,

15 LAKE STREET,

[See page 96.]   CHICAGO.

MYRON L. OSGOOD,
HOWLAND BLOCK, Room 25,
182 DEARBORN ST.,
Real Estate. CHICAGO.
[See page 52.]

S. F. WRIGHT & CO.
S. F. Wright. G. N. Wright.
Livery and Boarding Stables,
248, 250 & 252 KINZIE STREET,
CHICAGO.
Telephone 8008. [See page 161.]

J. A. SHEPARD,
Portrait & Copying House,
289 WABASH AVE.
CHICAGO, ILL.
[See page 98.]

GEHR & GARDNER,
T. E. Gehr. Wm. Gardner.
Hide Brokers,
178 MICHIGAN STREET,
References: Stephen Kistler's Sons, N. Y.; Loeb, Messer & Co., N. Y.
CHICAGO, ILL.
New York Office: 91 GOLD ST. [See page 171.]

S. A. MAXWELL & CO.
Booksellers, Stationers,
And Wall Paper Dealers,
134 & 136 Wabash Ave.,
[See page 175.] CHICAGO, ILL.

PETERSON & OVESON,
B. C. Peterson. C. A. Oveson.
MANUFACTURERS OF
Center, Library and Parlor Tables and Flower Stands,
Nos. 140 TO 151 NORTH SANGAMON STREET,
Corner Austin Avenue. CHICAGO, ILL.
[See page 170.]

CANFIELD & CO.
H. S. Canfield. F. E. Canfield.
MANUFACTURERS OF
Show Cases.
Drug-Store Fixtures and Wall Cases for All Purposes.
7, 9, 11 & 13 WABASH AVE.,
[See page 171.] CHICAGO.

H. G. MEDCALFE & CO.
ESTD. 1859
Prescription Druggists
72 NORTH CLARK STREET,
Bet. Michigan and Illinois Sts. CHICAGO.
TELEPHONE NO. 3158. [See page 71.]

→ M. THOME, ←
Importer of
Hair Goods
HAIR BAZAAR: 157 STATE STREET.
WHOLESALE DEPOT: 138-140 WABASH AVENUE.
CHICAGO, ILL.
[See page 72.]

Young, Gatzert & Co.,
SUCCESSORS TO ANDREW YOUNG,
PLUMBERS AND GAS-FITTERS,
965 WEST MADISON ST.,
SANITARY PLUMBING A SPECIALTY.
CHICAGO.
ALL WORK GUARANTEED. [See page 179.]

TELEPHONE No. 1616.

C. H. GURNEY & CO.,
Steel, Heavy Hardware
RAILWAY, MACHINISTS' AND MINING SUPPLIES.

247 & 249 Lake St. and 7 & 9 Market St.,
CHICAGO.

[See page 74.]

RIVERDALE DISTILLING CO.
DISTILLERS AND RECTIFIERS,
264 to 270 EAST KINZIE ST.,
Foot of Cass,

DISTILLERY
LOCATED AT
RIVERDALE, COOK CO., ILL.
Chicago.

[See page 74.]

JOSEPH BLAKEMORE,
Manufacturer and Gilder of

Gold and Metal Leaf Frames,
MOULDINGS MOUNTED FOR THE TRADE.

OFFICE AND FACTORY:
234 EAST LAKE STREET.
CHICAGO, ILL.

[See page 175.]

"FERMENTUM"
THE ONLY RELIABLE

COMPRESSED YEAST
MANUFACTURED BY THE
RIVERDALE DISTILLING CO.
A. JUNKER, GENERAL AGENT,
264-270 Kinzie St., CHICAGO.

[See page 74.]

WM. GANSCHOW,
(Successor to John Kittel,)

GEAR ÷ CUTTING
MILLING WORK OF EVERY DESCRIPTION A SPECIALTY.
Machinery Made to Order.

31 AND 33 SOUTH CANAL STREET,
Near Washington,

Second Floor. Telephone 4157. CHICAGO.

C. H. JULIUS & SON
Merchant Tailors,
DYEING AND SCOURING,

16 East Jackson Street,
Under Leland Hotel. CHICAGO.

[See page 164.]

Jos. Deetsch, Prest. A. Hofman, Treas. Wm. Lange, Sec'y.

Northwestern Parlor Suit Co
MANUFACTURERS OF

PARLOR FURNITURE FRAMES,
687 to 701 Clybourn Ave. and 26 to 30 A St.,
Telephone 3456. CHICAGO, ILL.

[See page 178.]

H. D. CASTEEL,
Manufacturer of

HAVANA CIGARS
AND DEALER IN
LEAF TOBACCO,
95 & 97 ADAMS ST.,
Opp. Custom-House. CHICAGO.

[See page 193.]

Wolf, Beefier & Co.,
COMMISSION DEALERS

Wool, Pelts, Furs and Skins,
221 to 227 E. KINZIE STREET,

REFER BY PERMISSION TO
MR. W. A. HAMMOND, Cash
NAT'L BANK OF ILLINOIS
AT CHICAGO.
CHICAGO.
TELEPHONE 3148.

[See page 174.]

SCHREIBER & ANNAS,
Successors to Schreiber & Brown,
DESIGNERS AND MANUFACTURERS OF

Ornamental ÷ Cut ÷ Glass,
PLAIN AND FANCY BEVELED GLASS,

13 & 15 SOUTH CANAL STREET,
ORIGINAL DESIGNS FURNISHED ON APPLICATION.
Chicago.

[See page 175.]

A BUSINESS TOUR OF CHICAGO.

A. F. SEEBERGER. CHAS. D. SEEBERGER.
A. F. SEEBERGER & CO.
WHOLESALE HARDWARE,
Cutlery, Tinplate, Metals, Nails, &c.
38 & 40 LAKE ST.,
[See page 148.] CHICAGO.

J. H. PURDY & CO.,
Watch Materials, Tools, Etc.
——AND——
U. S. JEWELERS' GUILD JEWELRY.
170 State Street,
[See page 176.] CHICAGO, ILL.

IRA BROWN,
Real × Estate × Dealer
——AND——
PRIVATE BANKER,
177 La Salle St., Room 9,
Loans Money and Builds Houses to Order. CHICAGO, ILL.
[See page 147.]

H. F. VEHMEYER,
DEALER IN
BROOM CORN
Broom Manufacturers' Supplies,
206, 208 & 210 MICHIGAN ST., Near State,
[See page 164.] CHICAGO.

WM. EVERS & CO.,
GENERAL
Commission ⋄ Merchants,
215 SOUTH WATER ST.,
CREAMERY A SPECIALTY. CHICAGO.
TELEPHONE 489. [See page 150.]

Patent, Trade Mark and Copyright Law.? American and Foreign Patents Obtained.
CHARLES T. BROWN,
ATTORNEY AT LAW,
ROOM 33, 225 DEARBORN ST.,
Opp. Government Building. [See page 162.] CHICAGO.

1035 W. Madison Street.
ACME LAUNDRY
James Donnellan, Prop'r.
[See page 182.]

F. PRUSSING,
DEALER IN
FOREIGN **GROCERIES** DOMESTIC
51 & 53 NORTH STATE ST.,
TELEPHONE 3131. CHICAGO.
[See page 170.]

L. L. WADSWORTH,
MANUFACTURER OF
Spring Trucks and Wagons,
REPAIRING PROMPTLY ATTENDED TO.
252 Michigan Street,
[See page 142.] CHICAGO.

PORTMAN BROS. & CO.
MANUFACTURERS OF
Traveling Bags
88 & 90 LAKE STREET,
[See page 53.] CHICAGO, ILL.

A BUSINESS TOUR OF CHICAGO. xiii

TREMBLE & ALBERDING,
—:WHOLESALE AND RETAIL:—
MANUFACTURING CONFECTIONERS,
→CARAMELS A SPECIALTY,←
NO. 64 NORTH CLARK STREET,
CHICAGO.

PETER SMITH & CO.,
MANUFACTURERS OF
CARRIAGES, BUGGIES, &C.,
→78 & 80 MICHIGAN STREET,←
CHICAGO.
Prompt Attention Paid to Repairing.
[See page 74.]

MOORSHEAD & CO.,
Manufacturers' Agents and Jobbers of
JEWELRY SPECIALTIES,
[In Men's Fine Rolled Plate Sleeve Buttons, Sleeve Links, Collar Buttons, Scarf Pins, Studs, &c.
A Full Line of the Celebrated FULL DRESS STONINE Sleeve Buttons, Studs and Links, Constantly on Hand.
161 La Salle St., Rooms 74 & 76,   →CHICAGO.

MATTSON & AEPPLI,
→TANNERS,←
AND MANUFACTURERS OF
GLOVES & MITTENS,
13 & 15 SLOAN STREET,
Salesroom, 89 Franklin Street.   CHICAGO.

C. F. WEBER.   W. J. WEBER.
WEBER BROS.,
METAL SPINNERS,
→Manufacturers of all Kinds of←
METAL GOODS,
85 N. Clinton Street,   →CHICAGO.
(National Tube Works Building.)
JOBBING PROMPTLY ATTENDED TO.

McCORMACK BROS.,
Homœopathic Pharmaceutists,
Rooms 34, 35 & 36 Quincy Building,
113 Adams St., Opposite Post-Office,
CHICAGO, ILL.
[See page 77.]

B. GARCIA & CO.,
Spanish Cigar Manufacturers
IMPORTERS AND DEALERS IN
→**Havana Leaf,**←
44 & 46 La Salle St.,   CHICAGO.
[See page 147.]

JOHN GARETTI,
✠**FRESCO PAINTER**✠
AND MANUFACTURER OF
ROMAN MOSAIC MARBLE FLOORING,
→42 N. STATE STREET,←
[See page 139.]   CHICAGO, ILL.

NEW YORK.   FACTORY TROY, NEW YORK.   BOSTON.
JAMES K. P. PINE,
MANUFACTURER OF
"LION BRAND"
Men's Linen Collars & Cuffs,
→128 FIFTH AVENUE,←
W. M. WADSWORTH, Manager.
[See page 52.]   CHICAGO

D. BAKENHUS.   A. MUESELER.
BAKENHUS & MUESELER,
MANUFACTURERS OF
CARRIAGES, TRUCKS and WAGONS,
95 & 97 E. INDIANA STREET,
CHICAGO.
Every Description of Work Made to Order.   Repairing Promptly Done.
[See page 64.]

M. D. RIDER,

Wholesale and Retail Dealer in

BLANK BOOKS AND STATIONERY

OF EVERY DESCRIPTION,

120 LASALLE STREET,

Four Doors North of Madison.   CHICAGO.

SOCIETY AND COMMERCIAL PRINTING.

[See page 72.]

CHARLES RAISER,

Manufacturer of

CHILDREN'S CARRIAGES.

SPECIALTY: Selling Direct to Private Parties.

62 & 64 CLYBOURN AVE.,   CHICAGO.

[See page 145.]

R. P. LAYTON,

CITY AND SUBURBAN

REAL ESTATE

Room 23,

182 Dearborn Street,

(HOWLAND BLOCK.)   CHICAGO.

[See page 115.]

MEATH BROS.

Wholesale and Retail Dealers in

FURNITURE, CARPETS,

STOVES, OIL CLOTHS, CURTAINS,

And everything in the house-furnishing line for cash or on our easy payments.

265 & 267 W. MADISON ST.,   CHICAGO.

[See page 162.]

Isaac Shillington,

LIVERY, BOARDING and SALE STABLE

210 & 212 INDIANA STREET,

Between Clark and Dearborn.

Telephone 3077.   CHICAGO.

[See page 96.]

N. D. SWANSEN,

DEALER IN

Cigars, Tobacco,

CONFECTIONERY, STATIONERY AND PERIODICALS,

1047 Madison Street,

CHICAGO.

[See page 174.]

R. H. SANBORN & CO.

Western Agents for

CELLULOID

COLLARS AND CUFFS

NO. 143 FIFTH AVENUE,

Jobbers Supplied from Chicago Stock.   Chicago, Ill.

[See page 79.]

MRS. A. MOLLER'S

HOME LAUNDRY,

No. 10 RUSH ST.

ALL WORK DONE BY HAND.

[See page 64.]

Thos. S. Cruttenden,

AGENT FOR THE SALE OF

GARNER & CO'S GOODS

252 MONROE STREET,

[See page 101.]   CHICAGO.

U. S. HOME MFG. CO.

INVENTORS AND MANUFACTURERS

Specialties

37 Lakeside Building, Cor. Clark & Adams Sts.,

P. O. BOX 443.   CHICAGO, ILL., U. S. A.

[See page 157.]

A BUSINESS TOUR OF CHICAGO.

H. W. JENNEY, President.   C. L. GRAHAM, Sec. & Treas.

JENNEY & GRAHAM GUN COMPANY,

Fire Arms, Fishing Tackle,

—AND—

→GENERAL SPORTING GOODS,←

53 STATE STREET,

Former Stand of E. E. EATON.

CHAS. STATTMAN & CO.,

Manufacturers and Importers of

→Sealskin Garments,←

Fine Furs, Caps, Gloves, Muffs, Trimmings,

→ROBES AND COATS,←

216-218 MONROE STREET,

RAW FURS BOUGHT.   CHICAGO.
[See page 137.]

STEPHEN PADDON & CO.,

CHEMICAL AND DRUG IMPORTERS,

GLASSMAKERS', SOAPMAKERS',

PAPERMAKERS' SUPPLIES,

156 WASHINGTON STREET,

[See page 133.]   CHICAGO.

+ROUNDY & SON,+

MANUFACTURERS OF

→Lodge Supplies, Banners and Flags,←

Regalia and Uniforms for all Societies,

188 & 190 S. CLARK ST.,

[See page 119.]   Chicago, Ill.

JOS. DOWNEY,

→MASON CONTRACTOR & BUILDER←

OFFICE:

No. 161 La Salle Street, Room 94,

CHICAGO.

Office Telephone: No. 167.   Residence Telephone: No. 7141.

[See page 67.]

ESTABLISHED 1874

+McEWAN'S+

Temperance European Hotel & Coffee House

95 W. MADISON STREET.

Transient Rooms, 50 Cts. to $1.00.   Meals at all Hours.

[See page 158.]

+CLUB HOUSE CIGAR FACTORY.+

CASS F. MAURER,

—DEALER IN—

CIGARS & TOBACCO,

→DOMESTIC AND IMPORTED.←

103 Adams Stree.
Opposite Post-Office.   [See page 101.]   **CHICAGO.**

G. A. MARINER.   ESTABLISHED 1856.   WM. HOSKIN.

G. A. MARINER & CO.,

Analytical and Consulting

CHEMISTS & ASSAYERS,

81 South Clark Street, CHICAGO,

Top Floor, take Elevator

—ASSAYS AND ANALYSES OF ALL KINDS.—

Chemistry applied to Mining, Geology, Agriculture, Useful Arts, Metallurgy, Patents, Inventions, Medical, Legal, Commercial and Domestic Affairs.

[See page 64.]

IF YOUR HOUSE IS INFESTED WITH

COCKROACHES, BED BUGS, MOTHS, ANTS, &C., &C.

CALL ON OR ADDRESS

+I. BLUMENTHAL,+

+INSECT + EXTERMINATOR+

07½ N. WELLS STREET,   CHICAGO.

The Best Reference Given.   Contracts Accepted.

[See page 69.]

GEORGE M. BOGUE.   HENRY W. HOYT.   HAMILTON B. BOGUE.

BOGUE & HOYT,

+REAL ESTATE AGENCY.+

No. 182 Dearborn Street, Room 1, Second Floor.

Real Estate Bought and Sold on Commission. Special Attention Given to the Care and Management of Property. Taxes paid and Rents Collected. Interests of Non-Residents Carefully Looked After. Mortgage Loans.

Telephone 030.   [See page 78.]

A BUSINESS TOUR OF CHICAGO.

ESTABLISHED 1880.   INCORPORATED 1885.

THE G. M. JARVIS CO.,
~SAN JOSE, CAL.,~
Growers, Distillers & Dealers
Wines & Brandies,
Jarvis Riesling Grape Brandy Our Specialty.
80 North State St.,
[See page 149.]
CHICAGO.

GEO. C. FINNEY.   JAS. CHANNON

FINNEY & CHANNON,
Ship Chandlers & Sail Makers,
Manila, Hemp and Wire Rigging, Blocks, Anchors,
~CHAINS, PAINTS, OILS, ETC.~
Special Attention Given to Outfits and Repairs.
270 & 272 South Water St., CHICAGO, ILL.
[See page 146.]

JAMES H. RICE COMPANY,
Importers of and Dealers in
Polished, Rough and Crystal Plate Glass,
FRENCH PLATE AND GERMAN MIRRORS.
Also English, French and American Window Glass,
13, 15, 17 Quincy Street,
Telephone 506.
[See page 70.]
CHICAGO.

E. NORCOTT,
Manufacturer of and Wholesale and Retail Dealer in
TIN & COPPER WARE,
COR. STATE AND ILLINOIS STREETS (Basement).
ROOFING AND GUTTERING.
Job Work Done Easily and Promptly.
Furnaces and Stoves Repaired.
CHICAGO, ILL.
[See page 171.]

PHILLIPSON DECORATIVE CO.,
Designers, Importers, Manufacturers,
~245 WABASH AVE.~
Frescoing, Paper Hanging, Painting, Papier Mache,
Stained Glass, Drapery.
Telephone 3634.   [See page 151.]

ALFRED C. KEMPER COVERING CO.
Room 920, Opera House Building, CHICAGO.
GENERAL WESTERN AGENCY
MAGNESIA SECTIONAL AND PLASTIC COVERING,
AINSWORTH WOOD PULP PLASTIC COVERING,
FLEECE FUR SPACE COVERING.
Dealers in Asbestos and Hair-Felt Covering.
DEPOT, HIRAM SIBLEY'S WAREHOUSE.   TELEPHONE 1284

The Sigwalt Mfg. Company,
MANUFACTURERS OF
Seal Presses, Check Protectors and Engravers' Supplies,
11 to 13 N. Canal Street,
J. SIGWALT, Manager,   CHICAGO.
[See page 49.]

BUCKLEY'S
CHEAP CASH MARKET
Fresh Fish, Oysters and Game in Season.
BOARDING HOUSES AND RESTAURANTS SUPPLIED
AT THE VERY LOWEST TERMS.
[See page 141.]   1307 West Van Buren Street.

U. E. ATWATER & CO.,
Real Estate and Furnished House Agency,
Room Renting & Boarding House Directory,
~CHATTEL MORTGAGE LOANS.~
Room 9, Adams Express Building.
105 Dearborn St.,   CHICAGO.
Special Attention Given to Hotels, Lease and Furniture for Sale.
[See page 144.]

TOM. N. DONNELLY & CO.
Loan & Diamond Brokers,
118 DEARBORN ST.,
Corner Calhoun Place,
Bet. Madison and Washington,   CHICAGO.
Highest Cash Price paid for Old Gold, Silver and Precious Stones.
[See page 175.]

A BUSINESS TOUR OF CHICAGO.

S. E. BLISS.   E. C. TRACY.

BLISS & TRACY,

Iron and Steel Shafting,

Steel Rim Pulleys, Friction Clutch Pulleys,
Hangers, Couplings, Etc.

51 S. CANAL ST.,   CHICAGO.

[See page 119.]   TELEPHONE 4485.

JAS. HOLLINGSWORTH.   THOS. COUGHLAN.   JOHN COUGHLAN.

HOLLINGSWORTH & COUGHLAN,

OLD ∴ PIONEER ∴ CONTRACTORS

For Raising, Lowering and Removing BRICK, STONE AND IRON BUILDINGS.

Thirty years' experience in handling the heaviest and most costly structures without accident or damage.

Office, 159 La Salle St., Room 73, CHICAGO.

Office Hours, 10 to 11 and 3 to 4.   Telephone 905.

[See page 123.]

BYRON A. BALDWIN,   WALTER S BALDWIN,
Member Chicago Real Estate Board.   Notary Public.

BYRON·A.·BALDWIN·&·Co.

154 Washington Street, - CHICAGO.

Real Estate and Loan Agents.

Rents Collected, Money Loaned, Taxes Paid,
Investments Made and Property Sold.

Telephone No. 890.   [See page 125.]

HAMBURG HOUSE

M. MARKS,   Proprietor.

First-Class Accommodations   Special Inducements
for Transient Public at   for
Moderate Prices.   Weekly Arrangements.

184 AND 186 RANDOLPH ST.,

[See page 109.]   CHICAGO.

C. F. WARDELL,

Automatic Engines, Slide Valve Engines

— AND BOILERS, —

METAL-WORKING MACHINERY,

MANUFACTURER' AGENT FOR

FITCHBURG MACHINE WORKS
PROSPECT MACHINE AND ENGINE CO.
TAYLOR MANUFACTURING CO.

[See page 93.]   50 S. CANAL ST.

GINN & CO.,

PUBLISHERS OF

School & College Text Books

180 WABASH AVENUE,

M. S. SMYTH,   CHICAGO.
MANAGER.   [See page 115.]

RICHARD ROBINS.   ED N. KIRK TALCOTT.

ROBINS & TALCOTT,

BUILDING SPECIALTIES

Ornamental Iron Work, Terra Cotta, Granite,
Marble, Sandstone, Magneso Calcite.

Agents for Fireproofing, Bowls Architectural Bronze and Iron Works (New York and Brooklyn); Boston Terra Cotta Co. (Boston, Mass.)

115 Monroe St., R. 11 Montauk Bl'k, CHICAGO.

TELEPHONE 1714.   [See page 103.]

J. B. HASSETT,

WHOLESALE AND RETAIL GROCER,

— JOBBER IN —

FINE TEAS AND COFFEE, FLOUR,
FRUITS AND PRODUCE,

No. 9 NORTH CLARK ST.,   CHICAGO.

[See page 108.]

WM. G. BERGER.   ROBT. BERGER.

BERGER BROS.

Wholesale and Retail Dealers in

MICHIGAN AND INDIANA CHARCOAL,

Car Loads and Cases of CHARCOAL shipped to any part of the Country.

OFFICE, 170 MICHIGAN ST.,
B. R. TE. With car Central Pt. of S. Water St.   CHICAGO, ILL.

CONTRACTS A SPECIALTY.   TEL. No. 3181.

[See page 111.]

Chas. F. Gifford.   J. C. Gifford.   C. E. Gifford, Jr.

CHAS. H. GIFFORD & CO.

COMMISSION,

Grain and Provisions,

Rooms 62 and 63,

238 & 240 La Salle Street,

[See page 112.]   CHICAGO.

A BUSINESS TOUR OF CHICAGO.

GASLER'S

DRESS PLAITING

—AND—

BUTTON HOLE BAZAR,

99 EAST MADISON ST.,

[See page 156.]   **CHICAGO.**

JACOB P. GROSS.   *A. H. GRUNEWALD.*

J. P. GROSS & CO.,

Dealers in

BROOM CORN

HANDLES, WIRE, TWINES, TOOLS AND MACHINERY,

Nos. 249 & 251 Kinzie St.,   **CHICAGO.**

ESTABLISHED 1872.

Chicago Weekly Occident,

155 & 157 WASHINGTON ST., CHICAGO.

THE LEADING JEWISH NEWSPAPER OF THE GREAT NORTHWEST.

JULIUS SILVERSMITH, M. A., - Editor.

[See page 166.]

J. F. FREITAG,

Manufacturer of

CARRIAGE AND CAB LAMPS,

NO. 4 LA SALLE AVE., CHICAGO.

Coach, Carriage, Hearse and Dash Lamps, Hook and Ladder, Truck and Hose Cart Lamps, Fire Engine Signals and Trumpets, Hub Caps, Curtain Rollers and Carriage Candles of all Sizes.

Old Work Repaired and Replated.   [See page 140.]

Ruddock & Seymour,

YELLOW PINE

AND RED CYPRESS,

CYPRESS SHINGLE,

—CHICAGO.—

H. GOETTSCHE,

Wholesale and Retail Dealer in

Imported, Key West AND Domestic Cigars

TOBACCOS, MEERSCHAUM AND BRIAR PIPES AND SMOKERS' ARTICLES.

271 E. MADISON ST., Cor. Market,

FACTORY:

239 East Division Street.   **CHICAGO.**

MEERSCHAUM PIPES BOILED AND REPAIRED.

[See page 152.]

L. HELLER & CO.,

WHOLESALE JEWELERS,

NOVELTIES IN BUTTONS AND PINS.

A FULL LINE OF AMBER AND RHINE STONE JEWELRY.

240 ADAMS STREET,

[See page 65.]   —CHICAGO.

ESTABLISHED 1877.

L. HIRSCHBERG.   E. DRISCOLL.

DIAMOND PALACE,

119 East Madison St.,

Wholesale and Retail Dealers and Importers of

GENUINE DIAMONDS AND PRECIOUS STONES,

Also Fine Watches and Jewelry.

[See page 174.]

ADAM SIEBERT,

PRACTICAL

CARRIAGE, WAGON AND SIGN **PAINTING**

95 & 97 E. Indiana Street,

[See page 166.]   **CHICAGO.**

M. H. LOWELL,

—Artist,—

Dealer in Oil Paintings and Frames,

183 MADISON STREET,

[See page 66.]   **CHICAGO.**

A BUSINESS TOUR OF CHICAGO.

xix

GUS. LINDHOLM'S
City Express AND Parcel Delivery,
FOUR TRIPS DAILY.
Englewood, Stock Yards, Hyde Park, Ravenswood, Cicero, Lawndale and Oak Park,
—ONE TRIP DAILY—
TRUNKS, 25c.   PARCELS, 10c.
Also Dealer in COAL, WOOD AND COKE.
72-74-76 N. State Street,   CHICAGO, ILL.
Telephone 3165.   [See page 62.]

J. P. MALLETTE,   R. E. BROWNELL,   C. B. EGGLESTON, *Special*.
J. P. MALLETTE & CO.,
Real Estate Loans AND Insurance.
OFFICES:
CHICAGO—ROOM 616, ROYAL INS. BUILDING.
TELEPHONE NO. 1932.
ENGLEWOOD—ROOMS 1 & 3 CENTRAL BL'K.
TELEPHONE NO. 15.
[See page 119.]

T. E. COPELIN,
37 N. State Street, CHICAGO, ILL.
Stoves, Furnaces, Ranges, and Builders' Hardware,
Repairing and Jobbing in Tin, Copper and Sheet Iron.
FINE GRINDING, NICKEL-PLATING AND POLISHING.
Agents for Wm. RESOR & CO'S "Monitor" Stoves and Ranges.
[See page 64.]

CHAS. RASCHER,
—MANAGER—
THE RASCHER MAP PUB'G CO.
162 LA SALLE STREET.
FIRE INSURANCE MAPS OF ALL WESTERN CITIES.
—CHICAGO.—
[See page 67.]

TUCKHORN & CO.,
MANUFACTURERS OF
BILLIARD AND POOL TABLES.
Importers and Dealers in all kinds of Billiard Material. Second-hand Tables to sell or storage. Balls Turned and Re-colored in the cheapest and best manner. Second-hand Balls bought and sold.
In all kinds of Repairing we agree to do First-class Work.
Send Postal Card and I will call.   92 Fifth Ave., CHICAGO.
BRANCH: 29 Mifflin St., MADISON, Wis.   (TIMES BUILDING.)
[See page 164.]

GALE & BLOCKI,
DRUGGISTS AND IMPORTERS OF
ARTIFICIAL EYES
PROPRIETORS OF THE
White Rock Spring Water and Ginger Ale.
111 Randolph St.,
44 & 46 Monroe St., PALMER HOUSE,
126 N. Clark St., 200 Lake St., OAK PARK.
[See page 144.]

REVERE HOUSE,
American and European Plans.
Cor. Clark and Michigan Street,
TWO BLOCKS FROM C. & N. W. R'Y DEPOT.   CHICAGO.
—J. D. FANNING, Proprietor.—
A Finely Appointed Cafe Run in Connection with the Hotel.
Best Furnished and Best Appointed Hotel for the Price in America. The Safest Hotel in the World.
Nine Exits in case of Fire.
PRACTICALLY FIREPROOF.   [See page 154.]

ALBURGER, STOER & CO.,
MANUFACTURERS AND IMPORTERS OF
TAILORS' TRIMMINGS,
228 & 230 FIFTH AVENUE.
CHICAGO.
PHILADELPHIA.
BRADFORD, ENG.   CHICAGO.
J. R. TERHUNE, Manager.   [See page 136.]

JAMES H. SHIELDS.   FREDERICK E. BROWN.
SHIELDS & BROWN CO.,
MANUFACTURERS OF
Sectional Insulated Air Coverings.
For Steam, Gas and Water Pipes, Drums, Heaters, &c.,
143 Worth Street,   78 & 80 Lake Street,
NEW YORK.   CHICAGO.
[See page 116.]

JACOB KOEHLER,
SALE AND EXCHANGE STABLES,
—61 & 63 N. Wells St., CHICAGO.—
Have Constantly on Hand a Full Line of Horses and Mules Suitable for all Purposes.
For Fair Dealing During the past Fifteen Years, we refer to Respectable Business Men.
Telephone 3059.   [See page 110.]

A BUSINESS TOUR OF CHICAGO.

JOHN V. FARWELL & CO.

WHOLESALE

DRY GOODS,

Notions Woolens,

CARPETS AND UPHOLSTERY.

Monroe and Market Streets,

CHICAGO.

[See page 50.]

P. W. GATES, President.   RALPH GATES, V. P. and Supt.
J. S. FARGO, Sec'y and Treas.

GATES IRON WORKS,

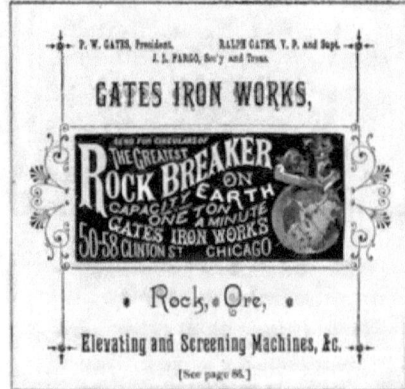

SEND FOR CIRCULARS OF
THE GREATEST
Rock Breaker
ON EARTH
CAPACITY ONE TON A MINUTE
GATES IRON WORKS
50-58 CLINTON ST.   CHICAGO

• Rock, • Ore, •

Elevating and Screening Machines, &c.

[See page 85.]

SAMUEL SIMPSON,   ANDREW ANDREWS,
President.   Secretary.
CLARENCE H. BROWN,   GURDON W. BULL,
Treasurer.   Gen'l Manager.

NEW YORK STORE
NO. 20 E. 14th STREET.

FACTORIES AT WALLINGFORD, CONN.

SIMPSON, HALL, MILLER & CO.

MANUFACTURERS OF

FINE ✢ SILVER-PLATED ✢ WARE

ALSO WM. ROGERS'

Spoons, Forks, Knives, Etc., Etc.

137 & 139 STATE ST.,

M. H. BURCHARD,
Manager.   ✦———CHICAGO.

[See page 76.]

THE

CHALCEDONY COMPANY

MANUFACTURERS OF

✢ SAXOLIN ✢

AND

CHALCEDONY SOAPS,

FINE TOILET SOAPS.

GRIT SOAPS A SPECIALTY.

OFFICE:
93 DEARBORN ST.   CHICAGO, ILL.

[See page 100.]

H. J. SMITH & CO.,

PUBLISHERS,

Chicago and Philadelphia.

Our Great Benefactors.
    Wife and Mother.
        Beautiful, Wonderful and Wise.
Brave Men and Women.
    Pleasant Hours for Home and School.
        Mother, Home and Heaven.
Happy Days of Childhood.
    Pictures for the Wee Ones.
            Bibles.   Albums.

AGENTS WANTED EVERYWHERE.

[See page 141.]

THE

Continental Hotel,

G. COLLINS,   •   PROPRIETOR.

$2.00 PER DAY.

S. E. COR. WABASH AVE. AND MADISON ST.,
CHICAGO.

Thoroughly cleansed, refitted and furnished, is now open under the former management of St. Denis Hotel. It is located in the business center, convenient to all the large wholesale houses, theaters and railroad depots, and is the best $2.00 per day hotel in the city. Merchants and travelers will find clean, pleasant rooms and first-class table. Merchants' Sample Rooms on office floor.

[See page 140.]

A BUSINESS TOUR OF CHICAGO.

Sprague, Warner & Co.

IMPORTERS AND JOBBERS OF

GROCERIES

Randolph Street and Michigan Avenue,

CHICAGO ILL.

BOWMAN DAIRY CO.

(Successors to M. A. DEVINE,)

Pure Milk and Cream,

68 & 70 North State Street,

TELEPHONE 3187 — CHICAGO.

[See page 106.]

Heath & Milligan Manf'g Co.

PAINT

MANUFACTURERS

AND JOBBERS IN

Paints, Oils, Varnishes, Brushes, &c.,

170, 172 & 174 Randolph St.,

[See page 55.] CHICAGO ILL.

Inland Architect & News Record

A CHICAGO MONTHLY
(With an "Intermediate News" number and a "Photogravure" edition.) Devoted to
ARCHITECTURE, DECORATION AND FURNISHING.

ADVERTISE IN IT.
SUBSCRIBE FOR IT.

Illustrations Unequaled.
BEST ADVERTISING MEDIUM IN THE WEST.
[19 TRIBUNE BUILDING.]

E. M. HENDERSON & CO.

MANUFACTURERS OF

BOOTS AND SHOES

—AND—

RUBBER AGENTS.

Salesrooms Cor. Adams and Market Sts.,

CHICAGO.

[See page 51.]

O. W. RICHARDSON & CO.

O. W. RICHARDSON. E. C. RICHARDSON. M. M. CURRY.

Jobbers of CUT

CARPETS,

MATTINGS, OIL-CLOTHS and LINOLEUMS,

Smyrna Rugs,

261 & 263 State St., CHICAGO.

Richardson's Patent Carpet Exhibitor controlled exclusively by us for entire Northwest.
Merchants Wanted to Sell Carpets and Rugs by Sample.

[See page 190.]

A BUSINESS TOUR OF CHICAGO.

New York.   **Chicago.**

IVISON, BLAKEMAN & CO.

—PUBLISHERS OF—

The : American : Educational : Series

Of School and College Text Books.

CHICAGO BRANCH, 149 Wabash Avenue.

JOHN C. ELLIS, Manager.

[See page 72.]

Judd's College of Commerce,

116 MONROE STREET, CHICAGO.

Day, Special Afternoon and Evening Sessions.

BOOKKEEPING, ☆ SHORTHAND,
PENMANSHIP, ARITHMETIC, ETC.,

TAUGHT INDIVIDUALLY, TO CLASSES, BY MAIL, AND TO PRIVATE STUDENTS.

Believing that we offer the very best advantages to a limited number, we invite your inspection and solicit your patronage.

EVA N. JUDD, Stenographer,   F. F. JUDD, Accountant,
SECRETARY.   PRINCIPAL.

[See page 67.]

WILSON & BAYLESS,

General House Furnishers,

Furniture, Carpets, Stoves, Crockery.

FOLDING BEDS A SPECIALTY

314-316 W. Madison St.,

Chicago, Ill.

[See page 177.]

ACME COPYING CO.,

302 & 304 West Van Buren Street,

CHICAGO, ILL.

WE MAKE THE CELEBRATED

ACME PORTRAITS.

Good Agents Wanted in Every Town in
→THE UNITED STATES.←

DELTA
Transportation Company's

CHEBOYGAN, MACKINAW

—AND—

SAULT STE. MARIE

DAILY LINE OF STEAMERS.

W. R. OWEN, + Manager,

210 South Water Street, CHICAGO, ILL.

TELEPHONE 922.   [See page 103.]

THE GUARANTEE COMPANY
→OF NORTH AMERICA.←

→The Oldest and Largest in America.←

BONDS OF SURETYSHIP.—NO OTHER BUSINESS.

Paid up Capital, - - - $300,000
Assets 31st Dec., 1886, - 528,317
Annual Revenue over, - 250,000

It has deposited in the United States, for the sole security of all Policy-holders therein $85,000 of U. S. 4½ per cent Bonds, the value of which is over - - - $112,000

Head Office: ST. JAMES STREET, MONTREAL.

President, Hon. JAMES FERRIER, Senator.
Vice-President, SIR ALEXANDER T. GALT.
Managing Director, EDWARD RAWLINGS.

CHICAGO BRANCH.—*Office*, 175 La Salle Street,—*Directors:* L. J. GAGE, Vice-Pres't First National Bank; R. R. CABLE, Pres't C. R. I. & Pac. R. R.; HON. JOHN RUSSELL JONES, Pres't West Side Ry.; C. T. WHEELER, Pres't Continental National Bank; E. NELSON BLAKE, Ex-Pres't Board of Trade. *Counsel:* HON. JUDGE BECKWITH. JAMES GRANT, Secretary and Attorney.

With Branch Offices and Agencies in the principal cities throughout the United States and Canada.

[See page 135.]

LAWRENCE AMES & CO.

MANUFACTURERS OF

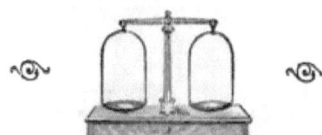

FINE SCALES AND WEIGHTS

81-83 N. Clinton Street.

DRUGGISTS' SCALES A SPECIALTY.

[See page 86.] ———CHICAGO.

JAMES C. BROOK'S, *President.*   NATHAN MEARS, *Vice-President.*

OCONTO COMPANY
—AND—
BAY DE NOQUET CO.
◁NAHMA, DELTA CO., MICH.▷

MANUFACTURERS AND DEALERS IN

Lumber, Lath, Shingles,

CEDAR POSTS AND TIES.

Telephone No. 853.   Office, 234 So. Water St.

Fresh School Books.   Shopworn School Books.

C. M. BARNES,

WHOLESALE DEALER IN

School & Miscellaneous Books,

STATIONERY, ETC.

Nos. 75 and 77 Wabash Ave.,

Miscellaneous Books and Stationery.   CHICAGO, ILL.   Second-Hand School Books.

[See page 108.]

THE ARCADIAN

MINERAL SPRING CO.

WAUKESHA, WISCONSIN.

O. W. HINCKLEY,

SOLE AGENT.

76 & 78 MARKET STREET.

Telephone 807.   CHICAGO, ILL.

GEO. D. WHITCOMB,
PROPRIETOR

HARRISON MINING MACHINE.

Commercial Bank Building, Rooms 32 and 33,
Dearborn and Monroe Sts.

Mining properties examined, estimates made, and machines furnished subject to sale after having worked on the basis of the estimate.

[See page 78.]

THE
Catholic Normal School
Of the Holy Family and

Pio·Nono·College.

ST. FRANCIS, WIS.

[See page 167.]

INDEX.

A.

	PAGE.
Academy of Music, Dan'l Shelby, Proprietor	54
Acme Engraving Co., L. H. Crumb, Manager	128
Acme Laundry, James Donnellan, Proprietor	152
Alburger, Stoer & Co., Tailors' Trimmings	136
Alcock, J. R., Plumber and Gas-fitter	112
Allen Co., Frank L., Shirt Manufacturers	109
Allen, Chas. B., Druggist	127
Alsip Brick Co., Manufacturers of Brick	80
Ambs, L. & Co., Scales and Weights	56
Ames & Frost, Manufacturers of Wire Mattresses	143
Andrews, A. H. & Co., Furniture Manufacturers	71
Angell, E. F. & Co., Brass and Bronze Workers	176
Anna House, A. B. Young, Proprietor	158
Arnold, Geo. A. & Co., Carpenters and Builders	126
Atwater, U. E., Real-Estate and Renting Agency	144

B.

Baldwin, Byron A. & Co., Real Estate	123
Ball, James, Fine Boots and Shoes	157
Barnes, A. S. & Co., School Books and Supplies	73
Barnes, C. M., Wholesale Books and Stationery	168
Barnett, Napoleon, Coal Dealer	63
Bakenhus & Mueseler, Carriage Manufacturers	64
Baumann, Frederick, Architect	139
Baumann & Lotz, Architects and Engineers	114
Beaumont, G., Architect	83
Beck, Geo. L., Publisher	151
Bee-Hive, Dry Goods, Notions, Etc.	76
Berger Bros., Charcoal Dealers	142
Bigelow, H. S., Music Typographer	78
Blair, W. E., Sign Manufacturer	172
Blakemore, Joseph, Picture Frame Manufacturer	175
Blake Patent Doubletree, O. D. White & Co.	131
Blatchford, E. W. & Co., Shot Tower	85
Blatz, Valentin, Brewer and Malster	135
Bliss & Tracy, Machinery Depot	119
Blumenthal, J., Vermin Exterminator	69
Boal, C. T., Wholesale Stoves	117
Boesch, John O., Manufacturer of Tables, Etc.	98
Bogue & Hoyt, Real Estate	78
Bolten, P. H & Co., Commission Merchants	159
Bookwalter, Kelley & Co., Commission Merchants	91
Born, Rudolph, Hardware, Cutlery, Etc.	94
Boser, Jacob, Coal Yards	129
Bowman Dairy Co., The, Pure Country Milk	126
Brainerd, E. L., Real Estate	67
Braun, David J., Spun Metal Goods, Etc.	63
Bremner Baking Co., The D. F.	150
Breuer, Adam, Cigars, Tobacco, Etc.	157
Brevoort Hotel, Hubbard & Field, Proprietors	165
Brown, Chas. T., Patent Attorney	162
Brown, Pettibone & Co., Blank Books, Printing, Etc.	106
Brown, Ira, Real Estate	147
Brown & James Heating Co.	104
Buckley, W. & Co., Groceries	141
Buell, Fred. P. & Co., Fire Insurance	76
Burke, Augustus, Felt and Composition Roofer	153

C.

	PAGE.
Cameron, A. J. & Co., Worsted and Woolen Yarns	134
Campfield, A. L., Printer	131
Canada Fur Manufacturing Co., Simon Minchrod & Co.	101
Canfield & Co., Show Cases, Etc.	171
Carettl, J., Roman Mosaic	129
Carse, J. F., Stained Glass Works	104
Casler, W., Dress Plaiting Bazar	156
Casteel, H. D., Havana Cigars	133
Catholic Normal School, The	167
Chalcedony Soap Co., The	120
Charles Creamery Co., F. R. Jackson, Manager	74
Charles, G. F., Photographer and Artist	120
Chase, B. F. & Co., Sign Painters	52
Chicago Desk Manufacturing Co.	86
Chicago Foundry Co., Heavy Castings	93
Chicago Herald Co.	147
Chicago, Milwaukee & St. Paul Railway	80
Child Adjustable Parlor Chair Co., The Geo. F.	73
City of London Fire Insurance Co., L'd, E. A. Simonds	145
Cleveland, S. E. & Sons, Livery Stables	125
Close Bros. & Co., Western Lands	110
Clottu, John & Son, Wringers, Carpet Sweepers, Etc.	100
Coder, M. D. & Co., Real Estate	174
Columbia Rubber Stamp Works	73
Commercial Laundry, Mrs. Sinclair, Proprietor	57
Continental Hotel, C. Collins, Proprietor	142
Cook, Hallock & Gammon, Lumber and Planing-Mill	140
Copelin, T. E., Stoves, Furnaces, Etc.	64
Corey Car Manufacturing Co.	69
Coughlin, M. T., Oils and Engineers' Supplies	153
Cowan, W., Wood Turner	109
Crooke Co., The John J., Capsule Manufacturers	118
Cruttenden, Thos. S., Garner & Co's Goods	101

D.

Dale, Wm. M., Drugs and Medicines	83
Dauchy & Co., Vault and Sidewalk Lights	152
Davis, John J. & Co., Jobbers of Cigars	81
Davison, John & Son, Ship Chandlers	119
Delta Transportation Co.	103
Devlin, J. B., Dental Surgeon	119
Diamond Palace, Diamonds, Watches, Etc.	174
Dietmann, L., Meerschaum and Amber Goods	128
Donnelly, Tom N. & Co., Diamond Brokers	174
Douglas Club Stables, H. Mather, Proprietor	128
Downey, Joseph, Contractor and Builder	67
Dunlap & Co., J. P., Brewster, Manager	89

E.

Eagle Carriage Works, J. B. Thomas, Proprietor	148
Earnshaw, E. & Son, Contractors and Builders	114
Eastland & Duddleston, Butchers and Packers	81
Eaton, L., Dentist	70
Eaton, T. W., Sawing Machines	96
Eberhart, Ira A., Real Estate	60
Edwards & Fitzgerald, Family Market	152
Eisendrath, B. W. & Co., Plate-Glass Importers	141
Elgin National Watch Co.	84
Ellicott, J. P., Mechanical Engineer	170

INDEX.

	PAGE.
Elmer & Anderson, Commission Merchants	65
English Bros., Market House	174
Enterprise Nickel-Plating Works	105
Enterprise Wire Cloth Mfg. Co., T. Voss, Proprietor	82
Ernesti, R., Artist	156
Eureka Foundry, Kolben Johnson, Proprietor	140
Evers, Wm. & Co., Commission Merchants	130
Exhaust Ventilator Co., The	56

F.

Fargo, C. H. & Co., Wholesale Boots and Shoes	65
Farm, Field and Stockman, The	127
Farwell, J. V. & Co., Wholesale Dry Goods	59
Farwell, Simeon & Co., Men's Furnishing Goods	89
Feld, W. T., Artist	108
Ferry, A. D. & Co., Broom Corn	108
Finney & Channon, Ship Chandlers	146
Fisher, H. C., Teas, Cigars, Etc.	127
Fitch, B. F., Paper Hanging, Paints, Oils, Etc.	84
Fitchburg Machine Works, C. F. Wardell, Manager	93
Fitch, H. A., Druggist	146
Flint, C. W., Manufacturer of Picture Frames	169
Fogg, J. Leland, Garden Seeds	109
Foster, Roe & Crone, Printers	98
Fowler, Ed. L., Photographer	123
Frank, Fred. E. & Bro., Bond and Stock Brokers	72
Frech, Wm., Metal-Working Machinery	114
Freiberg's Music Hall, H. Freiberg, Proprietor	121
Frieman, H. J., Bakery and Coffee House	154
Freitag, J. F., Carriage and Cab Lamps	140
Fullerton, C. W., Attorney-at-Law	71
Fyfe & Campbell, Printers	99

G.

Gale & Blocki, Druggists	144
Galloway, Albert, Steam Heating	94
Gannott's Laundry, E. Gannott, Proprietor	63
Garcia, B. & Co., Cigar Manufacturers	147
Garden City Cigar Manufacturing Co.	66
Garden City Stool Co.	91
Gardner, H. H. & Co., Lumber Dealers	98
Garlick, H. M., Real Estate	105
Garnett, Wm. & Co., Real Estate	150
Gates Iron Works	86
Gaw, Wm. A., Bookseller and Binder	173
Gaylord, Fred'k, Real Estate	81
Gay & Culloton, Plumbers	108
Geehr & Gardner, Hide Brokers	171
Gehman, A. B. & Co., Publishers	97
Germania Fire Insurance Co., E. G. Halle, Agent	121
Gibbs, Dr. L. O.	155
Gifford, C. E. & Co., Commission Merchants	112
Ginn & Co., Publishers	113
Globe Foundry, R. M. Eddy's Sons	87
Goodman, James B. & Co., Real Estate	168
Goodrich, A., Attorney-at-Law	138
Goes, Oscar & Co., Manufacturers of Saws, Knives, Etc.	129
Goettsche, H., Wholesale Cigars and Tobacco	102
Gowan, Victor D. & Co., Tailors' Trimmings	106
Great Atlantic and Pacific Tea Co., The, J. L. Crist, Mgr.	163
Great Western Wire Works, Theo. Spangenberg	152
Grier & Jack, Wholesale Lamps, Glassware, Etc.	36
Griswold, Palmer & Co., Cloaks, Trimmings, Etc.	147
Grubey, William H., Merchant Tailor	171
Guarantee Company of N. A., The	226
Gunderson & Lindberg, Livery Stables	108
Gustorf, F., Lumber Commission	160

H.

Haake, J. H., Fancy Groceries	126
Hall, William, Cigars, Confectionery, Etc.	109
Hall, John B. & Co., Tailors and Gents' Furnishers	168
Hamburg House, M. Marks, Proprietor	109
Harris, Geo. F. & Bro., Copper and Brass Work	93
Harroun Manufacturing Co., Sewing Machine Supplies	124
Haskins, J. S., Florist	112
Hassett, J. B., Groceries	108
Hathaway, J. L., Coal Dealer	106
Hat Palace, The, S. C. Nichols, Manager	107

	PAGE.
Headen & McAuley, Stills, Tanks, Etc.	118
Heath & Milligan Manufacturing Co., Paints, Colors, Etc.	55
Heer & Seelig, Engineers' and Surveyors' Instruments	140
Heggie, A. W. & Co., Cigars and Tobacco	163
Heinold Bros., Fishing Nets, Hammocks, Etc.	133
Heller, L. & Co., Wholesale Jewelers	95
Henderson, C. M. & Co., Wholesale Boots and Shoes	51
Henning, Wm., Vinegar Manufacturer	51
Henrici, Philip, Cafe and Bakery	155
Hewett, A. D., Fire Insurance	116
Hill's National Builder, T. E. Hill, Proprietor	87
Hilmrod, Chas. & Co., Pig Iron	65
Hindshaw, H. H., Taxidermist	176
Hirschfield, Aug., Merchant Tailor	62
Hobert, E. S., Dentist	112
Hoffman, H. C. & Co., Granite Work	116
Hogey, Julius H., Pharmacist	129
Holbrook Manufacturing Co.	115
Holbrook, Francis W., Expert Accountant	166
Hollingsworth & Coughlan, Contractors	123
Home Laundry, A. Moller, Proprietor	64
Home Mfg. Co., The U. S., N. B. Little, Manager	159
Horn, John, Clothes Cleaning	176
Horn, W. H., Corn Merchant	160
Hostetter, J. N., Coal and Wood Dealer	122
Hoyt, Geo. W. & Co., Dry Goods Commission	138
Hoyt, Mrs. E. M., Artist	156

I.

Illinois Terra Cotta Lumber Co.	99
Inkersell, J. J., Grocer	69
Irwin, Richard, Tailor	63
Ivison, Blakeman & Co., Publishers	72

J.

Jackson, Walter M., Real Estate	146
Jacobs, Henry C., Real Estate	145
Jansen, H., Rhine Wines	80
Jarvis Co., The G. M., Wine Growers	149
Jerusalem, J., Brewer	160
Jewish Occident, The, J. Silversmith, Publisher	166
Johnson, P. & H., Curtain Cornices, Etc.	102
Johnson & Metzler, Manufacturers of Carriages	143
Jonas, I., Merchant Tailor	70
Jones, R. Ralston, Mechanical Engineer	73
Jones City Express and Transfer Co.	124
Judd's College, F. F. Judd, Proprietor	67
Julius, C. H. & Son, Merchant Tailors	143

K.

Kaempfer, Fred, Bird Store	75
Katholischer Jugen-Freund	176
Kean, S. A. & Co., Bankers	124
Kehl, Mrs. L., Masquerade Costumer	157
Keller & Co., Manufacturers of Tables, Pedestals, Etc.	152
Kesler Bros., Real Estate	79
Kimball, Geo. F., Plate Glass	85
Koehler, Jacob, Livery Stables	110
Koehnke, C., Music Dealer	128
Kroscheil Bros., Steam Fittings	60
Kuh, Nathan & Fischer, Wholesale Clothing	127
Kurz, Adolph, Carriage and Sign Painter	132

L.

Lafrentz & Karstens, Feed Mill	138
Lansing & Sickler, Restaurant	157
La Pierre House, Mrs. S. Dunn, Proprietor	156
Lassagne, Victor, Restaurant	68
Layton, R. P., Real Estate	115
Lazier, W. W., Dentist	114
Lee, A. A., Shoe Manufacturer	128
Levinson, N. G., Wholesale Jeweler	62
Levy, W. & Son, Provision Dealers	170
Lewis Bros. & Co., Wholesale Dry Goods	106
Lewis & Howard, Wool Merchants	177
Lindholm's Express	62
Lindstrand, F. A., Jeweler	117

INDEX.

	PAGE.
Linington, C. M., Fancy Goods, Notions, Etc.	79
Lipman, A., Diamond Broker	155
Liverpool & London & Globe Insurance Co.	97
Living Church, The, C. W. Leffingwell, Editor	119
Lorenz, A. & Co. Engravers on Wood	117
Lowell, M. H., Oil Paintings	68
Lucke Bros., Merchant Tailors	156
Luetgert, A. L., Sausage Manufacturer	136

M.

MacLachlan & Co., Market House	178
Mallette, J. P. & Co., Suburban Homes	149
Mantonya, L. B. & Co., Wholesale Boots and Shoes	52
Mariner G. A. & Co., Chemists and Assayers	64
Marks, Phil. N. & Co., Hosiery, Notions, Etc.	104
Marshall, J. D., Sole Leather	120
Marsh, E. T., Harness, Collars, Etc.	162
Masury, John W. & Son, Paints and Varnishes	75
Mather, A. C. & Co., Manufacturers of Kid Gloves	90
Maxwell, S. A. & Co., Books, Stationery, Etc.	175
Maurer, Cass F., Cigars and Tobacco	101
May, Bernard H., Rattan and Willow Ware	92
McCormack Bros., Homœopathic Specialties	77
McEwan's Hotel	158
McHugh & Enright, Iron Foundry	86
McNamara & Dick, Trunk Manufacturers	115
Mears, C. & Co., Lumber and Brick Dealers	108
Meath Bros., Furniture House	162
Medcalfe, H. G. & Co., Drugs and Medicines	71
Merchants Safe Deposit Co.	91
Merchant & Co., Tin-plate, Metals, Etc.	188
Metcalf's Dancing Academies	111
Michener Bros. & Co., Packers and Provision Dealers	81
Mikkelsen & Bendtsen, Furniture Manufacturers	139
Montgomery, W. H., Artificial Limbs	116
Moorhead, McCleane Co., Iron Warehouse	55
Morper, Dernburg & Co., Cloak Manufacturers	102
Muchmore & Muchmore, Oils	100
Mullen Bros. & Co., Woolens and Tailors' Trimmings	87
Murphy & Co., Varnish Manufacturers	82
Myers, John, Palace Pharmacy	176
Myers, S. & Co., Jobbers in Whiskies	173

N.

Nagle, H. J., Confectioner and Caterer	134
National Boiler Works, Jos. Bee, Proprietor	90
National Tobacco Review, F. S. Anderson, Publisher	144
Needham's Sons, D., Clover Blossom Preparations	153
Neff, Wm., Flour, Meal, Hay, Etc.	92
Nelson, H. C., Banjo Maker	154
Newman Bros., Organ Manufacturers	96
Newgard, Henry, Locksmith	156
N. Y. C. & H. R. Ry., and B. & A. R. R., W. B. Jerome.	58
Nichols, H. T. & Co., Ales	135
Nitchkowski, L., Merchant Tailor	62
Norcott, E., Tin and Copper Ware	171
North Side Restaurant, Mrs. Williams, Proprietor	159
Northwestern Boiler Works, Chris. Pfeiffer, Proprietor	107
Northwestern Parlor Suit Co.	178
Noyes, L. W., Dictionary Holders	141

O.

Ohlman, A. R., Glass Engraver	158
Orvis, H. F. & Co., Grain Commission	128
Osgood, M. L., Real Estate	52

P.

Packard, E. E., Sewing Machines	96
Paalden, Steven & Co., Chemical and Drug Importers	159
Paine, W. M., Meats, Poultry, Etc.	161
Pank, J. H. & Co.	132
Parsons, John, Chemist and Perfumer	125
Payne, Leroy, Livery Stables	178
Payne, Alfred, Artist	134
Peters, Mathus, Upholstery and Drapery Manufacturer	86
Peterson & Ovesen, Parlor Tables, Etc.	170
Philippi, H., Bar Glassware	139

	PAGE.
Philipson Decorative Co.	151
Phrenological Institute, Prof. Thayer, Proprietor	168
Pine, J. K. P., Lion Brand Collars	52
Pittaway, James, Teas, Coffees, Etc.	63
Piano Manufacturing Co., The	107
Portman Bros. & Co., Manufacturers of Traveling Bags	53
Potter & Kisselburg, Hay Dealers	161
Prussing, F., Grocer	170
Purdy, J. H. & Co., Watch Materials, Etc.	159
Purtell & Kienzle, Saddlery Hardware	102
Putnam Clothing House, C. M. Babbitt, Resident Partner.	93

R.

Racine Wagon and Carriage Co.	110
Racine, Chas., Pattern Maker	162
Kaiser, Charles, Manufacturer of Children's Carriages	145
Randall, T. D. & Co., Commission House	100
Rand, Charles E., Real Estate	135
Rand, McNally & Co., Publishers	55
Raphael, Phil. L. & Co., Wine House	101
Rascher Map Publishing Co., The	67
Raymond, F. L. Co., Gummed Labels, Etc.	106
Red Star Line, Wasmansdorff & Heinemann, Agents	136
Regan, Joseph, Confectioner and Baker	118
Reid, W. H., Draper and Tailor	85
Remington Type-Writer	111
Revell, A. H. & Co., Furniture House	95
Revere House, J. D. Fanning, Proprietor	154
Rice, James H. Co., Plate Glass	70
Richardson, O. W. & Co., Carpets, Oil-Cloth, Etc.	150
Rider, M. D., Blank Books, Stationery, Etc.	72
Ries & Co. Furnishing Goods	90
Riverdale Distilling Co.	74
Roberts, J. D., Glass Beveler, Etc.	179
Robins & Talcott, Building Specialties	120
Rogan, J. B. & Co., Commission Merchants	138
Rogers, Brown & Co., Iron Commission	116
Rogers, I. C. & Son, Commission Merchants	146
Rosback, F. P., Manufacturer of Planers, Presses, Etc.	132
Rose, Charles W., Tailor and Draper	160
Roseboom, W. L. & Co., Commission Merchants	107
Rounsavell, George, Cooperage	180
Roundy & Son, Regalia and Uniform Manufacturers	113
Ruprecht, John, Broadway Market	169
Russell, J. K., Planing-Mills	149
Ryan, D. W., Cooperage	129

S.

Salisbury & Cline, Rubber Goods	100
Salvesen, George, Carriage Trimmer, Etc.	144
Sanborn, R. H. & Co., Celluloid Collars	79
Sandberg & Co., Engravers' Wood and Tools	158
Sautter & Apking, Boot and Shoe Manufacturers	89
Schmitz, Wm., Musical Instruments	119
Schoellkopf, Henry, Grocer	155
Schrader, A., Bakery and Confectionery	68
School of Art Embroidery, Mrs. E. D. Hodge	112
Schreiber & Annas, Ornamental Cut Glass	175
Schwalbach, M., Tower Clocks	163
Schwarz, Aug., Dye House	137
Schweitzer, F., Jewelry Cases	172
Sears & Sears, Designers and Engravers	141
Seeberger, A. F. & Co., Wholesale Hardware	148
Selz, Schwab & Co., Manufacturers of Boots and Shoes	89
Seng, W. & Co., Manufacturers of Furniture Fixtures	57
Servoss Furnace Co.	53
Seydell, Wm., Contractor	117
Shepard, J. A., Portraits	98
Shields & Brown Co., Pipe Coverings, Etc.	146
Shillington, Isaac, Livery Stables	66
Sibley Fireproof Warehouse, The Hiram	87
Siebert, A., Carriage and Sign Painting	106
Sievert, Henry, Cigars and Tobacco	166
Sigwalt Manufacturing Co., The, Seal Presses, Etc.	169
Simonds Manufacturing Co.	113
Simpson, Hall, Miller & Co., Silver-Plated Ware	76
Smith, H. J. & Co., Publishers	121
Smith, James P. & Co., Ice Dealers	167
Smith, Joshua, Dental Surgeon	168
Smith, Peter & Co., Carriage and Buggy Manufacturers	74
Snitzer, John, Merchant Tailor	155

INDEX.

	PAGE.
Snyder & Rathbone, Commission Merchants	146
Spalding Lumber Co.	82
Staiger, C. M., Publisher	176
Star Chemical Works, J. E. Landell, Proprietor	151
Stattmann, Chas. & Co., Sealskin Garments	137
Stein, S. & Co., Woolens	125
Stevens, J. K., Photographer	77
Stevenson, Robert & Co., Wholesale Drugs	133
Stotz, Woltz & Co., Furniture Manufacturers	92
Straus, M., Artist	97
Strauss, Goodman, Yondorf & Co., Wholesale Clothing	99
Svenska Tribunen	162
Swansen, N. D., Bakery and Confectionery	172

T.

Ternand, C. W. & Co., Jewelry Manufacturers	142
Thurber, W. S., Fine Art Dealer	145
Tiffany Pressed Brick Co.	130
Thorne, M., Hair Goods	72
Thomson & Taylor Spice Co., The	82
Townsend & Yale, Commission Merchants	148
Troy Steam Laundry, H. W. Howe, Proprietor	139
Truppel, R., Pharmacist	118
Tuckhorn & Co., Billiard and Pool Tables	164

U.

Union Steamboat Co., The, T. T. Morford, Agent	66

V.

Van Buren, B., Druggist	122
Vehmeyer, H. F., Broom Corn	164
Vessel Owners Towing Co.	94

W.

	PAGE.
Wadsworth, L. L., Manufacturer of Trucks, Wagons, Etc.	142
Waldo, J. Frank, Artist	99
Wallace, Chas. S., Sanitary Plumber	173
Wallace, J. H., Lumber Merchant	85
Wallis, F. J., Artist	158
Walsh, Mrs. E. T., Fine Millinery	105
Washington Foundry and Machine Shop	138
Wasmansdoff & Heinemann, Bankers	137
Wehle, Peter, Merchant Tailor	117
Wells & Nellegar Co., Wholesale Hardware	149
Western Furniture Co., W. C. McDonald, Manager	163
Western Patent Agency, H. P. Crawford & Co.	161
Whitcomb, Geo. D., Harrison Mining Machine	78
Whitman, Geo. B., Lumber Commission	136
Wilber Mercantile Agency, Mercantile Reports	70
Wilson & Bayless, House Furnishers	177
Wilt, Chas. T., Trunk Manufacturer	62
Wisconsin Central Line	61
Wold & Wolf, Undertakers and Livery	92
Wolf, Becker & Co., Wool Commission	174
Woodruff Hotel	66
Wright, S. F. & Co., Livery Stables	161
Wyman, W. W., Dealer in Meats	172

Y.

Yerbury & Barry, Laundry	172
Young, Gatzert & Co., Plumbers and Gas-fitters	179

Z.

Zengeler, John, Dye Works	131

WHETSTONE & CO.,

Chicago Agents for

The Standard Rotary Shuttle Sewing Machine.

BEST ON EARTH!   BEST ON EARTH!

BEST for the rich, because it is the finest finished and does the finest work.
BEST for the poor, because more work can be done on the "Standard" in two days than on other Machines in three.

BEST for the invalid, because it is the easiest-running Machine made.
BEST for the nervous, because it is noiseless.
BEST for the manufacturer, because it will outwear any other Machine made.

NOVEL!   BEAUTIFUL!   PRACTICAL!

2500 Stitches Per Minute.   Fastest Lock-Stitch Machine Made.   Attachments Entirely New Style.

Solid Steel Ruffler and Tucker.   Wood Work Finest in the World.

THE STANDARD SHUTTLE is Wheel-Shaped, and Revolves on Its Own Axis.

→ Main Office, 285 Wabash Avenue. ←

We carry a Complete Stock of McCALL'S BAZAR GLOVE-FITTING PATTERNS at our Main Office, 285 Wabash Avenue, and at our Branch Offices, 458 West Madison Street and 471 Ogden Avenue. THE BAZAR DRESS-MAKER, the best and most complete Fashion Album published. For sale at all of our Offices.

ORGANIZED 1845.   PURELY MUTUAL.

NEW YORK LIFE INSURANCE CO.

The NEW YORK LIFE INSURANCE COMPANY will sell a *Contract* that GUARANTEES *to pay 100 per cent. of the premiums with the face of the policy.* By sending your name, address and the date of your birth (day, month and year in which you were born), *to the undersigned, a statement will be sent you giving a full explanation of this form of policy.*

All the policies issued by the NEW YORK LIFE since 1850 have not contained a clause making them void in case of suicide or self-destruction; the policies of nearly all the other companies still contain a suicide clause.

The NEW YORK LIFE has a lower rate of mortality than any other company over forty years old.

The NEW YORK LIFE was the first company to recognize the policy-holders' right to paid-up insurance in case of discontinuance of payment of premiums, by originating and introducing in 1860 the first non-forfeiture policy.

The NEW YORK LIFE was the first company (many companies do not yet do it) to attach to each policy issued a copy of the application upon which the contract is based.

RECORD FROM APRIL 12, 1845, TO DECEMBER 31, 1886.

Period—Dates Inclusive.	Average Amount of Insurance Written Yearly.	Insurance in Force, End of Each Period.	Average Amount of Premiums Received Yearly.	Average Amount to Policy-holders Yearly.	Average Amount Paid in Death Claims.	Average Amount Received Yearly in Interest.	Cash Assets, End of Each Period.
1845–1859 . . 15 years,	$2,181,504	$15,284,718	$258,237.47	$132,212.10	$108,422.02	$37,106.14	$1,767,133.24
1860–1869 . . 10 years,	16,549,764	102,132,513	2,120,671.14	958,759.27	418,551.23	347,683.08	13,025,561.23
1870–1879 . . 10 years,	22,250,984	127,417,762	6,014,812.89	4,059,839.99	1,489,027.16	1,586,299.42	38,906,952.66
1880–1884 . . 5 years,	42,029,979	229,382,586	9,213,561.48	5,847,273.34	2,044,096.95	2,646,610.02	59,283,753.57
1885, . One Year.	68,521,452	259,674,500	12,722,103.03	7,681,873.75	2,999,109.64	3,399,069.71	66,864,321.32
1886, . One Year.	85,178,294	304,373,540	15,507,906.04	7,627,230.09	2,757,035.97	3,722,502.24	75,421,453.37

Received from Policy-holders in Premiums, in 42 years, 1845–1886, - - - - **$159,525,918.92**
Paid to Policy-holders and their representatives, 1845–1886, $96,714,644.67
Assets held as security for Policy-holders, January 1, 1887, 75,421,453.37
Total Amount paid Policy-holders, and now held as security
for their contracts, - - - - - - - - - - - - - - **$172,136,098.04**

Amount paid and held exceeds amount received, - - - - - $12,610,179.12

Received from Interest, Rents, etc., in 42 years, 1845–1886, $40,251,099.32
Death-losses paid in 42 years, 1845–1886, - - - - - - - 36,678,744.66

Interest and Rents exceeded Death-losses paid, - - - - - $3,572,354.66

Dividends paid in 42 years, 1845–1886, - - - - - - - - $30,294,550.62
Legal Surplus over Liabilities, under State Law, Jan. 1, 1887, 15,549,319.53

Amount Saved Policy-holders from table-rates, - - - - - $45,843,870.15

CASH ASSETS, *January 1, 1887,* - - over Seventy-Five Million Dollars.
INSURANCE IN FORCE, *January 1, 1887,* over Three Hundred Million Dollars.

A. J. FLITCRAFT, General Agent,
107 DEARBORN STREET, CHICAGO, ILL.

A. H. Andrews & Co.

Telephone No. 3430.   195 Wabash Avenue, CHICAGO, ILL.

—— LARGEST MANUFACTURERS OF FINE ——

Office Desks, Bank Counters and Railings, Office Chairs, Interior Fittings in Hard Woods.

Court House and Commercial Furniture. **BANK FITTINGS.**

Workers in Wood and Metals.

Andrews' Celebrated Office Desks	FINE BRASS & WIRE WORK,
Of Best Kiln-Dried Lumber.	Railings, Gates, Wickets,
We Claim Great Superiority.	Partitions, Screens, Etc.,
OUR DESKS	FOR COMMERCIAL AND PUBLIC
Are of Improved Design and Reduced in Price.	BUILDINGS.
LIBRARY TABLES.	Send for Illustrated Catalogue.

Andrews' Folding Beds
OUR UPRIGHT BED takes the Lead for Elegance and Comfort.
A. H. Andrews & Co.
Chicago & New York.
Bank Office Fittings

Opera Chairs.
— PATENTED. —

Upholstered or Plain; Newest Styles with Foot Rest, Tilting Back, and Hat Rest. Send for Catalogue.
School Desks, Library Tables, Etc.

The G. F. Child Adjustable Chair Co.
281 Wabash Avenue, CHICAGO.

THIS CHAIR
Is the most complete Adjustable Chair made.

IS EASILY ADJUSTED
To All Positions Desired.

For Invalids or General Easy Chair
IT EXCELS ALL OTHERS.

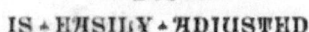

FACTORY: - - - - FUERTH, BAVARIA.

EUGENE ARNSTEIN,
IMPORTER OF
Bronze Powders, Lustre
AND

❧ GOLD PAINT ❧

No. 110 Dearborn Street, - - - - CHICAGO, ILL.

On Application will Send Catalogue and Price List.

On Application will Send Catalogue and Price List.

Established 1840.   Incorporated 1886.
The DeGolyer Varnish Co.
(Successors to DEGOLYER & BRO.)

Offices and Warehouses, Nos. 377 to 391 Illinois St.,
Factories, Nos. 410 to 422 Indiana Street,   - - CHICAGO, ILL.

MAKERS OF

Fine Varnishes
—AND—
JAPANS.

The DeGolyer Varnish Works are the oldest and most extensive in the West, and their manufactures are celebrated for their excellent qualities.

London, Eng., Branch Office:
No. 49 FINSBURY PAVEMENT.

ESTABLISHED 1855.
MARR & RICHARDS,
WOOD ENGRAVING,

Book Illustrations, Landscapes, Buildings, Portraits, Maps, Catalogue Work of All Kinds, Etc.

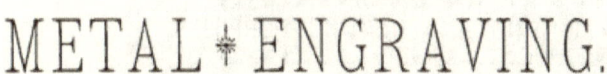

METAL ✦ ENGRAVING.

Seals, Steel Stamps, Lettering on Jewelry, and Medals, Rubber Stamps, Etc.

Mack Block, MILWAUKEE.   ✤   Gilfillan Block, ST. PAUL.

☞ We produce Cuts and Electrotypes by the processes of Wood Engraving Relief Line Engraving, or Photo Engraving, and are enabled to furnish all kinds of work in the best manner and by the Cheapest Process. We refer to the Cover and many of the Illustrations in this History as specimens of our work.

Douglas's
Patent Instantaneous Water Heater,
FOR
Baths, Offices and Domestic Purposes.

THE MOST
CONVENIENT
AND
ECONOMICAL
Water Heater Yet Invented.

No. 2 HEATER—*Diameter 15 inches, Height 42 inches.*

Will Heat 3 Gallons of water per minute, to 100 deg., taking the water at 60 deg. Consuming less than one cent's worth of gas for a large bath, allowing the price of gas at $1.00 per 1,000 feet.

MANUFACTURED BY
THE INSTANTANEOUS WATER HEATING CO.,
87 Dearborn Street,
CHICAGO.

Bursting or Explosions Impossible.

Simple and Effective.

THE
Combination Gas Machine Co.

CHICAGO BRANCH:
87 DEARBORN STREET.

FACTORY AND MAIN OFFICE:
DETROIT, MICH.

MANUFACTURERS OF

GAS MACHINES
FOR · LIGHTING · AND · HEATING · PURPOSES.

Gas Cooking and Heating Stoves,
    Weber Straight Way Valves,
  Rider's Improved Pumping Engines,
      Laboratory Burners, Etc.

The Eldredge "B"

150,000 IN USE!

The only Machine ever made where the Shuttle will thread itself by the action of the Machine.

WARRANTED
—FOR—
FIVE YEARS.

Light running and very quiet.

Sold with the guarantee of being the best that can be made.

SEWING ⁑ MACHINE.

Eldredge Manufacturing Company,
363 & 365 Wabash Avenue, CHICAGO.

www.ingramcontent.com/pod-product-compliance
Lightning Source LLC
Chambersburg PA
CBHW031814220426
43662CB00007B/641